The Book of Gladness / Le Livre de Leesce

The Book of Gladness /
Le Livre de Leesce

*A 14th Century Defense
of Women, in English and French,
by Jehan Le Fèvre*

TRANSLATED, ANNOTATED AND WITH
AN INTRODUCTION BY LINDA BURKE

6-26-14

*To David Jordan,
a great
colleague + fellow
Francophile. We
enjoy your books
as well —
Linda Burke*

McFarland & Company, Inc., Publishers
Jefferson, North Carolina, and London

LIBRARY OF CONGRESS CATALOGUING-IN-PUBLICATION DATA

Le Fèvre, Jean, approximately 1320–approximately 1390, author.
The book of gladness / le livre de Leesce : a 14th century defense
of women, in English and French / by Jehan Le Fèvre ; translated,
annotated and with an introduction by Linda Burke.
p.   cm.
Includes bibliographical references and index.

ISBN 978-0-7864-7427-1

softcover : acid free paper ∞

1. Women's rights—History—To 1500.   2. Man-woman relationships—
To 1500.   I. Burke, Linda, 1953– translator.   II. Title.
III. Title: Livre de Leesce.

HQ1143.L4 2013   305.42—dc23   2013033809

BRITISH LIBRARY CATALOGUING DATA ARE AVAILABLE

On the cover: artwork *Portrait of a Woman, Titian*
(© 2013 PicturesNow)

Manufactured in the United States of America

*McFarland & Company, Inc., Publishers
Box 611, Jefferson, North Carolina 28640
www.mcfarlandpub.com*

For Allan
mieux vaut tard que jamais

Contents

Acknowledgments

Over my years of work on *The Book of Gladness*, an extended labor of love, I have incurred many debts of gratitude. From the beginning, C. David Benson and Regina Schwartz gave encouragement when I needed it most. Without my cousins Tom and Elisa Harkness and Michael Steinberg, IT experts who helped with the technical aspects of the production, there would be no book. My dissertation advisor, Robert W. Hanning, gave important feedback as well as crucial encouragement and endorsement for the project. Thanks to Robert F. Yeager, I had the chance to organize my thoughts by presenting several papers on related topics to the Gower sessions at meetings of the International Congress of Medieval Studies at Kalamazoo, Michigan. Emmanuelle Bonnafoux of the University of Chicago provided expert help with the nuances of the French text; in this she was graciously assisted by Peter Dembowski. Lee F. Sherry gave his indispensable assistance in unraveling the perversities of Mahieu of Boulogne's Latin *Lamentations*. Benjamin Semple of the Christine de Pizan Society has also taken time from his busy schedule to share his insights on textual challenges. His collegial support, and the kind assistance of Bernard Ribémont, are further acknowledged in the appendix to this volume. Throughout our magical summer of 2011, Mike Monheit and Diane Garden provided many wonderful insights and encouragement on various aspects of the manuscript. Well into the process, the work was expertly fine-tuned by free-lance copy editor Susan Tarcov. I also thank Tina-Marie Ranalli for her expert advice on particular terms in Middle French and especially on manuscripts of the work. On rare occasions, I have disagreed with my advisers, and any errors in the text are of course my own.

At Elmhurst College, English department chairs Ted Lerud and Ann Frank Wake each granted me a semester of book leave without which the project could never have seen the light of day. Kathy Willis and Ang Romano of Elmhurst College Interlibrary Loan and all the fine staff of the Elmhurst College Library provided services without which the project could not have been completed. During breaks from school, I have also been expertly assisted by the reference librarians of the Hinsdale Public Library. With unfailing good cheer, Grace Burzynski of the campus printing office took the time to provide me with countless hard copies, so necessary (to me, at least) for correction of text.

A special word of thanks is owed to Petr Slouka of the Lobkowicz Collections and Jindřich Marek of the National Library of the Czech Republic for their help in locating the manuscript discussed in the appendix.

I also thank my parents, Duane and Virginia Barney, for every good thing in my life, especially the education they provided for me, and for never expecting me to do anything practical. Fortunately my mother is still here to celebrate publication. I am equally blessed in Estelle Burke, my mother of thirty-nine happy years and counting. My children, Daniel and Marjorie Burke and Gordon and Shuli Burke, now fine young adults, have enriched my life in more ways than they can possibly know. Dear baby Elizabeth Anne, I will have more time for you now. My dear friend Kristine Lang will be happy to see the project finished at last — she has put up with a lot. Other dear ones have been equally patient with my years of preoccupation and supplied me with all kinds of encouragement: Mary Barney, Alan and Natalie Sandler Berger, Maria Dering, Carla Feinkind, Cynthia and all the Harkness family, Ken and Shelly Hoganson, Sheila Kaptur and all her family, Judy Mazzei, Barbara Millman, the late Deborah Palmer, Carmen Quintana, Jim and Roseanne Rosenthal, and Chloe Tyler Winterbotham. Please forgive me if I am forgetting anyone. Finally, no words can do justice to my husband, Allan M. Burke, for putting up with "Smitty" all these years, and for his support and encouragement at every stage of the project. He has proved, contra Heloïse et al., that marriage is no hindrance, but an outright blessing, to literary study.

Abbreviations

Ars am.	Ovid, *Ars amatoria*
DMF	ATILF *Dictionnaire du Moyen Français* (see bibliography)
L	*Les lamentations de Matheolus*, trans. Jehan Le Fèvre
LGW	Chaucer, *Legend of Good Women*
LL	Jehan Le Fèvre, *Le livre de Leesce*
MercT	Chaucer, *The Merchant's Tale*
Met.	Ovid, *Metamorphoses*
PL	*Patrologia Latina*
Rem. am.	Ovid, *Remedia amoris*
RR	Guillaume de Lorris and Jean de Meun, *Le roman de la Rose*, ed. Félix Lecoy
Van Hamel	A.-G. Van Hamel, ed., *Les lamentations de Matheolus et Le livre de Leësce de Jehan Le Fèvre, de Resson*, 2 vols. (Paris: Émile Bouillon, 1892, 1905
WBPro	Chaucer, *The Wife of Bath's Prologue*
WBT	Chaucer, *The Wife of Bath's Tale*

Introduction

Than mote we to bokes that we fynde,
Thurgh whiche that olde thinges ben in mynde ...
— Chaucer, *Legend of Good Women*

A Neglected Classic — the Challenges

Le livre de Leesce (1380–87) by Jehan Le Fèvre, no less than its companion poem the *Lamentations of Matheolus,*[1] is one of the foundational texts of the late medieval literary tradition, especially the extended debate on the nature and status of women and marriage. Chaucer drew on *Leesce* as a paradigm for the dialectic in his *Wife of Bath's Prologue* and freely copied both its phrasing and its arguments in several of the *Canterbury Tales*.[2] John Gower's *Confessio Amantis* very likely owes a debt to the poem.[3] In the early works of Christine de Pizan, especially her entire series of polemics on the misogyny and misogamy of the thirteenth-century *Roman de la Rose*, the influence of *Leesce* is even more profound and pervasive. Shedding light on the most important legacy of the poem, Maureen Cheney Curnow has documented how *Leesce* provided the "basic pattern" and much of the content for Christine's masterful profeminine polemic, *Le livre de la cité des dames* (The Book of the City of Ladies)[4]; unnoted to date, Christine also responded to *Leesce* in her sequel to the *Cité*, the *Livre des trois vertus*, in two polemical passages on widows and prostitutes.[5] Sometimes as the companion poem to *Lamentations*, less often as a separate and independent work, *Leesce* spread through England and France in manuscript form and was printed in several editions as late as 1518.[6]

Given the importance of *Le livre de Leesce* to the history of literature and ideas, this work has been surprisingly little recognized in recent decades, especially in critical/historical studies where it would be most expected to appear.[7] The probable reasons for this relative neglect are worthy of discussion as a basis for understanding the historical context of the poem as well as its literary posterity.

Le livre de Leesce is the direct sequel, retraction, and rebuttal to its companion poem, Jehan Le Fèvre's translation into French of the notoriously misogynistic *Lamentations of Matheolus*. The vast majority of lines in *Leesce* (92–3468) are composed of alternating "points" and "counterpoints": invective against women, sometimes quoted, more often summarized, from the *Lamentations*, intercalated with profeminine counterarguments by Le Fèvre and his author-persona Dame Leesce/Lady Gladness, whose character is discussed below. All medieval literature is proudly intertextual, but Le Fèvre carried this quality to a

1

fault in *Leesce*, his final work. In at least ten passages of *Leesce*, most of them substantial, material carried over from the *Lamentations* is abridged so drastically, and in some cases so carelessly, that the basic literal meaning of the passage is impossible to decipher without consulting the text of the earlier poem.[8] Of course, when the author's "points" are opaque to the reader, his "counterpoints" will tend to be equally obscure. This problem is only imperfectly addressed by the only modern edition of the poem, to be found in the otherwise excellent two-volume edition by A.-G. Van Hamel of the Latin *Lamentations*, French *Lamentations*, and *Le livre de Leesce* (published in Paris, 1892–1905). Evidently for reasons of space, Van Hamel restricted his notes on *Leesce* to material found exclusively in that poem; for an explanation of the passages borrowed from the *Lamentations*, about one-third of the lines in *Leesce*, the reader must follow the cumbersome process of checking the corresponding lines from the earlier poem, and often the densely formatted notes to his edition of the *Lamentations* as well.

Aside from the roadblocks thrown up by Van Hamel's *Leesce*, the obscurity of the work has been condoned and enabled by its readers, starting with the contemporaries of Jehan Le Fèvre himself. For example, Chaucer at no time so much as mentions the name "Matheolus" or "Matheolule," as the French *Lamentations* was generally known in the Middle Ages, much less its sequel *Leesce*, although as noted above, he was notably indebted to both of these poems. Christine tells us how she leafed through "Matheolus" as a diversion from her more serious studies, but she never mentions *Leesce*, much less admits to the extent of her borrowings; in a tactic familiar to instructors of composition, she even takes care to obfuscate her debt by slightly rewording the material she appropriates.[9] The medieval authors' motives for this "silent treatment" of Le Fèvre are not difficult to guess. Dating from about 1380 or slightly later, the companion poems were too recent to carry much prestige in an age that generally valued the ancient over the contemporary. Furthermore, the very qualities that made the *Lamentations* and its sequel so popular — their sensational personal details, obscenity, near-pornography, and novelty — were exactly of the type to ensure that the works would be publicly treated with scorn, when they were mentioned at all. Christine calls "Matheolus" a mere "petit livret ... de nulle auctorité,"[10] while her ally in controversy, the theologian and preacher Jean Gerson, singles out "Matheole" as "le sot" (the stupid one) among the licentious books (including the works of Ovid and *Le roman de la Rose*) that he exhorts his parishioners to keep far from the eyes of their impressionable children, or even to tear up or burn.[11] Of course, Gerson's public attack on the *Lamentations* (in a series of vernacular sermons) is compelling evidence for its popularity, which could hardly have been hurt by the free advertising.

In recent scholarship as well, *Le livre de Leesce* has received very little recognition, especially for its place in literary history. Although its influence on the *Canterbury Tales* has been documented in several articles and portions of books, now decades old,[12] the *Riverside Chaucer Third Edition* contains no reference to *Leesce* in connection with the *Tales*. There is virtually no published analysis to date of possible allusions to the work in Gower's *Confessio Amantis*.[13] A handful of studies (mainly articles) examine the participation of *Leesce* in the late medieval debate on *Le roman de la Rose* ("la querelle de la Rose")[14] and the defense of women,[15] but the discussion of Le Fèvre in these works, while strong in quality, is of necessity limited in scope. Where Christine is concerned, there may be a residual defensiveness (based on past sexist disparagement of her work) that makes her present-day critics understandably hesitant to acknowledge her borrowings, especially from an author so preeminently linked with misogyny. Yet it surely in no way detracts from Christine's unique and brilliant achievement to recognize her intertextuality, a trait she shares with her great medieval contemporaries.

"Poor Smith": His Life and Writings

... for he doesn't know how to work on iron, but his effort is all on parchment.
— *The Book of Gladness* 3977–78

As noted above, *Le livre de Leesce* is the sequel and point-by-point rebuttal to *Les lamentations de Matheolus*, Le Fèvre's French translation of the Latin *Lamentations* (1290 or 1291)[16] by Matheus or Mahieu of Boulogne, known derisively as "Matheolus" or even "Matheolulus/Matheolule" after his demotion to the laity and the resulting anguish that inspired his 5,614-line complaint in verse form.[17] As he writes in the *Lamentations*, Mahieu was a prosperous cleric until he married Petra (also called Perrenelle or Perrette), a beautiful young widow. This marriage to a widow rendered him "bigamous" according to the recent edict by Gregory X, even though he was married only once. (The stigma of "bigamy" also applied to remarriage after the death of a spouse and—no more and no less—to the concurrent plural marriages of certain Old Testament worthies.)[18] Beyond the trauma of losing his benefice and thereby his rank in society, the life of a husband is a torment to Mahieu. His household with children is misery and chaos; worse still, Perrenelle is now old, ugly, and quarrelsome. She demands her "marriage debt" even though he is now impotent, and when he is unable to satisfy her, she grows even more bitter and hostile. He writes the Latin *Lamentations* both as a catharsis for his pain and in the hope of dissuading his fellow men from falling into the snare of matrimony. In a disorganized and irregular style that he excuses on the grounds of his intense suffering (42–69), Mahieu interpolates an intimate personal account of his marital troubles with misogynistic topoi from a farrago of sources, including the Bible, the church fathers, secular history, and racy new stories in the *fabliau* style.[19] The closest prototype to his work, as acknowledged by Mahieu himself,[20] is Jerome's *Adversus Jovinianum* (Against Jovinian),[21] a seminal text in the medieval debate on women and marriage; in turn, the latter was heavily influenced by the admonitions of Saint Paul in 1 Corinthians 7–9, although the misogyny and misogamy of *Against Jovinian* are far more extreme and pervasive than anything in the writings attributed to Paul. Jerome's purpose was to refute the heresies of Jovinian, who claimed (among other opinions not relevant to this volume) that virginity is no better than faithful marriage, that no stigma should attach to remarriage after the death of a spouse, and that the Bible supports an overwhelmingly favorable view of matrimony. Jerome was ferociously hostile to these opinions. In order to make his case that marriage, chaste widowhood, and virginity exist in a hierarchy, with virginity far superior to the others, he wove into his argument a misogynistic discourse that denigrated marriage per se, especially "digamy," a concept that includes remarriage after the death of a spouse.[22] In order to discredit matrimony, he also used examples from the Bible and other sources to disparage women as a class, especially widows who remarry. Mahieu lamented his personal predicament by embroidering at length upon all of these preoccupations.

Van Hamel knew only one manuscript of the Latin *Lamentations*; four more have been discovered[23] since he edited the poem and included it in dual language format with Le Fèvre's French translation. However, it is safe to say that the Latin *Lamentations* was never very popular, perhaps because of the opacity and downright weirdness of its Latin style.[24] It would be Le Fèvre's translation (of 1380 or not much earlier)[25] that would go down to posterity as the widely popular, and just as widely reviled, *Lamentations* of Matheolus, or (as it was often cited) just plain "Matheolus" or "Matheolule."

As we turn to the life records of Jehan Le Fèvre, including the evidence of his works, it is important to note the conventions of medieval autobiography, or as Lawrence de Looze has described it, "pseudo-autobiography."[26] Although couched in the first person, with an author-persona sharing the author's name, the late medieval narrative *dit* may not represent the author's personal experience in every precise detail. For example, was the lament of the *mal marié* both intended and generally understood as a literary fiction, in whole or in part? This is possible even in the case of Mahieu and his Petronilla the stony-hearted. While generally accepting the Latin *Lamentations* as factual, Ch.-V. Langlois notes the inconsistency of Mahieu's complaint over his old age and impotence, as interrupted by his account of a quarrel with his wife and their baby's wet nurse: "La scène de la nourrice est-elle 'une expérience ancienne' de Mahieu ou un simple morceau de la littérature (cf. Pers[ius] Sat., V, 182)?/is the scene with the wet nurse a distant memory for Mahieu, or simply a literary borrowing?" He notes that either is possible, as Mahieu must have married in 1274, some sixteen years before he wrote the *Lamentations*.[27] All that said, however, it would be misguided to assume no factual basis at all for the voice of the author-persona in late medieval literary productions. Many details from the writings of Mahieu, Le Fèvre, and their contemporaries can be verified from other surviving documents and even used to determine the dating and chronology of their works. In place of "pseudo"-autobiography, a more accurate description might be "selective, stylized and, in certain passages, fabricated." Protomodern authors used the details of their life stories as strategically, and often as playfully, as they were careful to showcase their real names within the text of their poems.

Through archival research and a thorough investigation of his writings, editor Geneviève Hasenohr has provided a definitive chronology of the Le Fèvre's life and works,[28] with the striking exception of any documentation (outside of his poems) that he ever actually married. (Given the historical precision of Le Fèvre's other references to contemporary persons, it is noteworthy that the very existence of his much-maligned wife cannot be verified.) As he tells us in his poem *Le respit de la mort* (ll. 39–45 and 375–78), he was at least fifty years old by the time he produced that work in late 1376. In homage to his provincial hometown, he frequently styled himself "Jehan Le Fevre, de Ressons-sur-le-Mas." There he owned a vineyard, which he rented out for an annual sum to the abbess and nuns of the neighboring convent of Nostre Dame de Soissons.[29] However, in accordance with his profession of "Procureur en Parlement," he would have resided in Paris for most of the year, from November to August. As explained by Hasenohr, a "Procureur en Parlement" was a lawyer who represented clients in court proceedings or who drew up documents on their behalf.[30] Addressing the female readers of *Leesce* in the closing lines of the poem, Le Fèvre alludes to both of these functions with a self-deprecating pun on his name:

> Mercy, mercy au povre fevre
> Qui plus grant soif seuffre a la levre
> Que n'ot le riche homme en enfer;
> Car il ne scet ouvrer en fer
> Mais en peaulx est toute sa cure.
> Pour vous a fait ceste escripture
> [3974–79].

Have mercy, mercy on poor Smith, who suffers a greater thirst on his lip than did the rich man in hell; for he doesn't know how to work on iron, but his effort is all on parchment. He has made this book for you.

Mostly unregulated in the fourteenth century, the profession followed by Le Fèvre was not much respected, nor was he terribly successful at his job. Compared with other *procureurs* of his time who were involved with scores of cases per year, Le Fèvre did little business, only about one case per year. Thus, his frequent complaints of poverty[31] should probably be taken at face value. He evidently supplemented his income with the proceeds of his literary works, although nothing specific has been discovered about his patrons. (Perhaps they didn't wish to be identified.) Seemingly proud of his creations, he frequently used his own name, for example: "Je, Jehan Le Fevre, claud qui ne sçay forgier" (I, John Smith, a lame man who doesn't know how to forge).[32] In this case, he manages to flaunt his acquaintance with Greco-Roman mythology (by linking himself with Hephaestus, the ancient god of metalworkers), while adroitly deflating the boast with a joke about his disability and the trademark pun on his surname. Of course, the poet's wordplay on his lameness may be self-promoting as much as self-deprecating; it served to distinguish him from others named "Jehan Le Fèvre."

Despite his mediocre performance as a *procureur*, Le Fèvre seems to have been quite knowledgeable in civil law, canon law, and common law, to judge from the evidence of his writings. As explained below, his poem *Le respit de la mort* takes the form of a legal document, and *Le livre de Leesce* is organized around the dramatis personae and process of a trial, complete with plaintiff, defendant, and judge, and with the deployment of lawyer-speak (often humorously pretentious) at strategic points in the poem.[33] In keeping with his expertise in canon law, our author was a spirited if slightly unorthodox theologian and biblical exegete, as will be discussed below.

Le Fèvre authored seven works, five of them translations. (I refer here to the extant works generally accepted as his; for doubtful or putative works, see the section on the works of Jehan Le Fèvre in the annotated bibliography to this volume.) As noted by Pierre-Yves Badel, his active lifetime coincided with "l'âge d'or de la traduction" supported by King Charles V. However, Le Fèvre seems to have worked on his own, without royal sponsorship, and he shied away from direct contact with the gold-standard primary sources tackled by the better-educated court-supported translators, e.g., Aristotle, Livy, and Augustine. Instead, he liked to engage with more popular works that offered a measure of diversion to the busy professional reader along with a smattering of classical learning in a palatable narrative form[34]; addressing this market, he achieved a measure of success. As explained by Hasenohr, his first translation ("très fautive ... une oeuvre de jeunesse"), was based on the Latin *Ecloga Theoduli*, a versified debate between partisans of Greco-Roman and biblical theology,[35] followed shortly thereafter by a new rendition of the often translated *Disticha Catonis*, also (like the *Ecloga*) a medieval primary schoolbook. Extant in over thirty MSS and several early printed editions, Le Fèvre's "Cato" became the most popular version of the text in French.[36] Sometime before 1376, Le Fèvre produced his translation of the pseudo–Ovidian *De vetula* (The Old Woman), in which the author (who was apparently believed by Le Fèvre to be Ovid himself) recounts in two books the dissipations of his youth and his sexual encounter with an old woman when he was hopefully stalking a girl, followed in the final book by a digest of medieval theology and cosmology that purports to be a description of Ovid's program of studies undertaken as penance on his (obviously apocryphal) conversion to Christianity.[37] With his appropriation of *De vetula*, our author had hit upon the sort of material that would ensure his immortality as the translator of "Matheolule": an engrossing story with elements of obscenity, gossip, and intrigue, leavened with enough "educational" interpolations (popularized excerpts from ancient philosophers, the Bible, and the church fathers) to keep it just within the margin of respectability and ensure its preservation.

Le Fèvre produced his first original work, the partly autobiographical *Le respit de la mort*, in late 1376, shortly after his recovery from a near-fatal illness and evidently in fulfillment of a pledge to atone for his sins. The poem is organized as a legal document, specifically an appeal for reprieve from paying a debt, i.e., a postponement of returning the soul lent to him by God. One legitimate excuse for such an extension is war damages, and Le Fèvre (as he claims) has long been in combat with the world, the flesh, the devil (2971–3028), and his loud, contentious wife (2955–70). The author describes how he discussed his petition with two friends who appear to be the only visitors at his sickbed, one Parviller, who has hope for his recovery, and Sire Robert le Pelletier, who doubts that such a respite is possible. In a curious display of personalized exegesis *ad literam*, their conversation focuses (not without out a sense of humor, at least on Le Fèvre's side) on interpreting the evidence of the Bible as it applies to the situation at hand. For example, the well-meaning Parviller advises his friend to consider the curative treatment attempted on the elderly King David, who had a beautiful young virgin placed in his sickbed as a warming device but didn't have sex with her (254–76).[38] He should also try to emulate Enoch and Elijah (321–34),[39] who were transported directly to heaven. Le Fèvre bats back that even though he is fifty or more, he is not as old as was David when the charms of the Shunamite girl left him cold (375–76), and he would love to follow in the footsteps of Enoch and Elijah if he only knew how (475–78)! When the dour Pelletier interjects that David's illness was incurable because he was worn out by his concubines, and in any case, there is no reprieve from death (487–559), the lawyer-patient counterargues (more or less accurately) that it was Solomon, not David, who had all those concubines (567–80),[40] and the pious David and Hezekiah were actually granted such a respite by God for their prayers (591–683),[41] while the incorrigible Ahaziah was denied (684–710).[42] After an extended digression on the macrocosm, microcosm, and estates of society, Le Fèvre closes his poem with a meditation on the biblical Jacob, his celebrated ladder, and its allegory (3195–3680). This portion begins with a statement on the spiritual utility of translating the Bible into the vernacular:

> Aux laiez gens grans biens feroit
> qui en franchois leur metteroit
> les exemples et lez figures
> que on list es Saintes Escripturez
> [3195–98].

It would be a great benefit to the lay people if someone would put into French the examples and the allegories that we read in Holy Scripture.

Le Fèvre explains the five steps of Jacob's ladder to heaven as an allegory of the five stages of penance: contrition, confession, and satisfaction, with the latter subdivided as prayer, almsgiving, and fasting (3313–41), all of which he discusses in detail (3342–3680) and declares his intention to practice (3724–27). Not long after his plea for recovery was granted by the merciful God, Le Fèvre evidently produced his translation *Hymnes de la liturgie*, which he may have undertaken in thanksgiving for his respite from death.[43]

By around 1380, however, Le Fèvre appears to have regressed from his sickbed resolutions, for it was then that he decided to translate the scurrilous, salacious, and often blasphemous[44] *Lamentations* of "Matheolule." With elements of genuine creativity as well as momentary lapses into carelessness, this is not an especially close or literal translation. Van Hamel and later critics have documented the poet's occasional inaccuracies, his topical updates to the thirteenth-century Latin poem (e.g., the famous catalogue of Parisian churches frequented by women on the prowl, 2.976–99), and — perhaps most intriguing — his interpolations, including details of his personal life, fictitious or otherwise (like Mahieu, he is unhappily married, 1.1–82). Clearly intrigued with modernity, he even adorned his polemic with a reference to eyeglasses, then a recent invention (2.415).[45] However, Le Fèvre made one revision to the *Lamentations* that outweighs all the others in its importance: he explicitly and prolifically borrowed from the thirteenth-century *Roman de la Rose*, especially its digressive and encyclopedic continuation by Jean de Meun. It is possible that Mahieu knew the *Rose*, although the French poem is never mentioned in the Latin *Lamentations*. Scholars have documented two short passages that might, but only just might, be borrowed from Jean de Meun.[46] There is no such doubt in the case of Le Fèvre's French *Lamentations*. It was he, at least more than anyone else, who established the late medieval reputation of the *Rose* as a misogynist work, and of "Matheolule" as its partner in crime. Le Fèvre first associates the two earlier authors in his original lines that precede the translated *Lamentations*: there he laments his own unhappy marriage and wishes he had followed the advice of "le livre de la Rose" (1.22) and "maistre Mahieu" (1.33) by evading the tortures of matrimony. His extensive borrowings from the *Rose*, both in the *Lamentations* and *Leesce*, are documented in Van Hamel's introduction and notes, Yves Badel's *Le roman de la Rose au XIV siècle: Étude de la réception de l'oeuvre*, Karen Pratt's "Translating Misogamy," and of course, the notes to the translation in this volume.

Le Fèvre's final work was *Le livre de Leesce*, his other original creation. (The date of his death is unknown.) From the topical references in the poem, some of which were misunderstood by Van Hamel, Hasenohr has dated the composition of *Leesce* to some time between 3 February 1380 and 22 April 1387.[47] Several critics have defined the work as a "palinode," that is, an author's extended retraction and refutation of his own previous antifeminist work. Like others of this already ancient genre, *Leesce* begins with an apology to women readers whom his earlier work has supposedly offended, words in their praise, excuses for the earlier work, a promise to make amends, and examples of good women both ancient and contemporary, all questionably serious in tone and intention. Florence Percival has provided a history of the palinode beginning with ancient Greece (where the term originates, with works Le Fèvre could not have known), to the poetry of Ovid, especially his *Ars amatoria* book 3, to the palinodes and palinode-like interpolations found in medieval poetry. She provides a brief discussion of *Leesce* and an extended analysis of its analogue, Chaucer's *Legend of Good Women*.[48] While her commentary is most enlightening, it should be noted that the term "palinode" is not used by the Western medieval authors themselves. Le Fèvre called his poem a "livre" (19, 28, 31), an "escripture" (3979), or a "dit" (3956), the latter being the Middle French term for a fairly lengthy work (usually around 4,000 lines) of intermingled narrative and exposition, pleasure and profit.[49] He refers to the bulk of the poem (81–3467), the lines between his introduction and closing argument, as a "dialogue" (3489), an obvious reference to its dialectical structure of profeminine "counterpoints" alternating with "points" quoted or abridged from the *Lamentations*. Perhaps the medieval genre of retraction and correction might best be characterized as *contredit*, the descriptive term used by at least three of the scribes in their *explicits* to MSS of *Leesce*.[50] Another possible name for the genre that echoes the vocabulary of the medieval authors themselves is "defense of women,"[51] although, to be precise, Le Fèvre and his author-persona Dame Leesce/Lady Gladness speak out as the plaintiffs, not the defendants, in the case of "my ladies versus the poets" (at 742; see below). Le Fèvre's palinode/*contredit* also overlaps with and borrows from other works containing multiple examples of good women, such as the Bible, Ovid's *Heroïdes*, portions of *Against Jovinian* and *Le roman de la Rose*, Boccaccio's *De mulieribus claris*, and the *Legenda aurea* (Golden Legend). Many of these works are termed "catalogs of good women" in the helpful study by Glenda McLeod[52] (which doesn't mention Le Fèvre).

Lady Gladness Puts the *Rose* on Trial

> If Truth sits on the throne, and Reason hears me, I have no cause to doubt that the trial will go my way.
>
> — *The Book of Gladness* 3481–84

Whatever we choose to call it, the medieval *contredit* or "defense of women" is not just intertextual but pugnaciously reactive and derivative. Very often, Le Fèvre is quite explicit about whom and what he (or his author-persona) is reacting against: the unhappy "bigamist" Mahieu of Boulogne and the misogyny of his "libelle diffamatoire" (libelous little book) (3522). Over the course of *Le livre de Leesce*, the summaries of the *Lamentations* are introduced with a phrase such as "Maistre Mahieu ... se complaint" (92–93) or just "Or dit il" (Then he says) (351 et al.) or more pointedly "Item le mesdisant fait noise que" (Then the evil-speaker grumbles that) (1629), while the profeminine counterpoints start with a phrase such as "Si di contre maistre Mahieu" (So I argue against Master Mahieu) (775) or "Leesce respont en riant / A ce qu'il va contrariant" (Gladness answers his argument with a laugh) (823–24). This "dialogue" actually comprises a kind of lawsuit — a series of complaints against the author of the *Lamentations* for the crime of "mesdire" (slander)[53] against women. As discussed above, however, Le Fèvre's response to literary misogyny is far from being addressed to "Matheolule" alone. In introducing the heart of his argument, he cites a list of other offenders, including Ovid and Jean de Meun:

> Et pour ce que il despisoit
> Mes dames et qu'il m'en desplaist,
> J'ay contre luy meü tel plait
> Dont il sera grant mencion
> Se j'en vieng a m'entencion.
> Mais j'ay sur moy maint adversaire
> Et a forte partie a faire.
> Maistre Mahieu a en aïde
> Gallum, Juvenal et Ovide
> Et maistre Jehan Clopinel
> Au cuer joli, au corps isnel,
> Qui clochoit si comme je fais;
> Sur moy en est pesant le fais;
> J'ay contre moy bourdes et fables
> Et poëtries delitables;
> Car de mençoignes y a maintes
> En ces histoires qui sont faintes,
> Que je voy contre moy plaidier
> Et dont ceulx se vouldront aidier

> Qui soustendront maistre Mahieu.
> Mais j'ay tout mon recours a Dieu
> [740–60].

And because he despised my ladies and thus displeases me, I have lodged such a case against him that it will give me great fame if I succeed in my intent. But I have many an adversary against me, and the opposing side is strong. Master Mahieu has on his side Gallus, Juvenal, and Ovid, and Master Jean Clopinel [Jean de Meun] of the merry heart and swift body, who limped just as I do. The burden on me here is heavy; I have against me deceitful tales and myths and delightful poetry; for there are many lies in these fictitious stories that I see arguing against me, and those who support Master Mahieu will resort to them for help. But I have all my help in God.

In fact, the poet will have almost nothing to say about Gallus or Juvenal; rather, he directs his accusations at a mere trio of poets, whose works he claims to be pervasively misogynistic: Ovid (including the pseudo–Ovidian *De vetula*), Jean de Meun, and Mahieu of the Latin *Lamentations*. (Of the three, only "Matheolule" is truly deserving of such a broad-brush categorization. The erudite *Rose* expounds upon many topics besides Jean de Meun's notorious *blasme des femmes*, while Ovid's multifaceted corpus is often downright sympathetic to women.) Thus, *Le livre de Leesce* plays a vital role in the medieval controversy over the meaning and value of *Le roman de la Rose*, especially the misogynous and misogamous passages in Jean de Meun's portion. Christine McWebb has rightly noted that this discussion took place over the better part of a century and is not at all limited to the 1401–2 epistolary debate among Christine, Pierre and Gontier Col, Gerson, and others, which is known as the "querelle de la *Rose*."[54] Nor did the combatants in this literary free-for-all (of the fourteenth century and later, including Le Fèvre) limit themselves to debating the *Rose*; they also argued over the evidence of the Bible (especially the personal behavior and canonical writings of David and Solomon), Ovid, "Matheolule," and others. In all the "querelle" documents thus broadly defined, including *Le livre de Leesce*, the subject of women is inseparable from the interpretation of texts, both sacred and secular, and the critic's judgment on the moral standing (and thus, the credibility) of their authors, both ancient and contemporary.[55]

This brings us to the discussion of Le Fèvre's complex engagement with the *Rose* and especially with Jean de Meun, whom (as he tells us, above) he finds to be sympathetic as a person and admires on artistic grounds. Although Le Fèvre is explicit in his counterarguments to certain of the opinions expressed in the works of the earlier poet,[56] his usual response to the *Rose* is more complex and subtle: an *hommage*, but a revisionist or subversive *hommage*.[57] The preeminent example of this tactic is the title character of his poem, the defender of women and author-persona Dame Leesce/Lady Gladness herself. Her character is borrowed from Guillaume de Lorris's portion of the *Rose*, where she appears as the beautiful young woman who personifies erotic pleasure amid the carefree delights of the rose garden. There she is escorted by her boyfriend Deduit/Mirth on one side and the God of Love on the other:

> Et savez vos qui est s'amie?
> Leesce, qui nou haoit mie,
> L'envoisie, la bien chantanz,
> Que, des qu'el n'avoit que .vii. anz,
> De s'amor li dona l'otroi.
>
> ...

> A li se tint de l'autre part
> Li dex d'Amors, cil qui depart
> Amoreites a sa devise
> [830–33, 863–65].[58]

And do you know who his [Deduit's] sweetheart was? It was [Gladness], who hated him not at all, the gay girl, the sweet singer, who, when she was no more than seven years old, had given him the gift of her love.... On the other side the God of Love stayed near to her. It is he who apportions the gifts of love according to his desire.[59]

"Leesce" can be translated as "joy," but I have followed Chaucer's translation of *Le roman de la Rose* (847) in rendering it as "Gladness." Aside from its Chaucerian provenance, my use of "gladness/glad" for "leesce/lié/liée or lie," thus far unique to this translation, has other important advantages. It allows me to render the poet's recurring dyad "tristesce/leesce" with the equally felicitous "sadness/gladness," and to translate "joye," which he uses interchangeably with "leesce" in all its range of meanings, with its English cognate. Le Fèvre actually refers to his author-persona as "Joye" at line 1925. In Le Fèvre's reimagining, Lady Gladness retains her erotic associations from *Le roman de la Rose*. She is "leesce, l'amoureuse" (2667), the alliterative counterpart to the "lamentations" of the misogynist "Matheolule." The author's allegory is transparent here: woman haters live in sadness/lamentations, while gladness is bestowed by women and their love. However, Le Fèvre's Gladness is no mere personification of sexual pleasure[60] or even of earthly happiness,[61] although she certainly incorporates both of these values. Le Fèvre explains the sacred component of her character in his opening argument against Matheolule:

> Le sage dit en l'Escriture
> Qu'entre toute mondaine cure
> Il n'est riens qui tant doye plaire
> Que d'estre *lié* [from Latin *laetus*] et de bien faire
> Et d'eschever debat et noise
> [81–85, emphasis added].

The wise man [Solomon] says in Scripture that in all the concerns of this life there is nothing which ought to please so much as to be *glad* and to do good and to avoid debate and quarrel. (Emphasis added)

This passage contains several echoes from the biblical books attributed to Solomon "le sage," but its most direct source (unnoted up to now) is a verse from the author's beloved Vulgate Ecclesiastes: "homini bono in conspectu suo dedit Deus sapientiam et scientiam et *laetitiam*" (2:26a, emphasis added)[62] (For to the one who pleases him God gives wisdom and knowledge and joy).[63] Unlike the authors of the *Rose*, Le Fèvre clearly alludes to the derivation of "leesce/lié/liée or lie" from Latin *laetitia/laetus,a*, and "joye" from *gaudia*, both words (and their variants) often used in the Vulgate Bible with honorable reference to godly living. Building up to his final argument, Le Fèvre underscores the Christian legitimacy of the concept by describing how Jesus sent his Paraclete/Holy Spirit to encourage the disciples "en joye" (3378); at 3487, he clearly uses "joye" with reference to a virtuous earthly happiness compatible with marriage. In a different connection, Karen Pratt notes how "by employing Latinisms LeFèvre's version profits from the linguistic authority of the source"[64]; this is clearly the case with his valorization of Lady Gladness through her verbal association with the biblical "gladness" and "joy."

Le Fèvre has not obliterated the erotic connotation of "Leesce," quite the contrary, but he has explicitly harmonized her qualities with *laetitia* as the reward for a life of obedience to God. How is this possible? Lady Gladness explains:

Ne nuls homs ne doit soustenir
Qu'il peüst fors que bien venir
Quant homs par bone affection
Pour lyen de dilection
Prent sa femme bonne et honneste
Si com nostre foy l'amonneste
[221–26].

nor should any man maintain that anything but good can happen when a man freely chooses to take his good and honest wife in a bond of love, just as our faith advises us to do.

For Le Fèvre, and he was far from the only medieval author to see the potential here,[65] the *Rose* can be domesticated by bringing its encomiums on erotic love and procreation into harmony with Christian teachings on marriage, and by extension with the moral guidelines of Reason, allegorically described in the *Rose* as the "semblance" and "image" of God (2975). The God of Love and his entourage have nothing to do with Lady Reason in the *Roman de la Rose*; the lover rejects her advice (to abandon his pursuit of the Rose) at 7155ff., and she departs from him at 7199–7200. While Jean de Meun's Reason is orthodox in her opposition to unregulated sexual passion, she notoriously advises the lover that "it is better to deceive than to be deceived" (4369–70), while disparaging the love of women (6376–77), especially compared with platonic friendship between men (4650ff.) In striking contrast, Le Fèvre restores Lady Reason to her more usual status as the voice of moral judgment in harmony with Christian teachings (763–68).[66] As Lady Gladness argues and Christine and Gerson would so passionately agree, a proper respect for marriage rules out the misogynous discourse of Jean de Meun as anti–Christian, a ban that surely extends to slanderous satire on widows.[67] A scholarly verdict on Christine's thinking applies just as accurately to Lady Gladness: "It is a historical fact that [she] saw in Christianity a means of overcoming oppression,"[68] including the defamation of women.

Le Fèvre's revisionist homage to the *Rose* can also be illustrated through the many exempla of good women that he adapts from the earlier poem. He tells the stories of Lucretia and Penelope as typical examples of women's chastity and marital fidelity (1459–73, 1474–86), while Jean de Meun — in the notorious persona of Le Jaloux (the Jealous Husband) — recounted their stories with a sneer: these women are extraordinary for their sex, not the norm, and even Penelope could be seduced by an artful male (8578ff., 8622). Le Fèvre returns several times to the exempla of Medea and Dido, two women of accomplishment who were used and abandoned by their lovers. In Jean de Meun's *Rose*, La Vieille/the Old Woman tells these stories to her young female charge with a cynical "moral": since men will be unfaithful to you, you do not have to be faithful to them (13235ff.). Lady Gladness detaches the stories of Medea, Dido, and other lovelorn heroines from any such disreputable context. She praises Medea for her generosity, her faithful love, and her intelligence, while heaping opprobrium on the opportunistic Jason; likewise, he tells how Dido rescued the ungrateful Aeneas in his hour of need. They and others like them are presented as evidence of the intelligence, generosity, and fidelity of women as a class.[69]

Le Fèvre/Lady Gladness appropriates many other teachings and personal examples from the *Rose* to substantiate her case for women. As a rule, these materials were used in the earlier poem with a different context and purpose, although not invariably misogynistic. Perhaps the most interesting of these borrowings is Le Fèvre's reworking of the story of Heloïse, which Jean de Meun had done much to popularize.[70] In the *Rose*, the advice of

Heloïse to Abelard is placed within a series of warnings against marriage in the tradition of Jerome's *Against Jovinian*:

> et li provoit par escritures
> et par resons que trop sont dures
> condicions de mariage,
> conbien que la fame soit sage;
> car les livres avoit veüz
> et estudiez et seüz
> et les meurs feminins savoit,
> car tretouz en soi les avoit
> [8739–46].

and she proved to him with texts and reasons that the conditions of marriage are very hard, no matter how wise the wife may be. For she had seen, studied, and known the books, and she knew the feminine ways, for she had them all in herself.[71]

Le Fèvre draws a different significance from the well-documented brilliance and erudition of Heloïse; she is a credit to women in general and an example of women's capacity for practical intelligence as well as philosophy:

> Les femmes eüssent la victoire
> Se cy avec dame Leesce
> Feüst Heloïs, l'abeesse
> Du Paraclit, qui tant fu sage
> Du droit de coustume et d'usage;
> Et si estoit philosofesse
> Combien que elle fust professe
> [1130–36].

Women would have had the victory if here with Lady Gladness were Heloïse, the abbess of the Paraclete, who was so wise in the law of custom and tradition[72]; thus she was a philosopher even though she was a nun.

Instead of focusing on Heloïse as a lover whose passion for Abelard brought calamity to them both, Le Fèvre brings forward the impressive details of her later life story in order to present her as a wise and capable administrator; he knew from his personal experience that an abbess would need a range of intellectual attainments in order to fulfill her responsibilities, which included large-scale financial transactions and attention to the physical facilities of her convent, as well as the pastoral care of her nuns.[73]

This is a good place to note that *The Book of Gladness* follows the *Roman de la Rose* in its apportionment of generic conventions between allegory, i.e., the personified abstractions (such as Leesce/Gladness) who frame the narrative, and the many short stories or exempla presented within the frame as a form of moral instruction on the literal level. For example, we have Le Fèvre's Lady Gladness, an allegorical figure, recounting the historically "true" examples of women both ancient and contemporary to substantiate her thesis that females are generally beneficent and thus worthy of love and respect. The remarks of A. J. Minnis on Jean de Meun's *Roman de la Rose* can be applied just as accurately to the *Book of Gladness*: "Jean was a plain-style poet whose main (though by no means only) modes of procedure are narration and exemplification rather than enigmatic fable and allegory."[74] Le Fèvre was familiar with the allegorical approach, as evidenced by his explication of Jacob's ladder as the stages of penance in *Le respit de la mort*, but to judge from his sickbed hermeneutics on the biblical books of Kings (to give just one example), he was more passionately attracted to the *sensus literalis*, both as a guide to moral conduct and as a possible source of encouragement. He was not alone. For medieval authors in general, the literal meaning of a narrative — especially a story from the Bible or other respected source — was highly valued for the moral education provided by its case studies of human behavior both good and bad, although the actual "take-home lesson" of a complex narrative might be endlessly debated, not least where the subject of women was concerned.[75] With ambivalent homage, Lady Gladness tells many of the same stories as did Jean de Meun, and she draws instruction from their literal meaning as he does, but as discussed above, she generally presents her own quite different conclusion on the moral teaching to be inferred from these stories.

Without directly mentioning the issue, Le Fèvre also weighs in on a notorious controversy generated by the *Rose* and taken up by its defenders and detractors: is it acceptable for a writer to mention the "secréz membres/private parts" of the human body by their "proper" names,[76] i.e., to discuss them plainly, without evasion or euphemism? His analysis implies that the answer is yes, at least when the mention of body parts is essential to the moral intention of a passage. Jean de Meun's Lady Reason had named "les coilles" (the balls)[77] in retelling an episode from Greco-Roman mythology, only to be scolded for her frankly sexual talk by the Lover (of all people!) in a spirited exchange of views on the ethics of speaking "proprement" on such a sensitive subject (6920; see 5507, 6899–7200). The controversy would be argued on different grounds in the 1401–2 "querelle de la Rose," where the poem's defenders argue that Jean de Meun's explicit naming of body parts was necessary and proper in its context, while Gerson and Christine maintain that these words must be avoided, almost without exception, because they tend to inspire the unclean thoughts that lead to illicit sexual activity, especially by the young and undisciplined.[78]

In *Leesce*, the disputed word occurs only once (2711), and its use is clearly strategic. To sustain her case for women, Lady Gladness must attack and discredit the poetry of Ovid, the alleged arch-misogynist. Among the weapons in her arsenal is the argument ad hominem:

> Ne cuidiés pas que je devine;
> Oncques chapon n'ama geline.
> Pour Ovide l'ay recité.
> Car on raconte en verité
> Qu'on lui coupa ambdeux les couilles;
> Aux estoupes et aux oeufs douilles
> Furent restraintes et sanées;
>
> ...
>
> Si puet on presumer et dire
> Que, haïneus et tout plain d'ire,
> Femmes après ce fait blasma
> N'oncques depuis ne les ama
> [2707–13, 2719–22].

Don't think I am imagining things; "a capon never loved a hen." I said this about Ovid. For the true story is that he had both his balls cut off. They were bandaged and healed with pieces of flax and soft eggs.... Thus we can understand and say that being hateful and brim-full of wrath, he blamed women after this and never loved them afterward.

As Lady Gladness explains, Ovid's motive for his literary attacks on women was personal and disreputable — he began to write in this fashion because he could no longer enjoy a normal sex life. The passage implicitly justifies the use of questionable language when its purpose is to reinforce a good moral. Lady Gladness says "couilles" to adorn her quite orthodox argument that Ovid's non–Christian teachings on women and sexual morality are not to be trusted. In so doing, she pays homage to Jean de Meun's plainspoken Lady Reason in her manner of naming the body parts, but without echoing the misogyny and sometimes questionable morality of her thirteenth-century prototype.

Lady Gladness Questions Authority

> It isn't such a great offense if one were to object to what he says about Saint Ambrose; it isn't worth a raspberry. For Saint Paul says just the opposite. Which one is better to follow?
>
> —*The Book of Gladness* 1705–10

Lady Gladness has a laudable purpose in recounting the story of Ovid's castration, but is it really, as she claims, "verité"? The medieval debate on women is just as surely a debate on the moral status and credibility of authors and their writings. Along with his strategic reconstructions of the *Rose*, Le Fèvre deploys an array of interpretive strategies in his engagement with a literary patrimony that he recognizes as overwhelmingly hostile to women. Only once or twice does he challenge the misogynist tradition through an allegorical reading of sources; for example, the creation of Eve from Adam's rib "ne pourroit plus proprement/Figurer/could not more truly prefigure" the emergence of Holy Church from the wounded side of the crucified Jesus.[79] Much more commonly, he passes judgment on whether a story understood on the literal level should be accepted as "vraye ystoire" (2495) or distrusted as "truffes" (frivolous stories) (668), mere fiction (e.g., 756), or, most often, "fable," from Latin *fabula*, which I generally translate with its Greek-derived equivalent "myth." His verdict is based on the credibility of the source. He is careful to note when an exemplum is taken from the Bible, and thus unquestionably true (81, 1022, 1270, 1544, 1939, 2492, 2495, 2948); other unimpeachable sources are the *Legenda Aurea* (Golden Legend) (2582) and the serious secular histories known to Le Fèvre at least at second hand.[80] By contrast, the tales of the classical poets, especially Ovid,[81] and more especially the unsourced *fabliaux* so beloved by "Matheolule,"[82] can be dismissed as fictions of no instructional value. In many cases, Lady Gladness points to the improbability of the events recounted in ancient *fables* as proof positive that the story is just not true. One example will suffice to illustrate this method. In Mahieu's distorted retelling of a story from Ovid's *Metamorphoses*, Eurydice serves as a typical example of women's disobedience[83]: although instructed not to turn and look back into hell as Orpheus escorts her to safety, she does so anyway and is forced to return there for good (1975–89). The response of Lady Gladness to this story is grounded in rationalism:

> D'Orpheüs et de s'espousée
> C'est fable de bourde arrousée.
> Car ce seroit contre nature
> S'une mortele creature
> Après sa mort venoit a vie.
> Quant l'ame est hors du corps ravie
> Il convenroit bien flajoler
> Et violer et citoler,
> Qui pour ce la pourroit ravoir!
> En luy a moult pou de savoir;

> Homs qui de tels exemples use,
> Il fait bien entendre la muse.
> Tels dis aux femmes point ne nuisent
> Ne leurs bontés n'en amenuisent
> [2088–2102].

It's a myth replete with falsehood about Orpheus and his wife. For it would be against nature if a mortal creature came to life after its death. When the soul is seized from the body, it is all very well to play the flute, the viol, and the harp: who could get her back that way? There is very little knowledge in him — the man who uses such examples is just giving us a song and dance.[84] Such stories in no way discredit women or take away from their good deeds.

In *The Book of Gladness*, a story classed as fictitious can simply be dismissed out of hand. By contrast, in expounding upon examples regarded as true, Le Fèvre uses a range of interpretive strategies that vary with the moral caliber of the woman discussed in the source. His argument can easily accommodate the respected heroines of the Bible, the *Legenda aurea*, and secular history; these women are cited straightforwardly as typical of their sex and thus as supporting his case: Judith (1761ff.), Esther (2123ff.), Jephthah's daughter (2492ff.), Virginia (2522ff.), female saints (2810–53), female worthies (2889ff.), Hannah (2913), Susanna (2914ff., the series of brave, accomplished, and virtuous women introduced at 3528, and the catalog of ancient heroines introduced at 3820. A bad woman, if acknowledged as historical, may be discounted as atypical of women in general, as in the examples of Carfania (1162) and the *fabliau* widow (1409ff.). In several cases, her failings are rationalized as necessary to the workings of providence: see the stories of Vashti (2115ff.), Eve (2141ff.), and Lot's wife (2180ff.); in other examples, her guilt is minimized by calling out the man involved with her crime. These include the knight who abetted the disloyalty of the *fabliau* widow (1421–22); Samson, who abandoned his wife to take up with the seductress Delilah (1545–51); and the devious husband responsible for his wife's death by poisoning (2071ff.).

At times, Le Fèvre offers a detailed rebuttal to the received interpretation of a source accepted as "vraye ystoire." This is especially the case with his repeated discussions of the biblical David and Solomon, whose eventful biographies were cherrypicked by a long line of theologians to "prove" that even the greatest of men have been lured to their moral ruin by the well-nigh irresistible enticements of women.[85] For example, Mahieu of Boulogne was only channeling the commentary of Jerome and others when he attacked Bathsheba as the cause, intentional or otherwise, of King David's fall from the exemplary piety of his earlier years, to the moral cesspool of his adultery and the murder by proxy of her husband, Uriah.[86] Bathsheba, in his hateful commentary, is typical of women:

> Quid damnabilius? Maledicantur mulieres
> Omnes! Expertas, si vis hoc scire, vide res.
> En! Fuit Urie mortis promotio David
> Cui Bethsabee per eum viduata jugavit [886–89].

What is more damnable [than for a woman to take a second husband and love him more than her first]? Ugh! May wives be cursed — all of them! If you want to know about this, look at the established facts. The instigator of Uriah's death was David, whom Bathsheba married on being widowed by him. (translation mine)

Some interpreters avoided the question of personal responsibility for the murder by allegorizing the story away; in this approach, King David becomes Jesus, who rescues

Bathsheba (the church) by killing Uriah (the devil).[87] Le Fèvre engages in no such hermeneutics of evasion. Instead, he "pulls rank" on Mahieu and his patristic sources by appealing directly to a close literal reading of their ultimate authority, the Bible, specifically the story of David and Bathsheba in the book of Kings[88]:

> Puis parle de la mort Urie
> Par Bersabee, sa moullier;
> David l'aperçut despoullier
> Et laver dedens la fontaine.
> ...
> Et se David donna la lettre
> Pour Urias a la mort mettre,
> Bersabee n'en fu coulpable;
> Ce fist Joab, le connestable.
> Des hommes treuve on ces desroys
> En la Bible, ou livre des Roys.
> ...
> Sa femme en fist, tant esploita,
> Et orent de leur mariage
> Un fil, roy Salemon le sage.
> Et s'il ot en ce aucun vice,
> David fu cause du malice;
> La dame n'en fu point coulpable;
> Cest exemple n'est mie fable
> [1505–9, 1539–44, 260–66].

Then he [Mahieu] talks of the killing of Uriah by Bathsheba his wife; David saw her undress and bathe in the fountain.... And if David gave the order for Uriah to be put to death, Bathsheba was not guilty of this—Joab the general did it. We find these sinful acts by men in the Bible, in the book of Kings.... He [David] took her [Bathsheba] to wife, he succeeded at that, and they had a son from their marriage, Solomon the wise. And if there was any fault in this, David was the cause of the crime; the lady wasn't guilty at all. This example is no myth.

Le Fèvre's defense of Bathsheba against the slurs of the misogynistic exegetes is morally serious and biblically well founded. As he surely knew well, the prophet Nathan accused David and no other person of guilt for the murder of Uriah, and David obeyed the prophet by repenting before God without any attempt whatsoever to shift the blame for his actions.[89]

Lady Gladness is equally faithful to the letter in discoursing on Solomon "le sage," especially his sexual promiscuity and his worship of foreign gods at the instigation of his wives:

> Il dit pis, que femmes vainquirent
> Salemon et le desconfirent.
> Par femmes et par leurs desroys
> Fu pris le plus sage des roys;
> Salemon, plain de sapience,
> Lors abusa de sa science:
> Si fu seduis et ordenés
> Que par blandices fu menés
> ...
> Hors de sa loy s'estut vuidier
> Pour les idoles aourer
> ...

Leesce respont en riant
A ce qu'il va contrariant
Et met ceste solucion:
...
Salemon fu riche homme et sage;
De nature savoit l'usage;
Il fu roy et non pas hermite,
Si ne voult estre sodomite;
Sodomite est plus lais pechiés
Dont l'omme puist entechiés.
Pour ce prist il des concubines
Et des femmes et des roïnes
Et jouvenceles a plenté
En usant de sa voulenté.
Il compila par grant science
Ecclesiastes, Sapience,
Et Proverbes et Paraboles,
Dont on lit en maintes escoles;
Et aussi fist il les Cantiques;
Beaulx livres sont et autentiques
[645–52, 654–55, 823–25, 847–62].

He [Mahieu] says worse, that women conquered Solomon and put him to shame. The wisest of kings was ensnared by women and their excesses; Solomon, full of wisdom, misused his learning then. He was so deceived and controlled that he was led by their enticements.... He was made to leave his religion and worship idols.... Gladness answers his argument with a laugh and poses this solution: ... Solomon was a rich man and wise; he knew the custom of nature; he was a king, not a hermit. He didn't want to be a sodomite![90] Sodomy is the ugliest sin with which man can be defiled. So he took concubines and wives and queens and plenty of young girls, using them as he pleased. With great learning he composed Ecclesiastes, Wisdom, Proverbs, and Parables, which we read in many schools; he also wrote the Song of Songs. These books are beautiful and true.

While in no way distorting the letter of Scripture here, Lady Gladness — notably described in the passage as "answer[ing] ... with a laugh" — may be suspected of speaking tongue in cheek, perhaps with good-natured satire on the exegetical contortions involved in rationalizing any story, but especially a sexy story, to serve as a morally improving exemplum. Solomon's amatory excesses offer a positive moral example for — avoiding sodomy! And anyway, his scandalous lifestyle didn't stop him from authoring books that are "beautiful and true," and, the passage implies, it may even have helped him to write more discerningly. While this may be the most shocking, it is not the only case where Lady Gladness attaches a rather unconventional moral to an exemplum of unquestioned prestige and veracity. For example, when Aristotle allowed himself to be mounted like a horse, he simply exemplified the power of love, and anyway, his enormous literary output was unhurt or even helped by the situation (867ff.); Lot's wife needed to get out of the way so that Lot could replenish the earth by impregnating his daughters (2167ff.); the moral of the story of "the woman taken in adultery" is that one shouldn't speak ill of women (2949–51). While the lawyer-poet never strays into outright heresy, at times he seems to play fast and loose with his self-expressed goal of creating a vernacular translation of the Bible for the lay reader's edification.

This discussion of Lady Gladness and her case against the authors would not be complete without noting how Le Fèvre sometimes assumed the role of author himself, and in a most radical fashion: he simply fabricated at least a few of his stories out of whole cloth to support his polemic, evidently hoping they would be accepted as "vraye ystoire" and enter the canonical tradition. To give the most egregious example, I can find no trace of the claim that Ovid was punished by castration in any source prior to *The Book of Gladness*. Le Fèvre may have conceived the idea by combining the fact that Ovid was sent into exile for unspecified misbehavior, with a willful misreading of his "mutacion" as described in *De vetula*, which refers to religious conversion, not dismemberment.[91] Thus altered by a literary "cut-and-paste" operation, the life story of Ovid now conveniently serves as a foil to the positive exemplum of the castrated Abelard, champion of women:

> L'en n'oï oncques en nul art
> Que maistre Pierre Abaëlart,
> Sages et bien araisonnés,
> Combien que il fust chaponnés,
> Des femme nul blasme deïst
> Ne de sa langue y mesfeïst.
> Mais fist le Paraclit faire,
> Ou suer Heloïs voult attraire;
> Elle y vesqui moult chastement,
> Sagement et honnestement
> [2785–94].

You never hear in any way that Master Peter Abelard, wise and eloquent, ever spoke ill of women or did them wrong with his speech, even though he was castrated. Instead, he had the Paraclete built, where he brought Sister Heloïse; she lived there very chastely, wisely, and honorably.

No subsequent author appears to have accepted the cock-and-bull story of Ovid's castration except for Christine de Pizan, who tells it with a similar ad hominem agenda.[92] She also repeats as fact, while softening the scurrilous detail, Le Fèvre's self-created embellishment on the exemplum of a certain Carfania: she exposed her posterior while pleading a case in court, and by thus disgracing all women, she caused their permanent disbarment from the legal profession.[93]

Le Fèvre also anticipated the arguments of Christine (and feminist discourse in general) by subjecting his literary patrimony to the counterforce of "modern empiricism,"[94] that is, to real-life experience, especially his own. Not only does the author declare his allegiance to "truth" in the opening lines of *The Book of Gladness* (43ff.); he questions whether this "verité" is to be found within authoritative texts or in conflict with them. If ancient authority and truth disagree, as well they might, he will choose the truth (73–74, 760–74), by which he means that he will firmly oppose the misogynistic tradition (43–80). Within *The Book of Gladness*, the author's first foray into this evidence-based hermeneutic is the remarkable catalog of contemporary men and women, some of whom he must have known personally, who happened to be "bigamous," that is, they married widows or they remarried after the death of a spouse (267–324). Notwithstanding the harsh attacks on "bigamy" by Jerome and "Matheolule," these contemporary Parisians are universally acknowledged, by Le Fèvre and others, to be accomplished, wise, and honorable. This passage has the unmistakable ring of a thoughtful observer's *cri de coeur* against the sheer cruelty of stigmatizing widows and remarriage, especially in an era when premature death was all too common. Le Fèvre refrains from mentioning outright, but surely expected his readers to know, that one of the ladies included on his honor roll was twice a war widow, from the battles of Crécy and

Poitiers.[95] How could it be acceptable, he implies, to ridicule and condemn such a tragic victim of circumstance? In response to Mahieu's bitter satire on women religious, summarized at *Leesce* 2595ff., Le Fèvre provides the true story of Abbess Jehanne de Neuville, a "tres vaillant pastourelle" (very valiant shepherdess) (2877), who was probably a personal acquaintance, along with two of her nuns (2885–88). Other real-life contemporary heroines are described in some detail to support his profeminine case: a female professor of law ("the daughter of Jehan Andrieu," 1140–54, also cited by Christine de Pizan),[96] a young wife who died for her chastity (1437–58), and the healer Calabre of Paris (3778–85). Also empirically based are his encomiums on the beneficent everyday activities of actual contemporary women: their domestic industry (545–49, 3694–98, 3738–41, 3751–57, 3763–67), their affinity for childrearing (3746–49), their aid to the sick (3758–61), their noninvolvement with violent crime (3692–93, 3927–30), and their frequent churchgoing (1781–1800, 3707–8).[97] Le Fèvre was clear and outspoken in his sympathy for two especially maligned categories of real-life women: widows who remarry (because they are assailed by unscrupulous wooers and need a protector, 1717ff.), and women forced into prostitution:

> Et quant il en y a aucunes
> Qui de leurs corps sont trop communes
> Et se vendent par povreté,
> Il ne leur doit estre reté.
> Car les hommes qu'elles reçoivent
> De tout leur pouoir les deçoivent
> Et sont plains de si grant malice
> Qu'il ne tendent qu'avarice.
> Car les femmes chuent et flatent
> Ou les tourmentent et les batent
> Quant elles ne peuent accomplir
> Leur vouloir et bien raemplir
> Les bourses des houliers gloutons
> Qui ne valent pas deux boutons [2327–40].

And if there are some women who are too common with their bodies and sell themselves from poverty, it shouldn't be blamed on them. For the men whom they pick up defraud them with all their might, and they are full of such great malice that they care only for profit. For they caress and flatter the women, or they torment and beat them when they can't accomplish their desire by stuffing the purses of those lecherous thugs who aren't worth two hoots.

In rebuttal to Mahieu's ranting argument that women are lascivious money-grubbers, Le Fèvre dares to note the obvious, with equal parts compassion and common sense: it is pimps, and not the desperate women under their control, who "stuff the[ir] purses" with the earnings of prostitution.

The Recurring Question of Sincerity: A "Dialogue"

> Truth knows well if I'm lying, but will be difficult to find, and this debate to be resolved.
> — *The Book of Gladness* 3965–67

With rhetorical weapons such as these, from the most exalted to the flagrantly risible, Lady Gladness argues her case of "my ladies against the poets." Although confident of a favorable verdict (what else is possible, with Reason as her judge?), the author leaves her case unresolved, inviting some future reader (preferably a woman) to complete his argument:

> Mes dames, je pri humblement
> Se j'ay sostenu foiblement
> Votre cause par ignorance,
> Employés cy vostre vaillance
> Et les deffautes ampliés
> ...
> Atant fineray mon propos
> Jusqu'a tant que plus sage viengne
> Qui ceste matiere soustiengne
> [3954–54, 3983–85].

My ladies, I ask you humbly, if I have pleaded your case weakly through my ignorance, use here your strength to make up for my defects.... So here I shall end my treatise until someone wiser comes along who may carry on this subject.

It may be this open-ended conclusion, with the feckless humanity of its appeal to the reader, that accounts for a remarkable ability possessed by *The Book of Gladness*: to call forth a natural human response from the serious scholar. Virtually every critic to engage with this work has expressed, in one form or another, the very same almost childlike curiosity: Is this writer serious? Is the poem a "real" defense of women? Is Lady Gladness a substantive creation with arguments intended to persuade, or is she supposed to be some kind of joke? Of course, as these critics know well, the question of an author's "real" motivation is ultimately unanswerable, sometimes even to the author herself. Nonetheless, a review of the major points of contention over the "sincerity" of the *Book* has insights to offer on its thematic content as well as its literary posterity.

Virtually every critic to engage with Le Fèvre's palinode/*contredit*, whatever her/his ultimate verdict on the seriousness of the work, has complained of the persistent voice of Mahieu through much of the poem. While the material carried over from the *Lamentations* does not in fact occupy as much as two-thirds of the sequel, as sometimes alleged,[98] there is no denying that *The Book of Gladness* provides an extended hearing for the misogynistic arguments that it claims to oppose. In my view, however, the author's resort to "point-counterpoint" format was virtually unavoidable in a work on this subject and is thus insufficient to discredit the sincerity of his case. Even as passionate an advocate for women as Christine de Pizan gives voice to the standard misogynistic allegations in many of the chapter headings to her *Book of the City of Ladies*, even as she goes on to demolish these rhetorical straw men with counterclaims developed at length within the text of the chapters themselves. In the patriarchal culture of premodern Europe, male supremacist discourse was virtually impossible to escape.[99] For example, on the subject of rape, Christine begins her rebuttal by summarizing the antifeminist position:

"Dame, ... m'anuye et me grieve de ce que hommes dient tant que fammes se veulent efforcier et que il ne leur desplait mie quoyque elles escondissent de bouche de estre par hommes efforciées. Mais fort me seroit a croire que agreeable leur fust si grant villenie.' Responce: 'N'en doubtes pas, amie chiere, que ce n'est mie plaisir aux dames chastes et de belle vie estre efforciées, ains leur est douleur sur toutes autres."

"My lady ... I am therefore troubled and grieved when men argue that many women want to be raped and that it does not bother them at all to be raped by men even when they verbally protest. It would be hard to believe that such great villainy is actually pleasant for them." She answered, "Rest assured, dear friend, chaste ladies who live honestly take absolutely no pleasure in being raped. Indeed, rape is the greatest possible sorrow for them."[100]

By contrast, Le Fèvre never once alludes to the claim that any woman, "chaste" or otherwise, would like to be raped. Where he does refer to the crime, it is with compassion for the victim: "Si amast mieulx estre escorchie/She would rather have been skinned alive" (1464), and a no-nonsense statement on who is at fault: "Je n'y en vois nulle qui blesce/Son ami n'a force le preigne/I see not one woman who wounds her lover or rapes him" (3927–28). In light of the evidence, it is clear that Le Fèvre did not invariably give voice to the hateful allegations of misogynistic discourse, even as a pretext for counterargument. In important cases, he allowed a strong profeminine statement to stand alone and unopposed.

Another time-honored observation on the *Lamentations* and its sequel is that the companion poems may actually amount to nothing more significant than an extended lawyer joke: in this reading, the author's most important purpose is to flaunt his cynical ingenuity in arguing both sides of the case.[101] As suggested above, *The Book of Gladness* does have its interludes of playfulness and parody that might be brought forward to justify such a claim. From ancient times, the palinode was associated with rhetorical virtuosity, juridical training, lack of conviction, and playful intentions, while paradoxically accommodating a serious subtext and/or interludes of profound conviction.[102] Where the polemic of Lady Gladness is concerned, the preponderance of the evidence (so to speak) weighs in favor of Blumenfeld-Kosinski's argument that the sacred "voice of reason" predominates.[103] In making his case for women, Le Fèvre calls on God as his help, repeatedly invokes the Bible and the doctrines of his faith, and expects a favorable verdict from the judgment of Truth and Reason. Thus, despite the leavening of humor and ribaldry, his position —*against* the misogyny of "Matheolule," and *for* "my ladies"— is hardly left open to doubt.

Another complaint against *The Book of Gladness* as a profeminine argument is that most of its exemplary women are distinguished for the "conventional," rather "passive" female virtues of virginity or fidelity, and/or they are celebrated mainly as helpers to men.[104] Such a critique, of course, is founded in anachronistic expectations of what was conceivable in a deeply patriarchal Christian culture. Even as outspoken a protofeminist as Christine de Pizan would base much of her defense on these same traditionally feminine qualities of fidelity and nurturing, which she proudly defines as "les trasses souveraines que Dieu commande a suivre" (the supreme footprints that God commands us to follow),[105] or no less than the imitation of Christ. This is a good place to remember how radical it was, by the standards of the time, to argue that women might surpass their male counterparts in any form of virtuous conduct, or for that matter even to associate the qualities of fidelity and fortitude in suffering with women. In Guillaume de Machaut's palinode *The Judgment of the King of Navarre*, the poet-persona initially attempts to defend his earlier case for the supremacy of males in emotional martyrdom (1703–68), although (within the fiction of the poem) he will be browbeaten into acceptance of the opposing argument, that women are better endowed with the capacity to suffer for love:

> On ne porroit trouver en homme
> Si grant loyauté comme en femme,
> Ne jamais d'amoureuse flame

> Ne seroient si fort espris,
> Comme seroit dame de pris.
> Car quant il y a meins d'amour,
> Il y a meins de dolour,
> Puis que ce vient a mal sentir [2810–17].[106]

> Loyalty as great as that of women
> Cannot be found in any man;
> Nor would men ever be as deeply
> Inflamed by the spark of love
> As a worthy lady would.
> For when there is less love,
> There is that much less suffering,
> Because it comes from feeling pain.[107]

Likewise, Christine in her *Book of the City of Ladies* considers the endurance of suffering to be a mark of superior virtue:

> Et les simples debonnaires dames, a l'exemple de pacience que Dieu commande, ont souffert amiablement les grans injures qui tant par bouche de plusieurs comme par mains escris leur ont esté faictes a tort et a pechié, eulx rapportant a Diue de leur bon droit.

> [Lady Reason:] And the simple, noble ladies, following the example of suffering which God commands, have cheerfully suffered the great attacks which, both in the spoken and written word, have been wrongfully and sinfully perpetrated against women by men who all the while appealed to God for the right to do so.[108]

Also eulogized for their patience are the "women trewe in loving al hir lyve" (F 438) of Chaucer's *Legend of Good Women*, a work often accepted in its own time and later as a serious argument[109]; five of the nine women are called "martyrs" in the titles to their legends. All things considered, Le Fèvre's encomiums to women for their loyalty and self-sacrifice should be understood within the Christian culture of their time as in no way belittling, but laudatory indeed.

Finally, the character of Lady Gladness herself has been called into evidence that Le Fèvre's profeminine discourse is less than pure and wholehearted. It is true that her character is not as developed as it might have been, "a cursory tutelary figure"[110] compared with the richly detailed portraits of her antecedents Lady Philosophy (Boethius), the Goddess Natura (Alan of Lille), and the personifications who inhabit *Le roman de la Rose*. Several critics have been troubled by the fact that Le Fèvre often appears to lose track of who is supposed to be speaking the "counterpoints" to "Matheolule," himself or Lady Gladness.[111] In this view, the frequent impossibility of distinguishing Le Fèvre's argument from that of his lady-persona is a signal that he is "presenting women's case without energizing her voice,"[112] or perhaps she merely represents "an aspect of the poet himself, namely, his desire for the solace that women provide."[113]

While partially justified, such reader responses fail to acknowledge the full range of associations, from the erotic to the sacred, in the concepts "leesce" and its interchangeable synonym "joye." The poet's identification with his female persona can more accurately be read as a signal of his respect for her qualities and his commitment to the case she presents. It was well understood in medieval literary theory that the views expressed by a fictional character (such as Le Jaloux [the Jealous Husband] in *Le roman de la Rose*) might or might not be identical with the views of the author. For example, Christine's antagonist Pierre

Col would argue that Jean de Meun created the character and put words in his mouth in order to discredit, not to endorse, the scurrilous misogyny of his fictional creation: "pour monstrer et corrigier la tres grant desraisonnableté et passion desordenee qui est en home jaloux" (in order to show and to correct the very great irrationality and unruly passion which resides in a jealous man.[114] Le Fèvre may have meant to remove all doubt of his intentions by "forgetting" who is supposed to be "speaking" the argument, himself or his lady-persona. In this view, Lady Gladness clearly speaks for the author; she is artfully crafted as the poet's true *altera sibi*. Through the range of her characteristics, he expresses his own irrepressible humor and *joie de vivre*, along with his serious concerns on textual authority, human relationships, and practical theology. In her challenge to literary authority, Lady Gladness personifies the Ovidian/medieval concept of "serious play" as elucidated by Robert W. Hanning in his book of that title. As noted by Hanning, this tradition is to be found in the mixed style and often subversive content of the palinode/*contredit* and defense of women.[115]

Of course, the degree of an author's "sincerity" is ultimately unknowable, and according to medieval literary theory, it may not be terribly important, except between the author and God. For Christine de Pizan, a work must be judged by its effect on the reader, whatever the supposed intentions (good or bad) of its author.[116] By this line of reasoning, Lady Gladness is a serious and powerful creation indeed, for she served as the prototype for at least two of the most memorable profeminine voices of the later Middle Ages. She provided the exact combination of elements — the wordplay, the joy, the exegetical high jinks, the serious moral argument — that Chaucer used to such brilliant effect in *The Wife of Bath's Prologue* and *Tale*. A. J. Minnis's recent insight on the Wife's multifaceted character applies just as accurately to Lady Gladness, her progenitor: "Chaucer took from Ovid's *Amores* and Jean de Meun's *Rose* the figure of the *magistra amoris* and transformed her ... she is capable of going beyond her mock-*magisterium* to exercise an extensive, and quite un-ironic, moral authority ... in effect she is brought into disputation with — and acquits herself well against — the mighty St. Jerome."[117] No such complexity is found in the prototypical characters of Ovid's Dipsas or Jean de Meun's La Vieille, nor do these earlier figures engage in a contentious "dialogue" with misogynistic literary authority, as Gladness and Alice of Bath would do. Not least among many others, Lady Gladness showed Chaucer the way.

Also to serve a profeminine polemic, Christine transformed Le Fèvre's singular author-persona into a trinity of God's daughters, the unequivocally serious Raison, Droitture, and Justice, who assist her in refuting the claims of misogyny and creating an alternate version of history in her *Book of the City of Ladies*.[118] In effect, Christine takes up the challenge put forward by Le Fèvre in his closing address to the *female* readers of his capstone work (3951–54, quoted above), and thereby creates a new and (in many ways) improved version of her predecessor's case for women.

Whatever the intention of its author, *The Book of Gladness* has proven to be anything but frivolous in the power of its literary legacy, which has been only imperfectly explored to date. Now that the book is available in a translation and format designed for clarity, there is hope that its author's desire for a spirited reader response, or to use his own expression, a "dialogue," can be more fully realized in the years to come.

Notes to the Introduction

1. There is one modern edition of *Le livre de Leesce*: in volume 2 of A.-G. Van Hamel, ed., *Les lamentations de Matheolus et Le livre de Leësce de Jehan Le Fèvre, de Ressons*, 2 vols. (Paris: Émile Bouillon, 1892–1905). This work also contains the Latin and French *Lamentations* and is still the only complete and fully annotated edition

of all three poems. All citations to the three poems in their original languages are drawn from Van Hamel's edition unless otherwise indicated. This edition has been published electronically at http://www.archive.org/details/leslamentations00hamegoog. For more recent editions of the Latin and French *Lamentations* (edited by Alfred Schmitt and Tiziano Pacchiarotti), see the annotated bibliography in this volume.

2. All references to the works of Chaucer are taken from *The Riverside Chaucer*, 3rd ed., gen. ed. Larry D. Benson (Boston: Houghton Mifflin, 1987). The bibliography on Chaucer and Le Fèvre, while not extensive, has established overwhelming evidence of influence; see Arthur K. Moore, "Chaucer and Matheolus," *Notes and Queries* 190 (1946): 245–48 (*Lamentations* only); Zacharias P. Thundy, "Matheolus, Chaucer, and the Wife of Bath," *Chaucerian Problems and Perspectives: Essays Presented to Paul E. Beichner C.S.C.*, ed. Edward Vasta and Zacharias P. Thundy (Notre Dame: University of Notre Dame Press, 1979), 24–58 (with detailed comparative charts, all on *Lamentations* except for brief comparison of Leesce and Alice of Bath, 45); Zacharias P. Thundy, "Chaucer's 'Corones Tweyne' and Matheolus," *Neuphilologische Mitteilungen* 86, no. 3 (1985): 343–47 (*Lamentations* and *Troilus and Criseyde* only); Helen Phillips, "Chaucer and Jean Le Fèvre," *Archiv für das Studium der neueren Sprachen und Literaturen* 232 (1995): 23–36 (29–36 has insightful comparison of *Leesce* with Chaucer's works including the *Wife of Bath's Prologue* and *Tale*); Susan L. Smith, *The Power of Women: A* Topos *in Medieval Art and Literature* (Philadelphia: University of Pennsylvania Press, 1995), 58–59 (brief comparison of Dame Leesce to the Wife of Bath); Jill Mann, *Feminizing Chaucer* (1991; rev. ed. Cambridge: D.S. Brewer, 2002), 1–2, 13, 27–31, 36 (takes insightful note of common themes and even word choices, while she does not argue that Chaucer knew Le Fèvre). Thundy's parallel passages are in some individual cases far-fetched, but collectively impossible to dismiss.

3. The only publication on this relationship to date is an abstract of my paper delivered at the International Congress of Medieval Studies, Kalamazoo, MI, 2001: Linda Barney Burke, "Counter-Defamation: Women and Truth in Gower's *Confessio Amantis* and Jehan Le Fèvre's *Le livre de Leesce*," *John Gower Newsletter* 20, no. 2 (2001): 20–21.

4. Maureen Cheney Curnow, introduction, "The 'Livre de la cité des dames' of Christine de Pisan: A Critical Edition," Ph.D. diss., Vanderbilt University, 1975, 128; the full discussion of *LL* as a paradigm for *Cité des dames* is at 127–38. Curnow's edition of the original Middle French *Cité des dames* is still the only fully annotated edition of that work, with (to date) the only systematic survey of its debt to various sources, including Le Fèvre. Thus, it remains indispensable as well as easy to obtain. Other critics have briefly noted Christine's debt to Le Fèvre; see Karen Pratt, "Analogy or Logic; Authority or Experience? Rhetorical Strategies for and against Women," in *Literary Aspects of Court Culture: Selected Papers from the Seventh Triennial Congress of the International Courtly Literature Society*, ed. Donald Maddox and Sara Sturm-Maddox (Cambridge, Eng.: D. S. Brewer, 1994), 62–63. Alcuin Blamires discusses the intertextuality of Christine's defense of women, including the contribution of Le Fèvre: see his ground-breaking study, *The Case for Women in Medieval Culture* (Oxford: Clarendon, 1997), esp. 3–5. Unlike Chaucer, Christine at least admitted to knowing the work of Jehan Le Fèvre, whom she refers to as "Matheolus": see *La città delle dame*, ed. Earl Jeffrey Richards, trans. Patrizia Caraffi (Milan: Luni, 1997), 40, 42, 70, 268; *The Book of the City of Ladies*, trans. Earl Jeffrey Richards, rev. ed. (New York: Persea Books, 1998), 3, 7, 19, 127. It is unlikely that Christine knew the Latin *Lamentations*, which was never very popular. In citing "Matheolus," she surely included a reference to *LL*, which was indisputably a major source for *The Book of the City of Ladies*. She almost certainly intended "Matheolus" to be understood as including Le Fèvre's French *Lamentations* as well; the companion poems were quite often bound as a unit (see n. 6, below), and might well have been considered two parts of a single work. M. Joy Young argues that Christine knew "Matheolus" only through *LL*: "Portraits of Woman: Virtue, Vice and Marriage in Christine de Pizan's *Cité des dames*, Matheolus' *Lamentations*, and Lefevre's *Livre de Leesce*," Ph.D. diss., Catholic University of America, 1992, 167–72, 211. While intriguing, this claim is impossible to prove.

5. On these two passages, see *Le livre de Leesce* 1717ff. and 2327ff. with their notes in this volume.

6. Van Hamel, 2.xxxi–xxxiii, describes two MSS, V and P, containing *LL* without *L*. For the MSS and early printed editions of *Lamentations* and *Le livre de Leesce*, see Van Hamel, 1.viii–xiii and 2: xxvii–xlvvii, and Tiziano Pacchiarotti, "Les Manuscrits du *Matheolus* et leur reception," *Le recueil au Moyen Âge: la fin du Moyen Âge*, eds. Tania Van Hemelryck and Stefania Marzano (Turnhout, Belgium: BREPOLS, 2010): 253–61, and Tiziano Pacchiarotti, ed., *Jean Le Fèvre de Ressons: Les Lamentations de Matheolus* (Alessandria: Edizioni dell'Orso, 2010), 35 ff. Van Hamel describes ten MSS containing *L*; Pacchiarotti describes all of ten of these, plus MS G, which Van Hamel had heard of, but never had the chance to examine (1: xii). On the rediscovery of what is now the Geneva MS, see Pacchiarotti, "Les Manuscrits du *Matheolus*," 255. Unknown to Van Hamel and Pacchiarotti, an additional MS of *L* and *LL* was discovered by Emil Freymond and designated by him as MS Lo.: "Eine Prager Handschrift der *Lamentations* Matheolus und des *Livre de Leesce*," *Prager Deutsche Studien* 8 (1908): 565–83. For further discussion of the MS discovered by Freymond, see the appendix to this volume. Another MS, Aug. 405, also unknown to Van Hamel and Pacchiarotti, is reported by Paul Lehmann, "Zur Überlieferung der Lamentationes Matheoli," *Zeitschrift für romanische Philologie* 46 (1926), 698. For a list of MSS containing *L* alone, *LL* alone, and both poems, see the bibliography in this volume.

7. For example, the vital contribution of *LL* to the *Rose* debate is unmentioned in both recent editions of

the "querelle de la Rose" documents for Anglophone readers, including selected works by Christine: Christine McWebb, ed., *Debating the* Roman de la Rose: *A Critical Anthology* (New York: Routledge, 2007), and David F. Hult, ed. and trans., *Debate of the* Romance of the Rose (Chicago: University of Chicago Press, 2010). Both works cite *L* only in passing and *LL* not at all.

8. At least the following passages, most of them extensive and important to the poet's argument, are impossible to understand without this kind of cross-reference: see *LL* 600, 615, 621ff., 921, 1401, 1581ff., 1596–97, 1599, 1844, and 2621ff. As indicated in Van Hamel's *varia lectio*, MS F provides a longer version (copied from *L*) of the stories at 600, 615, and 621. This is an exceptional case, however. Extreme abridgment of the source, to the detriment of clarity, is a frequent occurrence in *LL*.

9. Noted by Curnow, "'Livre de la cité des dames' of Christine de Pisan," 137. On the type of MS Christine might have known for *L* and *LL*, see the list of MSS in the bibliography.

10. *Città delle dame*, ed. Caraffi and Richards, 40, 42; *Book of the City of Ladies*, trans. Richards, rev. ed., 3.

11. Sermon of the Series "Poenitemini," December 24, the fourth Advent, in McWebb, *Debating the* Roman de la Rose, 368, 369; "Matheol." is also disparaged at Series "Poenitemini," December 10, 1402, McWebb, 364, 365.

12. See n. 2 above.

13. See n. 3 above.

14. The most complete discussion of *L* and *LL* and their crucial influence on the late medieval *Rose* debate (broadly defined) is the chapter "Le mépris des femmes — Une sagesse," in Pierre-Yves Badel, Le roman de la Rose *au XIV siècle: Étude de la réception de l'oeuvre* (Geneva: Droz, 1980), 178–200, esp. 199. Other discussions of the relationship, none of them exhaustive, are found at Jillian M. L. Hill, *The Medieval Debate on Jean de Meung's* Roman de la Rose: *Morality versus Art*, Studies in Mediaeval Literature 4 (Lewiston, ME: Edwin Mellen Press, 1991), 14–17; Karen Pratt, "Translating Misogamy: The Authority of the Intertext in the *Lamentationes Matheoluli* and Its Middle French Translation by Jean LeFevre," *Forum for Modern Language Studies* 35, no. 4 (1999): 421–35, esp. 433; Alastair Minnis, *Magister Amoris: The* Roman de la Rose *and Vernacular Hermeneutics* (Oxford: Oxford University Press, 2001), 211–12; and Helen J. Swift, *Gender, Writing, and Performance: Men Defending Women in Late Medieval France, 1440–1538* (Oxford: Clarendon, 2008), 148–52.

15. The most detailed and helpful overview of *LL* in the context of the late medieval "querelle des femmes" is Alcuin Blamires, *Case*, esp. 36–44. Other discussions are Jill Mann, *Apologies to Women* (Cambridge: Cambridge University Press, 1990), 23–25; Renate Blumenfeld-Kosinski, "Jean le Fèvre's *Livre de Leësce*: Praise or Blame of Women?" *Speculum* 69 (1994): 705–25; Helen Solterer, *The Master and Minerva: Disputing Women in French Medieval Culture* (Berkeley: University of California Press, 1995), 131–50; Florence Percival, *Chaucer's Legendary Good Women* (Cambridge: Cambridge University Press, 1998), 106–7; Karen Pratt, "The Strains of Defense: The Many Voices of Jean Lefèvre's *Livre de Leesce*," in *Gender in Debate from the Early Middle Ages to the Renaissance*, ed. Thelma S. Fenster and Clare A. Lees (New York: Palgrave, 2002), 113–34; and Swift, *Gender, Writing, and Performance*, 148–52. Martin Le Franc debated the views of "Mathiolet" among other misogynist authors in his *Champion des dames* (1440–42); see discussion by Steven Millen Taylor, ed. and trans., *The Trial of Womankind: A Rhyming Translation of Book IV of the Fifteenth Century* Le Champion des Dames (Jefferson, NC: McFarland, 2005), 4–5.

16. Editor Alfred Schmitt dated the Latin *Lamentations* to some time between 15 February 1290 and January 1291, based on his careful study of references to contemporary persons and events in that work; see his introduction in *Matheus von Boulogne: "Lamentationes Matheoluli" (Kommentierte und kritische Edition der beiden ersten Bücher)*, (Bonn: Druck Rheinischen Friedrich-Wilhelms Universität, 1974), 21.

17. As noted in n. 1 above, all references to the Latin *Lamentations* are taken from the Van Hamel edition. As Schmitt edited only the first half of that text, his edition has not displaced Van Hamel's. Pacchiarotti's edition of the Latin (which he calls *Lamenta*), included in his *Les Lamentations*, is based on Van Hamel's, with no acknowledgment of MSS discovered since Van Hamel's work.

18. For a detailed discussion of Mahieu of Boulogne and his "bigamous" plight, see V.-J. Vaillant, *Maistre Mahieu (Matheolus), satirique boulonnais du XII siècle: Essai de biographie* (Boulogne-sur-mer: Simonnaire, 1894); Ch.-V. Langlois, *La vie en France au moyen âge de la fin du XII au milieu du XIV siècle d'après des moralistes du temps*, vol. 2 (1926–28; Geneva: Slatkine Reprints, 1970), 241–46, 285–87; Van Hamel, 2: cvii–cxviii, and *Matheus von Boulogne*, ed. Schmitt, 13–18. The Wife of Bath discusses "bigamy" in its distinctively patristic and medieval sense in her *Prologue* 9–93; see notes on this passage in Benson, *Riverside Chaucer*.

19. In several cases, Le Fèvre draws attention to the novelty of Mahieu's *fabliaux* by calling them "nouveaulx exemples" (*LL* 3064) and a "conte ... tout neuf" (*LL* 3067). Comparison with possible sources and analogues will demonstrate that Mahieu was careful to "tweak" his renditions of stock *fabliau* plots to make them distinctive. In general, they do not very closely resemble their counterparts; for the difficulty of identifying the sources of Mahieu's *fabliaux* and other exemplary stories, see Van Hamel, 2: cxl–cxlv. Le Fèvre refers to or retells Mahieu's piquant new stories, mostly *fabliaux*, at *LL* 600ff., 607ff., 621ff., 963ff., 1073ff., 1347ff., 1581ff., 1966ff., 2621ff., 3067ff., 3079ff., and 3103ff.

20. Latin *Lamentations* 176.

21. Jerome, *Epistola adversus Jovinianum*, ed. J. P. Migne, *PL* 23, cols. 211–337; Jerome, *Against Jovinianus*, in *The Principal Works of St. Jerome*, trans. W. H. Fremantle (New York: Christian Literature Company, 1893), 346–416.

22. See *Against Jovinianus*, trans. Fremantle, 358–9 (1.14–15).

23. First reported in Lehmann, "Zur Überlieferung," 696–99; also see *Matheus von Boulogne*, ed. Schmitt, 22–27.

24. For a specimen of Mahieu's wordplay, see especially *LL* 593–667 and their notes in this volume, especially nn. 77. 78, 79, 90, and 93. The odd expression "master of the goals" (*LL* 664) has been only partially explained up to now; I unraveled it only with the help of classicist Lee F. Sherry.

25. For the probable date of *L*, see Geneviève Hasenohr, introduction, in Jean Le Fèvre, *Le respit de la mort*, ed. Hasenohr (Paris: A. & J. Picard, 1969), liii. She places it between the *Respit* of late 1376 and *LL* of no earlier than 3 February 1380.

26. See Lawrence de Looze, *Pseudo-Autobiography in the Fourteenth Century: Juan Ruiz, Guillaume de Machaut, Jean Froissart, and Geoffrey Chaucer* (Gainesville: University Press of Florida, 1997), which doesn't mention Le Fèvre.

27. Ch.-V. Langlois, *La vie en France au moyen âge*, 2: 254 n.1.

28. The biographical study in *Le respit de la mort*, ed. Hasenohr, has not been superseded, except that Hasenohr herself came to doubt that Le Fèvre ever wrote a now-lost *Danse macabré*: see Geneviève Hasenohr, "Jean Le Fèvre," *Dictionnaire des lettres françaises: Le moyen âge*, ed. Geneviève Hasenohr and Michael Zink (Brepols: Fayard, 1994), 802–4. For more on this putative work, see the entry for Jehan Le Fèvre, *La danse macabré* in the annotated bibliography to this volume.

29. As noted in detail by Hasenohr (*Le respit de la mort*, x), Le Fèvre styled himself this way in his *Theodolet*, *De vetula*, and *Respit de la mort* 3728–30. At x n. 2, she quotes the legal document of 1370 in which Le Fèvre accepted a "rente perpetuelle" for the use of his vineyard by the "religieuses dames et honnestes, madame l'abbesse et couvent de l'eglise Nostre Dame de Soissons."

30. Ibid., xi–xvi.

31. See the examples and discussion in ibid., xvi–xvii; Hippolyte Cocheris, ed., *La vieille ou Les dernières amours d'Ovide* (Paris: Auguste Aubry, 1861), xxxiii, quotes an example in the unedited "Théodolet." In *LL*, the poet alludes to his poverty at 462 and (probably) 3975–76.

32. See Jehan Le Fèvre, trans., *La vieille ou Les dernières amours d'Ovide*, ed. Hippolyte Cocheris, 3. For other examples of Le Fèvre's puns on his surname, see "Der Cato Jehan Lefevre's," ed. J. Ulrich, *Romanische Forschungen* 15 (1904): 70–106 (lines 25–29 and 701); *La vieille*, ed. Cocheris, lines 5985–86; and *LL* 3447 (hitherto unnoted) and 3474–78 with their notes in this volume. Cocheris (xxxiii–iv) notes a play on *forgier* in the prologue to the unedited *Hymnes de la liturgie*. Le Fèvre also alludes to his disability at *LL* 751; see n. 105 in the translation.

33. See *Le respit de la mort*, ed. Hasenohr, xii–xiii, and *LL* 160, 345–47, 742ff., 981ff., 3199–3208, 3247–48, 3317–18, 3481, 3482, with their notes in this volume.

34. On the type of semipopular work translated by Le Fèvre, see Badel, Le roman de la Rose *au XIV siècle*, 180–82.

35. See *Le respit de la mort*, ed. Hasenohr, xlix. Surviving in four MSS, Le Fèvre's translation of the *Ecloga* has not been edited. For the Latin text, see Joannes Osternacher, ed., *Theoduli eclogum* (Urfahr: Verlag des bischöflichen, 1902). For discussion of the Latin *Ecloga*, see G. L. Hamilton, "Theodulus: A Medieval Textbook," *Modern Philology* 7 (1909–10): 169–85; G. L. Hamilton "Theodulus en France," *Modern Philology* 8 (1911): 611–12; and R. P. H. Green, "The Genesis of a Medieval Textbook: The Models and Sources of the *Ecloga Theoduli*," *Viator* 13 (1982): 49–106. On the French versions, see G. L. Hamilton, "Les sources du *Tiaudelet*," *Romania* 48 (1922): 124–27, and Geneviève Hasenohr, "Tradition du texte et tradition de l'image: À propos d'un programme d'illustration du *Theodolet*," *Miscellanea codicologica F. Masai dicata MCMLXIX*, vol. 2, ed. Pierre Cockshaw, Monique-Cecile Garand, and Pierre Jodogne (Ghent: E. Story-Scientia, 1979), 451–67. For a catalog of medieval and early modern translations and commentaries on the Latin *Ecloga*, see Betty Nye Quinn, "Ps. Theoduli," *Catalogus translationum et commentariorum*, ed. Paul O. Kristeller et al. (Washington, DC: Catholic University of America Press, 1971), 2: 383–408. For more on the content of the *Ecloga* and its relevance to *LL*, see n. 10 to the translation.

36. See Ernstpeter Ruhe, *Untersuchungen zu den altfranzösischen Übersetzungen der Disticha Catonis* (Munich: Max Huber, 1968), 228–29. The French text is "Der Cato Jehan Lefevre's," ed. J. Ulrich. For discussion of the Latin "Cato" and its commentaries, see Richard Hazelton, "The Christianization of 'Cato': The 'Disticha Catonis' in the Light of the Late Medieval Commentaries," *Medieval Studies* 19 (1957): 157–73.

37. See *La vieille*, ed. Cocheris. According to Pacchiarotti, ed., *Les Lamentations* 123, this work has also been edited as a dissertation by Marie-Madeleine Huchet: *La Vieille de Jean le Fèvre* (Paris: École Pratique des Hautes Études, 2009). For the Latin original, see *Pseudo-Ovidius 'De vetula': Untersuchungen und Text*, ed. Paul Klopsch (Leiden: E. J. Brill, 1967), and *The Pseudo-Ovidian 'De vetula': Text, Introduction, and Notes*, ed. Dorothy M. Robathan (Amsterdam: A. M. Hakkert, 1968). For discussion of the Latin poem, see Dorothy Robathan,

"Introduction to the Pseudo-Ovidian *De vetula*," *Transactions and Proceedings of the American Philological Association* 88 (1957): 197–207, and Francesco Bruni, "Dal 'De vetula' al 'Corbaccio': L'idea d'amore e i due tempi dell'intelletuale," *Medioevo Romanzo* 1 (1974): 161–216.

38. From 1 Kings 1:1–5.

39. From Gen. 5:18–24; 2 Kings 2:11.

40. Although not as sexually hyperactive as his son Solomon, who had seven hundred wives and three hundred concubines (1 Kings 11:3), David was also polygamous (1 Sam. 25:43, 2 Sam. 3:2–5, 12:8).

41. David's petition and its success are described in 2 Sam. 24:1–20 and 1 Chron. 21:1–18. Actually, David sought a reprieve for his entire people, not specifically for himself. Hezekiah's case (which is much closer to the poet's situation) is described at 2 Kings 20:6, 2 Chron. 25:25, and Isa. 38:5.

42. From 2 Kings 1:2–6.

43. On the *Hymnes*, for which no modern edition exists, see *Le respit de la mort*, ed. Hasenohr, lii–liii, n. 32 above, the bibliography to this volume, and n. 496 to the translation.

44. Mahieu quotes 1 Thess. 5:21 in a scurrilous context at Latin *Lamentations* 816–17; see *LL* 1339–42 and note. As discussed by Van Hamel (2: xcviiiff.), he also presumes to bring an accusation against God for the sorry state of the world at 1295ff. Le Fèvre adds his own blasphemous touch by channeling Jesus in the Garden of Gethsemane as he laments his unhappy marriage (fictitious or otherwise) in the first line of his *L*: "Tristis est anima mea..."

45. Van Hamel (2: liv–lxviii) provides a detailed comparison of the Latin and French *Lamentations*. (Of course, Van Hamel knew only one MS of the Latin poem; for an edition based on all five surviving MSS, see *Matheus von Boulogne*, ed. Schmitt.) He notes omissions and additions (not always following any discernible pattern) at lxii–lxv, and mistaken or careless translations at lxv–lxvii. In "Translating Misogamy" (423ff.), Pratt argues that Le Fèvre intensified the misogyny of the Latin *Lamentations* by adding material from *RR*; he certainly amplified his source in this manner, but I disagree with her contention (422–23) that serious misogyny is absent from Mahieu's Latin; for example, see Mahieu's execration of Bathsheba, quoted in the introduction, above. Without acknowledging Pratt, Tiziano Pacchiarotti argues that Le Fèvre created an independent translator-persona in his version of *L*, partly in order to *distance* himself from the misogyny of the Latin *Lamentations* and *RR*: see "Traduction et écriture personelle dans les *Lamentations de Matheolus*," in *La traduction vers le moyen français: Actes du IIe Colloque de l'AIEMF, Poitiers, 27–29 avril 2006*, ed. Claudio Galderisi and Cinzia Pignatelli (Turnhout, Belgium: Brepols, 2007), 419. The reference to eyeglasses is hitherto unnoted; see n. 184 to the translation, below.

46. Van Hamel discusses the question whether Mahieu borrowed from Jean de Meun at 2: cxlvii–cliii, concluding that he almost certainly did; Badel, Le roman de la Rose *au XIVe siècle*, 179–80, leaves the matter inconclusive by consecutively quoting the two sets of similar passages (from *RR* and the Latin *Lamentations*) for readers to judge for themselves: Latin *Lamentations* 1555ff. (on keeping secrets from your wife) and 2833ff. (on the unnaturalness of monogamy), juxtaposed for comparison with *RR* 16317ff. and 13849ff.

47. See *Le respit de la mort*, ed. Hasenohr, xliii, xlv, liii; *LL* 309, 2853–88, and notes to these lines in this volume.

48. On *LL* as a palinode, see Percival, *Chaucer's Legendary Good Women*, 153, 156; the bulk of Percival's study, 173–323, is devoted to Chaucer's *LGW*.

49. The narrative works of Le Fèvre's contemporaries Machaut, Froissart, and Deschamps are also referred to as *dits*; for a discussion of these works and their descent from *RR*, see Badel, Le roman de la Rose *au XIVe siècle* 82–94. Machaut's *Judgment of the King of Navarre* is a palinode having commonalities with *LL*; their relationship merits investigation.

50. MS K, quoted by Van Hamel, 2: 127; MS Lo., quoted by Freymond, "Eine Prager Handschrift," 582; and MS Aug. 405, quoted in Lehmann, "Zur Überlieferung," 698.

51. Although acting as a plaintiff, Le Fèvre/Lady Gladness often uses *defendre* and its synonyms in presenting the case for women; see *LL* 35, 982, 1112, 1418, 2250, 2652. As the riposte to an earlier work, any palinode/*contredit* is bound to be defensive in its rhetorical strategy.

52. Glenda McLeod, *Virtue and Venom: Catalogs of Women from Antiquity to the Renaissance* (Ann Arbor: University of Michigan Press, 1991).

53. For misogyny as a crime, i.e., slander or defamation of women, in *L* and its sequel, see Helen Solterer's chapter titled "Defamation and the *Livre de Leesce*: The Problem of a Sycophantic Response," in her *Master and Minerva*, 131–50.

54. McWebb, *Debating the* Roman de la Rose, xiii. Her anthology begins with a response to the *Rose* by Petrarch (1340) and ends with a work by Laurent de Premierfait (1409).

55. For a helpful overview of medieval writing on women and the questioning of literary authority, see the subsection "Drawing into Memory: Women and the Written Record," in A. J. Minnis (with V. J. Scattergood and J. J. Smith), *Oxford Guides to Chaucer: The Shorter Poems* (Oxford: Clarendon, 1995), 379–89; Blamires, *Case*; Percival, *Chaucer's Legendary Good Women*; McLeod, *Virtue and Venom*; and Swift, *Gender, Writing, and Performance*; also Mann, *Feminizing Chaucer, passim,* esp. 5–38. Medieval *loci classici* for this discussion are found

in Chaucer, *WBPro*, esp. 669–787, and Christine de Pizan, *Città delle dame*, ed. Caraffi and Richards, 64–92; and *Book of the City of Ladies*, trans. Richards, rev. ed. 15–24. The intertextuality of the palinode is discussed in two enlightening studies of Chaucer's *LGW* (neither of which mentions Le Fèvre or *LL*): Lisa J. Kiser, *Telling Classical Tales: Chaucer and* The Legend of Good Women (Ithaca: Cornell University Press, 1983, and Sheila Delany, *The Naked Text: Chaucer's* Legend of Good Women (Berkeley: University of California Press, 1999). Laura Kathryn McRae makes an exaggerated claim for Christine's originality in her otherwise excellent article, "Interpretation and the Acts of Reading and Writing in Christine de Pizan's *Livre de la cité des dames*," *Romanic Review* 82 (1991): 412–33: "Christine's ideas on interpretation are a radical departure from earlier methods of interpretation codified by male theorists" (413). Le Fèvre also used the innovative method she describes, if not as extensively and brilliantly as Christine.

56. For examples of explicit and direct opposition to Jean de Meun's opinions, see *LL* 742ff., 1070–71, and 1072, and notes to these lines in this volume.

57. Le Fèvre's more usual strategy of simply rewriting objectionable material from *RR* (rather than explicitly refuting it) would prove to be influential. Christine's radically revisionist borrowing of characters and situations from the *RR* has long been recognized: see for example Sylvia Huot, "Seduction and Sublimation: Christine de Pizan, Jean de Meun, and Dante," *Romance Notes* 25 (1985): 4–28; Kevin Brownlee, "Discourses of the Self: Christine de Pizan and the *Rose*," *Romanic Review* 79 (1988): 199–221; and McRae, "Interpretation and the Acts of Reading and Writing." For the same revisionist strategy on Christine's part with regard to exempla found in Boccaccio's *De mulieribus claris*, see Liliane Dulac, "Un mythe didactique chez Christine de Pizan: Semiramis ou la veuve heroïque (du *De mulieribus claris* a *La cité des dames*)," *Mélanges de Philologie Romane offerts à Charles Camproux*, ed. Robert Lafont et al., vol. 1 (Montpellier: Université Paul-Valéry, 1978), 315–43; and Patricia A. Phillipy, "Establishing Authority: Boccaccio's *De claris mulieribus* and Christine de Pizan's *Le livre de la cité des dames*," *Romanic Review* 77 (1986): 167–93. In these otherwise excellent articles, neither Dulac nor Phillipy discusses *LL* as a possible model for this interpretive strategy.

58. All references to *RR* in French are taken from Guillaume de Lorris et Jean de Meun, *Le roman de la Rose*, ed. Félix Lecoy, 3 vols. (Paris: Honoré Champion, 1976–82).

59. *The Romance of the Rose*, trans. Charles Dahlberg (Princeton: Princeton University Press, 1971), 42. All English translations of *RR* are taken from this work.

60. Le Fèvre's concept of "leesce" is glossed as mere "jouissance" by Solterer, *Master and Minerva*, 148. "Rem leticie" does mean simply that in Latin *Lamentations* 1391, translated by Le Fèvre as "la chose joyeuse" in *L* 2.1881. In *LL*, however, the concepts "leesce" and "joye" are far from being limited to sexual gratification, although they do embrace it.

61. Karen Pratt's understanding of "Leesce" is more comprehensive but perhaps still too limited: she represents "the joy and pleasures his [Le Fèvre's] narrator hopes to enjoy as a result of courting female favor": "Strains of Defense," 128. It should be noted that as the personification of earthly happiness, Le Fèvre's Leesce may owe something to Dame Bonneürté, who rebukes the author-persona's earlier disparagement of women in Machaut's palinode *The Judgment of the King of Navarre* 3851ff.

62. *Biblia Sacra Iuxta Vulgatam Versionem* (Stuttgart: Deutsche Bibelgesellschaft, 1994). The poet also quoted Ecclesiastes at *Respit de la mort* 16–18.

63. *The New Oxford Annotated Bible*, ed. Michael D. Coogan, 3rd ed. (Oxford: Oxford University Press, 1991). Unless otherwise indicated, all references to the Bible in English are taken from this edition.

64. "Translating Misogamy," 427.

65. There are many examples of the attempt by later medieval authors (even before Gerson and Christine) to harmonize the encomiums to sex and fertility in *RR* with Christian teachings on marriage. In her definitive study, Sylvia Huot describes how this process began with scribes who recopied the *Rose* itself and in the process sometimes produced "remaniements" or revised versions: *The* Romance of the Rose *and Its Medieval Readers* (Cambridge: Cambridge University Press, 1993), esp. 37, 93, 104, 112, 118, 169–70, 172, 318, 328. Minnis, in *Magister Amoris*, provides more examples, especially at 304–12, where he discusses, e.g., the *Rose*-derived but marriage-friendly *Eschez amoureux*.

66. Likewise, other poets would emphatically associate Reason with their case for women, love, and marriage. Christine opposed Jean de Meun's Lady Reason for her cynical approval of deceitful tactics in love: "October 2, 1402: Christine's Response to Pierre Col," in McWebb, *Debating the* Roman de la Rose, 156, 157. Like Le Fèvre, she recreates Lady Reason as a morally orthodox figure in the opening chapters of her *Book of the City of Ladies*.

67. Both Christine and Gerson would argue that *RR* brought matrimony into disrepute with its scurrilous attacks on women as a class, and thus sinfully discouraged young men from taking a wife: Christine de Pizan, "October 2, 1402: Christine's Response to Pierre Col," in McWebb, *Debating the* Roman de la Rose, 176, 179, 180, 183; Jean Gerson, "Treatise against the *Roman de la Rose*," in ibid., 274, 275. A widow herself at twenty-five, Christine never stereotyped or disparaged widows; see the appendix to this volume. Gerson called for mutual humility and respect among all three classes of chaste people, that is, virgins, widows living in celibacy, and faithfully married couples: see "Poenitemini V, 31 December 1402," in McWebb, 370, 371.

68. *Book of the City of Ladies*, trans. Richards, rev. ed., xxxiii. As McLeod would express it, "[Christine's]

principal point is that misogynists, not women, speak from the margins of Christian tradition" (*Virtue and Venom* 116).

69. On Medea, see *LL* 2371, 2381, 2382, 2407, 3041, 3637; on Dido, see 2442, 2454, 2563, 2743. Circe is portrayed as wise and generous to Ulysses, who selfishly left her behind: 2415, 2416, 2421, 2432, 3043. Phyllis was the victim of Demophon's neglect: 2553, 2735. For discussion of lovelorn classical heroines and their varied but often sympathetic treatment in medieval sources (albeit without mention of Le Fèvre), see Götz Schmitz, *The Fall of Women in Early English Narrative Verse* (Cambridge: Cambridge University Press, 1990); also see Mann, *Feminizing Chaucer*, 5–38. For many examples of "the medieval Medea," although with perhaps undue emphasis on hostile portrayals, see Ruth Morse, *The Medieval Medea* (Woodbridge, Eng.: D. S. Brewer, 1996); Morse (220) briefly notes her appearance in *LL*.

70. Jean de Meun was seemingly the first to translate their famous correspondence into French: see *La vie et les epistres Pierres Abaelart et Heloys sa fame, traduction du XIII siècle attribuée a Jean de Meun avec une nouvelle edition des textes latins d'après le ms. Troyes bibl. Mun. 802*, ed. Eric Hicks (Geneva: Slatkine; Paris, Champion, 1991).

71. *Romance of the Rose*, trans. Dahlberg, 160. Here, Jean de Meun refers to Heloïse's antimatrimonial arguments as summarized by her husband Abelard in his autobiographical *Historia calamitatum*; see *The Letters of Abelard and Heloise*, trans. Betty Radice (Harmondsworth: Penguin, 1974), 70–74. As quoted by Abelard (71, 73), Heloïse approvingly cites Jerome's aspersions on marriage from *Against Jovinian*.

72. On my translation of this phrase, see n. 163 to the translation.

73. On Le Fèvre's personal acquaintance with nuns, see n. 29, above, and *LL* 2853–88 with notes 354–56 to the translation.

74. Minnis, *Magister Amoris*, 85. See also Blumenfeld-Kosinski, "Jean le Fèvre's *Livre de Leësce*," 714, quoted at n. 8 to the translation. Le Fèvre produced an original defense of arument by exemplum at *L* 2.2662ff.

75. For discussion, see Blamires, *Case*, esp. 65–69.

76. For a discussion of this controversy in *RR* and its literary posterity, including Christine and her interlocutors, see Minnis's chapter "*Parler proprement*: Words, Deeds, and Proper Speech in the *Rose*," in *Magister Amoris*, 119–63, and also his "Old Wives' Tales: Vetularity and Virtue," in *Fallible Authors: Chaucer's Pardoner and Wife of Bath* (Philadelphia: University of Pennsylvania Press, 2008): 294–307.

77. At *RR* 6917ff. For the current scholarly consensus that *couilles* was a "dirty" word in medieval French, and thus should be translated with an English vulgarity, see Minnis, *Magister Amoris*, 122 n. 12 and 168 n. 13; also David Raybin, "The French Fabliaux in MS Harley 2253," presented at the 46th International Congress on Medieval Studies, Kalamazoo, MI, 14 May 2011, where he discusses his forthcoming edition and translation of the MS (with Susanna Fein), including its use of *couilles* and other graphic anatomical terms.

78. For the bad moral influence of sexually explicit language, see "June–July 1401: Christine's "Reaction to Jean de Montreuil's Treatise on the Roman de la Rose," in McWebb, *Debating the* Roman de la Rose, 118, 119, 120, 121, 122, 123; Christine, "October 2, 1402: Christine's Response to Pierre Col," in ibid., 140–91, esp. 140–57; Gerson, "Treatise against the Roman de la Rose," in ibid., 276, 277.

79. Also in a kind of allegorical reading, he defends women's intelligence on the grounds that the names of all arts and sciences are feminine in grammatical gender (3655–61); here he may be less than serious. For more on Le Fèvre's preference for a straightforward and literal-minded defense of women, see Blumenfeld-Kosinski, "Jean le Fèvre's *Livre de Leësce*," 714. Le Fèvre's almost exclusive focus on a literal reading of ancient stories is very much at odds with the *Ovide moralisé*, a free translation of Ovid's *Metamorphoses* with interpolated allegories: see translation n. 296.

80. The story of Virginia, ultimately from Livy although Le Fèvre clearly borrowed it from *RR*, is labeled "chose veritable" (2522), and a series of examples taken from the historian Justin is introduced as "ystoire" (3586). In a parallel use of the topos, Christine's own life story would be retold as an "exemple ... vray" in a unique anonymous scribal interpolation to Le Fèvre's *L*; see appendix in this volume.

81. Unlike the stories of Jephthah's daughter and Virginia, Ovid's tale of Scylla (who murdered her father) is only "fable" (myth) (2521); see also 753–56, 780, 1516–22, 2090, 2474–75, 2483, 2692, 2697–2700, 2725, 2741–42. For Le Fèvre's use of "fable" to denote a "récit auquel on peut à la limite ne pas croire" (story you just can't believe), see Marziano Guglielminetti, "Jean le Fèvre et Machiavel: Matheolus et Belphégor," in *L'aube de la Renaissance*, ed. Dario Cecchetti et al., Bibliothèque Franco-Simone 18 (Geneva: Slatkine, 1991), 226, referring to *L* 2.3853ff.

82. Le Fèvre dismisses a series of Mathieu's misogynistic *fabliaux* as mere "truffes" (frivolous stories): 668, 753, 787, 797, 798, 1647, 2483.

83. *Met.* 10.3ff. According to Ovid, it was Orpheus, not Eurydice, who disobeyed the order not to look back.

84. For my translation of this phrase at *LL* 2100, see n. 263 to the translation.

85. See Smith, *Power of Woman*, esp. 23–35.

86. A range of patristic and medieval responses, mostly hostile to Bathsheba while not exonerating David, is documented in Alcuin Blamires, ed., with Karen Pratt and C. W. Marx, *Woman Defamed and Woman Defended:*

An Anthology of Medieval Texts (Oxford: Clarendon, 1992), *passim*, and A. J. Minnis, *Medieval Theory of Authorship*, 2nd ed. ((Philadelphia: University of Pennsylvania Press, 1988), 103–09.

87. For this type of reading, see Minnis, *Medieval Theory of Authorship*, 105–06.

88. The story is found in 2 Sam. (also known as 2 Kings) 11:2–12:25 and elaborated in Ps. 51 (Vulgate 50). God's special love for Solomon, the son of Bathsheba and David, is introduced at 2 Sam. 12:24–25.

89. 2 Sam. 12:13; also see Ps. 51 (Vulgate 50).

90. On my translation of this phrase, see n. 116 to the translation.

91. See Minnis, *Magister Amoris*, 167 n. 12. Another possibility is that Le Fèvre elaborated on Ovid's sexually charged pun on his missing "foot," i.e., his use of the metrically defective elegiac meter instead of the hexameters favored by serious poets, and his comic lament over his occasional attacks of impotence, discussed by Robert W. Hanning, *Serious Play: Desire and Authority in the Poetry of Ovid, Chaucer, and Ariosto* (New York: Columbia University Press, 2010), 16, 18, based on Ovid's *Amores* 1.1 and 3.7. Ovid despised eunuchs as perverse and wicked according to an extended rant on the subject in the pseudo–Ovidian *De vetula*, translated by Le Fèvre as *La vieille*, ed. Cocheris, 2.2087–2557. Another possible model for the emasculated Ovid is Mahieu's complaints over his impotence, repeated at *LL* 721ff.

92. *Città delle dame*, ed. Caraffi and Richards, 74; *Book of the City of Ladies*, trans. Richards, rev. ed., 21.

93. *LL* 1039ff.; see n. 149 to the translation. For Christine's reference to this character, see *Città delle dame*, ed. Caraffi and Richards, 92; *Book of the City of Ladies*, trans. Richards, rev. ed., 31. Martin Le Franc used the story as a set-up for rebuttal in his *Champion des Dames: The Trial of Womankind*, trans. Taylor, 129ff. (lines 3913ff.). Taylor agrees (204 n. 3913) that "the picturesque detail of her mooning the judges" was invented by Le Fèvre.

94. For the "empiricist" element in Christine's early feminism, see Joan Kelly, "Early Feminist Theory and the *Querelle des Femmes*, 1400–1789," *Signs: Journal of Women in Culture and Society* 8 (1982): esp. 15.

95. *LL* 314; see n. 54 to the translation.

96. *LL* 1140–54; see n. 167 to the translation.

97. Christine would repeatedly develop these *topoi*, especially in her "Letter of the God of Love," lines 168–77, in *Poems of Cupid, God of Love*, ed. Thelma S. Fenster and Mary Carpenter Erler (New York: E. J. Brill, 1990), and *Città delle dame*, ed. Caraffi and Richards, 82, 84; *Book of the City of Ladies*, trans. Richards, rev. ed., 26–27.

98. I find just one-third of the poem to consist of material carried over from *L*, not two-thirds as alleged by Solterer, *Master and Minerva*, 138–39. On the voice of Mahieu in *LL*, also see Blumenfeld-Kosinski, "Jean le Fèvre's *Livre de Leësce*," 723; Percival, *Chaucer's Legendary Good Women*, 153; and Pratt "Strains of Defense."

99. For examples of Christine's prolific quotation of antifeminist "points," see her chapter headings, transcribed in full in Curnow's edition of the *Cité des dames*, 597–615, and translated in full in *Book of the City of Ladies*, trans. Richards, rev. ed., v–xi. To give another example, Martin Le Franc's entire 24,384 profeminine polemic is formatted as a debate between "champion for ladies" Franc Vouloir and various personae who argue (at great length) in defense of the misogynistic position: *Le champion des dames*, ed. Robert Deschaux, 5 vols. (Paris: Honoré Champion, 1999). Of Le Fèvre's contemporaries, only John Gower in his *Confessio Amantis* would take the radical step of simply omitting misogynistic topoi and allowing his traditional Christian profeminine arguments to stand alone and unopposed: see Linda Barney Burke, "Women in John Gower's *Confessio Amantis*," *Mediaevalia* 3 (1977): 240.

100. *Città delle dame*, ed. Caraffi and Richards, 328; *Book of the City of Ladies*, trans. Richards, rev. ed., 160–61. Much like Le Fèvre, Gower would present the act of rape as utterly cruel and bestial: *Confessio Amantis*, "Tale of Tereus," 5.5569ff., and "Tale of Lucrece," 7.4754ff., as well as antithetical to love, 5.5531–32.

101. Van Hamel, 2: cxcv; Pratt "Strains of Defense," 119.

102. On the palinode as comic, see, e.g., Gorgias of Leontini, "Encomium to Helen" (both text and commentary), in Vincent B. Leitch, ed., *The Norton Anthology of Theory and Criticism* (New York: Norton, 2001), 29–33; Ovid's palinodic materials (*Ars amatoria*, book 3, and *Remedia amoris*) and their comic roots in the *disputatio ad utramque partem* of the Roman rhetorical schools, discussed in Hanning, *Serious Play*, 70ff.; and Machaut's "playful" or "seriocomic" intentions in *Judgment of the King of Navarre* (ed. and trans. Palmer, xxix; Hanning, *Serious Play*, 127). Percival notes the ludic nature of the genre, while acknowledging its interludes of deep sincerity (*Chaucer's Legendary Good Women*, esp. at 154–55, 328–29). Hanning, in *Serious Play*, also notes a serious subtext of challenge to authorities both literary and political.

103. Blumenfeld-Kosinski, "Jean le Fèvre's *Livre de Leësce*," 717. Jill Mann makes a spirited case for the "sincerity" of *LL* in *Feminizing Chaucer*, 28–29, although she questioned it in her *Apologies to Women*, 23–25; Karen Pratt argues more cautiously that "Christine's rehabilitation of women is sincere; Le Fèvre's may have been," in "Analogy or Logic," 66.

104. Blamires, *Case*, 6.

105. *Città delle dame*, ed. Caraffi and Richards, 84; *Book of the City of Ladies*, trans. Richards, rev. ed., 26. Christine develops her argument that these gentle and "passive" virtues are truly Christlike and thus worthy of honor, especially at Caraffi and Richards 82, 84, 86, and Richards, 25–27.

106. For the French text, see Guillaume de Machaut, *The Judgment of the King of Navarre*, ed. and trans. R. Barton Palmer (New York: Garland, 1998). For a summary of the two judgment poems, see *ibid.*, xxiv–xxxvii.

107. This translation is from *The Judgment of the King of Navarre*, *An Anthology of Medieval Love Debate Poetry*, trans. and ed. Barbara K. Altmann and R. Barton Palmer (Gainesville: The University Press of Florida, 2006), 132.

108. *Città delle Dame*, ed. Caraffi and Richards, 54; *Book of the City of Ladies*, ed. and trans. Richards, rev. ed., 10.

109. See Delany, *Naked Text*, 3–7, on Hoccleve and other early readers who viewed *LGW* as "a serious and accomplished poem in defense of women" (7). Mann, *Feminizing Chaucer*, 25–38, explores "the groundswell of seriousness beneath its [*LGW*'s] mannered surface" (26), a seriousness she finds analogous to the "sincerity" (28) of *LL*.

110. Blamires, *Case*, 37.

111. Ibid., 37; Pratt, "Strains of Defense," 122–23.

112. Blamires, *Case*, 37.

113. Pratt, "Strains of Defense," 119.

114. See McWebb, *Debating the* Roman de la Rose, 324, 325. On the medieval theory of literary *persona* and its possible relation to the author's intentions, see Minnis, *Magister Amoris*, 219–26, 229–32.

115. Although Hanning's *Serious Play* happens not to discuss *LL*, it does relate the title concept (including revisionist approaches to literary authority) to other medieval palinodes, specifically Machaut's *Judgment of the King of Navarre* and Chaucer's *LGW* (Hanning, 127–51). See also Robert W. Hanning, "The Question of Women in the *Decameron*: A Boccaccian *Disputatio ad utramque partem*," 46th International Conference on Medieval Studies, Kalamazoo, MI, 12–15 May 2011.

116. Gerson and Christine would indignantly reject the claim that an author's (allegedly) good intention in creating a character such as Le Jaloux in any way redeems the bad effects of a wicked and seductive text: as Gerson expresses it, "doit estre verité et honnesteté gardée es personages" (truth and decency must be maintained likewise in fictional characters), Eric Hicks, ed., *Le débat sur le "Roman de la Rose"* (Paris: Honoré Champion, 1977), 182; "Poenitemini Sermon 4, December 24, 1402," in Hult, *Debate of the* Romance of the Rose, 212. Christine rejected the "*persona*-excuse" for the immoral teachings of Le Jaloux and others in her "Reaction to Jean de Montreuil's 'Treatise on the *Roman de la Rose*," McWebb, 118, 119, and in her "Response to Pierre Col," ibid., 162, 164, 165. In *Book of the City of Ladies*, Christine's Lady Reason demolishes the claim that an author's good intention (or his speaking through a fictional persona) in any way compensates for the wrongfulness and bad influence of his views on women: *Città delle dame*, ed. Caraffi and Richards, 66, 68; *Book of the City of Ladies*, trans. Richards, rev. ed., 17–18.

117. Alastair Minnis, *Fallible Authors*, 249, 309. For earlier critics who noted the parallel roles of Lady Gladness and the Wife of Bath, see Thundy, "Matheolus, Chaucer, and the Wife of Bath," 45, and Phillips, "Chaucer and Jean Le Fèvre": "Lady Leësce picks up statements Matheolus has made and disputes them, and similarly Chaucer's Wife operates as a one-woman debate on these topics, picking up and refuting statements allegedly by her opponents" (33).

118. Blamires (*Case*, 43) notes Le Fèvre's "verité," "droiture," and "equité," all aligned with Lady Reason in *LL* 760–64, and their possible influence on Christine's holy trinity of God's daughters (Raison, Droitture, and Justice) who comfort and counsel the author-persona in the opening chapters of *The Book of the City of Ladies*.

A Note on the French Text
and Translation

The French text is based on A.-G. Van Hamel's edition of *Le Livre de Leesce*, to date the only modern edition of the poem, now published online at http://www.archive.org/details/leslamentations00hamegoog. I have silently corrected a few obvious typographical errors. In the handful of cases where I have based my translation on a variant reading (provided by Van Hamel's *varia lectio*) or otherwise emended the text (usually in agreement with a later judgment by Van Hamel himself, as expressed in his notes), I have provided an explanation in a note to the translation.

Regarding the translation, I have tried to be as literal as possible, consistent with clarity and readability in English. Therefore, I have sometimes changed the word order or verb tenses of the original to conform with standard English practice. Significant departures from literal translation and other special translation-related issues are discussed in the notes. As did Mahieu before him, Le Fèvre composed his work in a variety of styles, often juxtaposed for comic effect, from the elevated and mock legalistic, to the colloquial, plainspoken, and at times even frankly obscene. The translation attempts to capture the range of his voices without rhetorical excess or striving for effect.

Le Fèvre resorts very frequently to a periphrasis denoting a completed action by using *vouloir* (to wish, will, want) plus the infinitive. He may have followed this practice for the sake of meter. For example, referring to Abelard, he writes: "Mais bien fist le Paraclit faire, / Ou suer Heloïs *voult attraire*" (Instead, he had the Paraclete built, where he *brought* Sister Heloïse) (*LL* 2791–92). When translated literally into English, this construction may imply that the action was intended, but not actually accomplished, by the subject of the verb. Thus, I have omitted the verb "wish, will, want" in my English translation of these phrases, except where obviously called for by the context.

At various times in Le Fèvre's writing (and in Middle French in general), the subject of a verb not only is omitted but is unclear from the context. Where appropriate, I have discussed these ambiguous passages and explained my chosen translation in a note on the passage.

As explained in the introduction, n. 64, I have almost invariably translated *leesce/lié/liée* or *lie*) as "gladness/glad" and all forms of *joye* with their English cognates. (Chaucer rendered *leesce* as "gladness" in his *Romaunt of the Rose* 847). Thus, I have generally been able to translate Le Fèvre's frequent strategic coupling of "tristesce/leesce" with the equally felicitous "sadness/gladness."

I have generally translated proper names from history, pagan mythology, and the Bible with their current English spellings. However, I have retained Le Fèvre's "Mahieu" for referring to the author of the Latin *Lamentations*.

While *mesdisant* can be translated "slanderer," I have generally used "evil-speaker" for the sake of euphony.

On rare occasions, I have inserted explanatory material in brackets for the sake of clarity.

My debt to Van Hamel's excellent notes to his edition of the *Lamentations* and *Leesce* will be obvious throughout. I have thoroughly updated and amplified his annotations in several important ways. First, Van Hamel's notes to *Leesce* are limited to material found exclusively in that work. By contrast, I have provided sufficient annotation on all parts of *The Book of Gladness* to render the work intelligible throughout, although I have offered more extensive commentary on material peculiar to *The Book of Gladness*.

I have expanded Van Hamel's notes with reference to sources unnoted by him, especially Boccaccio's *De claris mulieribus*. I have also improved his often fragmentary source notes by providing a complete bibliographical reference whenever possible. Given that Van Hamel's edition is over one hundred years old, I have cited modern editions of Le Fèvre's probable sources and analogues wherever it was feasible to do so. Following Van Hamel's helpful practice, I have provided a cross-reference to the *Lamentations* in every case where a passage in *Leesce* is based on a corresponding passage in the earlier poem. Thus, the reader can easily check the source passage in the online Van Hamel edition or in Tiziano Pacchiarotti's 2010 edition of *Lamentations*, which uses the same line numbers as Van Hamel's. Unlike Van Hamel, I have provided a summary of the source passage from *Lamentations* in every case where Le Fèvre's response to that passage in *Leesce* would otherwise be unclear.

Also, I have annotated the translation with a summary of critical commentary (what little there is to date) in a manner so complete as to constitute a variorum edition of *Le livre de Leesce*. My notes are thoroughly cross-referenced to recurring or related material within the text of *Leesce* itself. Finally, I have provided extensive annotations on works influenced by *Leesce*, especially those of Chaucer and Christine de Pizan.

Le Livre de Leesce (French text)

Mes dames, je requier mercy.
A vous me vueil excuser cy
De ce que sans vostre licence
J'ai parlé de la grant dissence
5 Et des tourmens de mariage.
Se j'ay mesdit par mon oultrage,
Je puis bien dire sans flater
Que je n'ay fait que translater
Ce que j'ay en latin trouvé;
10 Assés pourra estre prouvé
Ou livre de Matheolule.
Si me semble que femme nulle
Ne personne qui soit en vie
N'en doit sur moy avoir envie.
15 Dont, se je m'en suy entremis,
Je suppli qu'il me soit remis
Et pardonné par vostre grace.
Car je suy tout prest que je face
Un livre pour moy excuser;
20 Ne le me vueilliés refuser.
Il n'est riens qui n'ait son contraire,
Qui en voulroit les preuves traire
Et penser justement aux choses:
Les espines sont près des roses;
25 Aussi est l'ortie poingnant
Jouste l'erbe souef joingnant.
Sans vostre grace ne vueil vivre.
Et s'aucun requiert de cest livre
Comment entitulé sera,
30 Je dy que l'en l'appellera
Par droit nom «Livre de Leesce»;
Car pour l'amour de celle est ce
Qu'ay fait cest livre, pour complaire
Par argument de sens contraire.
35 Pour vous excuser loyaument
Et monstrer especiaument
Que nul ne doit femmes blasmer;
On les doit loer et amer,
Cherir, honnourer et servir,

40 Qui leur grace veult desservir.
La raison y est bien apperte;
Cy après sera descouverte.

Or me doint Dieu prosperité
Que je soustiengne verité,
45 Si com jadis fist Alithie,
Qui soustint la vraye partie
Contre Pseuti, le fauls d'Athaines;
Sur le rivage des fontaines
De fauls et de vray disputerent
50 Et par leurs instruments gagerent;
Mais Alithie ot la victoire;
Car verité doit avoir gloire
Tout aussi que mieulx vault leesce
Que ne falt courroux et tristesce.
55 Verité vainct contre mençoingne,
Verité est noble besoingne,
C'est la plus fort chose qui soit,
Si com Zorobabel disoit
A la demande du roy Daire,
60 Qui voult une question faire;
Car de force estoit a descort.
L'un dist que le roy estoit fort,
L'autre dist que fort est le vin,
Et le tiers, qui fist le devin,
65 Dist que les femmes sont plus fortes.
Zorobabel contre leurs sortes
Mist verité plus fort trouvée;
Sa sentence fu approuvée.
Aristote ama verité;
70 En ses dis est bien recité
Qu'il dist a ceulx qui le prioient
Et pour Socratès supplioient:
«J'aim Socratès, n'en doubtés mie,
Mais verité est plus m'amie.»
75 Priés Dieu que ma langue tiengne,
En cest fait de moy luy souviengne,
Et me face si bien respondre

Que nul ne puist mes dis confondre
Et que chose ne puisse dire
80 Ou il ait occasion d'ire.

Le sage dit en l'Escriture
Qu'entre toute mondaine cure
Il n'est riens qui tant doye plaire
Que d'estre lié et de bien faire
85 Et d'eschever debat et noise.
Car longue voye et pluye poise
Et on s'esjoïst de briefté;
Si ne me sera pas griefté
De ceste matiere abregier.
90 Qu'en ne me tiengne pour bregier,
Proceder vueil sommierement.
Maistre Mahieu premierement
Se complaint fort de bigamie
Et dit: mieulx vault avoir amie
95 Que d'espouser vefve mouillier;
Ses yeulx font sa face mouillier
Car il perdi son previlege
Et devint bon homme de neige,
Quant il demoura sans tonsure
100 De clerc; lors luy sembla trop sure
De Gregoire la decretale.
D'autre part estoit triste et pale
Qu'il ne pouoit en nule guise
Recouvrer des clers la franchise;
105 Trop se lya de fors lyens.
Exemple met des anciens,
Comment Jacob avec Lya
Et puis a Rachel se lya
Et Helcana espousa Anne
110 Et puis ot a femme Fenanne.
Les sains peres du temps jadis,
Que Dieu mette en son paradis,
Ainsi le faisoient adés
Sans estre d'onneur degradés.
115 De Lameth apres nous raconte
Et dit que bien dut avoir honte
Du corps et grant tourment a l'ame,
Quant il fu le premier bigame;
Lameth espousa Selle et Ade;
120 Pour ce meffait fu plus malade
Que pour ce que Caïn tua.
Bigame pou de vertu a;
Il est subgiet a la gent laye
Et ne puet guerir de sa playe,
125 Dont Mahieu moult se desconforte
En son livre, auquel me rapporte.
Ad ce respont dame Leesce,
Pleine de sens et de noblesce,
Car elle est de meurs aornée,

130 Dont noblesce lui est donnée,
Et monstre par argument fort
Que maistre Mahieu avoit tort
De lamenter et de plourer,
Et plus grant tort de labourer,
135 Pour imposer aux femmes blasme.
Trespassés est, Dieux en ait l'ame!
Quant il prist vefve a mariage,
Des lors estoit il en aage,
Regnans entre les advocas;
140 Tels paroles sont bien au cas.
Il savoit les drois exposer
Et les distinctions gloser
Et savoit en loy crestienne
La sanction Gregorienne
145 Et pourquoy l'omme est fait bigame.
Sur luy en doit tourner le blasme
Se blasme y avoit d'aventure,
Qui n'est pas blasme par droiture.
Et s'il y ot decepcion,
150 N'y chiet point restitucion;
Deboutés est du benefice.
Et d'autre part je luy obice
Qu'en ce n'avoit fraude n'injure,
Si com il meïsme le jure.
155 Il savoit bien ce qu'il faisoit
Et que le contrait luy plaisoit;
Il le voult, il le consenti.
Dont, se depuis s'en repenti,
Raison puet bien apercevoir
160 Qu'a ce ne fait a recevoir.
«Tart main a cul, quant pet est hors.»
Cils proverbes est assés ors.
Il convoita tant Perrenelle,
Pour ce qu'elle luy sembla belle
165 De façon et de contenance,
Qu'au dire prenoit grant plaisance
En remirant la pourtraiture
D'un des plus beaux vouls de nature
Qu'il sceüst lors en tout le monde:
170 Car la cheveleüre blonde,
Resplendissant, bien aornée,
Qui lors sembloit estre a or née,
Le front ample, net et poly,
Le sourcil plaisant et joly,
175 Les beaux yeulx vers, doulx et rians,
Amoureusement guerrians,
Le nes bien fait et la bouchette
Vermeillette, riant, doulcette,
Souef flairant, et par dedens
180 Tres bien ordenée de dens
Bien assis et plus blans d'ivire,
Le beau mentonnet pour deduire,

Les oreilles et les buffetes
Bien colourées et bien faites,
185 La gorgete polie et plaine
Ou il ne paroit nerf ne vaine,
Le col blanc, rondet par derriere,
Les espaules et la maniere
Des bras souples pour acoler,
190 Qu'en ne porroit plus beaux doler,
La main blanche, les dois traitis,
Les costés longs, le corps faitis,
Et la façon de la poitrine
Parée de double tetine,
195 Rondette, poignant a eslite,
Ne trop grande, ne trop petite,
Du port la maniere seüre
Et des rains la compasseüre
Ne trop large ne trop estroite,
200 Les beaux piés et la jambe droite,
Et tout ce qui dehors paroit
De si grant beauté la paroit
Qu'il n'y avoit point de deffaulte.
Ne fu trop basse ne trop haulte.
205 Se dehors fu belle sans lobe,
La beauté de dessoubs la robe
Dut bien estre considerée:
Car sa noble taille esmerée
Designoit sa belle char nue
210 Ne trop maigre ne trop charnue;
La mote et les choses secretes,
Que scevent personnes discretes
Convenables a leurs delis;
Les roses et les fleurs de lis
215 Estrivoient pour sa couleur.
De la sourdi la grant douleur
Dont Mahieu fist un grand chapitre.
Sa complainte n'a point de titre;
On ne doit mie tant amer
220 Qu'en face de son doulx amer
Ne nuls homs ne doit soustenir
Qu'il peüst fors que bien venir
Quant homs par bone affection
Pour lyen de dilection
225 Prent sa femme bonne et honneste,
Si com nostre foy l'amonneste.
  Et des exemples qu'il la met
Et de Caïn et de Lameth,
Ils n'ont point lieu ou cas present,
230 Ja n'en deüst faire present.
Car les gens lors sans loy estoient
Et toute leur cure mettoient
A acomplir leur voulenté;
Des maulx faisoient a plenté
235 Tant qu'on dit qu'a Dieu en desplut;

Pour ce sur eulx tonna et plut
Et noya tout par le deluge;
En l'arche en mist uit a refuge
Pour le siecle continuer;
240 Et puis leur fist insinuer
Loy qu'en dit la loy ancienne;
Or avons nous loy crestienne,
De Crist fondée en raison.
Se ses commandemens faison
245 Et nous tenons les bons usages
De l'eglise et des mariages,
Ce sera notre saulvement.
Et se d'exemples autrement
Vielz et nouveaulx voulés savoir,
250 Par David en porrés avoir,
Qui de son gré se bigama
Pour Bersabée, qu'il ama,
Qui pour lors estoit femme Urie,
Un chevalier de sa mesnie.
255 En un jardin estoit venue;
Le roy choisy la dame nue,
Qui se lavoit a la fontaine.
De si grant beauté estoit pleine
Que par amour la convoita;
266 Sa femme en fist, tant esploita,
Et orent de leur mariage
Un fil, roy Salemon le sage.
Et s'il ot en ce aucun vice,
David fu cause du malice;
265 La dame n'en fu point coulpable;
C'est exemple n'est mie fable.
  Aussi le conte d'Alençon
Tout par amour et sans tençon
Ama d'Estampes la contesse,
270 Qui de beauté sembloit deesse.
Par honneur espousa la dame;
Nuls homs n'en pourroit dire blasme,
Car en eulx fu toute largesce,
Beauté, bonté et gentillesce.
275 Qui contredit, il est coquart.
Je vi messire Anceau Choquart,
Bon clerc, joli, faitis et droit;
Bien savoit l'un et l'autre droit,
Et le canon et le civil.
280 N'ot pas mariage si vil
Qu'il ne preïst Marote a femme.
Depuis la belle sans diffame,
Quant messire Anceau deceda,
En bons meurs si bien proceda,
285 Com celle qui est sage et bonne,
Que pour amour de sa personne
Messire Estienne de la Grange
D'elle ne se fist pas estrange,

Mais l'espousa comme s'amie,
290 Non contrestant la bigamie.
Maistre Pierre de Rochefort,
Sage de lois, bel homme et fort,
Espousa une damoiselle
De Dormans, avenant et belle;
295 Fille fu mon seigneur Guillaume,
Un des plus sages du royaume.
Entre eulx orent des biens assés;
Et quant Pierre fu trespassés,
Messire Philebert Paillart,
300 Sage, discret, riche et gaillart,
La prist a femme a mariage;
Point ne doubta le bigamage.
Ces deux, qui furent bigamés,
Sont moult honnourés et amés;
305 Dedens Paris sont residens
Et ou parlement presidens,
Chevaliers, et leurs femmes, dames;
Dieux leur doint paix de corps et
d'ames!
Messire Guillaume de Sens,
310 Riche d'avoir et plein de sens,
President ou dit parlement,
Se bigama pareillement.
Aussi puis je dire sans guile
De maistre Pierre de Mainville,
315 Vaillant homme et de grant prudence;
Ou parlement ot residence
Et y fu president jadis;
Dieux ait son ame en paradis!
Il se mist avec les bigames;
320 Successivement ot trois dames
Espousées en sainte eglise,
Belles et bones a devise,
Sages et de noble renon;
De chascune ne sçay le non.
325 Pluseurs grans clers a l'en veüs,
Sages, discrès et pourveüs,
Qui de leur gré se bigamerent;
Oncques pour ce ne diffamerent
Les femmes ne il n'en mesdirent
330 Ne les blasmerent ne despirent.
Maistre Mahieu s'en est doulu
Et dit tout ce qu'il a voulu.
Toutesvois se vault il mieulx taire
Que sur autruy mordre ou detraire.
335 Car il n'y a autre action
En ceulx qui font detraction
Fors qu'il soufflent pour affoler;
Mais il font la pouldre voler
Et dedens leurs yeulx asseoir;
340 Verité ne peuent veoir

Ne prononcier vray jugement.
Certes, Dieu scet bien se je ment,
Tant sont espris d'envie et d'ire
Qu'a paines peuent il bien dire;
345 Et pour ce le droit en fait doubte
Et de tesmoingnier les deboute,
Car il dient leur ataïne;
Et pour faveur ou pour haïne
Mahieu soustenoit leur partie,
350 Et ne vault rien chose qu'il die.
Or dit il que par la veüe
Fu sa science deceüe,
Et que beauté son cuer navra
Parmi l'ueil, dont ja mais n'avra
355 N'oncques puis n'ot un jour repos;
Et fonda sur ce son propos
De rioter et de plourer
Et de femmes deshonnourer.
Certes, trop monstra sa folie;
360 Car quant femme est belle et jolie,
Com plus est doulce creature,
Tant plus a des dons de nature
Et tant plus donne de leesce
Et boute hors toute tristesce;
365 L'omme assouage et met en voye
De pais, de doulceur et de joye
Et met son cuer en si grant aise
Que lors n'est riens qui luy desplaise.
A parler proprement, sans glose,
370 Femme est la plus tres doulce chose
Que Dieu pour homme formast
oncques.
Il est vray, si puis dire doncques
Que fols est qui en fait complainte;
Car il en est aujourd'uy mainte
375 Par qui leurs maris sont hauciés
Et bien vestus et bien chauciés,
Honnourés et mis en chevance,
Moyennant la bonne ordonnance
Des femmes et leur industrie,
380 Dont leurs maris ont la maistrie
Par vraye amour et par concorde,
Si com bonne foy s'y accorde.
Mal ait es dens qui mal en dit
Et les fievres jusqu'au lendit.

385 Item il dit que du proverbe
Du serpent qui gisoit en l'erbe,
Qui muce et repont son venin,
Ne du malice femenin
N'avoit il pas lors congnoissance.
390 Puis raconte sa mescheance
Et sa douloureuse aventure

Et dit assés honte et laidure;
Mais il n'est homme qui ne peche
Ne si belle fleur qui ne seche,
395 Et que celle qu'il espousa,
Pour qui tant debatu nous a
Et qui le fist mu et taisant,
Estoit si belle et si plaisant,
Femenine, doulce et benigne,
400 Que d'un roy avoir estoit digne
S'a luy se deüst marier,
Mais depuis le fist varier;
Car elle devint tant ripeuse,
Courbée, boçue et tripeuse,
405 Desfigurée et contrefaite
Que ce sembloit une contraite;
Trop estoit laide devenue,
Hideuse, ridée et chenue
Et a regarder moult orrible,
410 Et par dedens trop mal paisible,
Du pis qu'il pouoit en disoit
Et en tous cas la despisoit.
Tout courroucié et mal estable
Mist en son livre mainte fable,
415 Pour ses dis en vertu tenir,
Qui ne sont pas a soustenir,
Ou prejudice de mes dames,
Que Dieu vueille garder de blasmes!

420 A quoy on puet respondre et dire,
Pour son propos tout desconfire,
N'est pas temps que nous nous taisons:
Il a en l'an quatre saisons
Printemps y a, qu'en nomme ver,
Esté, automne et yver.
425 Printemps florist et donne fleurs
Et herbes de maintes couleurs;
Esté fleurs et plante meüre
Et d'avoir fruit nous asseüre,
Freses, cerises et pommettes,
430 Qui naissent de tendres florettes,
Et autres fruis de mainte guise,
Dont cy ne feray pas devise;
Legiere chose est a congnoistre
Que Dieu les fait venir et croistre;
435 Automne les fait enveillir
Et permeürer et cueillir;
Yver en fait merveilleus change;
Car quant tout est mis en la grange,
Et en grenier et es maisons,
440 Quanque donnent les trois saisons,
De printemps, d'esté et d'automne,
Et les vins sont mis en la tonne,
Yver met paine du despendre:

Fleurs met a fain et herbe tendre,
445 De l'arbre fait cheoir la fueille,
N'y a verdeur qui ne s'en dueille.
Pour ce le fourmy en esté
Par grant sens est amonnesté
Des grains en sa caverne attraire,
450 Pour resister au temps contraire.
Prudens est et pourveüs en ce,
Et en luy a tant de science
Que de son bec ronge forment
Dessus chascun grain de fourment
455 Pour obvier que il ne germe
Dedens la terre a son droit terme.
Il scet bien reporter son grain
Hors de sa fosse au temps serein,
Pour sechier et pour essuer;
460 Bien scet quant le temps doit muer.
Aussi se pourvoit le fourmy;
Tant de bien ne sçay pas pour my.
    D'autre part maintiennent leur guerre
Le feu et l'air, l'eaue et la terre;
465 Chaut et sec, moisteur et froidure
Gouvernent toute creature
Et font homme et femme muer.
A ce pouons attribuer
Les saisons dont je fais parole,
470 Si come on en lit en l'escole.
Printemps, comparé a jeunesce,
Est plein de joye et de leësce
Jusqu'a vint ans ou environ.
De la saison d'esté diron:
475 D'autres vint ans avoir s'efforce;
C'est quant l'omme a beauté et force.
Mais automne après le gouverne;
En ce temps par raison discerne
Les choses et vit sagement
480 Homme de sain entendement;
Et par autres vint ans luy dure.
Yver, qui est plein de froidure,
Comparé au temps de vieillesce,
Met au neant et a feblesce
485 Le corps de creature humaine,
A decrepité le remaine.
Ainsi fu il de Perrenelle:
En son printemps fu josne et belle,
Et en esté plaisant et sage
490 Selon l'estat de son aage;
Ainsi fu elle sage et bonne,
Selon son cours, au temps d'automne.
Mais quant vieillesce l'assailli,
Beauté et vigueur ly failli;
495 Quant de ses fleaux fu tastée,
Elle devint feible et gastée.

Les membres furent tous roidis,
Retrais, courbés et refroidis.
Le pis ot dur, et les mamelles,
500 Qui tant souloient estre belles,
Furent souillies et noircies
Come bourses de cuir froncies.
Ainsi va d'umaine figure:
La beauté moult petit y dure,
505 Car il ne puet autrement estre.
Pour ce Mahieu, qui estoit maistre,
N'avoit cause ne action
D'en faire lamentacion.
S'elle estoit vieille, il estoit vieulx;
510 Dont en tous cas luy venist mieulx
Qu'il eüst pris en pacience
Que de monstrer sa grant science
Pour femmes blasmer egaument.
Cils est fols especiaument
515 Qui en mesdit oultre mesure
Et qui au blasmer met sa cure.
Car nous, hommes gros et menus,
Sommes tous de femmes venus.

A un orloge a comparée
520 Femme, ja n'iert si bien parée,
Et dit que la femme noiseuse
N'est oncques de sonner oiseuse;
Et s'il y a faulte de vivre
Et le mary assés n'en livre,
525 Les femmes dient et maintiennent
Que les deffauls des hommes viennent;
Et s'il y a des biens assés,
Elles les dient amassés
Par elles, par leur diligence,
530 Par leur sens et par leur prudence.
Ainsi est il, en verité,
Tout vient de leur prosperité,
Biens fais a elles attribuent;
Car puis qu'elles filent et buent
535 Et de tout l'ostel ont la cure,
On puet bien veoir par droiture
Que gaaing en l'ostel feront,
Et que plus y proffiteront
Trois toiles par elles filées
540 Et par leurs euvres empilées
Plus que tous les emolumens
Fais a chevaulx ou a jumens
Ne pourroient par labour rendre;
Car il convient ailleurs despendre.
545 Mais ce qui vient de la quelongne,
Que l'en soustient jouste la longne,
Tient l'ostel par nuit et par jour;
Elles labourent sans sejour,

Et la quelongne rien ne couste;
550 Et qui a la charrue ajouste
Deus beufs, il convient es greniers
Foing, avoine, mailles, deniers,
Herse, crible, rastel et beche,
Pour labourer la terre seche,
555 Fourche, flael, van et houel;
Tousjours y fault ou un ou el
En despens, avant ou arriere.
Et se l'aguille a cousturiere
Y euvre avecques la quelongne,
560 Elle fait trop bien la besongne;
Tout l'ostel soustient et gouverne.
Le mari boit en la taverne
Et despent fort, vaille que vaille;
Il ne lui chault comment tout aille.
565 Si n'est pas merveille trop dure
Se le chetif mari endure
Et est rioté de sa femme,
Qui pour ses deffaultes le blasme.
Assés en est de tel courage
570 Qu'ils n'ont cure de faire ouvrage
Pour leur mesnage soustenir.
Pour ce ne leur puet bien venir;
Car ils sont paillars et oiseus
Et contre leurs femmes noiseus.
575 Dont, se rioteuses les treuvent,
Pluseurs raisons a ce les meuvent;
On le voit par experience.
Doncques, par droit et par sentence,
Les hommes sont plus a blasmer
580 Et les femmes plus a amer,
Quant elles font mieulx leur devoir.
Bien le puet on dire de voir.
Or dit il par sa grant rudesce,
Plain de courroux et de tristesce,
585 A quoy il se veult arrester,
Que nul ne pourroit contrester
Contre la tençon venimeuse
De la femme trop rioteuse.
Non feroit Dieux, a son cuidier;
590 La place luy feroit vuidier.
Et pour plus blasmer et mesdire,
Dit qu'il n'est riens de femme pire
Et qu'a cinq metes maine l'homme;
Par fallaces ainsi les nomme.
595 Par la langue et par la veüe
Et par touchier est deceüe
De l'omme la fragilité
Par faulx et par iniquité.
Si convient que nous en dyon.
600 Exemple nous met de Guyon,
Qui disoit sa femme trouvée

Dessoubs Simon toute prouvée,
Et respudier la vouloit;
Pour ce la femme s'en douloit;
605 Blasme luy mettoit sus sans cause
Et en racontoit grande pause.
  Avec la langue est la veüe
Par le sophisme deceüe,
Si com il dit et le tesmoingne
610 Que Werry vit en la besoingne
Sebille, sa femme espousée,
Dessoubs un homme supposée.
Sebille le fait luy nya
Et jura que coulpe n'y a.
615 Une voisine de la rue
A Werry vint a sa charrue
Et l'osta hors de jalousie;
Car cil est fols qui s'en soucie.
  Après dit subrepticement
620 Et parle de l'atouchement,
Comment Framery se prouva;
L'ami de sa femme trouva
Près de son lit par nuit obscure;
Il se leva et mist grant cure
625 Au trouver, moult s'esvertua,
Tant fist que son asne tua
D'un grant pestail parmi la teste.
Non coupable en estoit la beste,
N'autre chose n'y pot trouver
630 Et failli a son fait prouver.
Mais sa femme, dont Dieux ait l'ame,
Par les voisines en ot blasme.
Je croy bien que ce fu a tort,
Et toutesvois l'asne en fu mort.
635   Encor disoit en son langage,
Perseverant en son oultrage,
Que le mari mal assené
Est a mete de faulx mené;
De femme ne se scet defendre,
640 De la lune luy fait entendre
Que soit une peau de veel,
Par paroles ou par revel,
Et veult prouver que c'est loisible,
Combien que ce soit impossible.
645   Il dit pis, que femmes vainquirent
Salemon et le desconfirent.
Par femmes et par leurs desroys
Fu pris le plus sage des roys;
Salemon, plain de sapience,
650 Lors abusa de sa science:
Si fu seduis et ordenés
Que par blandices fu menés
Jusques a mete de cuidier.
Hors de sa loy l'estut vuidier

655 Pour les idoles aourer,
N'oncques ne sçot tant labourer
Qu'il y peüst remede mettre.
  Encor dit Mahieu en sa lettre,
En continuant sa riote,
660 Et nous raconte d'Aristote
Comment femme le seurmonta
Alors que par dessus monta;
Ou chief lui mist frain et chevestre
Et vainqui des metes le maistre.
665 En ce fu grammaire traïe
Et logique moult esbaïe.
  Maistre Mahieu, pour soy esbatre,
A mis de truffes plus de quatre,
Pour colourer s'opinion;
670 Et en après fait mention
Comment la femme, pour troubler
L'omme, fait la chose doubler
Et repeter par pluseurs fois;
Ne luy souffist n'en deux n'en trois;
675 Semblant fait que point ne l'entent;
Lors voit on bien qu'elle ne tent
Fors a son mary courroucier;
Le bon homme n'ose groucier;
Veuille ou non, fault que la paix quiere,
680 Pour doubte qu'elle ne le fiere.
  Après dit que les sens de l'omme
Se deulent tous en une somme
Par femmes et par leur oultrage;
Si tost qu'homs est en mariage,
685 La tençon, ce n'est pas merveille,
Nuist et fait assourdir l'oreille,
Et leur orloge tousjours sonne,
Tout estourdist et tout estonne;
Et après l'omme ainsi demaine
690 Il n'est riens qui puist traveillier
Les yeulx tant que fait le veillier;
Et en après, pour la feblesce
Du rume qui le cervel blesce,
Le nés ne puet rien odourer;
700 Roupies luy convient plourer.
La narine est d'umeurs emplie
Que la corise multiplie
Et fait aler le materel
Jusqu'au col ou au haterel;
705 Car l'umeur y assemble toute,
Par quoy le nés souvent degoute.
On voit, quant le chief est enferme,
Qu'il n'y puet avoir membre ferme;
Tous se deulent avec le chief
710 Et tous partissent au meschief.
  De la langue desordenée,
Mal parlant et mal affrenée,

Disoit Mahieu des mauls assés
Qui cy ne seront trespassés.
715 Disoit qu'il n'osoit babouillier
Pour la langue de sa mouillier,
C'estoit la langue Perrenelle,
De tencier estoit trop isnelle,
Et que trop lui faisoit de honte.
720 En cel chapitre nous raconte
Comment jadis fouïr souloit
Puissamment, mais or se douloit
Quant plus ne pooit labourer;
C'est ce qui le faisoit plourer
725 Du temps qui ly estoit contraire,
Et qu'il ne le pooit plus faire,
Mesmement ou courtil Perrette;
Car vuide estoit sa pharette
Et son arc ne pooit plus tendre.
730 Ainsi n'ot de quoy se deffendre.
Qui n'a de quoy faire sa paix,
Souffrir l'estuet des ore mais.
       Pour ce maistre Mahieu plouroit
Et les femmes en devouroit
735 Et disoit en sa grant misere:
«Las! pourquoy fuy je nés de mere?
«Il m'estuet languir en griefs paines.»
De lamentacions sont plaines
Toutes les choses qu'il disoit.
740 Et pour ce que il despisoit
Mes dames et qu'il m'en desplaist,
J'ay contre luy meü tel plait
Dont il sera grant mencion
Se j'en vieng a m'entencion.
745 Mais j'ay sur moy maint adversaire
Et a forte partie a faire.
Maistre Mahieu a en aïde
Gallum, Juvenal et Ovide
Et maistre Jehan Clopinel,
750 Au cuer joli, au corps isnel,
Qui clochoit si comme je fais.
Sur moy en est pesant le fais;
J'ay contre moy bourdes et fables
Et poëtries delitables;
755 Car de mençoingnes y a maintes
En ces ystoires qui sont faintes,
Que je voy contre moy plaidier
Et dont ceulx se vouldront aidier
Qui soustendront maistre Mahieu.
760 Mais j'ay tout mon recours a Dieu.
Bien sçay que Dieu est verité
Et veult droiture et equité.
Et si me trairay a refuge
Vers raison, qui est nostre juge.
765 Car je voy proprement a l'ueil

Qu'un pou de ray de vray soleil
Fait fuïr une grant bruïne
Et la remet toute en ruïne.
Si ne lairay pour mesdisans
770 Ne pour les envieus nuisans
Que je n'en parle a mon aaise,
Non obstant que leur en desplaise.
Car je ne les prise un torchon;
Ou il cherra, si l'escorchon.

775   Si di contre maistre Mahieu
Que chose qu'il ait dit n'a lieu
Et qu'il n'y fait a recevoir.
Les femmes font bien leur devoir,
Ne ce n'est pas chose creable
780 De Simon ne de l'autre fable,
Ne de Werry ne de Sebille
Ne de quanqu'on dit par la ville.
En tel cas ne font pas a croire.
Il fait de Framery memoire,
785 De son asne et de sa chandeille;
De tout fait une grant merveille;
Ce sont truffes, saulve sa grace.
Et si advient bien que l'en brace
Choses assés plus semilleuses
790 Et a oïr plus merveilleuses,
De peau de veel et de lune,
Ou il dit qu'il en y ot une
Qui son mary le fist entendre,
Et l'omme ne se sçot deffendre.
795 C'est pou de chose a proposer;
L'en n'y porroit gueres gloser;
Rien n'y valent teles frivoles;
Ce sont truffes assés plus moles
Que ne soit un coignet de burre.
800 Il ne puet pas pour ce conclure,
S'il veult partie diffamer,
Qu'il puist le tout pour ce blasmer.
Il ne s'ensuit pas vrayement;
En logique est tout autrement,
805 Posé qu'il deïst verité.
Car s'il y a fragilité
Ou meffait en une partie,
La chose seroit mal partie,
Se le tout en estoit coulpable.
810 Si soit son dit compté pour fable;
Car tels truffes soubs faulse esconse
Ne sont pas dignes de response.
Et ou il dit une autre note,
De Salemon et d'Aristote,
815 Deux des plus sages de ce monde,
Sur quoy Mahieu son propos fonde,
Que Salemon moult s'abaissa

Quant pour femmes sa loy laissa,
Et qu'Aristote, le grant maistre,
820 Ot en son chief frain et chevestre
Et que femme le chevaucha
Et par dessus luy se haucha,—
Leesce respont en riant
A ce qu'il va contrariant
825 Et met ceste solucion:
Dieux, qui voult generacion,
L'omme fourma et puis la femme
Et en leurs corps inspira l'ame.
Amour y mist et compaignie
830 Pour faire et pourcreer lignie.
Et ne fait pas a oublier
Qu'il commanda multiplier
Et croistre pour remplir la terre.
Ce ne fu pas signe de guerre;
835 Il voult que propagacion
Venist par delectacion.
Homme et femme sont raisonnables
Et plus discrès et plus notables
Que ne soit autre creature.
840 Amour puissant avec nature
Les fait mouvoir a deliter
Et a charnelment habiter
Pour continuer nostre espece,
Que la mort corrompt et despece;
845 Car qui s'en tenroit pour tencier,
Tout seroit a recommencier.
Salemon fu riche homme et sage;
De nature savoit l'usage;
Il fu roy et non pas hermite,
850 Si ne voult estre sodomite;
Sodomite est plus lais pechiés
Dont l'omme puist estre entechiés.
Pour ce prist il des concubines
Et des femmes et des roïnes
855 Et jouveuceles a plenté
En usant de sa voulenté.
Il compila par grant science
Ecclesiasastes, Sapience
Et proverbes et paraboles,
860 Dont on lit en maintes escoles;
Et aussi fist il les cantiques;
Beaulx livres sont et autentiques.
Se par amour, qui le lya,
Aux femmes tant s'umilia
865 Que leur plaisir voult du tout faire,
Maistre Mahieu s'en doit bien taire.
Aristote fu plain de grace;
Et ot une cité en Trace
Qui Stragire estoit appelée;
870 Cele cité fu grant et lée

Et estoit de son patremoine.
Il fu extrait de Macedoine;
En science n'y ot greigneur;
Ce fu le prince et le seigneur
875 De tous philosophes gregois;
En Grece servi a deux roys,
A Phelippe et a Alixandre,
Auxquels fist moult de biens aprendre.
Bien savoit force de nature
880 Et fist mainte belle escripture:
Periarmeinnes et Elenches,
D'argumens sont toutes les branches,
Priores, Posteres, logique
Et science mathematique.
885 Plain estoit de grant charité;
Par tout soustenoit verité,
Dont on le doit moult essaucier.
Et s'il se laissa chevauchier,
Ce fu par joye et par deduit;
890 Amour a ce faire le duist
Par sa grant debonnaireté;
Si ne doit pas estre reté.
Bien monstra qu'on doit amer femmes
Sans leur dire lait ne diffames;
895 Car pour ce ne sont point coulpables,
Mais les dis Mahieu sont dampnables,
De ce ne convient point doubter,
Et si ne fait a escouter
Quant il allegue sa laidure.
900 Se Perrenelle n'avoit cure
De luy, ce estoit par sa coulpe;
Bien luy devoit faire la loupe.
Perrette de luy se douloit
A bon droit, car il ne vouloit
905 Payer celle debte amoureuse.
Elle en estoit plus dangereuse
Quant il refusoit a payer;
Le sourt faisoit pour delayer;
Lors estoit sa honte anoncie,
910 Et disoit la bourse froncie;
Ne puet payer et n'a que rendre
Ne le membre ne le puet tendre.
On se courrouce bien pour mains;
Pour ce le prenoit elle aux mains,
915 S'il ne fuyoit hors de la presse,
Si come il le dit et confesse;
Dont il estoit coquart et nice.
Puis raconte de sa nourrice,
Qui riotoit avec sa femme;
920 Bien y avoit cause, par m'ame
S'elle ne se vouloit lever.
Car on ne porroit trop grever
L'omme qui ne puet besoingnier.

Aussi doit il moult ressoingnier
925 Quant il n'a de quoy sa paix faire.
Pour ce se doit tel homme taire
Sans mesdire des damoiselles
Ne des dames ne des pucelles
Ne de quelque femme vivant;
930 De ce ne voist nul estrivant!
   Nous avons assés a respondre
A autres fais qu'a berbis tondre.
Mahieu mettoit toute sa peine
Et sa pensée fole et vaine
935 A toutes femmes courroucier;
Vers la sienne n'osoit groucier.
Trop s'acoustuma a mesdire,
Je croy qu'il le faisoit par ire,
Et disoit: s'il est papelart
940 Qui des femmes ne sache l'art,
Que il leüst dedens son livre,
Et des femmes seroit delivre.
Trop en mesdist, trop en parla
En ses dis par ça et par la,
945 Principaument de leur tençon;
En ce n'a point de raençon;
Lors convient que l'omme s'en fuye.
Il dit que fumiere et la pluye
Et femme tençant sans raison
950 Chacent l'omme de sa maison.
Car la femme tence et debat
Souvent commence le debat,
L'eaue pourrist, et la fumiere
Empire des yeulx la lumiere
955 Et les fait par force plourer;
Ainsi n'y puet plus demourer.
Et afin que la tençon meuve,
Elle faint souvent qu'elle treuve
Son mary pris en avoutire
960 Et contre luy content et tire.
D'exemples mettre se traveille,
Tant en met que c'est grant merveille.
Il dit qu'en puet bestes saulvages
Donter par lyens et par cages
965 Et mener a humilité
Par art ou par subtilité.
Ce ne puet homs faire d'espeuse,
Car son viés ploy a pris la heuse.
Example nous met d'un jeune homme,
970 Je ne sçay comment on le nomme,
De Monstereul; moult merveilleus,
Fumeus estoit et batailleus
Et ne queroit que la bataille,
Il ne doubtoit estoc ne taille.
975 Tant ala et tant charia
Qu'en la parfin se maria.

Quant il fu du lyen lié,
Donté fu et humilié;
Il n'osoit le sourcil lever;
980 Pour tant pouoit de dueil crever.

   Leesce dit: j'ay entendu
Et petitement deffendu
Jusques cy, mais ne vous desplaise,
Preste suy que vous en rapaise,
985 Car j'ai assés temps et saison
Et je m'en rapporte a raison.
Si useray de grans maximes
Pour donner couleur a mes rimes
Et pour les mesdisans destruire,
990 Que ja mais ne nous puissent nuire.
Je respondrai de clause en clause.
Le Decret, en l'onziesme cause
Et en la tierce question,
Nous fait ceste narration:
995 Quant on veult loer ou blasmer
Ce qu'on veult haïr ou amer,
Chascun doit, pour loyal secours,
A sa pensée avoir recours,
C'est, a sa propre conscience
1000 De bien et de mal; ainsi en ce
Que, se bien n'est en nous trouvé
Tel dont nous sommes approuvé,
Nous devons grant tristesce avoir;
Car nos meffais pouons savoir.
1005 Aussi devons de joye rire
Se le mal que nous oyons dire
De nous n'y est aperceü
Et n'y est trouvé ne sceü.
Saint Pol en fait bonne memoire
1010 Et nous dit que c'est nostre gloire
Tesmoing de nostre conscience;
Et Job, parfait en pacience,
Dit que son tesmoing est es cieulx;
Car cil qui tout scet ce est Dieux;
1015 Ou ciel est tesmoing nostre Sire,
Si gardons que nous devons dire.
   Comment est dont homme mortel
Si hardi qu'il donne mors tel
Qu'il ose femme desprisier
1020 Ne sa faulse langue aguisier
Pour en dire mal ne laidure?
David en dit en l'Escripture:
Les pecheeurs sout estrangiés,
Car hors du ventre sont changiés
1025 Et ont erré contre nature.
Ne souvient a la creature
Dont elle vient, quant elle est née;
C'est faulseté desordenée.

Fols est qui soy meïsme blasme
1030 Et le lieu dont il naist diffame.
Uns proverbes nous est donnés;
C'est que cil qui coupe son nés
Trop laidement sa face empire.
Aussi ne puet homme mesdire
1035 De femme qu'il ne se mesface;
Fols est donc qui coupe sa face.
    Mahieu dit: femme est tenceresse
Et mesdisant et jangleresse.
Cafurne ouvra trop nicement,
1040 Son cul moustra en jugement;
Car par luy fit femme chacie
Et privée d'avocacie;
A toutes femmes fist dommage
Par sa langue et par son oultrage.
1045 Par droit, si com j'ay entendu,
Leur est a tousjours deffendu
Des jugemens examiner
Et des causes patrociner.
Aussi dit il qu'une Juïse,
1050 Marie, qui fit suer Moïse,
Jangleuse fu et orguelleuse;
Par sa jangle devint lepreuse.
Et la corneille, qui fu blanche,
Devint noire et d'autre semblance;
1055 Il advint par sa janglerie
Et par sa faulse menterie.
Et qui vouldroit Dieu accuser,
Il ne se pourroit excuser
Qu'il n'armast les femmes perverses,
1060 Et leur donna langues diverses.
    Mahieu a son entencion
Fait après une question:
Pourquoy femmes sont plus noiseuses,
Plaines de paroles oiseuses
1065 Et plus jangleuses que les hommes?
Car elles sont d'os et nous sommes
Fais de terre en nostre personne,
Et l'os plus hault que terre sonne.
Ses exemples met un a un,
1070 Et suit maistre Jehan de Meun,
Quant est ou fait de jalousie,
Que cil est fols qui se marie.
Autre exemple en faisoit savoir:
Uns homs voult trois femmes avoir;
1075 Toutesvois en espousa une;
Ce fu a sa male fortune.
Si advint ou il demouroit
Que le leu aux agneaulx couroit;
Pris fu; les veneurs enqueroient
1080 De quel mort mourir le feroient.
L'omme marié l'entendi

Et son avis leur en rendi,
Que, qui marier le pourroit,
Le loup de male mort mourroit.
1085 Grief tourment est de mariage;
Ainsi disoit par son oultrage,
Et que la femme a l'omme estrive;
Car char de femme est corrosive
Et la char de l'omme degaste
1090 Quant par mariage la taste,
Et semble que les noces nuisent;
Les vertus de l'omme amenuisent.
Et dit qu'il fait bon estriver
A son pouoir pour eschiver
1095 Lyen qui fait homme despire
Et toutes les vertus empire.
Des femmes disoit maint lait dit,
Assés pis que je n'en ay dit.

    Or venons aux conclusions
1100 Et laissons les illusions
Des exemples que Mahieu baille,
Et de tençon et de bataille
Et de la femme rioteuse
Et de perverse et de jangleuse
1105 Et du cornart qui se marie
Et de Cafurne et de Marie
Et pourquey la corneille est noire.
Tels exemples font pou a croire;
Mais Leesce les veult debatre
1110 Pour les faulx mesdisans abatre,
Qu'aux femmes ne facent offense.
Leesce y met ceste deffense:
Se Cafurne fist malefice,
Ce luy soit imputé a vice,
1115 Car seule en doit estre punie;
Une autre point n'y a unie,
Les autres n'en sont point coulpables.
Une legion de diables
Anges jadis estre souloient;
1120 Mais on dit, pour ce qu'il vouloient
Estre dieux et s'enorgueillirent
Et tel pechié en eulx cueillirent
Com d'estre pers a Dieu, leur maistre,
Qui tous nous fait mourir et naistre,
1125 Dieu les fist des cieulx trebuchier
Et en tenebres embuschier.
Les autres anges demourerent,
Cest pechié point ne comparerent;
Ils sont es cieulx lassus en gloire.
1130 Les femmes eüssent victoire,
Se cy avec dame Leesce
Feüst Heloïs, l'abeesse
Du Paraclit qui tant fu sage

Du droit de coustume et d'usage;
1135 Et si estoit philosofesse,
Combien que elle fust professe.
Car Mahieu a methe menassent
Et ses argumens ordenassent
Qu'envers elles n'eüssent lieu.
1140 La fille maistre Jehan Andrieu,
Qui lisoit les lois et les drois,
Se leva matin une fois,
Pour monstrer par vraye science
Devant tous en plaine audience
1145 Que femme est a l'omme pareille,
Et proposa mainte merveille
Pour l'onneur des femmes garder
Et pour leur blasme retarder.
Tout le jour dura sa lecture
1150 Jusques bien près de nuit obscure.
Des raisons mist plus de soissante,
Voire, ce croy, plus de septante,
Et si bien y continua
Qu'homme ne l'en redargua.
1155 Femmes sont de noble matere,
L'engin et la science ont clere,
Plaine de grant subtilité.
Si puis conclure, en vérité
Que les hommes moult les doubterent;
1160 Pour ce toutes les debouterent
De l'office d'avocacie.
Se Cafurne en fu hors chacie,
Son fait aux autres point ne touche
Et n'en doivent avoir reprouche.
1165 Si ne fait la jangle Marie;
On puet dire que cils varie
Quant dit qu'elle devint lepreuse
Pour ce qu'ainsi estoit jangleuse.
Et quant a la corneille noire,
1170 Certes, ce n'est pas chose a croire
Qu'elle eüst oncques esté blanche;
Si est du dire grant enfance;
Aussi puet on dire du cigne,
Qui est grant oysel et benigne,
1175 Qu'il avoit jadis noire plume,
Or est blanc par droit coustume.
    Et se tout estoit verité
Quanque Mahieu a recité
Et dit pour les femmes blasmer,
1180 En tous ses dis n'a fors amer,
Et procede par si grant ire
Qu'a paines pourroit il bien dire.
Si ne vault son entencion;
Et se c'estoit solucion
1185 Des inconveniens doubler,
J'ay bien cause de le troubler

Et de dire les maulx des hommes,
Dont ils sont chargiés a grans sommes
De murdres et de roberies,
1190 De larrecins, de pilleries,
D'arsins et de faulx tesmoignages,
D'avoultires en mariages,
De sortileges, de poisons,
De faulsetés, de traïsons
1195 Et de pluseurs enormes crimes,
Que bien savroye mettre en rimes;
Mais a present je m'en tairay
Et en espace les lairay
Jusqu'a tant que j'en aye a faire;
1200 Car on dit bien que par trop taire
Et par trop parler de sa bouche
Aquiert on dommage et reprouche.
    A ce que Mahieu nous assaut
Et dit que femme parle haut
1205 Pour ce qu'elle est d'un os fourmée,
Je di, tant plus doit estre amée
La chose quant elle est plus noble.
Ainsi comme azur et sinoble
Valent mieulx que charbon ne croie,
1210 Il n'est vivant qui ce ne croie
Que femme doit avoir le los
Pour ce que fu faite de l'os
Et l'omme fu fait de la terre.
Pour ce Mahieu en ce point erre;
1215 L'os est plus noble et si vault mieulx;
Et pour ce l'en voult faire Dieux
Dedens le paradis terrestre,
A cest article je m'arreste;
L'omme fu fait d'un pou d'ordure,
1220 Du limon de la terre dure,
Ou val d'Ebron, enmi les champs.
Par ce point est homs plus meschans;
On puet monstrer par raisons vives
Que femme a des prerogatives
1225 Assés plus nobles que n'a l'omme.
La premiere noblesce nomme
Que dedens paradis fu faite,
Des mains Dieu fourmée et pourtraite.
Item, Dieu la fist d'une coste;
1230 Point de noblesce ne luy oste;
Plus noble en est en toutes places.
Dieu fist a femmes tant de graces
Que dedens femme voult descendre
Pour nous et nostre fourme prendre
1235 Dedens sa mere vierge et pure.
De ce fu a descort nature
Et s'en esbaï, ce me semble,
Comment fu mere et vierge ensemble.
Nostre foy monstre par doctrine

1240 Que ce fu par euvre devine.
      Mulier en latin langage
      Est dite, car l'omme assouage,
      Ou *moulier*, l'omme amolie
      Qui en mesdit il fait folie.
1245 Et s'aucun quiert pourquoy fu faite
      La femme et de la coste extraite,
      La cause en est toute delivre
      De Sentences ou second livre:
      Faite fu du costé de l'omme
1250 Tant pour son adjutoire comme
      Pour amour et dilection,
      Si que par bonne affection
      Tenist a l'omme compaignie,
      Et aussi pour avoir lignie.
1255 Et ne fu pas faite du chief,
      Pour segnourir; et de rechief,
      Dieu ne la voult pas asservir
      Ne faite des piés, pour servir,
      Mais du moyen, par la maniere
1260 Que dame ne que chamberiere
      Avecques l'omme ne feüst,
      Et qu'elle seïst et geüst
      Delés luy, pour son plaisir faire,
      Comme sa compaigne et sa paire;
1265 Et sueffre qu'avec l'omme gise,
      Pour ce qu'en son costé fu prise.
      Et s'après leur transgression
      Elle fu en subjection,
      Par coulpe advint, non par nature.
1270 Ainsi le nous dit l'Escripture.
          Or y a bien cause affermée
      Pourquoy femme doit estre amée,
      Et pourquoy fu elle ainsi faite
      Et du costé de l'omme traite
1275 Plus en dormant que en veillant.
      Nul ne s'en voist esmerveillant
      Du fait ne du noble mistere
      Qui advint en ceste matere.
      Dieu tout sachant et tout puissant
1280 Et toute chose congnoissant
      Au faire voult endormir l'omme
      Et le mist en un si doulx somme
      Que, quant le costé luy ouvri,
      Si doulcement le descouvri
1285 Et en osta la coste saine
      Que l'omme n'ot douleur ne paine,
      N'oncques il ne le traveilla,
      N'oncques il ne s'en esveilla
      Ne son repos n'en perdi oncques.
1290 En cest ouvrage desadoncques
      Monstra la puissance devine
      Qu'a nous sauver seroit encline.

On ne pourroit plus proprement
Figurer le saint sacrement
1295 De Jhesucrist et de l'Eglise.
      Ceste figure nous est mise
      Et par ceste euvre est bien monstrée,
      Qu'aussi que femme fu fourmée
      Du costé de l'omme endormi
1300 Et que point n'en fu estormi,
      Tout aussi est l'Eglise faite,
      Issue, fourmée et extraite
      Des sacremens qui descendirent
      Et du benoist costé issirent
1305 De Jhesucrist dormant en croix,
      Ou il devint palles et frois.
      Pour nous saulver en crois pendi,
      Et sanc et eaue descendi
      Du costé, pour nous racheter
1310 Et des paines d'enfer geter.
          Veons s'on doit femmes haïr
      Ne par faulse langue envaïr.
      Certes non, qui sages seroit;
      Ja preudoms ne les blasmeroit
1315 Se n'estoit par correction
      Secrete ou en confession.
      Et aussi fait cils grant oultrage
      Qui diffame le mariage.
      Comme maistre Mahieu faisoit.
1320 Du blasmer point ne se taisoit
      Et disoit: s'aucun se marie
      Et avec femme s'aparie,
      Il devient chetis et cocus;
      Ses cheveulx meslés et locus
1325 Parmi ses espaules s'estendent,
      Ceulx derriere par devant pendent;
      Ses sollers et son vestement
      Sont descousus, et lentement
      S'en va, la face aval baissiée;
1330 Sa joliveté est plaissiée.
      Et ne puet estre alienée
      Femme en mariage donnée;
      Il convient que l'en la retiegne,
      Quelque meschief qu'il en aviegne
1335 Et que cil qui vuelt femme prendre
      Et qui voit qu'il ne la puet rendre,
      Devroit prendre yeulx de beril,
      Pour mieulx veoir le grant peril;
      Et dit que tempter ne puet nuire,
1340 Mais vault moult, car on se puet duire
      A prendre chose prouffitable
      Ou a laissier la dommagable;
      Et dit qu'il est bien pou de femmes,
      Soyent damoiselles ou dames,
1345 Qui leurs maris loyaument aiment,

Combien que se dueillent ou claiment.
Raconter voult d'un chevalier
Bel et appert et bon guerrier,
Qui espousa sa chamberiere,
1350 Et en dit en ceste maniere:
Le chevalier fu grans et fors,
Mais par un fait d'armes fu mors.
Sa femme forment le ploura
Et sur sa tombe demoura
1355 Et ne voult, par nulle raison,
Plus retourner en sa maison.
Ce jour fu, bien l'ay entendu,
Un larron au gibet pendu
Dont un chevalier renommé,
1360 Sire Gillebert fu nommé,
Pour son fief en devoit la garde.
En passant la dame regarde
Delés le seigneur enfouy.
Ses pleurs et son estrif ouy.
1365 Courtoisement luy a dit: «Dame,
«Rapaisiés vous, priés pour s'ame,
«On ne gaigne rien a dueil faire.»
Elle respont: «Ne m'en puis taire;
«J'ay perdu le meilleur du monde;
1370 «O luy en la fosse parfonde
«Vouldroie gesir toute morte.»
Sire Gillebert la conforte
Et dit qu'un autre en trouvera;
Aussi bon ou meilleur sera.
1375 Aux champs a sa voye tenue,
Car la nuit estoit ja venue.
Et le larron estoit emblé;
Adont a de paour tremblé
Et cuidoit que par son forfait.
1380 Ait son fief perdu et forfait,
Gillebert retourna arriere,
Tout pensif, droit au cimetiere;
A la dame dist s'aventure
Et puis de son fief la nature,
1385 Sa complainte luy publia;
Et elle tantost oublia
Son bon mari, en esperance
De renouveler aliance.
«Sire,» dist elle, «n'ayés soing,
1390 «Secourray vous a ce besoing
«Du meschief de quoy vous doulés,
«Se vous pour femme me voulés.»
—«Il dist: «oïl» a bonne chiere.
Maintenant deffouy la biere
1395 Et fu l'omme mort, ce sachiés,
Aux fourches destrais et sachiés,
Quant vint la, plus n'y attendi,
Elle meïsmes le pendi

Ou propre lieu et ou costé
1400 Dont on ot le larron osté.
Deux playes lui fist en la teste;
Et avec ce la male beste
Les yeulx luy fora et creva;
Par semblant moult pou luy greva.
1405 Sire Gillebert n'en ot cure;
Quant il vit la besongne oscure,
Oncques ne luy tint serement,
Mais la refusa laidement.
    Se par exemples haïneus
1410 De mesdisans ataïneus
Femmes sont egaument blasmées
Qui bien deüssent estre amées,
On leur fait tort contre raison.
Se male femme ou mauvais hom
1415 Fait aucun mal particuler,
On ne doit pas articuler
Qu'il soit pour tous a consequence.
Assés souffist ceste deffense.
Celle qui son mari pendi
1420 Sur ce coulpable se rendi;
Le chevalier pecha en tant
Qu'il fu du mesfait consentant.
Je di, et est chose prouvée,
Qu'en femme est loyauté trouvée,
1425 Principaument en mariage;
Car Dieux en fist l'appariage.
Et pour brieve response faire,
Vous en metray vray exemplaire.
Devers Laleue, en Picardie,
1430 Advint une grant coquardie
D'un chevalier de grant renom;
De Bailleul portoit le surnon.
Tant ama une damoiselle,
Pour ce qu'elle fu jeune et belle,
1435 Que de s'amour luy fist requeste.
Mais l'amour estoit deshonneste
Pour ce qu'elle avoit un mari.
La damoiselle au cuer marri,
S'elle estoit plaine de beauté,
1440 Encor avoit plus loyauté;
La requeste luy refusa.
Et le chevalier l'accusa
De crime par faulx tesmoignage,
Et fu de si felon courage
1445 Que il la fist ardoir en cendre,
A tort et sans raison entendre.
Le mari de la damoiselle
Au roy Phelippe en fist querelle.
Le chevalier fu en prison
1450 Et jugiés pour sa mesprison
A mener traïner et pendre.

Le roy Jehan l'en fist deffendre,
Qui estoit duc de Normandie.
Le chevalier, quoy qu'on en die,
1455 Fu appointiés sur une cloie,
Pour mener pendre droite voie.
Mais le bon duc en ot pitié;
Ainsi fu par luy respitié.
    Lucresse aussi, qui fu de Romme,
1460 Ot espousé un vaillant homme;
Loyauté luy fist en sa vie,
Mais a force luy fu ravie
Et oultre son gré esforcie;
Si amast mieulx estre escorchie.
1465 Son bon mari la rapaisoit
Et l'embraçoit et la baisoit
Et lui pardonnoit le meffait
Que de son gré n'avoit pas fait.
Rien n'y valu le conforter,
1470 Sa honte ne voult plus porter
Non obstant pardon ne confort;
D'un coultel se feri a mort.
Ainsi fina dame Lucresse.
Penelope, qui fu de Grece,
1475 Femme Ulixes, qui fu moult sage,
Se maintint bien en mariage.
Ulixes fu a la grant Troie,
Avec les Grieux, pour querir proie.
Maint peril souffri en la mer.
1480 Penelope fist a amer;
Par dix ans ou plus l'attendi.
Si loyaument se deffendi
Qu'oncques ne se voult marier
N'avecques homme aparier.
1485 Et si bien se garda la dame
Que nul n'en devroit dire blasme.
    Le mesdisant tousjours tençoit,
Sa riote recommençoit:
Sylla, ce dist, occist son pere.
1490 Avoir en dut grant vitupere;
En ce fait moult se diffama
Pour le beau Minos qu'elle ama.
Elle fu trop crueuse beste
Quant de son pere prist la teste.
1495 Encor dit il autre laidure,
Que femme est de tele nature:
Quant son mari est trespassé,
Paix n'avra jusqu'elle ait brassé
Tant qu'elle ait pris son ennemi,
1500 Et n'atent ne jour ne demi;
Ceulx que deüssent reprouchier
Font souvent en leurs lis couchier
Ou a mariage les prendent,
Ne bien ne raison n'y entendent;

1505 Et que chascune luxurie.
Puis parle de la mort Urie
Par Bersabée, sa moullier;
David l'aperçut despoullier
Et laver dedens la fointaine.
1510 Ainsi sa riote demaine;
Et sa douloureuse chançon
Nous ramentoit le fort Sanson,
Que Dalida tondi des forces,
Dont il perdi toutes ses forces.
1515 Que lui vault parler de Sylla?
On scet bien que mal dit il a.
Car, ou c'est fable controuvée,
Ou mençonge de faulx prouvée.
Trop bien est es fables Ovide
1520 Comment Sylla fu patricide
Et qu'elle occist Nisus, son pere;
Mais la mençonge est toute clere.
Il dit que Sylla fu chuëte,
Qui par jour se tient en muëte,
1525 Et Nisus devint esprevier.
Cela ne fait nul reprouvier.
Quant aux femmes vituperer,
L'en n'y doit point obtemperer.
Et s'aucunes se remarient
1530 Et par leur niceté varient,
Pour ce n'avient il pas a toutes.
S'il y a de mauvaises gloutes,
Plus y a de mauvais gloutons
Es hommes; de ce ne doubtons.
1535 Certes, femmes sont moult courtoises,
Dames, damoiselles, bourgoises
Et autres selon leur estat.
Dieu vueille amender le restat!
Et se David donna la lettre
1540 Pour Urias a la mort mettre,
Bersabée n'en fu coulpable;
Ce fist Joab, le connestable.
Des hommes treuve on ces desroys
En la Bible, ou livre des Roys.
1545   Se le fort Sanson fu tondu
Et par Dalida confondu,
Sanson en fu cause en partie.
De sa femme fist departie,
Maugré ses parents la laissa;
1550 De querir femme ne cessa,
Si trouva Dalida la fole.
Il se deçut par sa parole,
Car ses ennemis s'acointerent
De Dalide et luy presenterent
1555 Des dons pour le secret savoir,
Que Sanson peüssent avoir
Pour le lyer par force ou prendre

Si qu'il ne se peüst deffendre.
Elle fist tant par ses blandices
1560 Que Sanson, comme fols et nices,
De ses forces dist l'achoison.
Sa bouche n'ot point de cloison,
Car contre son bien respondi,
Et elle en dormant le tondi.
1565 Par ce fu pris et si grevés
Qu'il en ot les deux yeulx crevés.
A bon droit souffri son orage,
Quant il laissa son mariage
Pour une fole femme amer;
1570 De ce doit on Sanson blasmer
Qui estoit juge d'Israel;
Il fu batu de son flael.
Cest dit aux femmes point ne nuit,
Mais les hommes enseigne et duit
1575 Que leurs secres point ne revelent
Et au mieulx qu'il pourront les celent.
Nous avons chascun jour a prime
Les vers que suivent ceste rime:
«Linguam refrenans temperet
1580 «Ne litis horror insonet.»
    Mahieu par felonie dit
Que Salemon fist un edit
Que tous vieulx hommes de cent ans
Fussent mis a mort en son temps,
1585 Sur peine d'indignacion.
Apres la publicacion
Un jeune homme muça son pere,
Pour eschever celle misere;
Secretement luy queroit vivres.
1590 Son pere lui aprist ses livres
Tant qu'il devint discret et sage.
Salemon enquist de l'oultrage;
Le jeune homme fist ajourner
Et luy enjoinst, sans sejourner,
1595 Sur quanque a luy estoit tenus,
Qu'il ne venist vestus ne nus,
N'a pié, n'a cheval, n'a jument;
Et luy dist, par son argument,
Son seigneur, son serf, son amy
1600 Menast avec son ennemy.
Le jeune homme s'apareilla,
A son pere se conseilla.
D'une roys se vestit moult bien,
Son fils et son asne et son chien
1605 Et sa femme avec luy conduist;
Le pere sagement l'induist.
Au roy monstra au doy sa femme
Et jura qu'oncques, par son ame,
Plus grant ennemy ne senti.
1610 Elle tantost le desmenti;

Et il luy donna une buffe;
Mais elle nel tient pas a truffe;
Au roy dist: «Sire, faites prendre
«Ce larron et le mener pendre;
1615 «Certes, il a enclos son pere,
«Si doit mourir de mort amere.»
Le roy s'en rist, quant il l'oï,
Et en son cuer s'en resjoï.
    Ne sçay pourquoy homme s'en deult;
1620 Enne dit il pas qui ne veult
Ses secrès, oultre sa deffense?
Le bon homme fist grant offense
De ce que sa femme bati
Devant le roy, qui rabati
1625 Leur noise et ne s'en fist que rire.
Qu'en puet donc le mesdisant dire
Fors qu'en doit chascun jour apprendre
Qu'en se puist garder de mesprendre?
    Item le mesdisant fait noise
1630 Que, selon le dit saint Ambroise,
On ne doit nul homme prier
Ne ennorter de marier,
Pour les maudiçons qui en viennent;
Car pour mal conseillés se tiennent
1635 Ceulx qui se mettent en tel ordre;
Il ne cesseront ja de mordre
Et maudire comme ennemis
Tous ceulx qui s'en sont entremis.
Et quant le mary gist en biere,
1640 La femme et avant et arriere
Quiert comment se puist marier;
Et assés la fait varier,
Quant il convient que elle pleure.
A paines attent jour ne heure
1645 Et tant de marier se haste
Qu'elle en prent un qui tout li gaste.
Encor dit il mainte frivole,
Et dit qu'il n'est beste si fole
Que vefve femme reparée;
1650 Ne se tient pas pour esgarée;
Souvent se renouvelle et change
Et prent cheveleüre estrange;
Et, aussi que la louve gloute,
Se prent au pire de la route.
1655 Jadis souloit estre autrement:
Un an y avoit proprement
Que femme son mary plouroit
Et en lugubre demouroit.
Or n'y a mais trois jours d'espace;
1660 Et se plus, querés qui le face!
Les vefves par ardeur effrontent,
Sur les maisons rampent et montent
Aussi que les roynes d'Egipte;

N'ont cure de lit ne de giste
1665 S'il n'y a masles avec elles.
Qui cuidast qu'elles fussent teles,
De tel estat ne de tel estre?
Sains Acaires ama mieulx estre
Garde des dervés enragiés
1670 Que des vefves estre chargiés;
Dervées sont et sans lien,
Si n'en voult estre gardien.
Des femmes dit en pluseurs guises,
Et comment quierent les eglises
1675 Et se vont monstrant par la voye.
Chascune veult bien qu'en la voye,
Mais les reliques n'aiment gueres,
Les fiertres ne les saintuaires;
Plus aiment les clers et les prestres
1680 Et les suivent dedens leurs estres.
N'y a nulle qui s'en esfroye.
Les ribaus y quierent leur proye,
Aucunes en mettent souvines;
Ce ne sont pas euvres divines.
1685 Qui en l'eglise achateroit
Un cheval, il se mefferoit.
Mais assés plus est a deffendre
Que femme ne s'y doye vendre.
Elles font de la Dieu maison
1690 Bordel contre droit et raison.
Bien deüssent estre doubteuses;
Elles vont comme pou honteuses
Par les eglises de Paris;
Ce n'est mie pour leurs maris.
1695 Mahieu dit, par saint Nicolas,
Que c'est pour avoir leurs soulas.
La faignent estre catholiques;
Souvent visitent les reliques
Qui sont en la sainte Chapelle;
1700 Chascune sa commere appelle
Ou autre de son voisinage,
Pour aller en pelerinage.
  Liement y responderay;
Gueres sur ce n'arresteray;
1705 Ce n'est mie trop grant offense,
Qui trespasseroit la deffense
De ce qu'il dit de saint Ambroise;
Ce ne vault pas une framboise.
Car saint Pol dit tout au contraire.
1710 Lequel vaut il doncques mieulx faire?
Saint Pol loe le mariage:
Pour trop grant chaleur fait ombrage.
J'en parleray plus plainement
Ainçois que soye au finement;
1715 Vous orrés tout a une fois
Ce qu'en diray a haulte voix.

Se femme tost se remarie,
C'est bon, quant elle droit charie;
Maintes fois est a ce menée
1720 Qu'en l'appelle mal assenée:
Se mal en vient, c'est sa droiture!
S'il en vient bien, c'est aventure!
S'elle se haste, n'en puet mais;
El ne puet demourer en paix
1725 Pour les cornars qui la requierent.
Et tels leur avantage quierent
Qui y treuvent leur arrerage.
Ainsi est il du mariage.
Ce n'est rien d'une femme seule,
1730 Et souvent par mauvaise gueule
Pourroit pour pou estre blasmée.
Et elle est servie et amée
Quant elle a homme qui la porte
Et en ses fais la reconforte.
1735 Elle le fait en esperance
D'avoir tousjours meilleur chevance
Et d'estre en tous ses fais gardée.
Pour ce n'y vault rien la tardée;
Le sien ne fait que consumer;
1740 Ainsi le doit on presumer.
  Quant la vefve se remarie,
Pour ce que le temps se varie
Varier aussi nous convient.
Mahieu a dit, bien m'en souvient,
1745 Que vefve doit un an attendre
Ainçois qu'elle puist homme prendre.
Certes il n'en est ja besoing;
Car il convient qu'elle ait le soing
De traitier toute sa besoingne;
1750 Si n'a mestier de grant aloingne.
Com plus atent et plus se gaste;
Pour ce est il bon qu'elle se haste
Selon ce que elle se sent.
Car on voit que le temps present
1755 Au temps passé est tout contraire.
Et quant il dit que saint Acaire
Ne voult femmes vefves garder,
On ne doit pas pour ce tarder
A rentrer en bon mariage;
1760 Car en tel fait n'a point de rage.
Judich ne fu pas trop dervée;
Car sa cité fu reservée
Et deffendue d'estre prise
Des gens qui l'avoient assise.
1765 Olofernes, le mal estable,
Des Assiriens connestable,
Soupa avec la vefve dame;
Au cuer avoit d'amour la flamme,
Avec elle cuidoit gesir

1770 Pour acomplir son fol desir.
Il but trop et mal se garda.
Judich son fait bien regarda;
A Oloferne d'une espée
Ot tantost la teste coupée
1775 En dormant, car il estoit ivre;
Ainsi fu la cité delivre.
    Se les femmes, blanches et bises,
Hantent voulentiers les eglises,
De ce ne font point a blasmer
1780 Ne deça mer ne dela mer.
Elles vont aux processions,
Elles vont aux confessions,
Elles vont aux enfans lever
Et aux commeres relever,
1785 Aux espousées et aux festes,
Elles vont aux choses honnestes,
Elles vont pour messes ouïr,
Elles vont aux mors enfouïr,
Elles vont aux festivités
1790 En aumosnes et charités,
Elles vont par les cimetieres
En oraisons et en prieres
Et prient pour les trespassés,
Et font des autres biens assés.
1795 En tous leurs fais sont amiables
Et devotes et charitables,
Bonnes et vrayes catholiques,
Et aourent moult les reliques,
Les crucifix et les images;
1800 Je croy que ce sont bons usages.
Pour ce n'aiment ne clerc ne prestre;
Nul n'en doit parler a senestre,
S'il n'est espris de jalousie
Ou du pechié d'ypocrisie.
1805   Le mesdisant ne s'en taist mie
Sa langue est trop grant ennemie:
Femmes tiennent eschevinage
D'espouser, de concubinage,
Et de Martin et de Sebille,
1810 Et de quanqu'on fait par la ville.
Mahieu en a dit grans merveilles,
Oncques je n'oï les pareilles.
Il dit que femmes tiennent senne,
Agnès, Bietrix, Berthe et Jehanne.
1815 En leur senne n'a rien celé,
La est le secret revelé,
La devient chascune maistresse
D'estre jangleuse et tenceresse.
L'une veult amer par luxure,
1820 L'autre a son mary dit injure,
Et disoit, si luy aist Dieux!
Qu'on ne scet laquelle vault mieulx,

Ou la femme luxurieuse
Ou la moullier injurieuse.
1825 Grant sens y convenroit avoir;
Les femmes veulent tout savoir
De tel condicion sont toutes;
Elles veulent savoir les doubtes,
Les temps, les momens et les poins
1830 Par lesquels les hommes sont poins,
Et les causes parfondement
Dès le chief jusqu'au fondement.
    Et s'il y a chose secrete
De cy jusqu'en l'isle de Crete,
1835 Il convient que femme le sache;
Car son mary prent et le sache,
A soy le tire sur le lit
Et faint que vueille avoir delit.
Lors son mary baise et acole
1840 Et luy dit par fainte parole
«Je ne sçay que l'omme ressoigne;
«Car, ainsi que Dieu le tesmoigne,
«Pour femme laisse pere et mere;
«C'est tout un, si com je l'espere.»
1845 Lors se joint a luy pis a pis
Non obstant sarge ne tapis,
Et luy dit: « Vecy, je te donne
«Quanque j'ay je le t'abandonne,
«Et cuer et corps et tous mes membres
1850 «Si te pri que tu t'en remembres.
«Tu es mon mary et mon sire,
«Or me di ce que je desire;
«J'ameroye mieulx a grief paine
«Mourir de male mort soudaine
1855 «Que je tes secres revelasse
«Jamais ne le feroye, lasse!»
Lors le rembrace et le rebaise
Et l'aplanoye et le rapaise
Et le blandist et puis le flate
1860 Dessoubz luy se met toute plate
Et dit «je suy en ton demaine,
«Force d'amour a ce me maine.»
Et quant l'omme veult aprouchier,
Elle luy deffent le touchier,
1865 Arrier se trait, le dos luy tourne
Et ploure comme triste et mourne;
Semblant fait que soit moult troublée.
Lors est la riote doublée.
Quant elle s'est un pou teüe,
1870 Elle dit: «je suy deceüe,
«Lasse! je suy ta chamberiere;
«Je vouldroye estre bien arriere
«Noyee dedens une fosse.
«La chose par seroit trop grosse
1875 «Que je te porroye celer;

«Et rien ne me veulx reveler!
«Car nostre amour n'est pas pareille,
«Puis que tu fais la sourde oreille.»
L'omme s'esbaïst et s'apense,
1880 A l'encontre ne scet deffense,
Et luy dit: «Tournés vous deça!
«Si courrouciés ne fu pieça;
«Il n'est riens que j'aye tant chiere.»
Vers son mary tourne la chiere
1885 Et puis luy tent bouche et poitrine.
Bien le deçoit par sa doctrine.
Tant luy requiert, tant luy supplie
Qu'il luy dit tout, si fait folie;
Car depuis est dame et maistresse,
1890 Et il est serf a grant tristesce.
    La response en est assés brieve:
Tenir sa langue point ne grieve.
Se les femmes sont souvent prestes
De faire a leurs hommes requestes
1895 Qui puissent tourner a contraire,
Il n'y a fors que du bien taire;
Bien celer en est medecine.
Se femme est par nature encline
Que les secrès vueille savoir,
1900 L'omme doit tant de sens avoir
Que son secret puist bien celer,
Ou ne le doit point reveler.
De Sanson le poués aprendre
Qu'on se doit garder de mesprendre.
1905   Or dit qu'hom ne puet Dieu servir
Qui femme se veult asservir.
Car tousjours de plus de mil cures,
Qui lui sont greveuses et dures,
Est empeschiés en sa pensée.
1910 Il veult complaire a s'espousée
Querir luy fault vestir et vivre.
Ainsi n'est pas du tout delivre.
Hom sans femme puet mieulx entendre
A servir de cuer souple et tendre
1915 Nostre Seigneur en sainte Eglise
Que ne fait cil qui femme a prise.
Après raconte de la cene
Ou Dieu nous appelle et assene,
Et que la cene signifie
1920 Souper en pardurable vie
A la table de paradis,
Et que ja n'en y avra dix
De tous hommes que si marient,
Puisque femmes les contrarient.
1925   Joye respont incontinent
Que l'article est impertinent
A la fin ou Mahieu veult tendre;
Et s'il y convenoit deffendre,

Elle dit qu'hom qui femme a prise
1930 Ne doit pas servir en l'Eglise,
Mais cil y doit faire l'office
Qui est rentés du benefice;
Et l'omme mis en mariage
Doit procurer pour son mesnage;
1935 Bien voist au moustier, quant on sonne,
Selon l'estat de sa personne.
Et quant est au fait de la cene,
Ou il dit que Dieu nous assene,
De l'Evangile est la parole
1940 Par maniere de parabole:
Un homme fist un grant souper,
Ou païs n'ot pareil ou per,
Et a ses sergens commanda
Querir tous ceulx qu'il y manda.
1945 Uns, qui lors mariés estoit,
Que le sergent amonnestoit
D'y aler, pas ne refusa,
Mais courtoisement s'excusa
Et dist: «Aller n'y puis, par m'ame!
1950 «J'ay aujourd'hui espousé femme.»
Ce fu juste excusacion.
Que vault ceste narracion?
Se le marié ne pot mie
Aler en celle compaignie,
1955 Aux aultres ne fait prejudice,
Ne ce ne seroit pas justice.
Ne on ne se doit pas aherdre
Que les mariés doivent perdre
Le souper de la sainte table
1960 De paradis tres delitable;
Ne le dit que Mahieu en conte
Ne fait aux femmes point de honte.
    Item il dit en sa morsure
Que femme d'obeïr n'a cure.
1965 Tout ce qu'en luy deffent veult faire;
Et nous en met un exemplaire
D'un homme qui le voult prouver.
De fort venin qu'il pot trouver
Brassa, que plus n'y attendi,
1970 Et a sa femme deffendi
Qu'elle ne touchast au vaissel.
Elle doubta pou le faissel
Et en but contre sa defense;
Ce luy fu mortele despense.
1975 Orpheus savoit la theorique
De tous instrumens de musique.
Sa femme, Erudix appelée,
Estoit en enfer hostelée.
Orpheus ala a la porte
1980 D'enfer, pour avoir sa consorte;
A bien jouer moult entendi

Si bien joua qu'en luy rendi
Sa femme par tele maniere
Que, s'elle regardoit derriere,
1985 Que retourner la convendroit
Et que jamais n'en revendroit.
Erudix ot pout de science,
Si ne voult faire obedience;
Dedens enfer fu remenée
1990 La fole, de male heure née.
Assuerus, le roy de Mede,
Oncques ne pot mettre remede
Que sa femme, pour sa puissance,
Luy voulsist faire obeïssance.
1995 Vasty avoit nom la roïne;
Par orgueil tourna en ruïne.
Elle ne voult a luy venir
Ne son commandement tenir,
Mais plainement luy refusa;
2000 Et pour ce le roy l'accusa;
Du royaume fu hors boutée
Et des autres au doy monstrée.
Eve plus tost la main tendi
Au fruit que Dieu luy deffendi,
2005 Que s'il abandonné l'eüst
Et que du faire luy leüst.
La femme Loth mal se garda,
Quant par derrier soy regarda
Sodome, la cité bruïe,
2010 Dont elle estoit hors affuïe,
Un ange, qui les conduisoit,
De par Dieu la femme induisoit
Que plus illec ne sejournast
Et que point ne se retournast,
2015 Que mal n'en venist prestement.
Contre son amonnestement
Retourna pour veoir la flamme;
Roide devint comme une lame.
  Certes, qui ne responderoit
2020 Et les femmes n'escuseroit
Sur ceste désobeïssance,
Ce seroit trop grant ignorance;
Car bien y chiet response tele:
Quant Dieu ot mis l'ame immortele
2025 Dedens le corps d'omme et de femme
Par amour qui les cuers entame,
Il leur donna de bon courage
A chascun par franc arbitrage
Que bien et mal peüssent faire.
2030 Mais qui du bien fait le contraire,
Soit male femme ou mauvais hom,
Retourner s'en doit a raison,
Afin que, quant il se desvoie,
Que raison le remette a voie.

2035 Car voulenté a mal encline
Contre raison souvent domine
Toutes foys qu'a pechié le maine
Par inclinacion humaine;
Et qui en tous temps bien feroit
2040 Et point ne se desvoieroit,
Ce seroit par divinité,
Non mie par humanité.
Pour ce les femmes ont puissance
De faire desobeïssance
2045 En usant de leur franc vouloir.
Toutesvois se peuent douloir
Qu'elles sont en subjection
Des hommes par transgression.
Et qui commandement feroit
2050 Qui par droit juste ne seroit,
Il n'y avroit pas grant offense
A trespasser celle deffense.
Les hommes scevent bien par eulx
Qu'aux femmes sont assés pareulx,
2055 La subjection exceptée
Dont la femme est supeditee.
Et selon le droit de nature
La femme puet de sa faiture
Du mal ou du bien procurer,
2060 Se raison le veult endurer.
Et s'elle ne veult, si s'en aille
Ou elle trouveroit bataille.
Car Dieu a es femmes planté
Mains raison et plus voulenté;
2065 Si doit avoir plus de franchise;
Ne raison n'a point de maistrise
Ou voulenté veult estre dame.
Quoy qu'il en soit ou los ou blasme,
Voulenté en puet nul contraindre,
2070 Mais le fait puet on bien refraindre.
  Se l'omme qui avoit haïne
A sa femme, par faulx couvine
Luy apresta venin pour boire,
Et, en aumoire ou en ciboire,
2075 Le mist en vaissel par malice,
Et elle en but, ce fu le vice
De l'omme qui luy deffendi;
Car trop faulsement luy rendi
De sa haïne la vengence.
2080 Elle avoit du fait ignorance;
Car se le venin y sceüst,
La femme jamais n'en beüst.
Ainsi en fu l'omme coulpable
Par son vice et son fait damnable.
2085 Bien avoit desservi a pendre,
Quant le vray ne luy fist entendre,
Ou il avoit peril de mort;

Il machina contre elle a tort.
D'Orpheus et de s'espousée
2090 C'est fable de bourde arrousée.
Car ce seroit contre nature,
S'une mortele creature
Après sa mort venoit a vie.
Quant l'ame est hors du corps ravie,
2095 Il convenroit bien flajoler
Et violer et citoler,
Qui pour ce la pourroit ravoir!
En luy a moult pou de savoir;
Homs qui de tels exemples use,
2100 Il fait bien entendre la muse.
Tels dis aux femmes point ne nuisent
Ne leurs bontés n'en amenuisent.
    Et ou la roïne Vasti
Contre son mari s'aasti,
2105 Plaine d'orgueil et de desroy,
Ou temps Assuerus,— le roy
Un certain jour tint sa grant feste;
Elle ot couronne sur la teste;
Il la manda qu'a luy venist
2110 Et la feste en joye tenist;
Elle luy sot bien refuser
N'oncques ne s'en voult excuser;—
Puet estre qu'il li mescheï
Pour ce qu'elle desobeï,
2115 Ou Dieux ainsi en ordena
Et a ce faire la mena
Pour donner aux autres exemple;
Et la cause y est assés ample:
Se Vasti perdi sa couronne
2120 Ainsi com descent la personne
Par orgueil et fragilité,
Aussi par grant humilité
Monta Hester, qui fu roïne.
Elle fu a bien faire encline
2125 Et fist delivrer Mardochée,
Et Aman ot male soudée,
Car il fu au gibet pendu;
Mardochée en fu deffendu.
Hester fu d'hebrée lignie,
2130 Bien aprise et bien enseignie;
Au roy fist humble obeïssance,
Et il en ot bien congnoissance;
Car le peuple israelien
Fist delivrer hors du lien
2135 De prison de chetiveté.
Par sa grant debonnaireté
Contre Vasti doit estre mise
Hester, celle noble Juïse,
Et doit on honnourer les femmes
2140 Sans en dire mal ne diffames.

Tout ce que Mahieu a dit d'Eve
Ne monte pas a une feve
Quant aux autres femmes blasmer;
Car Dieu, qui tant nous voult amer
2145 Par dessus toutes creatures
Et savoit les choses futures,
Les passées et les presentes,
Avoit ja planté pluseurs entes
Dedens le paradis terrestre.
2150 Bien savoit qu'il en pouoit estre
Et comment l'omme mangeroit
Du fruit qui veé luy seroit.
Quant Eve induist le premier homme
A mordre dedens une pomme,
2155 Pour ce voult Dieu ça jus descendre
En femme et nostre fourme prendre,
Pour nous rendre nostre heritage
Et satisfaire de l'oultrage
Du delit et de la morsure,
2160 Pourquoy il souffri la mort sure
En croix. Si est drois qu'homs entende
Que Dieu pour luy paya l'amende;
Et quant Dieu le voult amender,
Hom n'en doit plus rien demander.
2165 Car la coulpe de l'omme y pent;
Du meffait fu participant.
Et se la femme Loth sceüst
Que pour soy retourner deüst
Devenir roide comme pierre,
2170 Point ne l'eüst fait, par saint Pierre;
Et se derrier soy regardoit
Sodome, qui en flamme ardoit,
Ce ne fu pas trop grant merveille;
Mains de chose le cuer esveille
2175 A regarder et a veillier;
Si n'en doit on esmerveillier.
Et l'ange qui l'amonnestoit,
Tousjours en fourme d'omme estoit;
Dont ne cuida pas tant mesprendre.
2180 Si puet on autrement entendre
Que Dieu le voult, qui tout savoit;
Car des lors pourveü avoit
Que Loth, le neveu Abraham,
Qui avoit souffert grant ahan,
2185 O ses filles habiteroit
Et d'eulx lignages ysteroit,
Et que, se Loth sa femme eüst,
Avec ses filles ne geüst.
Leurs deux fils nommeray a mon
2190 Pouoir: l'un Moab, l'autre Amon.
De Moab sont les Moabites
Et d'Amon sont les Amonites;
Ces deux la terre moult remplirent,

Dont maintes guerres en sourdirent.
2195 Par ce que j'ay dit et diray
Et que par droit sentier iray
Sont les femmes bien excusées;
Point ne doivent estre accusées
De blasme ne de vilenie,
2200 Et qui mal en dit, je le nie;
Car d'obeïr sont assés prestes,
Sages, courtoises et honnestes.
　　Maistre Mahieu de langue ague
Sur les femmes point et argue
2205 Et dit qu'elles sont envieuses,
Mesdisans et malicieuses.
Et qui veult savoir le covine
D'une femme ou de sa voisine,
Si die qu'elle est bonne et belle,
2210 Douce, simple, plaisant et telle
Qu'on la doit louer et amer:
Par les autres l'orrés blasmer
Et ses vices ramentevoir;
Lors fait envie son devoir.
2215 S'il y a une coustumiere
De seoir au moustier premiere
Ou d'aler devant a l'offrande,
Il convient qu'elle soit bien grande,
S'en son fait vouloit frequenter
2220 Sans rioter ou tormenter.
Et qui veult paix, si se pourvoye
Que, quant femmes vont par la voye,
Que son salut ne rende a une,
Mais salutacion commune
2225 Face a toutes en audience
Avec signe d'obedience.
La femme par envie encline
Reprouche tousjours sa voisine
Mieulx parée, dont il luy poise.
2230 Au mari en revient la noise.
«Chetif mari», ce dit la femme,
«Tu as grant honte et grant diffame,
«Quant tu me tiens ainsi vestue
«Que je n'ose aler par la rue.
2235 «Se ce qu'a moy affiert eüsse,
«O les greigneurs estre deüsse.»
Le mari n'ose contrester;
Des robes luy fait aprester
Pour ce que, s'il y avoit faulte,
2240 La noise trouveroit trop haulte.
Chascun jour vouldroit faire change
De la chanvre ou du lin estrange,
Et dit souvent que c'est merveille,
Qu'a sa voisine n'est pareille;
2245 Mieulx vault de sa vache le pis;
Ce dit quant ne scet dire pis.

　　Si convient que response die
Sur ce vice qui est d'envie,
Dont Mahieu mes dames accuse.
2250 Je di ainsi et les excuse:
Que les choses sont assés troubles
Et les entendemens sont doubles.
Il y a envie de bien
Et envie qui ne vault rien.
2255 Homme ou femme qui estudie
A bien faire, c'est bonne envie;
Ainsi le doit on raconter.
Qui puet les autres surmonter,
Soit en armes ou en science
2260 Et avoir bonne conscience,
C'est bonne envie, ce me semble,
De pouoir et savoir ensemble.
Mais qui d'autruy mal s'esleesce
Et qui d'autruy bien a tristesce,
2265 C'est envie faulse et mauvaise.
Cuer envieus n'est pas a aise,
Car il prent tout en desplaisance
Et ne puet avoir souffisance.
C'est maufait d'autruy a tort mordre,
2270 Car en toutes choses a ordre;
Le philosophe le tesmoingne.
Ce n'est pas mauvaise besoingne
De femme qui est bien vestue;
Car elle est plus chiere tenue
2275 Et honnourée en toutes places;
Et en yver, quant sont les glaces,
On a en soy plus grant chaleur.
La femme de plus grant valeur
Et qui de lignage est plus grande,
2280 Doit aller premiere a l'offrande
Et doit bien estre preferée
Selon l'ordre en honneur gardée.
Il m'est avis que bien se portent,
A honneur tendent et ennortent
2285 L'une l'autre par compagnie
A mieulx valoir; c'est bonne envie.
S'elles veulent du lin avoir
Ou de la chanvre ou d'autre avoir
Ou de la soye ou de la laine
2290 Ou une vache de lait plaine,
Ceste envie est assés commune,
Si n'en doit on blasmer aucune.
　　Or argue Mahieu d'un vice
Qui est appelé avarice.
2295 Contre les femmes par injure
Dit que sont de froide nature
Et que toute femme est avere.
Et après, en ceste matere,
Quant il en veult preuves atraire,

2300 A soy meïsmes est contraire.
Mais il le dit par yronie,
Par maniere de vilenie.
Des femmes dit, quant il en parle,
Que plus chaudes sont que le masle.
2305 De leur avarice tesmoingne
Qu'il ne leur chaut, mais qu'on leur
  doingne.
Argent veulent avoir et dras
De ceulx que tiennent en leurs bras,
Voire de leurs appartenans,
2310 Tant sont elles de près prenans.
Et dit que pour deniers se vendent
Et aux hommes plumer entendent,
Et que pis leur est advenu,
Ainsi comme il est contenu
2315 En son livre, ou je m'excusay,
Quant a le translater musay,
Pour ce que il me desplaisoit
Des complaints qu'il en faisoit.
  A tout quanqu'il en pourra dire
2320 Je respon sans dueil et sans ire,
Tout par le conseil de Leesce,
Qu'en femmes a assés largesce
Et ne sont ne folles ne nices,
Et especialment les riches
2325 Et celles qui ont leur chevance
Sans mal faire et sans decevance.
Et quant il en y a aucunes
Qui de leurs corps sont trop
  communes
Et se vendent par povreté,
2330 Il ne leur doit estre reté.
Car les hommes qu'elles reçoivent
De tout leur pouoir les deçoivent
Et sont plains de si grant malice
Qu'il ne tendent qu'a avarice.
2335 Car les femmes chuent et flatent
Ou les tourmentent et les batent
Quant elles ne peuent acomplir
Leur vouloir et bien raemplir
Les bourses des houliers gloutons
2340 Qui ne valent pas deux boutons.
En subjection les maintiennent
Et en si grant vilté les tiennent
Qu'a tout mal faire les induisent
Et de tout leur pouoir leur nuisent
2345 Et a perdicion les mainent
Et en toutes guises se painent
De femmes ainsi decevoir.
Je puis bien dire de ce voir;
Si n'est mie trop grant merveille
2350 Se femme encontre s'apareille

Pour resister a leur malice.
Car es hommes a plus de vice
De cent doubles qu'il n'a es femmes;
Et si en dient grans blafemes
2355 Mains justement, contre raison.
Et s'aucunes en leur saison
Aux hommes souffrir s'abandonnent,
Et les hommes des dons leur donnent
Pour leurs necessités trouver,
2360 On ne leur doit point reprouver.
S'il y a des mauvaises gloutes,
Ne s'en suit par pour ce que toutes
Soient generalment comprises
En leurs blasmes n'en leurs reprises.
2365 Certes, femmes sont assés larges;
Dieu leur envoit des biens cent barges
Toutes plaines a grant planté,
Pour user a leur voulenté!
  Qui veult leurs largesces trouver,
2370 Par exemples le puet prouver.
Quant Jason trouva l'achoison
De conquester d'or la toison,
Jamais avoir ne la peüst
Se par Medée ne l'eüst.
2375 Et si aloit, en tel peril,
Que, pour demourer en exil
En Colcos, une isle de mer,
Trop long seroit a exprimer
Tout ce qui advint en l'istoire.
2380 Mais on doit avoir en memoire
Comment Medée le reçut
Et comment Jason la deçut.
Medée estoit fille de roy
Et ne pensoit a nul desroy;
2385 Elle estoit belle, bonne et sage;
Jason promist qu'a mariage
La prendroit et seroit sa femme.
Jason en dut avoir le blasme;
Car elle s'amour luy donna
2390 Et de tout luy abandonna
Cuer, corps, richesces et avoir;
A mari le cuidoit avoir,
Puet estre qu'en celle esperance
Il l'engroissa par decevance.
2395 Et quant elle l'ot bien armé
Et de sors garni et charmé
Et oint de pluseurs oingnemens
Et baillié ses enseignemens,
Comment il pourroit a son oeus
2400 Vaincre le serpent et les boeus
Qui en l'isle la terre aroient,
Dont hommes armés apparoient,
Et qu'il ot le mouton doré,

Dont depuis fu moult honnouré,
2405 Il retourna en son païs.
De tous en doit estre haïs;
Car il laissa Medée enceinte,
De dueil descoulourée et tainte,
N'oncques puis d'elle ne cura
2410 Et faulsement se parjura.
Elle employa mal ses richesces
Et ses honneurs et ses largesces.
  Ulixes, conte de Duliche,
Sages homs et plains de malice,
2415 La roïne Circé deçut.
Circé bonnement le reçut;
Il et ses compaignons pilliés
Estoient en mer exilliés
Et en povreté revenus.
2420 Il fu grandement retenus.
Circé se vouloit marier;
Ulixes la fist varier;
Quant il vit qu'elle fu s'amie,
Les richesces n'espargna mie,
2425 Et elle assés luy en donna.
Mais trop mal luy guerredona;
Car toute grosse la laissa,
S'onneur de tant luy abaissa;
Si s'en revint en sa contrée,
2430 Quant en mer pot avoir entrée,
Et la morte saison passa.
Oncques Circé tant ne brassa
Qu'elle le peüst retenir.
Aux autres en doit souvenir.
2435   Eneas, l'exillié de Troye,
Par la mer avoit pris la voye
Et s'en venoit en Ytalie.
Chevance luy estoit faillie
Et a ceulx qui a lui estoient.
2440 Leurs nefs cassées raprestoient;
Ilz arriverent en Cartage.
Dido les vit sur le rivage
Qui venoient moult noblement;
Les reçut honnourablement;
2445 Elle estoit du païs roïne.
Eneas jut soubz sa courtine
Et tant y fu qu'il l'engroissa
Et que son serement froissa.
Et quant il ot des bien assés
2450 Et le temps d'yver fu passés,
Par dedens ses nefs bien refaites,
Qui hors du port estoient traites,
Passa en la terre Lavine.
Quand Dido perçut le couvine
2455 Et vit qu'ainsi estoit trompée,
Elle se tua d'une espée.

Ses largesces mal emploia
Quant desespoir la desvoia.
Ce fist la faulseté d'Enée;
2460 Par luy fu ainsi mal menée.
Des femmes et de leurs prouesces,
De leurs vertus, de leurs largesces
Et des bontés dont ont assés
Du dire ne suy pas lassés.
2465   Mais il me convient efforcier,
Car la queue est a l'escorchier.
Mahieu, qui mist toute sa cure
A blasmer femmes de luxure,
Dit que Pasiphé, la roïne,
2470 Soubz un torel se mist souvine
Et abandonna sa crevace
Ou simulacre d'une vache,
Couverte d'une peau velue.
Certes, vecy grant fanfelue!
2475 Ce ne puet estre vray, c'est fable,
Mais ce fu euvre de deable.
Comment pourroit femme souffrir
Qu'a un torel voulsist offrir
Le noble sexe femenin?
2480 Le mot est tout plain de venin.
Ce n'est pas a faire loisible,
Si croy que tout soit impossible,
Ou, sauve sa grace, c'est bourde;
Pasiphé ne fu pas si lourde
2485 Qu'elle soubzmesist son corps nu
Par dessoubz un torel cornu.
Et avec ce ne fait acroire
De Silla, dont il fait memoire,
Ne de Minos, ne de Nisus.
2490 J'y ay ja respondu cy sus.
Sa conclusion est inepte.
Mais je di qu'il est vray que Jepte,
Juge d'Israel et seigneur,
Qui ou peuple estoit le greigneur,
2495 Si comme on treuve en vraye ystoire,
Voua que, s'il avoit victoire,
En une bataille ancienne
Contre la gent philistienne,
Qu'il a Dieu sacrifieroit
2500 La chose qu'il encontreroit
A son retour premierement.
Il voult tenir son serement.
Sa fille encontra la premiere,
Qui luy venoit a lie chiere,
2505 Car joyeuse estoit la pucelle,
Doulce, plaisant et bonne et belle.
«Ha! dist- il,» je suy deceü;
«J'amasse mieulx avoir veü
«Autre chose;» et puis raconta

2510 De son veu a quoy il monta.
La pucelle, qui fut honneste,
Fist a son pere une requeste,
Qu'elle eüst possibilité
De plourer sa virginité
2515 Deux mois avecques ses compaignes
Par les bois et par les montaignes.
Jepté luy ottroia assés.
Quant les deux mois furent passés,
Il coupa la teste a sa fille.
2520 Ce n'est mie pareille bille
De Silla, ou il n'a que fable.
Aussi c'est chose veritable
Que le vaillant Virginius,
Ou despit de Tarquinius,
2525 Quan par faulx tesmoings luy prouva
Que sa fille serve trouva,
A sa belle fille Virgine,
Qui née estoit de franche orine,
En jugement coupa la teste.
2530 Les Romains n'en firent pas feste.
    Sur le pechié luxurieus,
Dont Mahieu estoit curieus
De blasme aux femmes imposer,
Tout quanqu'il en voult proposer
2535 Pour abregier repeteray,
Et puis aprés responderay.
Premiers a Mirra reproucha
Qu'avecques son pere coucha
Et souffri la couple charnelle
2540 Contre l'onnesté paternelle.
Se Mirra jut avec son pere,
Si fist Biblis avec son frere
Et Canasse avecques Macaire.
Encor ne s'en pouoit il taire
2545 Que Phedre, fille au roy de Crete,
Ne fu pas en amours discrete;
Elle ama le bel Ypolite;
Ce n'estoit pas chose licite;
Fils fu son mari Theseüs.
2550 Quant du pot ot les tes eüs,
Congnier se fist a son fillastre;
Venus en fist folle marastre.
Philis fist trop grant deablie;
Si folle ne fu establie,
2555 Si chetive, si forsenée.
A luxure desordenée
Trop honteusement se rendi,
Quant pour Demophon se pendi.
Je ne sçay qui la faisoit pendre,
2560 Mais elle ne pouoit attendre,
Pour desespoir qui la menoit
Et que son ami ne venoit.

Dido, roïne de Cartage,
Ce dit, refist trop grant oultrage
2565 Pour Eneas, qui fut son hoste
Et luy avoit congnié la coste.
Dido fist forment a blasmer.
Quant Eneas vit en la mer,
Qui s'en venoit en Lombardie,
2570 Elle fu trop fole hardie.
Toute grosse d'enfant sentant,
Plourant, criant et lamentant,
Par fole amour si se mua
Qu'a ses propres mains se tua
2575 De l'espée qui fu Enée.
Elle fu de fort heure née.
Ovides dit que femme est chaste,
Quant nul ne la requiert ne taste.
Attendu leur concupiscence
2580 Le pape leur donne licence
De marier sans delayer,
Pour le charnel treü payer.
Et dit que ne peuent attendre
Gueres sans eulx donner ou vendre;
2585 Et dit que femmes amoureuses
Ont condicions merveilleuses:
La noble voulentiers soulace;
Aux gentilz ne convient que place,
Mais que soit en lieux convenables;
2590 Femmes de cités sont prenables;
Vaincre les convient par donner,
Car rien ne veulent pardonner;
Aux villages sont les mains fieres;
Pluseurs se donnent par prieres.
2595   Les nonnains, les religieuses
Se tiennent pour trop precieuses
Pour leur espirituaulté.
Mais pou y a de loyaulté.
Ainsi dit Mahieu a sa guise;
2600 Et parle sur les gens d'eglise
Et dit que soubz turlupinage
Trouveroit on en tapinage
Envie, dol, ypocrisie,
Luxure par fraude brisie,
2605 Especialment es beguines,
Qui ne font pas euvres divines.
Des vieilles ne se voult pas taire;
Assés en disoit de contraire:
Que, quant elles sont devenues
2610 Vieilles, ridées et chenues
Et perdent leur propre chaleur
Et sont de petite valeur,
Lors couvoitent elles le joindre;
Vieille savate se veult oindre.
2615 Puis parle des macqueleries,

Des baras et des sorceries,
Des paintures et oingnemens
Et des autres enseignemens
Par quoy deçoivent les filettes
2620 Et livrent roses et florettes;
Et que par oignons et moustarde
Une vieille, que mau feu arde,
Faisoit sa chiennette plourer
Pour Galatée desflourer;
2625 Et comment son ami manda,
Si com la vieille commanda;
De luy souffri le jeu d'amours
Sans faire noise ne clamours;
Et comment fu despucelée
2630 Secretement et a celée;
Et que les vieilles macquerelles
Jouent souvent de tels merelles
Et de pis faire ne se feingnent:
Les enfans es ventres esteingnent;
2635 Et qui proye vouldra avoir,
Leurs mauvaistiés pourra savoir,
Et dit que, s'il est qui l'en croye,
D'elle meïsme fera proye.
Leurs fais sont prouvés et sceüs.
2640 Ovides en fu deceüs;
Il cuidoit trouver jouvencelle,
Car il amoit une pucelle;
Par nuit vint pour trouver le lit
Ou il cuidoit avoir delit;
2645 Mais la vieille s'y supposa;
Ne sçay comment faire l'osa.
    Or est il temps que je responde.
Les causes sur quoy je me fonde
Ne puis plus bonnement celer;
2650 Car il m'estuet tout reveler
Ce qui fait a m'entencion
Et a mon excusacion.
Omers fu uns clers merveilleus,
Sages, soutius et semilleus,
2655 Et fist de belles escriptures,
Des exemples et des figures
Et des ystoires anciennes,
Faites selon les loys payennes.
Il tint pluseurs opinions,
2660 Il traita en ses fictions
Et dist des tonneaulx la maniere
Desquels Fortune est taverniere,
Dont l'un estoit plein de leesce,
Et l'autre rempli de tristesce;
2665 Et en convient chascun jour boire,
Ou de tristesce, qui est noire,
Ou de leesce, l'amoureuse,
Qui en tous lieux est savoureuse.

Ceulx qui de tristesce ont beü
2670 Ont dit du pis qu'ilz ont peü
Des femmes et de leur affaire,
Mais Leesce leur est contraire
Et sera, s'il est qui m'en croye.
Omers traita de la grant Troye
2675 Et de tournois et de batailles,
De la fin et des commençailles.
Ne sçay se fu pour soy esbatre,
Mais par ses dis faisoit combatre
Les dieux de leur loy immortels
2680 Avecques les hommes mortels.
Mais Palas, Juno et Venus
Y estoient souvent venus
Pour porter armes en bataille
Et ferir d'estoc et de taille.
2685 Dame Venus y fu navrée,
Encor n'est sa playe sanée.
Ovides, qui le soustenoit
Et ses opinions tenoit,
L'ensuï en pluseurs manieres.
2690 Des choses deça en arrieres
Parlerent, chascun a sa guise;
Mainte belle fable y est mise
Qui raconte novacions
Et des fourmes mutacions.
2695 Il tenoient la loy payenne
Et nous tenons la crestienne.
Leurs fables et leurs poësies
En nostre loy sont heresies,
Et pour ce ne font pas a croire,
2700 Ne ceulx qui suivent leur ystoire,
Principaument quant il parlerent
Des femmes et qu'il les blasmerent;
Il en dirent moult de rebus,
De Jupiter et de Phebus
2705 Et des grans dames du païs;
S'en doivent bien estre haïs.
    Ne cuidiés pas que je devine;
Oncques chapon n'ama geline.
Pour Ovide l'ay recité.
2710 Car on raconte en verité
Qu'on lui coupa ambdeux les couilles;
Aux estoupes et aux oeufs douilles
Furent restraintes et sanées;
Puis vesqui par pluseurs années
2715 Et en exil fu envoyés
Et oultre la mer convoyés.
Ja n'en convient dire la cause,
Car loisir n'ay de faire pause.
Si puet on presumer et dire
2720 Que, haïneus et tout plain d'ire,
Femmes aprés ce fait blasma

N'oncques depuis ne les ama.
De Mirra dit grant vitupere,
Qu'elle coucha avec son pere;
2725 Sa bourde doit estre huée,
Car il dit qu'elle fu muée
En un arbre pour son pechié
Et que l'arbre est depuis sechié
Et que couverte fu d'escorce.
2730 Si n'en doit on ja faire force,
Ne de Biblis ne de Canasse,
Ne des exemples qu'il amasse,
Ne de Phedre ne d'Ypolite,
Ne de leur amour illicite,
2735 Ne de Philis, qui se pendi,
Qui Demophon trop attendi.
Ovides dit que c'est un tremble,
Un arbre dont la fueille tremble
Quant Demophon la vint baisier.
2740 Si s'en puet on bien rapaisier,
Car on voit bien que tout est fable
Et qu'il n'y a riens veritable.
     De Dido m'avés oï dire
Et d'Eneas et du navire
2745 Et comment elle fu fraudée
Et en son courage eschaudée
De ce qu'Eneas s'en fuï,
Et du fait qui s'en ensuï,
Et comment elle en prist la mort
2750 Par ire, qui a ce l'amort.
Certes, on voit bien qui tort a
Et qu'Eneas mal s'en porta;
Et se vrais estoient ces contes,
Sur les hommes en sont les hontes,
2755 Et de tous les autres meffais
Sur les hommes en sont les fais,
Puisque c'est par leur decevance.
Aux femmes font trop de grevance
Par barat et par tricherie,
2760 Pour soustenir leur lecherie.
     Mahieu par Ovide se haste
De dire qu'il n'est femme chaste
Et conclut jusques a la bonne
En disant qu'il n'est femme bonne.
2765 Je respons sur son jugement:
Ses mots sonnent trop largement
Et ne sont pas a droit tessus.
Car, si come j'ay dit dessus,
Qui dedens soy regarderoit
2770 De mesdire se cesseroit.
L'en ne doit pas parler d'ordure;
Cil qui allegue sa laidure
Ne fait en rien a recevoir.
On ne se puet mieulx decevoir.

2775 Qui dit mal sa bouche put; ains-
i seroient filz de putains
Tous ceulx qui sont de mere nés!
Ovides fu mal enfrenés
Quant sa bouche femmes blasmoit;
2780 Il meïsmes se diffamoit
Par courroux et par felonie;
Sur soy en soit la vilenie
Et sur Mahieu, qui le repete,
Car ce dire ne lui compete.
2785 L'en n'oï oncques en nul art
Que maistre Pierre Abaëlart,
Sages et bien araisonnés,
Combien que il fust chaponnés,
Des femmes nul blasme deïst
2790 Ne de sa langue y mesfeïst.
Mais bien fist le Paraclit faire,
On suer Heloïs voult attraire
Elle y vesqui moult chastement,
Sagement et honnestement.
2795   Je croy que mesdisans mourront
Quant toutes les causes orront
De la partie de Leësce,
Pour faulse envie, qui les blesce.
Car des preudes femmes avons,
2800 Les noms des quelles bien savons,
Et anciennes et nouvelles,
Dames, bourgoises, damoiselles,
Dont je mettray cy une annexe,
De celles du femenin sexe
2805 Qui furent et qui sont vaillans,
Maugré mesdis, aux cuers faillans,
Pour arguer coutre le Gal
Et contre Ovide el Juvenal
Et respondre a Matheolule:
2810 Des dames avons sainte Ursule
Avec les onze mille vierges;
De chasteté furent concierges;
Ursule en Bretaigne venoit
Et ses compaignes amenoit
2815 Pour marier selon l'Eglise
Si com chascune estoit requise.
Ursule estoit bien pourveüe
Pour espouser fut esleüe
Le roy Conain en mariage,
2820 Quant par tourment et par orage
En mer furent esparpillées
Et en divers lieux essillées.
Mais non obstant adversité
Garderent leur virginité.
2825 Nous avons sainte Katherine,
Sage, plaisant, vierge enterine,
Qui les maistres en rethorique

Vainqui par sens de theorique;
Par argumens les surmonta
2830 Et le roy Maxence donta.
Marguerite o sa panetiere
Bergiere fu, vierge et entiere;
Olibrium ne voult souffrir
Pour rien qu'il luy seüst offrir.
2835 Agnes, Luce, Agathe, Marine,
Genevieve, Gertrud, Cristine,
Perpetue et Felicité
Garderent leur virginité.
    Les nonnains, les religieuses
2840 Sont en leurs fais moult gracieuses,
Sobres, plaisans, bonnes et belles.
Des dames et des damoiselles
Y met on plus que d'autres femmes,
Si n'en doit on dire nuls blasmes;
2845 Car des saintes y a plus d'une:
Sainte Aurée et sainte Opportune,
Sainte Angadresme et sainte Bride
Sont saintes, en despit d'Ovide.
D'autres en nommeroye maintes,
2850 Vaillans femmes, bonnes et saintes,
Desquelles la vie honnorée
Est en la Legende Dorée:
Suer Jehanne de la Neuville,
D'emprés Ressons, en robe vile
2855 Et en habit de cordeliere,
De Dieu disciple et escoliere,
Entroduite en humilité,
Enflammée de charité
Et en vertus bien enseignie.
2860 Extraite de noble lignie,
En sa jeunesse fut menée
A Longchamp et a Dieu donnée.
Dieu a servi en celle eglise
Depuis le temps qu'elle y fu mise
2865 Et tellement s'y est portée,
Du Saint Esperit ennortée
Que Dieu l'a si bien pourveüe
Qu'en abeësse est promeüe,
A gouverner cinquante dames
2870 Moult devotes de corps et d'ames.
Encloses sont et emmurées
Et hors du monde asseürées,
Pour eschever pechié et vice;
Dieu loent en divin office.
2875 Dame Jehanne les gouuerne
En esté et quant il yverne.
Comme tres vaillant pastourelle
Du tout prent la cure sur elle;
Bonne dame est et debonnaire,
2880 A chascune veult plaisir faire

Et a toutes est chamberiere.
D'orgueil n'a point en sa maniere,
Mais est humble en sa face clere;
C'est la seconde sainte Clere.
2885 Celle de Gueux et la Moisie,
Qui en doulx chant est renvoisie,
Ensuivent de bien près sa trace.
Dieu les gart toutes par sa grace.
    Encor en nommeray de preuses,
2890 De bonnes et de vertueuses:
Avec Lucresse et Penelope
Puet on bien adjouster Sinope
Et Ypolite et Menalipe,
Pour mesdisans faire la lippe;
2895 Car il ne sont pas nos amis.
La roïne Semiramis
A une part eschevelée;
Thamaris et Penthasilée,
Teuca, Lampetho, Deïphile
2900 Et d'autres dames plus de mille,
Renommées de grant prouesce,
Sont de la partie Leesce
Et luy porteront sa banniere,
Pour aidier en toute maniere.
2905 Teuca fu chaste et gracieuse
Et aux armes moult courageuse.
Tous leurs fais ne pourroye escrire.
Longue chose seroit a dire,
Et si m'estuet ailleurs entendre
2910 Pour le droit garder et deffendre
Des femmes a qui Dieu doint joye
En tout chemin, en toute voye.
Pour les preudefemmes est Anne,
Mere Samuël; et Susanne,
2915 Qui des prestres fu accusée,
N'y doit pas estre refusée;
Car des bonnes la contenence
Monstra par vraye experience;
Jusques au feu fut esprouvée
2920 Et pour preudefemme trouvée.
Ceulx qui l'accuserent a tort
En moururent de male mort.
    L'en dit que jadis en Judée
Une femme estoit lapidée
2925 Quant elle faisoit avoutire;
Elle estoit menée a martire.
Les Juifs en trouverent une
Qui par sa mauvaise fortune
Avoit esté prise prouvée
2930 Et d'avoutire reprouvée.
A Dieu, pour jugier, la menerent
Et par fraude lui demanderent
Comment la femme jugeroient

Et comment mourir la feroient.
2935 Dieu, qui sait tout quanque cuer pense
Et bien se sot garder d'offense,
Congnut ce qu'il venoient querre;
De son doit escript en la terre:
«S'aucun de vous est sans pechié,
2940 «Et qui ne s'en sente entechié,
«Si gette la pierre premiere
«A la femme tant qu'il la fiere.»
De la response s'esbaïrent
Ne la femme point n'envaïrent
2945 N'oncques pierre ne luy geterent,
Ainçois paisible la laisserent.
La femme demoura delivre;
Des evangiles est ou livre.
  Dieu nous monstra par cest exemple
2950 Que de tres grant folie s'emple
Qui sur les femmes veult mesdire.
Ce dit ne porroit hom desdire,
Car il est vray et fait a croire.
Si ne sçay pourquoy hom prent gloire
2955 A blasmer femme de sa bouche
N'a en dire mal reprouche,
De mariée ou de pucelle,
De vieille ne de jouvencelle.
  Les vieilles les jeunes enseignent
2960 Et de bien monstrer ne se faignent
Comment se doivent maintenir
Et de tout mal faire abstenir.
Les vieilles ont plus de science
Et crement Dieu en conscience,
2965 Et est vray qu'elles ont grant joye
Quant les jeunes vont bonne voye.
Se les vieilles font sorceries,
Karaudes ou maqueleries
Ou choses qui vers Dieu leur nuisent,
2970 Les hommes a ce les induisent
Et leur ennortent et conseillent
Et, pour mal faire, se traveillent
Nuit et jour pour femmes frauder.
Les hommes veulent ribauder,
2975 Ja femme n'y fera meffait
Se moyennant homme n'est fait.
On voit trop bien, qui tout raconte,
Auquel en appartient la honte,
Ou au masle ou a la femelle,
2980 Mesmement en ceste querelle.
Les hommes ont vertu active
Et les femmes ont la passive.
L'omme doit assaillir et faire,
La femme doit souffrir et taire
2985 Chose raisonnable et honneste;
Et se l'omme luy amonneste

Chose qui soit contre droiture,
La femme par droit de nature
Luy puet sagement refuser
2990 Et soy loyaument excuser,
Car dame est de sa voulenté.
Et se Mahieu a lamenté
D'Ovide, qui fu deceü,
Il ne doit estre receü
2995 A femme blasmer d'aventure.
Le pere et seigneur de nature,
Dieu, qui toutes choses crea,
Auquel nostre fourme agrea,
La voult faire continuer.
3000 Pluseurs raisons insinuer
Voult pour la generacion
Et pour la propagacion
Des hommes et des bestes brutes.
Et entre les autres hatutes
3005 Y mist le delit, pour mieulx plaire
Et pour l'un envers l'autre atraire.
Par celle delectacion
Se fait continuacion
De toutes fourmes et especes,
3010 Soient menues ou espesses.
Si en doit on a droit user
Licitement, sans abuser.
Si conclu que il ne convient
Point blasmer le lieu dont on vient;
3015 Le proverbe dit des oiseaulx:
A chascun ses nis luy est beaulx.
  Et quant est au fait des sorcieres,
Dont Mahieu dit paroles fieres,
Et de leurs incantacions,
3020 De sors, de conjuracions
Et de crapaux vestus de robes,
De draps et d'autres faulses lobes
Et d'aucuns ymages de cire,
Que femmes font ardoir et frire
3025 Pour les cuers des hommes bruler,
Et du chat qu'elles font uler,
Vestu de sa grise cotelle,
Qu'elles mettent en la paelle
Et luy font les piés eschaufer
3030 Dedens a l'arain ou au fer
Et le lient a une late;
Neron, Belgibus et Pilate
Et d'enfer la puissance toute
Aourent et n'en ont pas doubte;
3035 Et comment vieilles font d'ennuis
Et s'en vont au gibet de nuis
Prendre les cheveulx et la corde
D'un pendu, c'est chose trop orde;
Et par nuit desfouent les corps

3040   Des enfans et des hommes mors.
      Il dit Medée enchanteresse,
      En magique devineresse,
      Et Circe fist grans derveries
      Par magique et par sorceries,
3045   Et Erithot, la vieille sale,
      De la bataille de Thessale,
      De Jule Cesar et Pompée
      Enquist, qui vaincroit a l'espée,
      Et en fist conjuracions
3050   Par sors et devinacions.
      Vieilles chevauchent les balais
      Par cours, par sales, par palais;
      Comme vent s'en vont par le monde,
      Au commandement dame Habonde.
3055   Il dit que Saül voult savoir
      Se Samuel pourroit ravoir;
      Mais riens n'y valut le plaidier,
      Car il ne luy pouoit aidier.
      Une phitonisse sorciere
3060   L'en fist response a mate chiere.
        Maistre Mahieu dit moult d'oultrages
      De femmes et de leurs ouvrages;
      Les maulx qu'il ot dit repetoit
      Et nouveaulx exemples mettoit,
3065   Comment les femmes rien ne celent
      Et tout quanq'on leur dit revelent.
      Un conte nous en fist tout neuf
      D'un preudomme qui post un euf.
      La femme dist a sa commere
3070   Que deux en y ot, par saint Pere!
      L'autre en ala a sa voisine
      Querir du feu en la cuisine
      Et dist qu'il en y avoit quatre;
      A mentir se sçot bien esbattre.
3075   Les femmes tant le publierent
      Et telement multiplierent
      Qu'on luy a mis des eufs cinquante,
      Voire, en la fin, plus de soissante.
        Après dit d'un autre preudomme
3080   Qui faint avoir tué un homme;
      A sa femme s'en descouvry
      Et elle son secret ouvry;
      Certes, gueres ne le cela;
      A ses voisines revela
3085   Que son mary, le mescheant,
      Avoit murdri un marcheant
      Et l'avoit mis dessoubz sa queste,
      Dont le juge en fist faire enqueste.
      Mais la mençonge fu prouvée,
3090   Car une truie fu trouvée
      En un sac ou il l'avoit mise.
      La femme en fu forment reprise

      Comme jangleuse et mençongiere,
      Car sa langue fu trop legiere.
3095   Mahieu disoit par faulse envie
      Que, quant Dieu vint de mort a vie
      Et a Pasques ressuscita,
      Que tout premier le recita
      Aux femmes pour le publier.
3100   En ce fait ne voult oublier,
      Quant il les visita premieres,
      Que de jangler sont coustumieres.
        Aussi disoit un autre tour
      D'un jalous, qui en une tour
3105   Gardoit si femme bien serrée,
      Mais ne l'avoit pas enferrée.
      Le jalous y fist troys huys faire,
      Et si avoit des cles troys paire;
      Mais en la fin fu deceü.
3110   Il avoit a un soir beü,
      Si s'endormi apres souper.
      Le boire le fist encouper;
      Sa femme ses clefs luy embla,
      Avec son ami s'assembla.
3115   Mais jalousie tost resveille
      Le jalous, qui petit sommeille.
      Quant la chose luy fu apperte,
      Moult fu courroucié de sa perte
      Et dist: «femme, ou es tu alée?»
3120   «Hors de la tour es avalée;
      «Bien est prouvé ton avoutire,
      «Demain en souffreras martire.»
      Lors revint la femme courant;
      A son mari dist en plourant:
3125   «Je vous pri, pour la Magdalaine,
      «Que vous ne me mettés en paine.
      «Espargniés moy, je jureray
      «Que plus ne vous courrouceray.
      «Je n'ay pas vostre tour minée;
3130   «Yssue suy par destinée
      «Et non mie par ribaudie,
      «Si n'est pas drois qu'on m'en mauldie.
      «Je me noieray en ce puis,
      «S'en vous mercy trouver ne puis.»
3135   Il respont pour la confuter:
      «Je te feray demain fuster.»
      La nuit estoit noire et obscure;
      Elle prist une pierre dure
      Et dedens le puis la lança.
3140   Adonc le mari s'avança,
      Qui la cuidoit noiée ou morte.
      Si tost qu'il fu hors de la porte
      Elle entra ens et l'uis ferma
      Et luy jura et afferma
3145   Qu'il comperroit ceste envaïe.

Elle ne fu pas esbaïe.
Aux guetes cria: «Ça venés!
«Ce vilain ribaut me prenés!»
Il fu pris et mis en prison,
3150 Oncques mais ne fu mieulx pris hom,
Et fu batu et escharni,
Car de sens estoit mal garni.
    Aussi dit il de dame Berthe,
Que Clement trouva descouverte
3155 Et dessoubz un prestre estoupée.
Clement tira sur eulx l'espée;
Si leur convient laissier leur euvre.
Berthe sault sus et se recuevre,
Son mari prist et tint a force,
3160 A pou les poins ne luy escorche.
Berthe, qui est faulse et qui ment,
Crioit sur son mari Clement:
«Bonnes gens, il est forsenés;
«Haro! pour Dieu, bien le tenés!
3165 «N'a gueres que sages estoit;
«C'est prestre aïde me prestoit;
«Pour moy aidier est cy venu
«Ou il me fust mal avenu.»
A Clement ne laissoit mot dire.
3170 L'un le boute, l'autre le tire,
Pris fu et a terre abatus,
Lyés et de verges batus.
Trois jours luy dura ceste haire,
Par force luy convint paix faire;
3175 Tant doubtoit les coups de Bertain
Qu'il pardonna tout pour certain.
    A tout quanque Mahieu propose
Et contre les femmes oppose:
D'aler hors en pelerinage,
3180 Ou elles vont en tapinage,
Du retour, quant leurs plantes plaignent
Et pour travaillies se faignent,
Des sacrifices et des veilles,
Qu'a leurs maris dient merveilles,
3185 Que chascune pas ne confesse
Comment elle a esté en presse,
Des sorceries, des karaudes
Et des sors que font les ribaudes,
De leur luxure, de leurs vices,
3190 De leurs fraudes, de leurs malices,
De leurs bourdes, de leurs mençoignes,
Et de toutes autres besoingnes
Dont on les pourroit diffamer,
Haïr, accuser ou blasmer,
3195 Soit par fables ou par exemples,
Posé qu'ilz fussent assés amples,
Et au pis qu'on en pourroit dire,
De tout ce que la femme empire,

3200 Qui contre la loy ne seroit
Et dont elle ne mefferoit
Crime capital ou damnable
Et qui ne seroit excusable,—
Dont je fay protestacion
Que ce n'est pas m'entencion
3205 De dire ne de soustenir
Que l'on ne se doye astenir
De pechié qui est deshonneste,
Si com nostre loy l'amonneste,—
Sans proceder vilainement
3210 Je respon ainsi plainement,
Pour femmes a droit excuser,
Qu'en doit bien de vertus user
Laissier le mal et le bien faire;
Si en diray vray exemplaire.

3215   Dieu, que est sans commencement,
Perdurable et sans finement,
Trois personnes en trinité
Par indivisible unité,
Pere, Fils et saint Esperiz,
3220 Qui puet relever les periz,
Les beaux anges crea jadis
Et les mist en son paradis
Pour servir a sa magesté.
Et quant ensemble orent esté,
3225 Par la devine prescience
Dieu, qui est vraie sapience
Et scet ce qui puet avenir,
Passé, present et avenir,
Voulant qu'on congneüst sa gloire
3230 A perpetuelle memoire
Et que homme fust congnoissant
Comment Dieu est juste et puissant,
Et pour reveler sa justice
A ceulx qui feroient malice,—
3235 Quant les beaus anges ot creés,
Lucifer fu si desreés,
Plus que soleil resplendissant,
Qu'a Dieu fu desobeïssant.
De la celeste mansion
3240 Lucifer o sa legion
Tresbucha ça jus en tenebres,
En repostailles, en latebres;
En enfer tresbucha sa route
D'anges et sa sequele toute
3245 Et furent mués en deables
Lais, hideus et espoventables,
Entroduis a punicion,
Pour faire leur relacion,
Pour les mauvais espoventer
3250 Et corrigier et tourmenter

Selon la justice divine,
Qui a nous sauver est encline.
　　Après Dieu de ses mains forma
L'omme, qui si belle forme a,
3255 Et la femme pour luy aidier,
Si com m'avés oï plaidier;
Ame leur donna sensitive,
Raisonnable et intellective,
Et entre les prerogatives
3260 Qui sont es creatures vives,
Trois choses y mist proprement:
Car memoire et entendement
Y mist avecques voulenté
Et des autres biens a plenté.
3265 Memoire remembre les choses
Et recole textes et gloses
Des passées et des presentes
Et des choses qui sont absentes,
Qui a venir sont et futures,
3270 Dont l'en prëesche es escriptures;
Par l'entendement fait entendre
Comment pouons choses aprendre
Qui nous sont aux yeulx invisibles
Et possibles ou impossibles;
3275 Voulenté si que du bien use
Et que mal a faire refuse;
Car l'un ou l'autre puet eslire,
Cy dessus l'avés oï dire.
Tels biens a l'ame raisonnable,
3280 De toutes vertus est prenable
Et entent les maulx a senestre.
Et si com Dieu ne pourroit estre
Compris par nulle creature,
Est l'ame de telle nature
3285 Que ne pourroit estre comprise
Ne dedens entendement mise
D'une creature visible;
Savoir ne luy est pas loisible.
L'ame sur quanqu'on puet veoir
3290 Et l'entendement asseoir
Puet comprendre visible chose;
Et l'ame ne puet estre enclose.
Car le ciel ne luy puet deffendre
Que traitier ne puist et entendre
3295 Sur les choses celestiennes
Et aussi quant aux terriennes;
Abisme ne la puet tenser
Que veoir ne puist par penser
Jusques aux choses infernaus
3300 Par esperitels gouvernaus
De substance esperituelle.
Et la substance corporelle
Des quatre elemens fait le corps

Ainsi comme j'en suy recors,
3305 Car la terre la char luy donne
Et l'eaue le sang qui randonne,
Et de l'air vient le soufflement;
Le feu, qui est quart element,
Par le corps espant la chaleur;
3310 Pour nourrir est de grant valeur.
Le chief, roont comme l'espere
Du ciel, est de noble matere
Et a deulx yeulx pour luminaire,
Qui aux tenebres est contraire.
3315 　Or il est vray qu'en jugement
Convient juge premierement
Et accuseur ou demandeur,
Et si y convient deffendeur.
Se Dieux eüst tousjours esté
3320 La dessus en sa magesté,
Sa gloire fust incongnëue
Et si ne fust jamais scëue
Sa justice ne sa puissance
N'omme n'eüst ja congnoissance
3325 De Dieu qui tout a surmonté
Par sa valeur, par sa bonté.
Pour ce voult il deux creatures
Creer de diverses natures;
L'une fu espirituelle
3330 Et l'autre si fu corporelle.
De tous deux voult estre loés
Et servis, si com vous oés.
Les anges sont espiritels,
Et les hommes sont corporels.
3335 Pour ce le voult il ainsi faire
Pour nous monstrer vray exemplaire,
Et voult que les anges pechassent
Et que ça dessoubz tresbuchassent.
Lucifer et toute sa route
3340 Fist tresbuchier ça jus sans doubte.
Ainsi voult il faire de l'omme,
Car il luy deffendi la pomme
Et le fruit de l'arbre de vie.
Adam en ot si grant envie
3345 Que sur la deffense attempta
Par sa femme, qui le tempta.
Il pechierent enormement
Et desservirent dampnement.
　Dire ne scet nulle ne nus
3350 Les grans biens que sont avenus
De ces pechiés dont je recorde;
Car Dieu par sa misericorde
Par ce nous a manifesté
La gloire de sa magesté
3355 Pour ce daigna des cieulx descendre
Ça jus et forme humaine prendre

Dedens la vierge precieuse
Saintefiée et glorieuse,
De toutes bontés pourvëue;
3360 Dieu l'avoit pour luy esleue;
Naistre en voult et la mort souffrir
En croix et soy pour nous offrir.
La mort d'enfer suppedita
Et au tiers jour ressuscita
3365 Puissamment et eureusement,
A prouffit merveilleusement,
Et vrayement ce devons croire;
Contre la mort obtint victoire.
Et quant il fu ressuscités
3370 Et ses amis ot visités
Et avec eulx ot fait sejour
Jusques au quarantiesme jour
Apres sa resurrection,
Es sains cieulx fist ascension,
3375 Qui aus desciples ennoia.
Dix jours après leur envoia
Saint Esperit pour conforter
Leurs cuers et en joye ennorter,
Si comme promis leur avoit.
3380 Lors chascun d'eulx parler savoit
Langage pour soy convenable.
Nostre foy tient, ce n'est pas fable,
Que sur nous, ou temps a venir,
Vendra son jugement tenir;
3385 Les mors et les vifs jugera.
De crimes nous accusera
Le deable, nostre adversaire;
Car en tous temps nous est contraire
Et quanqu'il puet le mal procure
3390 De toute humaine creature.
Si doit on de paour fremir
Et le puissant juge cremir
Qui est plus juste que balance;
Et si fu feru de la lance
3395 Pour nous saulver et racheter
Et des peines d'enfer geter.
Tous ces biens voult Dieu pour nous
    faire,
Pour nous dedens sa gloire attraire,
Doncques en son avenement
3400 De ce grant jour du jugement.
Tandis qu'en a ou corps la vie,
Ainçois que l'ame en soit ravie,
Doit homs adviser pour veoir
Comment il pourra pourveoir
3405 D'entrer en gloire pardurable
Et d'eschever chose dampnable.
Chose dampnable est pechiés;
Par pechiés sont biens fais sechiés

Et n'ont ne vertu ne vigueur.
3410 Et se Dieu monstroit sa rigueur
Quant il jugera mesdisans,
Leurs mos leur seroient nuisans;
Si seront il, ce doit on croire,
Car tout revendra a memoire
3415 Et convendra de tout respondre;
A Dieu ne puet on rien repondre
Ne de meffais ne de mesdis.
Si puis conclure par mes dis
Que c'est grant pechié de mesdire,
3420 Qui procede d'envie et d'ire;
Et pechiés est chose dampnable.
Doncques, par argument prouvable,
Cil qui mesdit aulcunement
Est en peril de dampnement
3425 Ne il ne puet saintement vivre.
Catons le nous dit en son livre
Que c'est la vertu primeraine
Que homme sa langue refraine.
Tholomées en Almageste
3430 En met une sentence preste
Et dit que sage doit pener
Que sa langue puist refrener.
Saint Pol dit que de l'abondance
Du cuer et par oultrecuidance
3435 Parle la bouche folement.
Si puet on oïr quellement
Les mesdisans sont entechiés
Et en peril pour leurs pechiés.
Doncques est il bon de soy taire
3440 Sans autruy mordre ne detraire.
Trop pourchace l'omme sa mort
Qui d'autruy mesdire s'amort.
Et qui ces dis mettra en terme
La querelle Mahieu enferme
3445 Trouvera et forment malade.
Si en ay fait ceste balade:

Je forgeray toute ma vie
Pour plaire a ma dame Leesce,
Et en soustenant sa partie
3450 Blasmeray courroux et tristesce.
Des dames et de leur haultesce
Diray bons mos clers et luisans,
Pour confondre les mesdisans.

Car es femmes, quoy que l'on die,
3455 Maint valeur, sens, los et noblesce;
Certes, qui bien y estudie,
Toute honneur, bonté et largesce
Vient d'elles et de leur prouesce.
Leurs fais sont bons et souffisans

3460   Pour confondre les mesdisans.

Se de leur bonté naist envie,
Qui d'autruy mesdit il se blesce;
Celui semble qui par folie
Souffle la poudre en la flamesce;
3465   Dedens ses yeulx souvent radresce.
Tels exemples sont bien gisans
Pour confondre les mesdisans.

    Or est temps que je m'entremette
De mon propos mener a methe;
3470   Pour abregier la question
Convient faire conclusion
Et eschever plait et discorde
Et nourrir paix avec concorde
Et en tous temps liement vivre,
3475   Car ainsi le veult nostre livre,
Et est la voye plus seüre.
Le maltalent qui tousjours dure
N'est mie bon a maintenir;
On doit verité soustenir
3480   Et faulseté bouter arriere.
Se verité siet en chaiere
Et raison me veult escouter,
Il ne me convient pas douter
Que n'aye pour moy jugement;
3485   Car je concluray sagement
Pour mes dames reconforter
Et elles a joye ennorter.
Vous orrés ja tost bonne gogue,
Et n'y a point de dialogue;
3490   Leesce seule parlera
Et ses fais prouvés monstrera
Par exemples et par figures
Des ystoires des escriptures
Puis que le monde commença,
3495   Des le temps Adam en ença.
    Et pour les hommes faire taire,
Pour avoir droit a fin contraire,
Propose ma dame Leesce
Et dit premier que vray est ce
3500   Que Mahieu a dit et conté
Que les femmes ont surmonté
Par leurs fais les plus grans du monde.
Le point sur quoy elle se fonde,
De Mahieu la confession,
3505   Fait assés a l'entencion
Des dames; si dit en ses rimes:
Mahieu de son propos meïsmes
Doit du tout en tout decheoir;
Ce puet on clerement veoir.
3510   Car, puis qu'il a ja dit que femmes

Sont par dessus les hommes, dames
Des plus fors, des puissans, des sages,
Que vaincus ont par leurs oultrages,
Si comme fu le fort Sanson,
3515   Le roy David et Salemon
Et le philosophe Aristote,
Chanter luy convient aultre note.
Car au surplus ne scet trouver
Chose dont il puist reprouver
3520   Les dames, quant au dire voir;
Pour ce ne fait a recevoir
Par libelle diffamatoire.
De nos dames dirons la gloire,
Les fais, les biens et les vaillances
3525   Des femelles et leurs puissances,
Qui sont dignes de reveler,
Et ne les doit on pas celer.
    Certes, a parler de prouesce,
Propose ma dame Leesce
3530   Que les femelles sont plus preuses,
Plus vaillans et plus vertueuses
Que les masles ne furent oncques.
Cest article prouverons doncques
Par Semiramis la roïne,
3535   Qui se pignoit soubs sa courtine;
De l'une part estoit treciée
Et sa chevelure dreciée,
Et d'autre part eschevelée,
Quant en ce point fu appelée
3540   D'un messagier, qui luy vint dire
Qu'en pluseurs lieux de son empire
Ses ennemis faisoient guerre,
Qui luy destruisoient sa terre,
Dommageoient et essilloient
3545   Et occioient et pilloient
Ses hommes. Dont, pour eulx
      deffendre,
Semiramis, sans plus attendre,
Hastivement enveloppée,
Son heaume prist et s'epée
3550   Et s'arma moult isnelement;
Sur eulx chevaulcha telement
Comme dame de grant courage,
Par prouesce et par vasselage
Ses ennemis suppedita
3555   Et sa terre bien acquita.
Contre elle en Perse ne en Mede
Masle n'y pot mettre remede.
    Le renon de Panthisilée,
Tant com la terre est grans et lée,
3560   Doit on tousjours ramentevoir.
Moult preuse fu, a dire voir;
Roïne estoit d'Amazonie;

Avec elle grant compagnie
De dames et de damoiselles,
3565 D'armes puissans, bonnes et belles
Et pour amour de la vengence
D'Ector, qui fu de grant vaillance,
Chevalier de noble memoire,
Duquel Achiles ot victoire,
3570 Vint aux Troïyens secourir
Et ne doubta point a mourir.
Achiles ot un fils, nommé
Pirrus, d'armes bien renommé;
La dame a luy se combati,
3575 Souvent du cheval l'abati
Et fist muer estat et place.
Aux femelles acquist grant grace
Au siege devant la grant Troye,
Dont elles doivent avoir joye.
3580 Thamaris, si com vous diron,
Vainqui le puissant roi Cyron.
Cyrus fu roy de Babiloine;
Thamaris luy fist tel essoine
Et son païs si revencha
3585 Qu'a Cyrus la teste trancha.
Et est bien trouvé en ystoire
Qu'en un bacin d'or le fist boire
Tout raëmpli de sanc humain;
Dedens le geta de sa main
3590 Et dist: «Or, boy ta felonie
«Et saoule ta tirannie.»
Que fist Lampethe et Arsionne ?
La renommee par tout sonne
D'Ypolite et de Deïphile
3595 Et des fais la noble Camille.
Hercules fu puissans de corps,
A son temps n'estoit hom plus fors;
Cacus, le geant, a la luite
Vainqui et si mist en fuïte
3600 Cerberus, le portier d'enfer,
Qui ne doubtoit acier ne fer.
On dit qu'il fist tant de merveilles
Qu'oncques homme ne fist pareilles
N'oncques ne pot estre vaincu
3605 Par homme qui portast escu.
Mais par femme fu tel menés,
Si vaincus et si ordenés
Qu'il se rendi, comment qu'il aille,
Par force d'armes en bataille.
3610 Grant los en ont toutes femelles
De leurs prouesces qui sont telles.
Tous pris d'armes, toute noblesce
Vient d'elles et de leur prouesce;
Plus d'un millier bien esprouvées
3615 En sont en ystoires trouvées,

Mais bien doit souffire pour preuve
De celles que cy endroit treuve.
Et s'il estoit qu'aucuns musars
Voulsissent arguer des ars,
3620 Aus femelles affiert le los;
Des sciences, bien dire l'os;
Prouver puis que femme est plus sage.
Car Carmentis trouva l'usage
Des lettres de nos escriptures,
3625 Toutes les vint et cinc figures
Dont on puet en latin escripre,
En françois, en tables, en cire,
En papier ou en parchemin;
Carmentis trouva le chemin;
3630 A chascune mist propre nom;
De sens doit avoir grant renom.
Les neuf Muses de la pratique,
De science et de rhetorique
Ont joye au cuer soubs les mamelles,
3635 Quant les noms portent de femelles.
Bien doit estre recommandée
La grant science de Medée;
Moult fu sage a grant merveille;
En son temps n'ot oncques pareille.
3640 De tous les sept ars fu maistresse
Et loée comme deese.
Celle valoit des hommes mille
Qui dist les secrès de Virgille
Et en declarant fist tele euvre
3645 Que la sainte foy nous descuevre.
Saffo fist les ditiés saffiques,
Qui sont vaillans et autentiques.
Vous, masles, avés vos poëtes
Qui fabloient de faulx prophetes.
3650 Dame Pallas doit bien souffire
Pour les femelles, a voir dire.
Car deësse est de sapience
Et a en soy toute science,
Et des femmes tient la partie.
3655 Si fait dame philosofie,
Grammaire, logique, musique,
Arismetique et rethorique
Et phisique et astrologie
Et la sainte theologie.
3660 Toutes portent noms de femelles;
Ce ne sont pas choses nouvelles.
Et Sebille, qui vrayement
Prenostica l'avenement
De nostre Seigneur Jhesucrist,
3665 Si com on le treuve en escript;
Et Cassandra, fille du roy
Priant, nonça le grant desroy
De Troye, la noble cité,

Et raconta la verité
3670 De la male destruction;
Bien en doit estre mention
Avecques les autres Sebilles,
Qui de sens furent tant habiles.
Se Dieu m'aïst, le roy Jhesus,
3675 Sage fu la fille Cresus;
Du roy son pere l'aventure
Conta de sa vision dure
Et comment il seroit pendu;
Onc n'en pot estre deffendu.
3680 Pour neant me travailleroie
Des exemples qu'en bailleroie.
Toutes ne puis mettre en memoire
Celles qui sont dignes de gloire,
Que dent d'envieus ne puet nuire
3685 Ne par sa fausseté destruire;
Car elles sont sages et preuses
Et en tous leurs fais vertueuses.
Les masles aiment pillerie
Et larrecin et roberie,
3690 Occision et convoitise
Et tout ce qui a mal atise.
Les femelles sont debonnaires
En tous cas et en tous affaires.
Chevaulx, mulès et cerfs et beufs,
3695 Oues et oiseaulx ponans eufs
Aiment des femmes la pasture
Et proufitent en nourreture
Plus que des hommes ne feroient.
Ce que femelles planteroient
3700 Vient mieulx que ce que l'omme
plante;
Assés est prouvé, je m'en vante:
Rainseaux, ceps et herbes le preuvent;
Ce tesmoignent ceulx qui le treuvent.
Femmes prient pour les bleciés
3705 Et pour ceulx qui sont es pechiés;
Les autels des eglises baisent
Et de leur pouoir Dieu rapaisent.
Les masles n'ont d'eglise cure;
Quant il y vont c'est aventure.
3710 Aux dés, aux tables, aux pelotes,
Aux marchiés, aux plais, aux riotes
Et aus bordeaulx est leur entente.
Qui diroit que Leesce mente
Et qu'on ne doit masles blasmer,
3715 Car il labourent en la mer
Et font des chasteaulx en ce monde,
Je suy tout prest que j'y responde.
S'en ce treuvent travail et peine,
Ce fait ardeur qui les demaine
3720 Pour le gaaing de convoitise,

Qui a ce faire les atise,
Et sont meüs par avarice
Qui en eulx est tres mauvais vice.
L'omme est fait du limon de terre
3725 Qui vers la femelle fait guerre.
La femme est nommée virage
Par la vertu de son courage.
Car la femme est superlative
Et a plus grant prerogative
3730 De lieu et de formacion;
Dessus en ay fait mencion,
Comment la femme fu jadis
Faite ou terrestre paradis,
Et comment Dieu, le roy de gloire,
3735 Fist la femme pour adjutoire.
La fureur des masles les blesce,
Leur gloutonnie et leur paresce
Et leur delit. Mais par nature
Chascune femelle procure
3740 Du mesnage bien maintenir
Et l'ostel a droit soustenir.
Dont par neuf mois leur enfant
portent
A l'enfanter se desconfortent,
Grant douleur ont a l'enfanter,
3745 Du contraire n'estuet chanter.
Les enfans nourrissent les meres
Et leur sont douces, non ameres,
Et leur alievent nourreture,
De tout le fais portent la cure.
3750 Elles filent et lins et laines,
De pluseurs grans vertus sont plaines,
Chascune femelle tant brace
Pour avoir du masle la grâce:
Tables, tresteaulx, couches et lis
3755 Appareillent pour leurs delis
El tout quanqu'elles peuent faire,
Afin qu'aux hommes puissent plaire.
Les femmes font des biens assés
Aux reposés et aux lassés,
3760 Les malades souvent rehaitent
Et amiablement les traitent.
Les hommes aiment miel et cire
Mais la femelle plus desire
Lin, laine, estoupes pour filer,
3765 Pour longues toiles empiler,
Et avec ce leur plaist l'ouvrage
De presser du lait le fromage.
Souvent boivent de la fontaine,
Mais les masles a longue alaine
3770 Boivent les vins de la taverne.
Dieu scet com chascuns se gouverne;
Les uns frequentent les boscages

Pour chacier les bestes sauvages,
Et les autres suivent oiseuse
3775 Et demainent vie noiseuse.
Mais les femmes font sagement
Leurs euvres; Dieu scet se je ment.
J'en tray a tesmoing la Calabre
De Paris, qui d'erbes ou d'arbre,
3780 Par mastic ou autre maistrie,
Dont elle scet bien l'industrie,
A fait maint con rapeticier
Et les mamelles estrecier,
Pour estre aux hommes plus plaisans,
3785 Pour les jalous faire taisans.
Se Leesce les bonnes nomme
Qui furent de Grece ou de Rome
Pour son entencion fonder,
A grant los luy doit redonder,
3790 Qu'il n'y a point de flaterie
De faveur ne de menterie;
Car on en trouveroit en France
Pluseurs vaillans de leur enfance.
Et s'on opposoit le contraire,
3795 Que Leesce, pour preuves faire,
Nomme les bonnes seulement
Et des mauvaises nullement
Ne fait aucune mencion,
Pour soustenir s'opinion,
3800 Elle respont, pour soy deffendre,
Que les masles veulent leur gendre
Lever en haut, soit tort ou droit.
Et qui repliquer y vouldroit,
Je diroye, par sens contraire,
3805 Mais qu'il ne leur doye desplaire,
Qu'en leurs libelles ne leurs fables
N'en leurs fais qui sont mal
    prouvables,
Ou il alleguent poësies
Et merveilleuses frenesies,
3810 Desquelles il ne font a croire,
Car en parlant de vraye istoire
Ils ne nomment pas Catelin,
Non font il, par saint Mathelin,
Denis le tirant ne Neron
3815 L'empereur, ne le fel Seron,
Qui moult greva les Macabieux,
N'Herode, qui ne vault pas mieulx,
Ruffin le faulx n'autres coulpables,
Desquels les meffais sont dampnables.
3820 Et nous taisons dame Antigone
Et Cleopatre, qui fu bonne,
Ruth, Rachel, Sarre et Octavie,
La noble Lucresse et Marie
Et Julie, femme Pompée

3825 Et Porcie a Caton donnée,
Susanne, Judich et Hester.
Celles durent bien conquester
Noble renon et seigneurie
Par les fais de leur bonne vie.
3830 Dessus en avons assés dit;
Trop est fol qui d'autruy mesdit.
    Vous dites femmes mal estables,
Vuides, faulses et decevables.
Mais Dieu scet quil est autrement
3835 Leur amour se tient fermement
Et droitement en chasteté.
Es masles est la faulseté,
Qui seulent femmes pervertir
A blasme leur doit revertir;
3840 Aux pucelles leur pucelage
Et aux femmes leur mariage
Tollent par fraudes et par dons,
Eulx mesmes s'en donnent pardons,
Car en ce ne cuident meffaire;
3845 Souvent desparient la paire.
On voit pou de femmes jolies
Prier les masles de folies,
Mais par prieres ou menaces
Les masles prennent en leurs naces
3850 Les femelles despourveües,
Qui souvent en sont deceües.
Nulle foy ne nulle constance
N'est en masle pour aliance
Tenir et garder vers femelle.
3855 Car leur condicion est telle
Que, quant faulsement les deçoivent,
Ils croient faire ce qu'il doivent.
Plus de mil femmes mariées
Femmes, sans estre variées,
3860 Tiennent aux maris foy estable;
Chascune est au sien veritable
Sans mal et sans encourir blasme.
Mais nuls ne tient foy a sa femme.
    Sans nombre est il femmes assés
3865 Qu'après leurs maris trespassés
Se contiennent honnestement
Et saintement et chastement;
Et ce vault bien virginité,
Combien qu'aient fecondité.
3870 Mais n'est hom, quant sa femme est
    morte,
Qui du jeu des rains se deporte,
Car des loingnes prennent deduit
Aux femelles et jour et nuit.
Se par les poëtes dampnés
3875 Les fais des femmes condampnés
Sont par masles aucunement

Et leur dient iniquement
Que ce soit deshonneur et honte,
Femmes scevent bien que ce monte;
3880 Car nuls homs ne blasme leur gendre
Tant que maistre jobart puist tendre.
On n'en mesdit en nulle place,
Mais veult bien que la paix se face,
Et les loe, sert et honnoure.
3885 Sages est qui a ce laboure
Et estudie a bien servir,
Pour paix et grace desservir.
    Quel pechié les femmes encombre?
Se roy Salemon fu soubs l'ombre
3890 De la beauté des femmes pris,
Aux dames en affiert grant pris,
Quant si sage fu surmonté
Par leur sens et par leur bonté.
Fureur qui es hommes habonde
3895 Les fait affoler en ce monde
Par ardeur et par lescherie.
Si com le lou en bergerie,
S'il puet, toutes estranglera,
Ja brebis n'en espargnera,
3900 Combien que d'une assés eüst
Qui de sa faim le repeüst,
Ainsi masles de mal courage
Ne peuent saouler leur rage;
Toutes veulent ahontagier
3905 Les femelles par leur dangier.
Quant leur plaisir n'en peuent faire,
Du blasmer ne se veulent taire.
S'Aristote, qui fu grand maistre,
Ne pot oncques si sages estre
3910 Qu'es las des femmes ne cheïst,
Non pas pour mal qu'il y veïst;
Se Virgille aussi, qui fu sage,
Fu mis par amour en servage
Et Achilles pour Polixene,
3915 Qui estoit belle comme Helene,
Fu si ravis qu'il en fu mort;
S'Hercules ou Sanson le fort
Furent par femmes abatus,—
En vain se sont ceulx debatus
3920 Qui femelles seulent blasmer;
Car en tous temps font a amer.
A elles n'en est point la coulpe;
Mais on en doit faire la loupe
A tout homme qui les desprise,
3925 Quant par femme fu entreprise
La fleur de sens et de prouesce.
Je n'y en voy nulle qui blesce
Son ami n'a force le preigne;
Ne rois ne filace d'araigne

3930 Ne las ne tendent pour les prendre;
Et si ne s'en peuent deffendre,
Ne doivent; s'a droit regardassent,
Jamais femelles ne blasmassent
Ne diffamassent par envie;
3935 Car elles sont salut et vie
Aux masles pour eulx conforter
Et pour compaignie porter.
Et si semble estre cruaulté
Des masles, se pour la beaulté
3940 Des femelles il se desvoient
En leurs fais et qu'il ne pourvoient
A leurs manieres ordener
Et a leurs langues refrener
Et eulx en raison contenir,
3945 Afin de vaincre et retenir
Leur constance, qui est trop mole,
Par volupté, qui les afole.
    Mes dames, je pri humblement,
Se j'ay soustenu foiblement
3950 Votre cause par ignorance,
Employés cy vostre vaillance
Et les deffautes ampliés
Et vostre honneur tant publiés
Que tous en aient congnoissance.
3955 Masles n'avront vers vous puissance
Quant cest dit leur sera leü.
Et afin qu'il soit reçeü,
Faites bien protestacion
De prouver vostre entencion,
3960 Et retenés, pour dupliquer,
S'aucun y vouloit repliquer:
Nyés fais de partie adverse.
Il n'a juge de cy en Perse
Qui osast faire jugement.
3965 Verité scet bien se je ment;
Mais a paine sera trouvée
Ne ceste querelle prouvée.
Vueilliés moy par grace advouer,
Ou je puis bien dire et vouer
3970 Que jamais jour n'avray leesce;
Ainsi demourray en tristesce,
Qui de mon las corps fera proie,
S'il mestuet payer la lamproie.
Mercy, mercy au povre fevre
3975 Qui plus grant soif seuffre a la levre
Que n'ot le riche homme en enfer;
Car il ne scet ouvrer en fer,
Mais en peaulx est toute sa cure.
Pour vous a fait ceste escripture.
3980 Car il scet bien qu'a tous les masles
Qui portent et bourses et males
Estes soulas, joye et repos.

Atant fineray mon propos
Jusqu'a tant que plus sage viengne
3985 Qui ceste matiere soustiengne,
Si croy je que jamais finée
Ne sera ne determinée;

Car venal est l'amour du monde
Et avarice est trop parfonde.
3990 Plus en diray a l'autre fois,
A Dieu vous commant, je m'en vois.

The Book of Gladness

[Jehan le Fèvre's Introduction]

(1) My ladies, I entreat your mercy. I would like to apologize to you here[1] for what I said without your permission about the great strife and the torments of marriage. If I slandered you through my insolence, I can truly say without fawning that I only translated[2] what I found in Latin[3]; this can be firmly proved in the book of Matheolus.

(12) So it seems that no woman or anyone alive should hate me for that. Therefore, if I was so occupied, I beg that it be pardoned and forgiven me by your grace. For I am all ready to write a book to redeem myself; please don't deny this to me. There is nothing without its opposite,[4] if we would observe and think rightly on these things: thorns are next to the roses; likewise, the sharp nettle grows amid the soft grass. Without your grace I don't want to live.

(28) If anyone wants to know how this book will be titled, I say that people will call it by its right name, *Book of Gladness*,[5] because I made this book for love of her, to give pleasure[6] by making the contrary argument,[7] in order to defend you ladies faithfully, and especially to show that no man ought to blame women; we ought to praise and love them, cherish, honor, and serve them, if we would deserve their grace. The justice of this is very clear, as will be explained[8] below.

(43) Then may God let me prosper so that I may uphold the truth,[9] just as Alithia did long ago,[10] when she defended her true case against Pseustis, the Athenian pagan: at the water's edge they argued between true and false and wagered their instruments. But Alithia won. For truth deserves the glory, just as gladness is better than vexation and sorrow.

(55) Truth prevails against lies; truth is a noble cause. It is the strongest thing there may be, as Zerubbabel[11] answered at the request of King Darius when he posed a question, for the topic of debate was "strength." One [courtier] said the king was strong, another said wine was strong, and the third, who posed as a prophet,[12] said that women are the strongest. Zerubbabel, opposing their group,[13] put truth in the strongest place. His judgment was approved.

(69) Aristotle loved the truth. It is clearly reported in his writings that he said to those who asked him and pleaded on behalf of Socrates: "I love Socrates, do not doubt it, but truth is more my friend."[14]

(75) Pray God that he may guard my tongue and remember this work of mine and make me answer so well that no one will defeat my arguments; and may I not say a thing that would give him cause for anger. The wise man[15] says in Scripture that in all the concerns of this life there is nothing which ought to please so much as to be glad[16] and to do good

74

and to avoid debate and quarrel. For a long journey in the rain[17] is tiresome, and brevity is a joy. So I will not be reluctant to shorten this material. Lest someone take me for a boor, I will proceed summarily.[18]

[Le Fèvre begins his response to the Lamentations *of Matheolus.]*

(92) In the first place, Master Mahieu[19] loudly complained of bigamy,[20] saying "better to have a mistress[21] than marry a widow woman."[22] His eyes wet his face with tears, for he lost his status and became a laughingstock[23] when he was left without the tonsure of a cleric: then the decretal of Gregory[24] seemed all too cruel to him. Besides, he was pale with sorrow, for he could not by any stratagem regain the privilege of the clergy; he had tied the knot too tightly.[25]

(106) He cites the ancients as an example[26]: how Jacob bound himself to Leah and then to Rachel,[27] and how Elkanah married Hannah and then had Peninnah as his wife.[28] The holy fathers of the old days — whom may God put in his paradise — they did this all the time without losing their honor. Then he tells us of Lamech[29] and says that he really ought to have disgrace of body and great torment of soul, because he was the first bigamist. Lamech married Zillah and Adah; for this deed he was worse off than when he killed Cain. The bigamist has little power; he is subject to the layfolk and cannot recover from his loss. Mahieu complains much about this in his book that I refer to.

(127) Lady Gladness replies to this, for she is full of wisdom and honor and instructed in good morals, for which she is praised. She proves by cogent argument that Master Mahieu was wrong to lament and weep, and much more wrong to labor in casting blame on women. He is dead, God save his soul![30] When he took a widow in marriage, he was of age and a prominent lawyer.[31] Such words are much to the point. He knew how to expound the laws[32] and explain the Distinctions.[33] He knew how a man becomes bigamous according to the edict of Gregory in canon law. One should assign the blame to him, if by chance there was any blame for something not rightly to be blamed.

(149) And if there was deception, there is no help for it at all; he was kicked out of his benefice. Besides, I object to him that there was neither fraud nor false pretense here,[34] just as he himself admits. He knew just what he was doing[35] when it pleased him to marry. He wanted it and he consented to it. Therefore, if he repented of it later, reason can clearly perceive that his case is not acceptable. "It's too late to cover your ass when the fart is out."[36] This saying is quite obscene.[37]

(163) He desired Perrenelle so much because she seemed beautiful to him in her bearing and in her face. He says that he took great pleasure in admiring the appearance[38] of one of the most beautiful faces that he had ever seen in all the world. For the blonde hair, shining and well adorned, that seemed to him made of gold, her forehead wide, clear, and smooth, her fine and pretty eyebrows, her beautiful gray eyes, sweet and smiling, lovingly assailing him, her well-made nose and little mouth, crimson, smiling, and sweet, softly curving, and well arranged inside with teeth, well placed and whiter than ivory, a beautiful chin for his pleasure, the ears and cheeks well colored and well made, the smooth and shining throat, showing neither line nor vein, the white neck, smooth all around, the shoulders and the contour of the arms, supple for embracing, more beautiful things than anyone could carve, the white hands, the graceful fingers, the slender sides, the graceful body, and the appearance of her bosom, adorned with two rounded breasts, tapered so perfectly, not too big or too small, her stately bearing and the dimension of her hips, not too broad or too narrow, the

beautiful feet and straight legs, and all that showed in her appearance, adorned her with such great beauty that there was not a single fault. She wasn't too short or too tall.

(205) If she was truly lovely on the outside, the beauty underneath her dress should also be considered: for her noble delicate figure set forth her beautiful naked flesh, not too thin or too fleshy, and her mound and secret things, which discreet persons know as fitting to their pleasures. Roses and lilies mingled in her complexion. From this arose the great sorrow to which Mahieu devotes a long chapter, but his complaint is quite invalid. "One should not love so much that he makes his good fortune bitter,"[39] nor should any man maintain that anything but good can happen when a man freely chooses to take his good and honest wife in a bond of love, just as our faith advises us to do.

(227) As for the examples that he cites there, of both Cain and Lamech, they have no bearing on the present case[40] and should not have been presented. For in those days, people were without the law, and they put all their effort into doing as they pleased. They did plenty of bad things, so much that God was said to be angry with them. For that reason he thundered and rained on them and destroyed everything in the flood; he gave shelter to eight people[41] in the ark to continue the human race, and then he made them understand the law we call the Old Law.[42] Now we have Christian law, ordained in reason[43] by Christ. If we follow his commandments and if we keep the good customs of the church and of marriage, that will be our salvation.

(248) And if you want to know more examples both old and new, you will have that of David,[44] who became bigamous of his own free will with Bathsheba, whom he loved, who at the time was the wife of Uriah, a knight of his retinue. She had entered a garden. The king saw the naked lady, who was washing in a fountain. She was so very beautiful that he desired her with passion. He made her his wife, he succeeded at that, and they had a son from their marriage, Solomon the wise. And if there was any fault in this, David was the cause of the crime[45]; the lady wasn't guilty at all. This example is no myth.

(267) Also[46] the count of Alençon,[47] all for love and without strife, loved the countess of Estampes,[48] who seemed a goddess with her beauty. He honorably married the lady. No man could speak ill of them for this, for they were generous, beautiful, kind, and noble; anyone who says otherwise is a fool. I saw messire Anceau Choquart,[49] a good scholar, handsome, elegant, and just, who was well versed in both kinds of law, canon and civil. He was not so averse to marriage that he did not take Marote to wife. After messire Anceau died, this beautiful and honorable woman conducted herself with such virtues, like the wise and good woman that she was, that for the love of her person messire Estienne de la Grange[50] did not estrange himself from her, but married her for love, even though it was bigamy.

(291) Master Pierre de Rochefort,[51] wise in the law, handsome and strong, married a young woman of Dormans, charming and beautiful, who was the daughter of my lord Guillaume, one of the wisest in the kingdom. Between them they had enough property. And when Pierre had passed away, messire Philebert Paillart, wise, discreet, rich, and strong, took her in marriage. He wasn't in the least afraid of bigamy. The [following] two men,[52] who were bigamous, are much honored and loved: these knights live in Paris, and preside at parliament, and their wives are ladies. God grant them peace of body and soul! Messire Guillaume de Sens,[53] rich in property and very wise, president of the said parliament, also became a bigamist. I can truthfully say the same of Master Pierre de Mainville,[54] a worthy man of much good sense; he was a member of parliament and once was president, God have his soul in paradise! He joined the bigamists. Three ladies in turn, completely beautiful

and good, wise and of noble renown, he married in holy church. I don't know any of their names.

(325) We have seen many great scholars,[55] wise, discreet, and prudent, who became bigamous of their own free will; still, they never defamed women or slandered them, or blamed or despised them. Master Mahieu complained about them and said whatever he pleased. It is always better to keep quiet than to backbite and slander others. For the evil-speakers accomplish nothing except for venting their folly. They make the dust fly and land in their own eyes. They can't see the truth or pronounce true judgment. Surely God knows if I'm lying. They are so oppressed with envy and wrath that they can't speak properly; therefore Justice is wary of them and prevents them from testifying,[56] for they speak to provoke a quarrel. Whether for favor or for hate, Mahieu defended their case,[57] and there is no truth in anything he says.

(351) Then he says that his mind was deceived through his sight,[58] and that beauty wounded his heart through his eye; therefore he does not and will not have a day's peace forever after, and on this he based his plan to rant and weep and dishonor women. Truly he showed his utter madness; for when a woman is beautiful and pretty, so much the more is she a sweeter creature, and the more she has the gifts of nature, the more she gives gladness, and drives away all sadness, and soothes the man and sets him on the way of peace, of sweetness, and of joy, and puts his heart in such great ease that there is nothing that displeases him. To speak plainly, without digressive commentary, woman is the sweetest thing that God ever formed for man. It's true, as I can firmly say, that he who complains about her is a madman. For there are many women today by whom their husbands are raised up, well dressed and well shod, honored and brought to wealth,[59] with the help of the good planning of women and their hard work, which their husbands control by true love and concord, just as good faith agrees. May he who speaks ill of them have a toothache and fevers until the Fair.

(385) Then he says he knew nothing then of the proverb about the snake lying in the grass[60] that hides and holds back its poison, or of feminine malice. Then he tells of his misery[61] and of his sad misfortune and says much that is shameful and nasty. But there is no man who doesn't sin, or flower so lovely that it doesn't wither. And she whom he married, of whom he complains so much to us, and who made him speechless and subdued, was so beautiful and so pleasant, womanly, sweet and kind, that she was worthy to be had by a king, if she could have married him.

(402) But then she made him change his mind, for she became so scabby,[62] sagging, hunchbacked and pot-bellied, disfigured and ill formed, that she seemed a cripple. She became extremely ugly, hideous, wrinkled, and white haired, both very horrible to look at and in her disposition, quarrelsome. He said the worst he could about her and despised her in every way. Very angry and disgruntled, he put many a story in his book to substantiate his claims, which are not to be defended, in disparagement of my ladies — may God keep them from blame!

(419) To which one can answer and say,[63] to utterly defeat his claim, for it's not time that we keep silent: there are four seasons in the year: there is spring, that we call vernal, summer, autumn, and winter. Spring beautifies and gives us flowers and plants of many colors. Summer ripens the flowers and the plants and makes us sure to have fruit, strawberries, cherries, and apples, which are born from little flowers, and other fruits of many a kind, which I will not describe here. It is an easy thing to know that God makes them come and flourish. Autumn makes them fully ripe and ready for the harvest. Winter makes a

striking change, for when all is stored in the barn and in the granary and in houses (all that the three seasons gave, spring, summer, and autumn), and the wine is placed in barrels, then winter turns its effort to destruction. It puts an end to flowers and the tender grass; it makes the leaves fall from the trees, and there is nothing green that doesn't suffer.

(447) Therefore in summertime the ant[64] is warned through his great wisdom to drag seeds into his den to withstand the harsh weather. He is prudent and wise in this. And there is so much knowledge in him that with his beak he bites hard on each grain of wheat to make sure it doesn't sprout in the earth at its due time. He knows well how to carry his grain back outside his den in the good weather, to dry it and wipe it; he knows well when the season is bound to change. The ant provides for himself; as for me,[65] I don't know how to do that so well.

(463) To continue, they keep up their war—fire and air, water and earth, hot and dry, wet and cold—they rule every creature and make man and woman age. We can attribute this to the seasons of which I speak, just as we learn of them in school. Spring, like youth, is full of joy and gladness, until twenty years or thereabouts. Let us speak of summer: it lasts for another twenty years. This is when a man has beauty and strength, but afterward autumn rules him; at this time the man of sound mind is rational in his affairs and lives wisely, and he stays like that for another twenty years. Winter, which is full of cold, is like old age: it weakens and destroys the human body and brings it to ruin.

(487) So it was with Perrenelle[66]; in her springtime she was young and beautiful, in summer, pleasant and wise, according to the state of her age; and then she was wise and good, following in due course the time of autumn. But when old age assailed her, beauty and strength failed her. When she was struck by its calamities, she became weak and ruined; her limbs were all stiff, contracted, bent, and cold. Her chest was hard,[67] and her breasts, which used to be so beautiful, were spotted and darkened, like purses of puckered leather. So goes the human form; its beauty lasts a little while, for it may not be otherwise. Therefore Mahieu, who was a scholar, had no just cause to complain about this. If she was an old woman, he was an old man. So in any case it would have been better for him to take it patiently than to show off his great learning in blaming all women. That man is truly mad who slanders them outrageously and puts his effort into blaming them. For we men, both great and small, have all come from women.[68]

(519) He has compared woman, no matter how well adorned, to a clock,[69] and says that an angry woman is never hesitant to strike. And if there is poverty, and the husband doesn't provide enough to live on, the wives say and insist[70] that the shortfalls are due to the men; and if there are enough possessions, they say they were amassed by themselves, by their hard work, their good sense, and their prudence. And truly, so it is[71]: everything comes from their good management. They take the credit for good things, for when they spin[72] and wash, and care for the whole household, in fairness we can truly see that they will make the household richer, and that three pieces of cloth spun by them and put together by their efforts will bring in more of a profit, more than all the income made with horses or oxen could yield by plowing the land—for you have to cover your expenses. But whatever comes from the distaff that she holds up next to her side supports the house by night and day. Women work without resting, and the distaff doesn't cost anything. But the man who joins two oxen at the plow,[73] he needs hay and oats from the granaries, farthings, pennies, harrow, sieve, rake, and spade to plow the dry land. He always has to spend for one thing or another, before or after—pitchfork, flail, winnowing basket, and trowel.

(558) But if a seamstress has a needle and works with a distaff, she has more than

enough to do the job; she supports and guides the whole household. The husband drinks in the tavern and spends a lot, win or lose; he doesn't care how it all goes. So it's no great wonder[74] if the worthless husband has a hard time and is scolded by his wife, who blames him for his faults. There are many men of such a nature that they make no effort to support their household. This is why they can't prosper, for they are worthless men and lazy, and obnoxious to their wives. So if their husbands find them quarrelsome, many reasons make them that way; thus we see it by experience, by justice and wisdom, that men are more to blame, and women more to love, since they do their duty better. We can surely speak the truth about it.

[Lady Gladness expounds on the five "met[h]es" (tricks or goals) by which, according to Mahieu, a woman misleads a man.]

(583) Then he says something in his great rudeness, full of anger and sadness, that he wishes to dwell on[75]: that no man would be able to resist the poisonous rage of the fighting woman. Even God would not be able to, in his opinion. She would make him give in. And to add more blame and slander, he says that nothing is worse than a woman,[76] and that she misleads her man to five goals.[77] Here is how he names them by their fallacies[78]: by the tongue and by the sight and by touch, by falsehood and by iniquity,[79] the weakness of man is deceived. Now it's time that we discuss it.

[The first "goal," the tongue.]

(600) He gives us the example of Guyon,[80] who said he caught his wife in plain sight underneath Simon, and wanted to repudiate her. So his wife complained about it; she put the blame on him unjustly, and talked about it for a long time.

[The second "goal," sight.]

(607) The eyesight[81] is deceived by the tongue with false logic, just as he says and bears witness that Werry saw his lawful wife, Sebille, in the act underneath a man. Sebille denied the act to him and swore she did nothing wrong. A neighbor woman from the street[82] came to Werry at his plow and relieved him from jealousy,[83] for any man who cares about it is a fool.

[The third "goal," touch.]

(619) Then he deceives by speaking of the touch, how Framery experienced it[84]: he found his wife's lover next to her bed in the dark of night. He got up and tried very hard to find him, he really used his strength; he did so much that he killed his donkey with a great blow to the head. The beast wasn't to blame for it. He couldn't find anything else there and failed to prove what had happened. But his wife, God have her soul, was blamed by the neighbor women for this. I do believe that this was wrong, and anyway the donkey died for it.

[The fourth "goal," falsehood.]

(635) He went on to say,[85] persisting in his insolence, that the unlucky husband is led to the goal of falsehood; he doesn't know how to resist his wife. Through her speaking or

her yelling, she gives him to understand that the moon is a sheet of vellum and tries to prove that this is true, however impossible it may be.

[The fifth "goal," false belief.]

(645) He says worse, that women conquered Solomon[86] and put him to shame. The wisest of kings was ensnared by women and their excesses[87]; Solomon, full of wisdom, misused his learning then. He was so deceived and controlled that he was led by their enticements to the goal of [false] belief.[88] He was made to abandon his religion and worship idols. He never knew how to work so hard that he could prevail against them.

(658) Mahieu continues his treatise, persisting in his tirade, and tells us how a woman subdued Aristotle when she mounted on top of him[89]; she put reins and bridle on his head and vanquished the master of the goals.[90] Thus was grammar betrayed and logic much abased.

(667) To amuse himself, Master Mahieu told more than four frivolous stories[91] to adorn his argument. And afterward, he mentions how the wife, to annoy her husband,[92] makes him say something twice and repeat it several times; two or three aren't enough for her. She pretends she doesn't hear him at all. We can see that she aims at nothing else except to make her husband angry. The good man doesn't dare complain; like it or not, he has to look for peace, for fear that she will hit him.

(681) Then he says that the man's senses suffer all together[93] because of women and their insolence. As soon as the man is married, it's no wonder that their quarreling hurts and deafens his ear. Their clock[94] always strikes — it totally shocks and stuns him. And then the husband lives in such a way[95] that he makes his eyes a fountain flowing down his face; hard crying hurts his eyes. And in quarreling, you have to do all that is bad for your eyes. There is nothing that can damage the eyesight as much as losing sleep; and later, with the misery of the head cold,[96] the nose can't smell anything; it has to weep drops of snot. The nostril is full of fluids that the head cold multiplies; it makes the mucus go into the throat or the neck, for all the fluid collects there, which is why the nose often drips. We see, when the head is sick, that no body part can be well; they all suffer with the head and share in its misfortune.

(711) Mahieu spoke about the many harms of the rebellious, evil-speaking, and uncontrolled tongue,[97] which will not be omitted here. He said that he didn't dare to speak up because his wife's tongue, that is, the tongue of Perrenelle, was too swift to argue, and she made him too ashamed. In this chapter he tells us how forcefully he used to dig long ago,[98] but now he complains that he can't plow anymore; this is what made him cry that times were bad for him, and that he couldn't do it anymore, even in Perrette's little garden,[99] for his quiver was empty and his bow could no longer stretch. So he had no way to defend himself. He who has nothing to make peace with must suffer forever after.

(733) Therefore Master Mahieu wept and cursed women for this, and said in his great misery: "Alas, why was I born of woman?[100] I have to suffer in grievous pains." All the things he said are full of lamentations. And because he despised my ladies and thus displeases me, I have lodged such a case against him[101] that it will give me great fame if I succeed in my intent. But I have many an adversary against me, and the opposing side is strong.[102] Master Mahieu has on his side Gallus, Juvenal, and Ovid,[103] and Master Jean Clopinel of the merry heart and swift body,[104] who limped just as I do.[105] The burden on me here is heavy; I have against me deceitful tales and myths and delightful poetry; for there are many

lies in these fictitious stories that I see arguing against me, and those who support Master Mahieu will resort to them for help. But I have all my help in God. I know that God is truth and wills justice and equity. And so I seek my refuge in Reason, who is our judge.[106] For I see clearly with my eye that a little ray of the true sun puts to flight a great fog and makes it disappear completely. So I will not leave off speaking freely, not for the evil-speakers or the envious wrongdoers, no matter if I displease them. For I do not hold them worth a straw — whenever he falters, we will skin him!

(775) So I argue against Master Mahieu that his statement is irrelevant[107] and his case is not acceptable. Women do their duty well, nor is his story credible — not of Simon or that other tale, or of Werry and Sebille — or whatever they say around town. In such a case they are not to be believed. He tells of Framery, of his donkey and his candle, and makes all that out to be a marvel; begging his pardon, these are idle tales. And it so happens that he cooks up many more foolish stories, and more amazing to hear — about a sheet of vellum and the moon, where he says there was a woman who made her husband believe it, and he didn't know how to resist. There is very little substance here; you could hardly make any sense of it. Such idle tales are worth nothing; these foolish stories are much less substantial than a piece of butter. He can't conclude for this reason, from the ill repute of one person, that he can blame all women for this.[108] It doesn't really follow; in logic it is quite the contrary, assuming that he told the truth. For if there is weakness or misconduct in one person, it would be a faulty judgment[109] if the entire group were blamed for it. Thus his poem may be counted as fiction; for such foolish stories in a misleading context aren't worthy of a response.

(813) And as for his other story,[110] of Solomon and Aristotle, two of the wisest men[111] in the world, on which Mahieu bases his claim that Solomon lowered himself when he left his religion for women, and that Aristotle, the great scholar, had on his head reins and bridle, and that a woman rode him like a horse and raised herself above him: Gladness answers his argument with a laugh and poses this solution: God, who wills procreation,[112] formed man and then woman, and breathed the soul into their bodies.[113] He put love there and companionship to make and generate offspring. He doesn't let us forget that he commanded us to be fruitful and multiply to replenish the earth.[114] This was not a hostile message. He wanted propagation to come about through pleasure. Man and woman are rational and wiser and more distinguished than any other creature. Powerful love along with nature causes them to seek pleasure and live together in the flesh in order to continue our species that death corrupts and destroys; anyone who would try to dispute this would have to start all over again.

(847) Solomon[115] was a rich man and wise; he knew the custom of nature; he was a king, not a hermit. He didn't want to be a sodomite![116] Sodomy is the ugliest sin with which man can be defiled. So he took concubines and wives and queens and plenty of young girls, using them as he pleased. With great learning he composed Ecclesiastes, Wisdom,[117] Proverbs, and Parables,[118] which we read in many schools; he also wrote the Song of Songs.[119] These books are beautiful and true. If by love, which bound him, he subjected himself to women, so much that he chose to do their pleasure in every way, Master Mahieu should just shut up about it.

(867) Aristotle was full of virtues. He had a city in Thrace, which was called Stagira; this city was great and large and was his by inheritance. He came from Macedonian descent; in learning there was no one greater. He was the prince and the lord of all the Greek philosophers. In Greece he served two kings, Philip and Alexander, to whom he taught many good

things. He knew well the power of nature and made many a beautiful book: *Peri hermeneias* and *Elenchi*[120] (they are the branches of argument), *Prior* and *Posterior Analytics*, logic, and mathematical science. He was full of great love; he always upheld the truth, for which we should praise him highly. And if he let himself be ridden like a horse, it was for joy and for pleasure. Love led him to do this by his great gentleness; so he ought not to be blamed. He clearly showed that we ought to love women, without slander or ill speaking, for they are not guilty at all for this, but the writings of Mahieu should be condemned — of this there can be no doubt at all, and so there is no need to listen when he makes his nasty claims.

(900) If Perrenelle didn't care for him, that was his fault. She had every right to despise[121] him. Perrette complained about him with good reason, for he didn't pay the debt of love. When he refused to pay, that made her more hostile. He played the deaf man to put her off[122]; then his shame was made known, when he said his purse was slack,[123] that he can't pay and has nothing to give,[124] nor can he get his member up for her. We get angry enough for less. For this she took him in hand, if he didn't flee from the fray,[125] just as he admits and confesses outright, which is stupid and foolish on his part.

(918) Then he tells of the wet nurse[126] who joined forces with his wife. She had good cause, by my soul, if she didn't want to get up.[127] No scolding is too harsh for the man who can't get the job done. Also, he should be very afraid, since he has nothing to make peace with. Such a man should keep quiet and refrain from slandering women or ladies or girls or any living woman. Let no man dispute this!

(931) We have many arguments to refute, on other things than mere trifles.[128] Mahieu applied all his effort and his foolish empty thought to attack all wives — he didn't dare complain to his own. He was much in the habit of slander; I believe he did it out of wrath. He went on to say: if there is a pious hypocrite[129] who doesn't know the wiles of women, then he should read his book, and he would be saved from them. He slandered them extremely, he spoke of them too much here and there in his poems, especially of their quarrelsome nature —[claiming that] there's no help at all for this.[130] A man should just run away from them. He says that smoke and rain, and a woman quarreling without reason, chase a man from his house.[131]

(951) For the woman rants and argues. Often the fight starts, the water makes things rot, and smoke impairs the sight and forces the eyes to weep, so he can't stay there anymore. And when the fighting spirit moves her, she often pretends that she catches her husband in the act of adultery and she fights and struggles against him. He tires himself out giving examples; it's amazing how many he gives. He says we can subdue the savage beast by bonds and by cages[132] and make them gentle by art or by subtlety. A man can't do this with his wife, for her nature is deeply ingrained.[133] He cites the example of a young man[134] — I don't know his name — of Monstereul, an amazing young man. He was fierce and warlike and he sought only battle; he didn't fear bludgeon or sword. He went out so much and rode so much that he finally got married. When he was bound in marriage, he became humble and submissive. He didn't dare raise an eyebrow[135]; therefore he could die of sorrow.

(981) Gladness says[136]: I have listened and offered little defense up to now, but don't worry. I am ready to set you at ease on this score, for the time is suitable and right,[137] and I make my case according to Reason.[138] So I will use great maxims to adorn my verses and destroy the evil-speakers so they can never harm us. I will answer him point by point. The *Decretum*, in the eleventh case and in the third question,[139] tells us this story: when one praises or blames what one loves or hates, each one should, for true support, have recourse to his thoughts, that is, to his own conscience, whether innocent or guilty; so that this way,

if the good that we are praised for is not found in us, we should be very sad, for we can know our own misdeeds. Likewise we should laugh for joy if the bad that we are accused of is not detected in us or discovered or known. Saint Paul gives us a good reminder when he tells us that our glory is the witness of our conscience[140]; and Job, perfect in patience, says that his witness is in the heavens, for God is the one who knows all[141]; the Lord is our witness in heaven. So let us consider what we ought to say.

(1017) How is it that mortal man is so bold with his biting words[142] that he dares to disparage woman, or sharpen his lying tongue[143] to say evil or nastiness of her? David says this of him in Scripture: sinners have gone astray, because once out of the womb, they changed and erred against nature.[144] If when he is born a creature forgets where he came from,[145] this is treasonous folly. He is mad who insults his own self by slandering the place he was born from. A proverb is given to us: that is, "he cuts off his nose to spite his face."[146] Likewise a man can't speak ill of women without disgracing himself. He is mad who disfigures his own face.

(1037) Mahieu says[147]: woman is quarrelsome and slanderous and indiscreet. Carfania acted very foolishly[148]; she showed her ass in court.[149] Because of her, woman was disbarred and deprived of advocacy; she did harm to all women by her tongue and her outrageous act. By law, just as I have heard, it is forever banned for women to study court sentences and to plead cases. He also says that a Jewess,[150] Miriam, the sister of Moses,[151] was a scold and a proud woman; she became a leper for her scolding. And the crow,[152] which was white, changed its appearance and became black; it happened for his scolding and for his wicked lying. And if one were to accuse God, he would not be able to deny that he armed wicked women by giving them facile tongues.[153]

(1061) Next, Mahieu posed a question[154] as part of his case: why are women more troublesome, more prone to idle words, and more quarrelsome than men are? Because they are of bone[155] and our bodies are made of earth, and bone makes a louder noise than earth. He gives examples one by one[156] and follows Master Jean de Meun when he writes in his chapter on jealousy[157] that the man who gets married is a fool.[158] He gives us another example of this[159]: a man had three wives; each time he married one of them, it turned out badly for him. So it happened that where he lived, a wolf was chasing the lambs. He was caught; the hunter asked how they should put him to death. The married man heard it and gave his opinion: that the wolf would die a terrible death if they could make him get married.

(1085) Heavy is the torment of marriage; so he said in his insolence. A woman is destructive to man,[160] for her flesh is corrosive; the flesh of man is ruined when he touches her in marriage, and it seems that marriage harms him and diminishes the strength of the man. He goes on to say that it is better to struggle[161] as best he can to avoid the bond that makes a man to be scorned and impairs all his virtues. He said many a nasty thing about women, much worse than I have said about them.

(1099) Now let's come to conclusions and leave the fictitious examples that Mahieu gives of the strife and battle, and of the scolding, perverse, and chiding woman, and of the fool who got married, and of Carfania and Miriam and why the crow is black. Such examples are scarcely credible. But Gladness wants to debate them in order to defeat the wicked slanderers so that they may not injure women. Here Gladness puts up this defense: if Carfania behaved badly, that fault should be blamed on her, for she alone should be punished for it — another woman has nothing to do with it. The others aren't guilty at all. A legion of devils used to be angels,[162] but (it is said) because they wanted to be gods and became proud and nursed such desire in themselves to be equal to God their master, who makes us all die and be born, God made them fall down from heaven and enter into darkness. The other angels stayed; they didn't share at all in the sin; they are up there in glory in the heavens.

(1130) Women would have had the victory if here with Lady Gladness were Heloïse, the abbess of the Paraclete, who was so wise in the law of custom and tradition[163]; thus she was a philosopher[164] even though she was a nun. They would have led Mahieu to [their] goal[165]; they would have overpowered his arguments so that they would have been useless against them.[166] The daughter of Master Jehan Andrieu,[167] who read the cases and the laws, got up one morning to show publicly in open audience through her great learning that woman is equal to man, and set forth many a good argument to guard the honor of women and protect them from blame. Her lecture lasted all day, almost until the dark of night. She put forth more than sixty reasons, and even, I believe, more than seventy, and she argued her case so well there that no man could refute it.

(1155) Women come from noble material; they have intelligence and clear knowledge, full of great subtlety. So I can truthfully conclude that men were much afraid of them; that is why they expelled all women from the legal profession. If Carfania was disbarred from it, her action doesn't taint the others at all, nor should they be blamed for it. So Miriam did not scold[168]; one might say that he errs when he says she became a leper just because she was a scold. And as for the black crow, it is surely not to be believed that it was ever white — that's a very childish thing to say. We might just as well say of the swan, which is a big and gentle bird, that it once had black plumage and now is white for good behavior.

(1177) And if it was all true, what Mahieu has written and said to blame women, in all his words is only bitterness, and he proceeds with such great anger that he can scarcely speak properly. So his plan is unsound; and if it were a solution to tell unhappy stories twice, I have good cause to trouble him by writing about the crimes of men, of which they are charged in great numbers: of murders and robberies, of arsons and false testimony, of adultery in marriage, of sorcery, of poisonings, of falsehoods, of treasons, and of many atrocious crimes that I know well how to put in verse. But for now I will be silent about it and leave them for a while,[169] until it is time for me to do that.[170] For it is a good saying that by too much silence and by too much speaking with the mouth one receives harm and reproach.

(1203) And when Mahieu attacks us by saying that woman speaks loudly because she was made of bone,[171] I say that a thing should be all the more loved insofar as it has more value. Just as azure and sinople are worth more than coal or chalk, there is no man living who doesn't believe that woman ought to have praise because she was made of bone and man was made of dirt. For Mahieu errs on this point; bone is more noble and so is worth more. This is why God chose to make her within the earthly paradise. I dwell on this point: man was made of a little slime, of dirt of the hard ground, in the valley of Hebron,[172] among the fields. For this reason man is more wicked. We can show by powerful arguments that woman has much more noble privileges than man has. Her first privilege was that she was made in paradise,[173] formed and finished by the hands of God. Furthermore, God made her of a rib; this takes nothing good away from her; she is more noble in all places. God gave to women so many graces that he descended into a woman for us, to take our form within his pure and virgin mother. Nature was at odds with this, and one is amazed, it seems to me, how she was both mother and virgin. Our faith shows through its teaching that this was by an act of God.[174]

(1241) Woman is called *mulier* in the Latin language because she soothes the man, or *moulier*, because she softens the man.[175] He who speaks ill of her is a fool. And if anyone asks why woman was made by taking her from the rib, the cause of this is explained in the second book of the *Sentences*[176]: she was taken from man's side as much to be his helper as for love and delight, so that by good affection she might keep him company and also have offspring. She was not made from his head to rule over him, and to repeat, God does not want her to enslave him; nor was she made[177] from his feet, to be his slave, but from his middle, in such a way that as a lady, not as a servant, she might be with the man, and that she might sit and lie down beside him, to do his pleasure as his companion and peer; and she agrees to lie down with the man because she was taken from his side. And if after their sin she was subject to him,[178] that happened by the Fall, not by nature. That is what Scripture tells us.

(1271) Now there is a real reason why woman should be loved, and why she was made this way — pulled from the side of man, more in sleeping than in waking. Let no one doubt this act or the noble mystery that proceeds from this story. Almighty and omniscient God, who knows everything, made the man sleep in order to do this, and put him into such a sweet dream that when his side was opened, he sweetly uncovered it and took from it the healthy rib, so that the man had neither sorrow nor pain, nor did he make him suffer at all,[179] nor did he wake up at all from this,[180] nor did he lose any rest at all. Through this act, from that time forth, Almighty God forever showed that he would be willing to save us. One could not more truly prefigure the holy sacrament of Jesus Christ and the church. This allegory is given to us, and by this act is clearly shown that just as woman was formed from the side of the sleeping man, without his waking up from this at all, just so the church was made, delivered, formed, and derived from the mysteries that descended and flowed from the blessed side of Jesus Christ sleeping on the cross, where he became pale and cold.[181] To save us he hung on the cross; both blood and water descended from his side, to redeem us and deliver us from the pains of hell.

(1311) Let's see if one should hate women or attack them with wicked speech. Certainly not, if he would be wise; the decent man would never blame them, except in secret reproof or in the confessional. Also, the man who slanders marriage, as Master Mahieu did, commits a great offense. He didn't refrain from blaming it at all, and he said: if any man gets married,[182] and joins himself with a woman, he becomes a wretch and a cuckold; his unkempt and shaggy hair hangs down on his shoulders, with the back of his hair hanging forward. His shoes and clothing are coming undone, and he walks slowly with his face cast down; his happiness is ruined. And a woman given in marriage can't be discarded[183]; he has to keep her, whatever misfortune may arise. And he who wants to take a wife, and who sees that he can't give her back, ought to get glasses,[184] the better to see his great danger. And he says that trying them out can do no harm,[185] but is quite worthwhile, because one can learn to take what is helpful and leave what is harmful; and he says that there are very few wives, be they girls or women, who love their husbands faithfully, however much they weep and lament.

(1347) He tells the story of a knight,[186] handsome and nimble and a good warrior, who married his servant, and the story goes like this: the knight was big and strong, but he died in battle. His wife wept bitterly for him and stayed at his tomb and would not for any reason return again to her house. One day, as I heard tell, a thief was hanged on a gibbet, which a famous knight, Sir Gilbert by name, had to guard in exchange for his fief. In passing, he saw the lady at her husband's grave. He heard her tears and her lament. He told her kindly, "Lady, calm yourself, pray for his soul, it doesn't do any good to mourn." She answered, "I can't stop crying for him; I have lost the best man in the world. I want to lie down deep in the grave with him, stone-dead." Sir Gilbert comforted her and said she would find another husband who would be just as good or better. He made his way to the fields, for the night was already come, and the thief had been stolen. Trembling with fear, he thought he had forfeited and lost his fief for his negligence.

(1381) Gilbert went back, very worried, straight to the cemetery; he told the lady what had happened and the terms of his assignment; he revealed his trouble to her. And right then she forgot her good husband, in the hope of getting married again. "Don't worry, sir," she said. "I will help you in your need, in the trouble you are sad about, if you will take me for your wife." He happily said yes. Now the bier was disinterred, and the dead man was, just so you know, pulled and dragged to the gibbet.

(1398) When she came there, she didn't hesitate—she herself hung him on the same place and on the same side from which someone had removed the thief. She made two wounds on his head,[187] and with that the evil beast dug and gouged out his eyes; this seemed to grieve her very little. Sir Gilbert didn't care for her, when he saw the evil deed. He never kept his promise to her but rudely rejected her.

(1409) If women, who ought to be well loved, are blamed as a class by the hateful examples of contentious slanderers, they are injured without reason. If a bad woman or a wicked man does some particular wrong, we should not insist that the consequence apply to all. This defense is quite enough. The woman who hung up her husband brought the guilt for this on herself; the knight sinned inasmuch as he consented to the crime. I say, and this is a proven thing, that loyalty is found in women, especially in marriage, for God made this partnership. And to make a brief answer, I will tell you a true story.

(1429) Near Laleue, in Picardy, a famous knight caused a very stupid thing to happen. He bore the surname De Bailleul. He loved a girl so much because she was young and beautiful that he asked her for her love. But his love was indecent, because she had a husband. The girl, who was sad at heart, if she was very beautiful, was still more faithful; she refused his request. The knight falsely accused her of a crime and was by nature so cruel that he had her burned to ashes, unjustly and without listening to reason. The husband of the girl made his complaint to King Philip.[188] The knight went to prison and was condemned for his crime to be dragged on a cart and hanged. King John,[189] who was duke of Normandy, protected him from this. The knight, whatever one may say about it, was placed on a hurdle, to be led out and hanged straightaway. But the good duke took pity on him, and so he was spared by him.

(1459) Lucretia[190] also, who was of Rome, had married an excellent man. She was faithful to him all her life. But she was taken from him by rape and violated against her will; she would rather have been skinned alive. Her good husband comforted her and hugged her and kissed her and pardoned her for the crime that was done without her consent. Comfort was to no avail; she didn't want to bear the shame anymore, regardless of pardon or comfort. She stabbed herself to death with a dagger. Thus ended Lady Lucretia.

(1474) Penelope[191] of Greece, the wife of Ulysses, who was very wise, was steadfast in marriage. Ulysses went to the city of Troy with the Greeks, in search of conquest. He suffered many a danger on the sea. Penelope was worthy to be loved; for ten years or more she waited for him. She kept herself so loyally that she always refused to marry or to wed a man. And the lady guarded herself so well that no one should speak ill of her.

(1487) The evil-speaker ranted without stopping; he started up again with his harangue: Scylla,[192] he says, killed her father. She deserved great blame for that; she disgraced herself much by this act, for handsome Minos whom she loved. She was a very cruel beast when she cut off her father's head. He says still another nasty thing,[193] that the woman's nature is such that when her husband has died, she will have no peace until she has contrived to take up with his enemy, and she doesn't wait a day or half a day. Those whom they ought to despise,[194] they often make lie in their beds or take them in marriage; they don't listen to right or reason. And [he says] that every woman is lustful.[195] Then he talks of the killing of Uriah[196] by Bathsheba his wife; David saw her undress and bathe in the fountain. So he continues his rant, and his mournful poem reminds us of Samson the strong, whom Delilah sheared with scissors, from which he lost all his strength.[197]

(1515) What good does it do him to speak of Scylla?[198] We know he has misspoken. For this is either a fictitious story or a proven lie in a false text. It's all too clear in the myths of Ovid how Scylla was a patricide, and that she killed Nisus, her father; but it's obviously a lie. He says that Scylla was an owl[199] who kept herself in a hideout by day, and Nisus became a sparrow hawk.[200] That proves no ill of anyone. As for blaming women, we should not give in to that at all.

(1529) And if some women remarry, and are fickle in their foolishness, this is not the case with all women. If there are some wicked licentious women, there are more wicked lechers among men; let us have no doubt of this. Surely women are very noble — ladies, girls, bourgeois women, and others according to their rank. May God reform the others! And if David gave the order[201] for Uriah to be put to death, Bathsheba was not guilty of this — Joab the general did it. We find these sinful acts by men in the Bible, in the book of Kings.[202]

(1545) If Samson[203] the strong was shorn and ruined by Delilah, Samson was partly to blame for that. He deserted his wife — he left her against his parents' will; he didn't stop looking for a wife, and so he found the wanton Delilah. He ruined himself by his talk. For his enemies got together with Delilah and bribed her to find out his secret so that they might capture Samson, to tie him up by force or trap him so that he could not defend himself. She did so much by her cajoling that Samson, like a madman and a fool, revealed the cause of all his strength. His mouth had no restraint at all,[204] for he answered against his own good, and she cut off his hair when he was sleeping. For this he was captured and so tortured that he had his eyes gouged out. It served him right to suffer his ordeal[205] when he left his marriage to love a lewd woman.

(1570) For this we should blame Samson, who was a judge of Israel; he was beaten with his own whip. This story in no way disparages women but teaches and instructs men not to tell their secrets at all[206] and to hide them as best they can. Each day at Prime, we have verses that rhyme like this: "May reining in control my tongue, and may the horror of strife not sound."[207]

(1581) Mahieu says in his wickedness that Solomon[208] made a law that all men of a hundred years old in his realm should be put to death under penalty of his wrath. After the proclamation, a young man hid his father to prevent this evil fate. Secretly he brought him food. His father taught him his books, so much that he became discreet and wise. Solomon discovered the crime. He had the young man summoned and ordered him without delay, on pain of losing all he held in fief, to come neither dressed nor naked, not on foot nor on horse nor on mare.[209] He told him that in his defense, he must bring his lord, his serf, and his friend, along with his enemy.[210] The man prepared himself and conferred with his father. He dressed himself nicely in a net and brought his son and his donkey and his dog and his wife with him; his father instructed him wisely. He pointed out his wife to the king and swore that never, by his soul, had he known a greater enemy. She quickly challenged him and he gave her a slap, but she didn't take it as a joke. To the king she said, "Sire, have this thief taken and led out to be hanged; truly, he has hidden his father, so he ought to die a painful death." The king laughed at them when he heard it and rejoiced in his heart.

(1619) I don't know why a man complains about this. Does he tell his secrets if he doesn't want to, except in his defense?[211] The good man did something very wrong when he struck his wife before the king, who disregarded their quarrel and did nothing but laugh about it. What can the evil-speaker say about this, except that we should learn each day that we can guard ourselves from acting foolishly?

(1629) Then the evil-speaker grumbles that according to the writing of Saint Ambrose,[212] one should never ask a man or persuade him to marry, because of the curses that result from it, for those who place themselves in that state[213] consider themselves to be ill advised. They will not desist from abusing and cursing as enemies all those who were involved with it. And when her husband lies on the bier,[214] his wife looks around in all directions to find herself a husband. But he says she's quick to change her tune when it's time for her to cry.[215] She hardly waits a day or an hour and hurries so much to get married that she takes a man who spends all she has. He goes on to say many a foolish thing,[216] that there is no beast so wild as a newly dressed-up widow woman; she doesn't behave herself as grief-stricken. She often changes and updates her style and gets a new hairdo; and, just like the hungry she-wolf, she joins up with the worst of the crowd.[217] Long ago it was different; it was for exactly a year that a wife would weep for her husband, and she would stay in mourning. Now it is only three days' time; look for someone who does more! The widows are brazen with desire; they climb and get up on their rooftops, just like the frogs of Egypt.[218] They don't care for bed or couch if there is no male with them. Who would have thought they were like that, of such a state or such a nature? Saint Acarius[219] preferred to be the keeper of raving lunatics rather than take charge of widows; they are crazy women out of control, and he didn't want to be responsible for them.

(1673) He speaks of women in several ways, both how they seek out the churches[220] and how they go around showing themselves in the street. Each woman wants very much to be seen. But they hardly love the relics, the shrines, or the sanctuaries — they prefer the clerks and the priests and follow them into their dwellings. Not one woman is afraid of them. The lechers seek their prey there and have sex with some of them. These are not holy acts! Whoever would buy a horse in church, he would do wrong. But it is much more forbidden that a woman should sell herself there; they make a brothel of God's house against law and reason. They should really be afraid. They go like shameless women through the churches of Paris — it's not for their husbands at all. Mahieu says, by Saint Nicholas, it's to have their fun. There they pretend to be Catholics; they often visit the relics that are at Ste. Chapelle. Each woman calls her close friend or someone else from her neighborhood to go on a pilgrimage.[221]

(1703) I will answer gladly here; I will hardly dwell on this. It isn't such a great wrong if one were to object to what he says about Saint Ambrose[222]; it isn't worth a raspberry. For Saint Paul says just the opposite. Which one is better to follow? Saint Paul praises marriage: "It is protection from too much heat."[223] I will speak of it more fully before I conclude[224]; you will hear all at once what I will say about it loud and clear. If a wife remarries soon, that is good, when she conducts herself wisely. But often she is led to this in such a way that they call her "unfortunate": if it turns out badly, "she got what she deserved!" If it turns out well, "it was pure luck!"[225] If she hurries, she has no choice; she can't live in peace because of the ne'er-do-wells who seek her out. Such men are trying to get ahead when they find themselves in arrears.[226] So it is with [re]marriage[227]: it is useless for a woman to be single.[228] And often, through evil talk, she could be blamed for something trivial. But she is cared for and loved when she has a man who supports her and comforts her in her burdens. She does this in hope of having a better livelihood and of being protected in all her affairs. Thus delay is worth nothing — it only serves to waste her assets. That is how we should understand it.

(1741) When a widow remarries, because times have changed, we must also change with the times. Mahieu said, as I remember well, that a widow should wait a year before she can take a husband. Surely there is no need for that now, because she has to be careful to deal with all her business, so there is no use in great delay. The more she waits, the more she loses; thus it is good for her to hurry according to what she feels. For we see that the present time is completely different from the past. And when he says that Saint Acarius didn't want to take charge of widows, that's no reason to delay remarrying well; for in doing so there is no folly.

(1761) Judith[229] was hardly a lunatic, for her city was saved and protected from being captured by people who had besieged it. Holofernes, the criminal, general of the Assyrians, had supper with the widowed lady; he had the flame of love in his heart. He planned to sleep with her in order to carry out his lewd desire. He drank too much and lost his self-control. Judith planned her action well; she quickly cut off Holofernes' head with a sword, while he was sleeping,[230] for he was drunk. Thus was the city saved.

(1777) If women of every description willingly haunt the churches, they are doing nothing wrong at all in this, neither here nor anywhere. They go to processions, they go to confessions, they go to christenings, and to churchings of their fellow women, and to weddings and celebrations, they go to honorable occasions, they go to hear mass, they go to bury the dead, they go to festivals, for alms and charities, they go to cemeteries, in orisons and in prayers they pray for the dead, and do many other good things. In all their deeds they are kind and devout and charitable, good and true Catholics. They often venerate the relics, the crucifixes and the images; I believe these are good customs. Thus they love neither cleric nor priest; no one would speak ill of them unless he is seized with jealousy or the sin of hypocrisy.

(1805) The evil-speaker doesn't shut up; his speech is very hostile: women get together and gossip[231] about married people and people living in sin, and Martin and Sebille, and whatever goes on around town. Mahieu says amazing things about them — I have never heard the like. He says that women hold court[232] — Agnes, Beatrice, Bertha, and Joan. In their assembly nothing is hidden. There the secret is revealed; there each woman becomes an expert at being a gossip and a scold. One woman wants an illicit love; another speaks ill of her husband. He also said, so help him God, that we don't know which is worse, the lecherous woman or the wife with a slanderous tongue.[233] Great discretion would be needed there; women want to know all. They are all that way.[234] They want to know the fears, the times, the moments, and the places with which their husbands are concerned, and all the issues in detail, from beginning to end.

(1833) And if there is a secret thing[235] from here to the isle of Crete, a wife has to know about it; she takes her husband and pulls him, she draws him to her on the bed and pretends she wants to make love.[236] Then she kisses and hugs her husband[237] and tells him with deceitful words, "I don't know what man is afraid of, for as God bears witness, he leaves father and mother for his wife; we're one flesh,[238] just as I long for." Then she joins herself to him chest to chest, with sheet or blanket no obstacle,[239] and tells him, "See here, I give you all that I have, I surrender it to you, my heart and body and all my members; I beg you to remember that. You are my husband and my lord; now tell me what I desire; I would rather die a sudden evil death in grievous pain than reveal your secrets. I would never do it, alas!"[240] Then she hugs and kisses him again, and strokes and soothes him, and cajoles him and then flatters him. She lies flat on her back underneath him and says, "I am in your power,[241] the force of love brings me to this." And when the man wants to get near, she forbids him to touch her, she pulls back, she turns her back on him,[242] and cries like a sad and mournful woman; she pretends to be terribly upset. Then she repeats her complaint. When she has quieted down a little,[243] she says, "I was deceived; alas, I am only your servant. I wish to be far out in back, drowned in a ditch. It would be too outrageous if I kept anything secret from you. You don't want to tell me anything! For our love is not equal, because you turn a deaf ear."[244]

(1879) The husband, stupefied, thinks it over; he knows no defense against this attack and tells her, "Turn back here! I wasn't so angry just now. There is nothing that I hold so dear." She turns her face toward her husband and holds out to him her mouth and bosom. She fools him well with her persuasion. She asks him so much, she begs him so much that he tells her all — a foolish mistake, for now she is lady and mistress, and he is a miserable serf.

(1891) The answer to this is brief enough: it causes no trouble to hold your tongue.[245] If wives are often ready to ask their husbands for things that can turn to their disadvantage, nothing works except to keep quiet; the cure for this is to keep secrets well. If a woman is so inclined by nature that she wants to know secrets, the man should have enough sense to hide his secret well when he shouldn't reveal it at all. From Samson you can learn that one should refrain from acting foolishly.

(1905) Then he says[246] that a man can't serve God if he chooses to serve a wife.[247] For he is always hindered in his intention by more than a thousand cares that are painful and hard for him. He wants to please his wife; he has to clothe her and support her. Thus he isn't free at all. A man without a wife can understand how to serve our Lord in holy church with a willing and tender heart, better than a married man. Then he tells of the banquet[248] to which God calls and summons us, and that the banquet signifies the supper in eternal life at the table of paradise, and that there won't be ten men there of all those who are married because their wives hinder them.

(1925) Gladness answers quickly that this point is irrelevant to the purpose Mahieu wishes to accomplish; assuming it worthy of reply, she says that a married man must not serve mass in church, but the man who is provided with a benefice should perform his function there. The married man should provide for his household. Let him go right to church when the bell rings, according to his status. And as for the real meaning of the banquet to which he says God calls us, it is the word of the Gospel in the form of a parable[249]: a man made a great supper — in that country he had no equal or peer. He commanded his servants to seek out all those he had invited. When the servant called one man, who was just married, to go there, he did not refuse but politely apologized, saying, "I can't go there, by my soul — today[250] I have married a wife." That was a fair excuse. How does this story apply? If one married man couldn't go into that company, it makes no judgment on the others, nor would that be fair. Nor should we claim that married men have to lose the joyful supper of the holy table in paradise, nor does this story told by Mahieu in any way put women to shame.

(1963) Then he says in his affliction that a woman is disobedient.[251] All that you forbid to her, she wants to do, and he gives an example[252] of a man who wished to prove it. He brewed the strongest poison he could find and without waiting any longer he ordered his wife not to touch the container. She little feared the vessel and drank of it against his order; that was a fatal dose for her.

(1975) Orpheus[253] knew how to play all the musical instruments. His wife, called Eurydice, was lodged in hell. Orpheus went to the gate of hell to bring back his wife; he knew how to play very well; he played so well that they gave him back his wife on the condition that if she looked behind her, she would have to return and never come back. Eurydice was not too bright, so she did not obey; she was taken back to hell — the fool, born in an unlucky hour.

(1991) Ahasuerus, king of Persia, could find no way at all to make his wife obey him, for all his power. Vashti[254] was the queen's name; she fell to ruin by her pride. She would not come to him or follow his command but flatly refused him. The king found fault with her for that. She was banished from the kingdom and made an example to the others.[255]

(2003) Eve[256] was quicker to reach for the fruit that God forbade to her than if he had left her alone and allowed her to do it. Lot's wife[257] lacked self-control when she looked behind her at Sodom, the burning city, from which she had fled. An angel, who was leading them, gave her instructions from God that she should not linger there or turn back at all, lest evil quickly come of it. Against this warning, she turned back to see the fire; she became hard like a tombstone.

(2019) Surely, if no one were to answer and defend women over this "disobedience," it would be extremely ignorant, for such an answer well applies: when God placed the immortal soul within the body of man and woman for the love that touched their hearts, he freely granted them to do both good and evil, each one by his free will.[258] But if someone does the opposite of good, whether it be a bad woman or a wicked man, he should return to reason, so that if he should err, reason would put him back on the right path.[259] For the will is inclined to evil and often rules against reason whenever it leads one to sin through human weakness. And if someone always does the right thing and errs not at all, that would be by God's help and not at all by human power. Thus women have the power to disobey by using their free will. They can always complain because they are in subjection to man, on account of their sin.[260] But if someone were to give [them] an order that wouldn't be lawful and right, there would be no great offense in breaking that rule.

(2053) Men know well among themselves that they are quite equal to women, except for the subjection in which woman is constrained. And according to the law of nature, a woman can bring about either good or bad through her actions, if Reason wishes to allow it — and if she doesn't, let her go away where she would get in trouble.[261] For God has placed in woman less reason and more will, so she ought to have more freedom.[262] Nor does reason have any control at all where will is the boss. Although it may result in praise or blame, no one can control the will, but one can certainly restrain the act.

(2071) When the man who hated his wife brewed poison for her to drink through his treachery, and in his storeroom or closet he deliberately placed it in a container, and she drank it, it was the fault of the man who forbade it to her; for he very wrongly punished her out of hatred. She was ignorant of what would happen; for had she known the poison was there, she never would have drunk it. Therefore the man was guilty of his crime and his damnable act. He really deserved to be hanged when he didn't let her know the truth, when there was mortal danger. He was in the wrong to plot against her.

(2089) It's a myth replete with falsehood about Orpheus and his wife. For it would be against nature if a mortal creature came to life after its death. When the soul is seized from the body, it is all very well to play the flute, the viol, and the harp: who could get her back that way? There is very little knowledge in him — the man who uses such examples is just giving us a song and dance.[263] Such stories in no way discredit women or take away from their good deeds.

(2103) And as for the time when Queen Vashti, full of pride and rebellion, provoked her husband Ahasuerus: the king held his great feast on a certain day.[264] She had a crown on her head. He ordered her that she should come to him and celebrate at the feast. However, she firmly refused him, nor did she bother to apologize at all. Maybe some disastrous impulse struck her and made her disobey, or God arranged it that way and led her to do this as an example to others.[265] There was good reason for this: when Vashti lost her crown, just as she fell through pride and weakness, so by her great humility Esther rose and became the queen. She was disposed to do good and caused Mordechai to be saved, and Haman was paid for his crime, for he was hanged from the gallows — Mordechai was protected from him. Esther was of Hebrew descent, well instructed and well taught; she humbled herself to the king,[266] and he paid good heed to her, for he had the Israelite people delivered from the order to arrest and imprison them. For her great meekness, the noble Jewess Esther should be contrasted with Vashti, and we should honor women without speaking ill or slander.

(2141) All that Mahieu said of Eve[267] doesn't amount to a bean when it comes to blaming other women, seeing that God, who loved us so much more than other creatures and knew all things future, past, and present, had already planted several seedlings within the earthly paradise.[268] He knew just what would come of it and how the man would eat of the fruit that was forbidden to him. When Eve prompted the first man to bite into an apple, God willed for this reason to come down here and take our form within a woman, to give us back our inheritance and pay for the crime of enjoying and tasting, for which he suffered bitter death on the cross. So it's right that man understand that God paid the price for him, and since God decided to redeem him, a man should ask for nothing more. For man's sin hangs there[269]; he shared in the crime.

(2167) And if Lot's wife had known[270] that she would have to get hard like a stone because she turned around, she wouldn't have done it at all, by Saint Peter![271] And if she looked behind her at Sodom which was burning in fire, that was no great wonder. The heart is alert to see and watch the slightest thing — no one should be surprised at that. And the angel who warned her was always in human form, so she didn't know how much she was mistaken. We could also understand it another way: all-knowing God wanted it to happen, for he had foreseen all along that Lot, the nephew of Abraham, who had suffered great loss, would have sex with his daughters[272] and beget nations from them, and that if Lot had had his wife, he wouldn't have slept with his daughters. I can and will name their two sons: one was Moab, the other Ammon. From Moab came the Moabites and from Ammon the Ammonites; these two filled up the earth and many wars were caused by them.[273]

(2195) Because of what I have said and will say and because I will go by the right path, women are well defended. They should never be accused of bad behavior or lewdness; and if anyone speaks ill of them, I deny it. For they are very quick to obey, wise, gracious, and honorable.

(2203) Master Mahieu of the sharp tongue aims his attack at women and says that they are envious and malicious gossips. And if someone wants to know what is thought about a woman or her neighbor, just let him say that she is good and beautiful, sweet, kind, and pleasant, and worthy to be praised and loved. You will hear her condemned by the others and her faults brought to mind — that's envy doing its job. If a woman is accustomed to sit first at church or go first to the offering, she'd better be a very important person if she expects to worship this way without being scolded or abused. And if a man wants peace, let him be sure that when a group of women are out walking, he doesn't greet just one of them, but he should make a common greeting for all of them to hear, with a polite bow.

(2227) The envious woman always complains about her neighbor who is better dressed, for it troubles her. Her tirade gets back to her husband: "Wretched husband," says the wife, "it's your great shame and great disgrace when you keep me dressed like this so that I don't dare go out on the street. If I could have clothes that suit me, I would fit in with the richer folk."[274] Her husband doesn't dare to argue; he has dresses made for her, because if anything should be wrong with them, he would find her noise too much to bear. Every day she wants to purchase some new hemp or linen cloth, and she often says it's a wonder that she's not as well off as her neighbor. "Her cow's teat produces more," she says when she can't think of anything worse.

(2247) So I need to make an answer on this sin of envy of which Mahieu accuses my ladies. I speak this way in their defense: these things are very complicated, and they have a double meaning. There is envy for a good purpose and envy that is worthless. If a man or woman is devoted to well-doing, that is good envy; that is how we should explain it. If someone can surpass other people, whether in arms or in learning, and retain a clear conscience, I think that's good envy both for strength and for knowledge. But if someone is glad at another's harm or sad at another's good, that is wrong and wicked envy. The envious heart is not at ease, for it is displeased with everything and can't be satisfied. It is a misdeed to blame other people wrongly, for there is order in all things, as the philosopher bears witness.[275] It is not a sinful practice for a woman to be well dressed,[276] for she will be more valued and honored everywhere. In winter, when it's icy, she will have a warmer body.

(2278) The woman of higher class and more noble lineage should go first to the offering and be rightfully preferred according to good custom and order. In my opinion they conduct themselves well; they strive for honor and each woman encourages the others to do better — that's good envy. If women want to have linen or hemp or other possession, or silk or wool or a cow full of milk, that desire is very common, so no one should blame any woman for it.

(2293) Then master Mahieu makes his argument[277] about a vice that is called avarice. He slanderously claims against women that they are cold by nature[278] and that every woman is stingy. And then when he brings in proofs on this subject, he contradicts himself — but he does it with irony, in a nasty way. Speaking of women, he says that they are hotter than the male.[279] He testifies on their avarice that they don't warm up unless you give them something.[280] They want money and clothes from those men whom they hold in their arms, even from their relatives[281] — that's how extremely grasping they are.[282] He goes on to say that they sell themselves for pennies, and they know how to fleece their men, so that an evil fate befalls them[283] — that's what he says in his book at the place where I apologized that I decided to translate it,[284] because he displeased me with the complaints he made about them.

(2319) To all that he can say about it, I answer without hard feelings, at all times with the help of Gladness, that there is much generosity in women, and they are neither wanton nor weak, especially the rich women who have their wealth without wrongdoing or fraud. And if there are some women who are too common with their bodies and sell themselves from poverty, it shouldn't be blamed on them.[285] For the men whom they pick up defraud them with all their might, and they are full of such great malice that they care only for profit. For they caress and flatter the women, or they torment and beat them when they can't accomplish their desire[286] by stuffing the purses of those lecherous thugs[287] who aren't worth two hoots. They hold them captive and keep them in such degradation that they teach them every kind of wrong and harm them with all their power and lead them to ruin and exert themselves with many tactics to exploit women this way.

(2348) I can speak clearly of this truth: it's no wonder at all if a woman for her part gets ready to resist their malice. For there is two hundred times more vice in men than there is in women. And so they harshly slander them, with little justice, against reason. And if any women in their prime give themselves up to men's will, and if men give them gifts to supply their needs, one shouldn't blame them at all. If there are wicked sluts, it doesn't follow from this that all women are generally included in their guilt or their reproach. Yes, women are quite generous. God send[288] them a hundred boatloads of goods, all full of great plenty, to use at their desire!

(2369) If you want to learn about their generous deeds, she can prove it by examples.[289] When Jason got the chance to win the Golden Fleece, he never could have had it if he hadn't had it through Medea.[290] And so he went, in such danger when he lived in exile on Colchis, an island of the sea, that it would be too long to tell all that happened in the story. But we should remember how Medea took him in and how Jason deceived her. Medea was the daughter of the king and didn't intend to do wrong; she was beautiful, good, and wise. Jason promised that he would take her in marriage and that she would be his wife. Jason should have the blame for this, for she gave her love to him and gave up everything for him — heart, body, riches, and possessions.[291] She thought she had him as a husband. Perhaps it was in this hope that he got her pregnant, through deceit. And when she had armed him well, furnished him with spells, given him charms, anointed him with several oils, and instructed him on how he could profit by defeating the serpent and the oxen who plowed the land on the island so that armed men appeared, so that he took the golden fleece, for which he has been much honored ever since, he went back to his native land. For this he should be hated by all, for he left Medea pregnant,[292] pale and wan from suffering. He perjured himself to her and never cared for her thereafter. She wasted her riches on him, her honors and her skills.

(2413) Ulysses, Count of Dulichium,[293] a clever and conniving man, deceived Circe the queen. Circe kindly took him in; he and his wretched crew were wandering on the sea and reduced to poverty. He was grandly entertained. Circe wanted to get married; Ulysses seduced her. When he saw that she was his mistress,[294] he didn't spare her wealth and she gave him much of it. But he repaid her very badly, for he left her very pregnant[295]; she debased her honor that much for him. He returned to his native land when he could embark on the sea and the winter had passed. Circe never plotted so well that she could hold him back. This should be a warning to others.

(2435) Aeneas, exiled from Troy,[296] had made a sea voyage on his way to Italy. He had no means of survival, nor did those who were with him. They repaired their damaged ships and arrived in Carthage. Dido saw them on the shore as they were coming very bravely; she graciously received them. She was queen of the land. Aeneas lay in her bedchamber and was there so much that he got her pregnant[297]; then he broke his oath to her. For when he had enough possessions, and winter was past, in his ships that were well restored and ready outside the harbor he crossed over to Lavinia's land. When Dido found out the plot and saw that she had been deceived, she killed herself with a sword. She wasted her lavish gifts on him when despair drove her mad. The treachery of Aeneas did this — she was so deceived by him. Of women and their brave deeds, their virtues, their generous acts, and their many good qualities, I am never tired of speaking.

(2465) But here I must exert myself, for my closing argument has yet to be addressed.[298] Mahieu, who put all his effort into accusing women of lust, says that Queen Pasiphaë[299] laid herself down on her back underneath a bull[300] and opened up her crack in the guise of a cow covered with a shaggy skin. See what a worthless trifle this really is! It can't be true; it's a myth, but it was the devil's work. How could a woman bear it, that she would offer her noble female parts to a bull? The tale is brim-full of poison. It's illegal to do that; I think not even possible; or, begging your pardon, it's a joke. Pasiphaë was not so insane that she would lay down her naked body underneath a bull with horns. And furthermore, he's not to be believed concerning Scylla, whose story he recalls, or Minos, or Nisus. I've already answered him on these, above.[301] His conclusion is invalid.

(2492) But I say it's true that Jephthah,[302] judge and lord of Israel, who was the greatest of his people — as we find in a true story — vowed long ago that if he were victorious in a battle against the Philistine people, he would sacrifice to God the first thing he would meet on his return home. He kept his oath. The first one he met was his daughter, who approached him smiling, for the girl was cheerful, sweet, pleasant, good, and beautiful. "Alas," he said, "I am ruined! I would prefer to have seen some other thing"; and then he told her the import of his vow. The maiden, who was chaste, made one request of her father: that she would be allowed to lament her virginity for two months with her companions in the woods and on the mountains. Jephthah granted this to her. When the two months were past, he cut off his daughter's head. This is not at all the same kind of story as the one of Scylla, which is only a myth.

(2522) It's also a true story that the brave Virginius,[303] in defiance of Tarquin, when he convinced him by false witness that he had found his daughter weak, cut off the head of his beautiful daughter Virginia as punishment — she was born of noble stock. The Romans made no joy over this.

(2531) Regarding the sin of lust, for which Mahieu tried to impose blame on women, I will briefly repeat all his claims, and after that I will respond. First he attacked Myrrha,[304] who slept with her father and allowed him to have sex with her[305] against paternal decency. As Myrrha lay with her father, so did Biblis with her brother, and Canace with Machaire.[306] Still he couldn't shut up about them — how Phaedra,[307] daughter of the king of Crete, was unrestrained in love. She loved the beautiful Hippolytus, which wasn't a lawful thing — he was the son of her husband, Theseus. When she had drunk that cup to the dregs,[308] she got herself laid by her stepson[309] — Venus made her a crazy stepmother.

(2553) Phyllis[310] did something terribly wrong; so deranged was she, so wretched, so beside herself. She yielded most shamefully to dissolute lust when she hanged herself for Demophon; I don't know who made her do it. But she couldn't wait for him because of the despair that drove her when her lover did not return.

(2563) Dido the queen of Carthage,[311] he says, did a very rash act for Aeneas, who was her guest and who had banged her box.[312] He said that Dido was much to blame. When she saw Aeneas on the sea when he was going away to Lombardy, she went mad with rage. Feeling herself great with child, weeping, crying, and lamenting, she was so moved with reckless love that she died by her own hand, with Aeneas's sword. She was born in a terrible hour.

(2577) Ovid says[313] that a woman is chaste as long as no one seeks her out or tries to.[314] As a concession to their lustfulness, the pope[315] gave them permission to [re]marry without delay, to pay their carnal debt. Then he says that without men, [women] can hardly wait to sell or give themselves away. Then he says that women grant their love[316] on some remarkable conditions: the noblewoman gives pleasure freely — the nobles just need a place, as long as it's somewhere nice. City women are available — you get them by giving them something. They don't give anything for free. In the small towns they're not so proud — many give themselves for the asking.

(2595) The nuns, the women religious,[317] think they're so superior because of their spirituality. But there's little chastity there. So Mahieu talks after his fashion about the women of the church and claims that underneath their show of piety,[318] you will find the hidden vices of envy, deceit, hypocrisy, and lust mingled with fraud, especially in the Beguines,[319] who don't do godly works.

(2607) He wouldn't shut up about the old women,[320] and says many hostile things about them: how, when they have become old, wrinkled, and white-haired, and lost their natural warmth and are of little use, then they long to hook up; the old shoe wants to get some oil. Then he tells of the pimping,[321] of the tricks and the witchcraft, of the cosmetics and the oils, and of the other teachings by which they lead young girls astray and solicit for women and young chicks; and how an old woman, may hell-fire burn her, made her little dog cry with onions and mustard[322] to deflower Galatea, and how she summoned her lover just as the old lady ordered, and how she let him make love to her,[323] without noise or shout, and how she was deflowered, secretly and in private; and how the old female pimps[324] often play at such tricks[325] and have no fear of doing worse things: they kill babies in the womb, and if a man wants to prey on women, he can take a lesson from their evil tactics. And he says, if anyone believes it, that she will make *herself* his conquest; their deeds are proven and well known. Ovid was tricked in this way[326]; he thought he'd found a young girl, for he was in love with a maiden. He came by night to seek her bed, where he expected to take his pleasure, but the old woman got herself down underneath him. I don't know how she dared to do that.

(2647) Now it's time for me to answer. I can no longer rightly hide the arguments that I rely on, for it behooves me to reveal everything that belongs to my plan and my defense. Homer was a wonderful scholar,[327] very wise, subtle, and quick. He made beautiful writings with examples and metaphors and ancient stories composed according to pagan doctrines. He held many opinions and explained in his fictions how Fortune is the tapster of the [two] kegs,[328] one of them full of gladness and the other full of sadness, and how each day you have to drink from them, either from Sadness, which is gloomy, or from Gladness the loving,[329] which is welcome everywhere. Those who have drunk from Sadness have spoken as badly as they could of women and their actions, but Gladness is opposed to them, and will be, if anyone should believe me about this. Homer wrote about the city of Troy and the fights and the battles at the end and the beginning. I don't know if it was just to amuse himself, but in his poems he made the immortal gods of their religion fight in combat with mortal men. Pallas, Juno, and Venus often went there to bear arms in battle and strike with their sword left and right. Lady Venus was wounded there[330]; her wound has not yet healed.

(2687) Ovid, who defended him[331] and held his opinions, followed him in many ways. They spoke of things like that long ago, each in his own style. Included [in their poems] is many a beautiful myth that tells of wonders and metamorphoses. They held the pagan religion, and we hold the Christian; their myths and their stories are heresies in our religion. Thus they are not to be believed, nor are those who repeat their stories, especially when they spoke of women and attacked them. They wrote much nonsense about them, about Jupiter and Phoebus and the great ladies of the land. For this they deserve to be hated.

(2707) Don't think I am imagining things: "a capon never loved a hen." I said this about Ovid. For the true story is that he had both his balls cut off.[332] They were bandaged and healed with pieces of flax and soft eggs; then he lived for many years and was sent into exile and transported overseas. It's not appropriate to talk about the reason, for I don't have leisure to digress. Thus we can believe and say that being hateful and brim-full of wrath, he blamed women after this and never loved them afterward.

(2723) He strongly condemned Myrrha,[333] saying she slept with her father; his lying should be called out to the world, for he says that she was changed into a tree for her sin, and that the tree then dried up and was covered with bark. So you shouldn't take any of it seriously now: not Biblis and Canace,[334] or the stories he collects of Phaedra and Hippolytus and their illicit love, or Phyllis, who hanged herself, who waited too long for Demophon — Ovid says it was an aspen,[335] a tree whose leaves shook when Demophon came to make love to her. We can rest easy about this because we see it's all a myth, and there's nothing truthful here.

(2743) You have heard me tell of Dido[336] and Aeneas and the ship and how she was cheated and angered in her heart because Aeneas left her, and of the act that followed that, and how she killed herself because of her wrath, which drove her to it. You surely see who was in the wrong — that Aeneas treated her badly. And if these stories are true, the shame in them is on the men, and the guilt for all the other crimes is on the men, because it happened by their treachery. They did much harm to women, using trickery and scheming to satisfy their lust.

(2761) Mahieu hurries along quoting Ovid,[337] saying there's no chaste woman,[338] and concludes at the very end by saying there's no good woman. I respond to his judgment: his words sound forth most rudely and are not rightly composed. For just as I said above,[339] he who would look within himself would desist from speaking slander. One shouldn't talk trash; he who declares his own nastiness will gain nothing by it — he couldn't be more deluded. He who slanders shames his own mouth; that way,[340] all men who were born of women would be sons of whores! Ovid was out of control when his speech attacked women; he defamed his own self by his anger and wickedness. May the shame of it be on him, and on Mahieu, who quotes him, for it wasn't right for him to say that.

(2785) You never hear that Master Peter Abelard,[341] wise and eloquent, ever spoke ill of women in any way or attacked them with his speech, even though he was castrated. Instead, he had the Paraclete built, where he brought Sister Heloïse[342]; she lived there very chastely, wisely, and honorably.

(2795) I believe the evil-speakers will die of wicked envy, which hurts them, when they hear all the arguments on the side of Gladness. For we have some virtuous women, whose names we know well, both ancient and modern[343]: ladies, bourgeois women, and girls. I will provide here a catalog of those females who were and are noble, despite the slanders of sinful hearts, to argue against Gallus and against Ovid and Juvenal[344] and respond to Matheolus: among the ladies we have Saint Ursula,[345] with the eleven thousand virgins[346] — they were defenders of chastity; Ursula went to Britain and led her companions to marry in the church as each one was asked to do. Ursula was well brought up; she was chosen to espouse King Conain[347] in marriage, when by tempest and by storm they were scattered on the sea and landed in different places. But notwithstanding hardship, they kept their virginity.

(2825) We have Saint Katherine,[348] wise, pleasant, a pure virgin who surpassed the masters of rhetoric in her knowledge of the subject; she outshone them in her arguments and defeated King Maxentius. Margaret[349] with her breadbasket was a shepherdess, a pure virgin; she wouldn't accept Olibrius for anything he knew how to offer her. Agnes, Lucy, Agatha, Marina, Geneviève, Gertrude, Christine, Perpetua, and Felicity[350] kept their virginity.[351]

(2839) The nuns, the women religious, are very gracious in their deeds, sober, pleasant, good, and beautiful. Noble ladies and girls are placed there, more than other women, so no man should speak ill of them at all. For more than one saint was a nun: Saint Aurée and Saint Opportune, Saint Angadresme[352] and Saint Bridget are holy, in spite of Ovid. I could name many others, brave women, good and holy, whose honored lives are in the Golden Legend.[353]

(2853) Sister Jehanne of Neuville,[354] from near Ressons, in humble clothing and in the habit of a Minorite, disciple and student[355] of Christ, [is] immersed in humility, on fire with charity, and well schooled in virtues. Descended from a noble line, she was brought to Longchamp in her youth and given to God. She has served God in that abbey from the time she was put there, and so conducted herself with the help of the Holy Spirit that God provided for her so well that she was promoted to abbess, to rule over fifty ladies, very devout in body and soul. They are enclosed and walled in and secured apart from the world, to avoid sin and vice; they praise God in the divine service. Lady Jehanne guides them both in summer and winter; as a very valiant shepherdess,[356] she takes the care of everything upon herself; she is a good and gracious lady; she wants to please each one and is servant to them all. She has no pride in her demeanor, but her fair face is humble; she is the second Saint Clare.[357] The lady of Gueux and the one called Moisie,[358] who delights in singing the liturgy, are following closely in her footsteps.[359] God keep them all by his grace.

(2889) I will name still more worthies,[360] good and virtuous women: along with Lucretia and Penelope, you can add Sinope and Hippolyta and Menalippe,[361] to make fun of the evil-speakers,[362] for they are not our friends. Queen Semiramis with disheveled hair on one side,[363] Thamiris and Penthesilea,[364] Teuca, Lampito, Deïphile,[365] and more than a thousand other ladies known for their great bravery belong to the party of Gladness and will carry her banner to support her in every way. Teuca was chaste and gracious and very courageous in arms.

(2907) I wouldn't be able to write all their deeds. It would be a long story to tell, so I must think of other [examples] to stand up for the right and defend the ladies — may God give them joy on every path, in every way. Among the good women is Hannah the mother of Samuel,[366] and Susanna,[367] who was accused by the priests: she should not be omitted here, for she shows by true experience the chastity of good women. She was tested by fire and found to be virtuous. Those who falsely accused her died an evil death for that.

(2923) It is written[368] that long ago in Judea a woman was stoned to death if she committed adultery; she was led to execution. The Jews found one woman among them who had the misfortune to be caught in the act and put on trial for adultery. They brought her to God to pass judgment and asked him (with evil intent) how they should sentence the woman and put her to death. God, who knows all the thoughts of the heart, and knew well how to keep himself from harm, saw just what they were after. He wrote on the ground with his finger: "If one of you is without sin, and if anyone feels himself unstained by it, let him cast the first stone at the woman until he strikes her." They were so stunned by his answer that they didn't hurt the woman, nor did they throw a stone at her at all, but they left her in peace. The woman lived on in safety; this is in the book of the Gospels.

(2949) God showed us by this example that whoever speaks ill of women commits a great crime.[369] One can't deny this story, for it is true and worthy of belief. So I don't know why a man takes credit for blaming women with his speech, or speaking evil or reproach against them — a married woman or a virgin, an old woman or a young one.

(2959) The old women teach the young ones and don't fail to show them how they ought to protect themselves and abstain from all wrongdoing. The old women have more knowledge and fear God in their hearts, and it's true that they rejoice when young women follow the right path.[370] If the old women practice witchcraft, spells, and pimping, or things that harm them in the sight of God, the men have prompted them to do this and urged them and persuaded them. They exert themselves night and day to mislead women for evil purposes. The men want to be debauched, for a woman will never commit a crime if a man is not involved. We can see very well, when the whole story is told, to whom the guilt belongs — to the male or to the female, in this debate as well. Men have the active strength and women have the passive. The man must go forth and act, the woman suffer and be silent — [as long as it is] something reasonable and decent. But if a man advises her to do something that wouldn't be right, the woman by natural law can wisely refuse him and rightfully decline, for she is in charge of her free will.

(2992) And when Mahieu complained about Ovid and how he was tricked,[371] it shouldn't be acceptable to blame women for this. The father and lord of nature — God, who created all things — was pleased with our form and wanted to make it multiply. He devises many stratagems to make us procreate, for the propagation of man and the lower animals. And among other motives he instilled pleasure,[372] the better to please us and attract us to each other. All forms and species, whether small or great, are continued by this pleasure, so one should practice it rightfully and lawfully, without abusing it. So I conclude that it makes no sense at all to blame the place you came from,[373] for the proverb says that to each one of the birds, its own nest is beautiful.

(3017) And as for the doings of witches[374] on which Mahieu has harsh words, and of their spells, of charms and conjurations, and of toads dressed in clothes and garments and other evil tricks, and certain figures in wax, which women cause to burn and fry to make the hearts of men grow hot, and of the cat that they roast in her gray coat that they put in the frying pan, and make its feet burn there against the bronze or on iron, and tie it to a board: they worship Nero, Beelzebub, and Pilate, and all the power of hell, and have no fear of them. And how the old women make bad things happen,[375] and go off to the gibbet at night to take the hair and the rope from a hanged man — it's a very nasty thing; and at night they dig up the bodies of children and dead men.

(3041) He says Medea was a witch[376] and a clairvoyant fortuneteller, and Circe did great crimes[377] by magic and by sorcery, and the dirty old woman Erychtho[378] tried to find out who would conquer by the sword at the battle of Thessaly, whether Caesar or Pompey: she made spells about it, by lots and incantations. Old women ride their broomsticks[379] through courts, halls, and palaces — they go around the world like the wind at the command of Lady Habonde.[380] He says that Saul wanted to know[381] if he could have Samuel back again; yet it did him no good to speak to him there, for he couldn't help him. A clairvoyant witch answered him with a frown.[382]

(3061) Master Mahieu wrote many insults about women and their actions; he repeated the bad things he said about them[383] and added new examples, on how women don't keep secrets[384] and give away everything you say to them. He told us a brand new story about it,[385] of a gentleman who laid an egg. His wife told her friend that there were two of them, by Saint Peter! The friend went off to her neighbor to get some fire for the kitchen and said there were four of them — she knew how to amuse herself by telling lies. The women spread the story so far and exaggerated so much that they chalked up fifty eggs to him — truly, in the end, more than sixty.

(3079) Then he tells of another gentleman[386] who pretended to have killed a man; he told his wife about it and she revealed the secret — she sure didn't hide it. She told her neighbors that her criminal husband had murdered a merchant and put him under his trunk, so the judge had an inquest made about it. But it was proved a lie, for a sow was found in the sack where he had put it. The wife was harshly reproved for this as a gossip and a liar, for her tongue was too reckless.

(3095) Mahieu said, from wicked envy,[387] that when God came from death to life, and rose up on Easter, that first of all he told it to women, in order to get the word out. In doing this he did not forget, when he appeared to them first, that they are prone to reckless talking.[388]

(3103) Also, he spoke another time of a jealous man[389] who kept his wife securely locked up in a tower, but he didn't have her in chains. The husband had three doors made there, and three sets of keys to match, but in the end he was fooled. He had drunk one evening, so he fell asleep after supper. The drink made him a cuckold; his wife took the keys from him and got together with her lover. But jealousy soon wakes up the jealous man, who sleeps little. When he saw what was happening, he was very angry at his loss and said, "Woman, where have you gone? You have flown outside the tower; your unfaithfulness is proven. Tomorrow you will die for it." Then the wife came running back and said weeping to her husband: "I beg you, by the Magdalene, that you don't make me suffer. Spare me, and I swear to you that I won't make you angry anymore. I didn't hurt your tower; I went out by fate and not for lechery at all, so it's not right that I be condemned for it. I will drown myself in the well if I can't receive your mercy."

(3135) He answered to distress her: "Tomorrow I will have you beaten." The night was black and dark; she took a heavy stone and threw it in the well. Then her husband went outside, thinking she was drowned or dead. As soon as he was out, she went inside and shut the door and swore to him and insisted that he would pay for this attack. She wasn't scared at all! She cried out, "Come here!" to the sentries. "Arrest this evil rapist for me!" He was taken and put in prison. Never was a man more justly captured. He was also beaten and mocked, for he was weak in the head.

(3153) He also writes of Lady Bertha,[390] whom Clement found naked and stuffed underneath a priest. Clement drew his sword on them, so they had to stop what they were doing. Bertha jumped up and put her clothes back on. She grabbed her husband and held him by force — she almost skinned his hands. Wicked liar that she was, Bertha cried out on her husband Clement: "Good people, he is out of his mind! Help! By God! Hold him fast! He's not in his senses; this priest hurried here to help me; he came here to help, or I would have been done for." She didn't let Clement say a word. One man pushed him and another pulled him; he was seized and thrown on the ground, tied up and beaten with sticks. His misery lasted three days; he was forced to make peace; he so dreaded Bertha's blows that he fully pardoned her for everything.

(3177) To all that Mahieu claims[391] and asserts against women: how they go out on pilgrimage,[392] where they go for secret purposes, and on returning say their feet hurt and pretend to be worn out from rituals and vigils (what amazing things they tell their husbands!) and how not one woman admits that she has been solicited, and of their sorceries and their witchcraft, and the charms that lechers make, and of their lust, their vices, their frauds, their scams, their tricks, their lies, and all the other actions for which one could attack, hate, accuse, or blame them (whether using myths or examples, assuming they were sufficient), and to the worst that one could say of every wrong a woman commits (except for anything against religion,[393] and assuming she would not commit a capital or mortal sin, which wouldn't be defensible, for on that subject I protest that it isn't my intention to say or to maintain that one should not refrain from actual sin, just as our religion teaches us), without speaking crudely, I strongly answer thus[394]: to defend women justly, one must truly practice virtues, avoid the bad and do the good; as proof, I will tell you a true story.[395]

(3215) God (who is without beginning,[396] eternal and without end, three persons in trinity through indivisible unity, Father, Son, and Holy Spirit, he who can raise the dead) long ago created the fair angels and put them in his paradise, to serve his majesty. And when they were all together, God (who is true wisdom and knows what is bound to happen, past, present, and future, willing that we might know his glory in everlasting memory, and that man should understand how God is just and powerful to show his justice to those who would do evil), when he had created the fair angels, Lucifer, brighter than the sun,[397] was so arrogant that he disobeyed God. From the heavenly home, Lucifer with his army fell right down into darkness,[398] into a secret hiding place. His crew of angels fell down to hell[399] with all his followers and were changed into devils, ugly, hideous, and frightful, and were commanded to make their report as a punishment,[400] in order to frighten the wicked and to punish and torment them at the orders of divine justice, which desires to save us.

(3253) After God molded man, who has such a lovely form, and the woman as a helpmate, just as you have heard me say,[401] he gave them a conscious soul, rational and understanding,[402] and among the privileges that belong to living creatures, three special things he gave them: he placed in them memory and understanding with free will and many other good things.

(3265) Memory remembers things and connects the texts and glosses of things past and present and things that are absent, things to come and future things[403] that are preached in the Scriptures; through the understanding he makes us understand how we can learn things that are invisible to our eyes, both possible and impossible.

(3275) [God gave them] free will so that they might practice the good and refuse to do wrong; for it can choose one or the other, as you have heard earlier.[404] The rational soul has such gifts; it is open to all the virtues and recognizes evil as such. And just as God may not be contained by any creature, the soul is of such a nature that it may not be contained or understood by a human being—this knowledge is not lawful for him. The soul can understand a visible thing—whatever one can see and pay heed to; and the soul can't be shut in, for heaven can't prevent her from being able to ponder and learn about both heavenly and earthly things. Hell can't obstruct her from being able to see right into the things of hell with her mind's eye, through spiritual control of spiritual substance.

(3302) And physical matter makes the body of four elements,[405] just as I remember it; for earth gives it flesh, and water the blood that flows, the breath comes from air, and fire, which is the fourth element, spreads warmth through the body—it is very strong to keep us healthy. The head, round like the vault of heaven, is of noble matter and has two eyes to give it light, which is the opposite of darkness.

(3315) Now it is true that at trial,[406] first you have to have a judge, then the accuser or plaintiff,[407] and there has to be a defendant there. If God had always been up there in his majesty, his glory would have been unknown,[408] and so neither his justice nor his power would have been known, nor would man now have knowledge of God who rules over all, by his strength and by his goodness. That is why he created two creatures with different natures; one was spiritual and the other was corporeal. He wanted to be praised and served by both, just as you hear. The angels are spiritual and men are corporeal. This is why he did this, to show us by true example how he wanted the angels to sin, and also to fall down there. He made them fall down there without a doubt—Lucifer and all his gang.

(3341) He did likewise with man, for he forbade him the apple and the fruit of the tree of life.[409] Adam had such desire for it that he broke the prohibition because of his wife, who tempted him. They sinned wickedly and deserved damnation.

(3349) No man or woman knows how to express the great good that resulted from these sins of which I write; for through these events, God in his mercy made clear to us[410] the glory of his majesty. This is why he lowered himself to come down from heaven right here and to take human form within the precious virgin, [who was] sanctified, glorious, and endowed with all the virtues; God had chosen her for himself. He was born from her and suffered death on the cross and offered himself for us. He conquered death in hell and on the third day rose again, in power and triumph, to our marvelous gain, and we should firmly believe it. He was victorious over death.[411]

(3369) And when he was risen, and had visited his friends and stayed with them until the fortieth day after his resurrection, he made his ascension into the pure heavens, which troubled his disciples. Ten days later,[412] he sent them the Holy Spirit to comfort their hearts[413] and encourage them in joy,[414] as he had promised them. Then each of them knew how to speak in a different language.[415]

(3382) Our faith maintains, this is no myth, that in time to come he will come to judge us; he will judge the living and the dead. The devil, our adversary, will accuse us of crimes,[416] for he is always against us and he brings to every human creature as much harm as he can. So we should tremble in terror and fear the powerful judge who is more just than a scale; he was pierced with the spear to save us and redeem us and rescue us from the pains of hell. God did all these good things for us to bring us into his glory at the time of his arrival on the great Day of Judgment. While man has life in his body, before his soul is seized from it, he should take care to see how he can prepare to enter into eternal glory and avoid mortal sin.

(3407) Sin leads to damnation; by sins good deeds are withered and have no force or power. And if God shows his firmness when he judges the evil-speakers,[417] their words will be harmful to them; so they will be, as we must believe, for everything will return to memory, and we will have to answer for everything; no one can hide anything from God, whether evil-doing or evil-speaking. So I conclude through my discourse that it's a great sin to slander, which proceeds from envy and wrath, and sin leads to damnation. So it follows logically that he who commits any kind of slander is in danger of damnation, nor can he lead a holy life.

(3426) Cato tells us in his book[418] that the most important virtue is for a man to control his tongue. Ptolemy[419] in his *Almageste* includes a useful saying on that: to wit, that a wise man should strive to rein in his tongue. Saint Paul says that from the abundance of the heart and wild thoughts the mouth speaks foolishly.[420] So we can understand how the slanderers are defiled and endangered by their sins. Then it is good to keep quiet without attacking or maligning other people. He who persists in slandering others is chasing after his own death. And anyone who puts these writings up for debate will find Mahieu's argument weak and extremely sick. So I have made this ballade about it:

(3447) I will hammer all my life[421]
To please my Lady Gladness,
And in defending her case
I will condemn anger and sadness.
Of ladies and their great worth
I will speak good words, clear and bright,
To defeat the evil-speakers.

(3454) For in women, whatever one may say,
Is much valor, wisdom, good fame, and honor;
Truly, if you consider it well,
All honor, goodness, and generosity
Come from them and their virtue.
Their good deeds are sufficient
To defeat the evil-speakers.

(3461) If their goodness gives rise to envy,
He who slanders other people hurts himself;
He seems like one who out of foolishness
Blows powder onto a fire[422];
It often flies back in his own eyes.
Such arguments are well established
To defeat the evil-speakers.

(3468) Now it is time[423] that I set myself to bring my treatise to the goal.[424] It is time
to conclude, in order to stop arguing, reject debate and discord, nurture peace with concord,
and at all times live gladly. For so my book is intended, and that's the best way. It isn't good
at all to hold a lasting grudge; we should uphold the truth[425] and put falsehood behind. If
Truth[426] sits on the throne, and Reason[427] hears me, I have no cause to doubt that the trial
will go my way. For I will make a good closing, to comfort my ladies and encourage them
in joy.[428] You will soon hear a merry jest[429] with no dialogue at all[430]; Gladness will speak
unopposed and will show the proven facts, through examples and metaphors from the stories
of the Scriptures since the world began, from the time of Adam long ago.

[Lady Gladness makes her final argument.]

(3496) And to silence the men, and put a clear end to the debate, my Lady Gladness
argues and says that in the first place, it is true what Mahieu has said and told: that women
have overcome the greatest men in the world[431] by their actions. The point on which she
bases her case — Mahieu's confession — is much to the advantage of women; so she says[432]
in her rhymes. By his own argument, Mahieu must completely lose the contest, as you can
clearly see. For since he has said that women are dominant over men, and that ladies sub-
jugated through their excesses the strongest, most powerful, and wisest men, among them
Samson the strong,[433] King David and Solomon, and the philosopher Aristotle, he has to
sing a different tune.[434] For he doesn't know how to find any further reason to accuse my
ladies, truth to tell. Therefore he has failed to make his case through his libelous little
book.[435] We will declare the glory of our ladies: of their feats, of their good deeds, and of
the bravery of females and their achievements, which are worthy to be told and should not
be hidden.

(3528) Surely, speaking of courage, my Lady Gladness argues that females are braver,
more valiant, and stronger than males ever were. We will prove this point now by Semiramis

the queen,[436] who was in her bedchamber dressing her hair. On one side it was braided and her hairstyle was finished, and on the other her hair was uncombed, when at that moment she was called by a messenger who came to tell her that her enemies were making war in many places of her realm and were ravaging her land, attacking and destroying, and killing and robbing her men. So to defend them, Semiramis dressed in a hurry without waiting any longer, took her helmet and sword, and armed herself very quickly; as a woman of great valor she rode out against them so that by courage and superior force, she defeated her enemies and defended her country well. Neither in Persia nor in Media could any male prevail against her.

(3558) The fame of Penthesilea[437] is as great and wide as the earth; we should always bring it to mind. She was very brave, to speak the truth; she was queen of the Amazons. With her there was a great company of ladies and girls, powerful in arms, good, and beautiful. In her desire to avenge Hector (who was very brave, a knight of noble fame), whom Achilles killed in battle, she came to help the Trojans without fearing death at all. Achilles had a son named Pyrrhus, very renowned in arms. The lady fought with him, often threw him from his horse, and made him fall down. She gained much honor for females at the siege before the city of Troy, for which they should rejoice.

(3580) Thamiris,[438] as we shall tell you, defeated the powerful King Cyrus. Cyrus was king of Babylonia; Thamiris made such trouble for him[439] and defended her country so well that she chopped off Cyrus's head. It is truly found in history[440] that she made him drink from a golden basin full of human blood; she pushed [his head] in with her hand and said, "Now drink your crime, and let your tyranny have its fill."

(3592) What did Lampito and Arsionne[441] do? The fame of Hippolyta and Deïphile[442] resounds everywhere, and the feats of noble Camilla.[443]

(3596) Hercules was strong of body — in his time there was no stronger man. He prevailed in a struggle with Cacus,[444] the giant, and put to flight Cerberus, the doorkeeper of hell, who feared neither steel nor iron. They say he did so many marvelous deeds that no man has ever done their equal, nor could he be defeated by a man of arms. But by a woman such a man was led,[445] so subdued and ordered around that he gave in, no matter what he had won by force of arms in battle. All women have great praise for that, for such brave deeds. All feats of arms and all bravery come from them and their courage; more than a thousand true examples of this are found in history, but it should be proof enough to cite the women I find right here.

(3618) And if it should happen that any fools want to argue about the arts, the praise for learning belongs to females, I dare well say; I can prove that woman is more intelligent. For Carmentis[446] invented the letters we write with, all the twenty-five symbols with which you can write in Latin, in French, on tablets, on wax, on paper, or on parchment; Carmentis found the way.[447] She gave its own name to each one; she deserves great fame for her intelligence.

(3632) The nine muses[448] of the arts of knowledge and of rhetoric have joy at heart under their breasts, for they bear the names of women. Medea's great learning[449] ought to be well praised; she was marvelously wise; in her time she had no equal. She was mistress of all seven arts and praised as a goddess.

(3642) The woman who told the secrets of Virgil[450] was worth a thousand men; she was so effective in declaring them that she revealed to us the Christian faith.[451]

(3646) Sappho[452] made Sapphic poems that are clear and truthful. You males have your poets who made myths of false prophets.

(3650) To speak truly, Pallas is quite sufficient for the female side. For she is the goddess of wisdom,[453] contains all knowledge, and defends the case for women.[454] So do Lady Philosophy, Grammar, Logic, Music, Arithmetic and Rhetoric, and Medicine and Astrology, and holy Theology. All bear the names of females[455]; this isn't news.

(3662) And Sibyl,[456] who truly foretold the coming of our Lord Jesus Christ, as we find it written, and Cassandra,[457] the daughter of King Priam, who announced the great ruin of Troy, the noble city, and told the truth of its terrible destruction — there should be note of these women with the other sibyls who were so wise. So help me God, King Jesus, the daughter of Croesus[458] was wise; in her cruel prophecy she told the fortune of her father the king, and how he would be hanged; he could not be saved from that.

(3680) I would tire myself out for nothing if I gave more examples of them. I cannot remember all the women who are worthy of fame, whom the rude speech of the envious man cannot harm or wickedly destroy; for they are wise and brave and virtuous in all their deeds. Males love pillage[459] and theft and robbery, murder and covetousness, and all that incites to evil. Females are gentle[460] in all matters and in all affairs. Horses, mules, deer and oxen, sheep and birds laying eggs love the nurturing of women, and they benefit from their care, more than they would from men. What females plant grows better than what man plants; this is well proved, I boast of it. Little branches, wine stocks, and herbs prove it; those who find it so bear witness.

(3704) Women pray for the injured and for those who are in sin; they kiss the altars of the churches and make peace with God through their efforts. Males don't care about church; when they go there, it's by chance. To dice, to gaming, and to ball games, to markets, to court, to brawls, and to brothels is their desire. If someone should say that Gladness lies, and that we shouldn't blame men, for they sail the sea and make castles on the earth, I am ready to answer this claim. If they find hard work and hardship there, it's because of the burning desire that drives them for excessive profit, which draws them to do this, and they are moved by greed, which is a very wicked vice in them.

(3724) Man is made of the slime of the earth, which is destructive to the female. Woman is called "virago" for the virtue of her heart. For woman is superior and has greater privilege for the place of her creation; I mentioned it above,[461] how woman was made long ago in the earthly paradise, and how God, the king of glory, made woman as a helper. The mad rage of men hurts them, their gluttony and sloth, and their lust. But each woman by her nature takes care to maintain the family well and support the household rightly. So they carry their child for nine months; they suffer in childbirth; great pain they have in childbirth; it's wrong to say otherwise.

(3746) Mothers care for their children and are kind to them, not cruel, and offer them food; they take care of the whole burden. They spin[462] both linen and wool; they are full of many great skills; each woman contrives so much to have thanks from the male. For their pleasure, they decorate tables, trestles, couches, and beds and do as much as they can so that they can please men.

(3758) Women do many good deeds for the deceased and the ill; they often cheer the sick and treat them kindly. Men love all the pleasures of life,[463] but a female prefers to spin[464] linen, wool, and flax to weave great cloths, and along with this they enjoy the work of pressing cheese from milk. They often drink water, but males drink wine from the tavern without coming up for air. God knows how each one of them behaves; some men go often to the woods to hunt wild beasts, and others follow idleness and lead a sinful life.[465] But women do their works skillfully; God knows if I lie. I call to witness Calabre of Paris, who with herbs or with plants, by resin or other skill, which she well knows how to practice, has made many a vagina small again and perked up the breasts,[466] to be more pleasing to men and to appease the jealous husbands.[467]

(3786) When Gladness names the good women of ancient Greece and Rome as the foundation of her argument, it should be counted much to her credit that she doesn't use flattery to seek advantage through deceitful talk; for you would find many women in France[468] who were worthy from their childhood. And if one puts forward the objection that Gladness, to make her case, names only the good women[469] and of the wicked makes no mention at all, she answers in her defense, to sustain her argument, that the males want to advance their gender, whether wrong or right. And to those who would object to that, I say to the contrary (please don't be offended), that neither in their little books nor in their myths, nor in their "facts" that are hard to verify, when they cite poetry and crazy stories, are they worthy of belief.[470] For in speaking of true history, they don't mention Catiline,[471] nor do they, by Saint Mathelin, the tyrant Dionysius or Emperor Nero or the cruel Siron[472] who greatly harmed the Maccabees, or Herod, who was no better, the traitor Rufinus[473] or other criminals, whose evil deeds were damnable.[474]

(3820) And we [men] don't talk about Antigone and Cleopatra, who was good,[475] Ruth, Rachel, Sarah, and Octavia, the noble Lucretia and Miriam, and Julia, wife of Pompey, and Portia, married to Cato, Susanna, Judith, and Esther.[476] These women stood firm to achieve their noble fame and high rank by the deeds of a virtuous life.

(3830) I said much about it earlier; he is mad who slanders other people. You say that women are fickle, empty-headed, false, and gullible, but God knows it's otherwise; their love endures firmly and faithfully and chastely. In males there is treachery, for they always seduce women; the blame should turn on them. By tricks and by bribes, they take from girls their virginity and from wives their fidelity; they grant themselves pardons for it, for they don't think they're doing wrong. They often break up a couple. You see few pretty women solicit men for immoral acts,[477] but by pleading or by threats, men catch in their traps[478] the unwary females, who are often deceived by them. There is no faith and no constancy in the male to keep and guard his promise to the female; for their nature is such that when they wickedly deceive them, they think they've done what they ought. More than a thousand married women, faithful and unchanging, keep faith with their husbands; each one is faithful to her own, without wrongdoing and without deserving blame. But no man is faithful to his wife.[479]

(3859) There are countless women who, after their husbands die, guard themselves honorably and devoutly and chastely; and that's just as good as virginity,[480] even if they've had children. But there is no man,[481] when his wife has died, who holds back from the game of love, for he takes pleasure with women, day and night, with his loins. And if the deeds of women are damned by poets and condemned by males in any way, and if they falsely tell them that this is to their shame and dishonor, women know well what this amounts to, for no man blames their gender as long as he can get his John Thomas up.[482] He maligns them nowhere, but tries hard to make peace, and praises, serves, and honors them. He is wise who works at this, and devotes himself to serving them well, to deserve their peace and favor.

(3888) What sin are women guilty of? If Solomon was subdued by the power of women's beauty, great praise belongs to women that such a wise man was overcome by their intelligence and their goodness. The wildness that abounds in men makes them go mad in this world with passion and with lechery. Just like the wolf in the sheepfold, he will devour them all if he can; he will not spare a single sheep, even though he would have enough with one to satisfy his hunger. So the males in their wickedness can't satisfy their lust; they want to disgrace all females with their strength. When they can't have their fun with them, they won't shut up with their slander.

(3908) If Aristotle, who was a great scholar, couldn't ever be so wise that he didn't fall into the traps of women,[483] not for the harm that he saw there; if Virgil also,[484] who was wise, was placed in servitude by love; and Achilles by Polyxena, who was beautiful like Helen, was so ravished that he died of it; if Hercules or Samson the strong was overcome by women, in vain they have argued with themselves, those who keep on slandering women, for they are at all times worthy of love. In women there is no guilt at all, but they are right to despise[485] every man who disparages them, since the bravest and wisest of men were caught by women. I see not one woman who wounds her lover or rapes him[486]; neither net nor spider web nor traps do they set out to catch them; and so they can't defend their case against them, nor should they try.[487] If they had considered rightly, they never would have slandered women, or defamed them in their malice; for they are health and life to males, to comfort them and keep them company.

(3938) And so it seems to be the depravity of males, if they act sinfully because of female beauty and can't bring themselves to keep their behavior in line and control their tongues and restrain themselves through reason, in order to guard and maintain their constancy, which is very weak because of lust, which drives them mad.

[Jehan Le Fèvre's farewell to the reader.]

(3948) My ladies, I ask you humbly, if I have pleaded your case weakly through my ignorance,[488] use here your strength to make up for my defects and publish your honor, that all may know of it. Males will not have power over you when this poem is read to them. And so that it will be accepted, state your opinion clearly to prove your case, and be ready to defend it if any man objects to it; deny the claims of the opposing side. There is not a judge from here to Persia who would dare to condemn you.

(3965) Truth knows well if I'm lying, but will be difficult to find, and this debate to be resolved. Please advocate for me, or I can truly say and promise that I will never have a day of gladness, but will remain in sadness, which will prey on my weary body, if I have to pay the expenses.[489] Have mercy, mercy on poor Smith,[490] who suffers a greater thirst on his lip than did the rich man in hell[491]; for he doesn't know how to work on iron, but his effort is all on parchment.[492] He has made this book for you, for he well knows that to all males who carry both purses and sacks,[493] you are comfort, joy, and rest. So here I shall end my treatise until someone wiser[494] comes along who may carry on this subject. I believe that it will never be concluded or resolved[495]; for worldly love is corrupt and avarice is too deep.[496] I will say more of it another time; I commend you to God and take my leave.[497]

Notes

1. (2) For the "apology to women" in *RR* and the medieval *querelle des femmes*, see Mann, *Apologies to Women*, especially 23–25, where she argues that this passage in *LL* is ironic.

2. (7–9) A topos apparently intended to deny responsibility for the translated material, especially for literary attacks on women; see parallel passages in Jean de Meun's *RR* 15184–15212, Chaucer's *LGW* F369–72, and Le Fèvre's *L* 2.1541–49, 1559–68. Pratt believes the excuse to be "amusingly disingenuous and reminiscent of the irony of [Le Fèvre's] favorite author," Jean de Meun: "Translating Misogamy," 425.

3. (9) Le Fèvre refers to the Latin *Lamentations* of Mahieu of Boulogne, which he had already translated as *L*, the companion poem to *LL*; on the Latin *Lamentations*, see introduction (nn. 1, 16, and 17).

4. (21ff.) See Ovid, *Rem. am.* 46; these lines may also allude to the doctrine of contraries and its relevance to the art of love in *RR* 21573–82. Pratt ("Strains of Defense," 119) believes this statement undercuts the apparent seriousness of his apology to women in the preceding lines, making *LL* "simply a rhetorical exercise." Helen Swift notes how Le Fèvre "appropriated" this material for "his own, self-publicizing purposes" (*Gender, Writing, and Performance*, 149 n. 154). Le Fèvre may be alluding to the classical/medieval rhetorical exercise "disputatio ad utramque partem" (arguing both sides of the case). For more on this tradition and its relation to the medieval debate on women, see the introduction (n. 102).

5. (31) Book of Gladness] "Livre de Leesce": Le Fevre provides a conventional announcement of the title of his work; for this and other examples see Jacqueline Cerquiglini-Toulet, *A New History of Medieval French Literature*, trans. Sara Preisig (Baltimore: Johns Hopkins University Press, 2011); 48–49. Leesce/Gladness is a female personification derived from *RR* 728, 830, 10425. She embodies happiness of every kind, both worldly and spiritual; see n. 15 to the translation. For more on the source of this character and my English translation of the word, see introduction (nn. 60–61). According to Thundy ("Matheolus, Chaucer, and the Wife of Bath," 45), "The [Wife of Bath's] name *Alys* bears a strong resemblance to Le Fèvre's Dame Leësce, the articulate defender of women and marriage."

6. (33) to give pleasure] "complaire": Wordplay on the beneficent association between *leesce, plaisir*, and the rightful praise of women. Le Fèvre also alludes to the famous Horatian dictum that poetry should be pleasurable (*dulce*) as well as instructive (*utile*); see Horace, *Ars poetica, www.thelatinlibrary.com/horace/arspoet.shtml* 343; *Norton Anthology of Theory and Criticism*, ed. Leitch et al., 132. In the prologue to his *La vieille*, he translated the duality as *proufiter* and *delecter*: see the transcription by Badel, *Le roman de la Rose au XIV siècle*, 181.

7. (34) by making the contrary argument] "Par argument de sens contraire": Le Fèvre explains that the sequel to his translation of the misogynistic *Lamentations* will be a *livre* defending women; for the possible allusion to the *disputatio ad utramque partem*, see n. 4 above.

8. (41–42) clear ... explained] "apperte ... descouverte": As noted by Blumenfeld-Kosinski, in "Jean le Fèvre's *Livre de Leësce*," 714, "Jean's rhyme, effectively using two synonyms for 'open,' rejects the need of uncovering a hidden truth by proposing a sense that is open from the very beginning." That is, Le Fèvre's defense of women will be devoid of allegorical obscurity.

9. (43–80) Of this introductory section, Blumenfeld-Kosinski ("Jean le Fèvre's *Livre de Leësce*," 716) notes that "the word 'verite' appears no fewer than six times in the space of thirty-seven lines. It is 'verité' that will be Jean's 'amie'; she will inform the text. The opposition of authentic (here represented by the Bible) and inauthentic (represented by myth) discourse — divided up by gender in this passage — will provide the ideological underpinning of the entire text." This reading introduces Blumenfeld-Kosinski's argument that *LL* is a serious and mostly successful defense of women.

10. (45–51) Alithia ("Truth," a Christian shepherdess) and Pseustis ("Falsehood," a pagan shepherd) debated theology in *Ecloga Theoduli*, which Le Fèvre translated as his earliest work; see the introduction (n. 35). Pseustis played the flute and Alithia the zither. The winner of the debate, judged by Fronesis (Intelligence), would be awarded the loser's instrument. Not surprisingly, Alithia won the contest. The *Ecloga* was a popular textbook throughout the Middle Ages and well into the sixteenth century. Blumenfeld-Kosinski ("Jean le Fèvre's *Livre de Leësce*," 716) argues that "Jean's [Le Fèvre's] portrayal of Alithie recalls that of eloquent female saints like Catherine of Alexandria, who appears later on in the *Leësce* [2825ff.]. Women, Jean shows us, can be the representatives of inspired true discourse." Always skeptical of Le Fèvre's motives, Pratt ("Strains of Defense," 121) notes that Alithia quotes "misogynistic exempla from the Bible" in her debate with Pseustis.

11. (58–67) "The Tale of King, Wine, Woman, and Truth" is found in the apocryphal 3 Esdras 3–4. According to the source, three courtiers argued which was strongest, king, wine, or woman. For more on this story as a medieval profeminine exemplum, see Linda Barney Burke, "The Sources and Significance of 'The Tale of King, Wine, Woman, and Truth' in John Gower's *Confessio amantis*," *Greyfriar: Siena Studies in Literature* 21 (1980): 3–15, and Blamires, *Case*, 55–57.

12. (64) who posed as a prophet] "qui fist le devin": Le Fèvre's summary of the story is a little confused here. In 3 Esdras, the prophet Zerubbabel was the third courtier to speak. After explaining that woman is stronger than wine or king, he ended by affirming that truth is stronger than all three. In Le Fèvre's version, three anonymous prophets speak the first three answers, while Zerubbabel correctly responds that truth is the strongest of all. It is unclear why Le Fèvre refers to the third speaker in such a disparaging manner. Given Le Fèvre's consistent association of the profeminine cause with truth (see the introduction n. 80) and translation (n. 9), there is grounds for questioning Pratt's contention that the exemplum ends with "a joke against women" ("Strains of Defense," 122).

13. (66) their group] "leurs sortes": Van Hamel believes that "leurs" (their) refers to women. I think it more naturally refers to the courtiers who answered incorrectly.

14. (69–74) This saying is not found in the works of Aristotle. Van Hamel (2: 235) attributes it to the *Vie d'Aristote* of Ammonius, known to the Middle Ages from the Latin translation of Nunnesius.

15. (81–85) Solomon, putative author of the biblical wisdom books Proverbs, Ecclesiastes, the Song of Songs, and the deuterocanonical Wisdom. Le Fèvre may be alluding to Eccl. 2:24, 3:22, or Proverbs 3:20. I believe the most important source for the passage is Eccl. 2:26, where the author praises "laetitia," ancestor of

French "leesce," as God's reward for virtuous living; see the introduction (nn. 60–61), and also lines 84, 2667, 3378, 3487, and nn. 16, 329, 414, and 428 below.

16. (84) glad] "lié," adjectival form of "leesce," and a clear allusion to the godly "laetitia" of Eccl. 2:26. For discussion of the biblical "laetitia" and its relationship to the title character of the poem, see n. 15, above.

17. (86) in the rain] "et pluie": I have translated somewhat freely for the sake of clarity.

18. (87–91) Le Fèvre will keep his promise to abridge the material he quotes and/or summarizes from *L*. The success of this practice, however, is questionable. In many cases, the recycled material is so drastically abridged that it makes no sense without reference to the source passage in *L* or the detailed set of notes provided in this volume; see introduction (n. 8).

19. (92) Mahieu or Matheus of Boulogne, author of the misogynistic Latin *Lamentations* (1290 or 1291), which Le Fèvre translated into French as the companion poem to *LL*; see the introduction. Mahieu himself (Latin *Lamentations* 20) informs us that he achieved the academic rank "magister." On Mahieu's education in logic and law at Orléans, see *Matheus von Boulogne*, ed. Schmitt, 14–15. At this line, Le Fèvre begins his direct response to the earlier poem (usually expressed through the persona of Lady Gladness) by alternating quotations from *L* with profeminine responses. This "point-counterpoint" format will continue until 3468, when Le Fèvre (with the help of Lady Gladness) begins his closing argument.

20. (93) Mathieu's marriage to a widow rendered him "bigamous" even though he was married only once; on Mahieu's disastrous marriage and the medieval understanding of "bigamy," see the introduction.

21. (94) See *L* 1.104.

22. (95) See *L* 1.154.

23. (98) laughingstock] "bon homme de neige," literally "a snowman." I have translated this phrase according to the context. Geneviève Hasenohr defines this expression, not attested elsewhere, as "perdre tout son crédit, toute son autorité": "La locution verbale figurée dans l'oeuvre de Jean Le Fèvre," in *La locution: Actes du Colloque International Université McGill, Montréal, 15–16 octobre 1984*, Moyen Français 14–15, ed. Giuseppe di Stefano and Russell G. McGillivray (Montréal: Ceres, 1984), 254. She notes other examples of "neige" referring to something useless or contemptible.

24. (101) For the decretal of Pope Gregory X against clerical "bigamy" and its ruinous effect on the career path of Mahieu of Boulogne, see Van Hamel, 2: cxii–cxvii, and *Matheus von Boulogne*, ed. Schmitt, 13–18.

25. (105) He had tied the knot too tightly] "Trop se lya de fors lyens," literally "he had bound himself too much in a strong bond," i.e., marriage. For similar play on "bond" and "ybounde" referring to marriage, see Chaucer's *MercT* 1260–61, 1285. Without citing this passage, Hasenohr ("La locution," 251) gives examples of wordplay on "lien" in *L* and its relation to "droit féodale."

26. (106–21) The moral to be drawn from this passage is just as confusing in *LL* as it is in the original passage from *L* 1.388–462 and its ultimate source, the Latin *Lamentations* 153–78. At *L* 1.389–417 and line 113 below, Le Fèvre (following Mahieu) describes polygamy in respectful terms by noting the Old Testament worthies who practiced it. At *L* 1.407–14, Le Fèvre explicitly envies them their freedom to engage in plural marriage under "la foy ancienne" (1.417). Without any kind of transition, he shifts to excoriating bigamy by slurring the biblical Lamech (see Genesis 4:19) as "le premier bigame" (*L* 1. 419; line 118 below) and lamenting the wickedness and misery of bigamy both ancient and modern. The source of the confusion is to be found in Jerome's *Against Jovinian*, to which Mathieu gives credit (Latin *Lamentations* 176, corresponding to *L* 1.45) as the source for his rambling and contradictory discussion of Old Testament bigamy; see lines 115–21 and n. 29 below.

27. (107) See *L* 1.396ff.; from Gen. 29:15–30.

28. (109–10) See 1 Sam. 1:2.

29. (115–21) See *L* 1.419ff.; from Gen. 4:19. Jerome excoriated the "first bigamist" Lamech as worse than a murderer: "Lamech, a man of blood and a murderer, was the first who divided one flesh between two wives. Fratricide and digamy were abolished by the same punishment — that of the deluge. The one was avenged seven times, the other seventy times seven. The guilt is as widely different as are the numbers." See *Against Jovinianus*, 1.14, trans. Fremantle, 358. With no attempt at consistency, Jerome notes several times that the bigamy of other Old Testament figures was justified by the law of their day, including the commandment to "be fruitful and multiply"; see especially *ibid.*, 1.24, trans. Fremantle, 363, 364.. The Wife of Bath notes this inconsistency in her defense of remarriage for widows; she prefers to honor the polygamous patriarch Jacob (as did Jerome) rather than censure the example of Lamech (as also did Jerome): see *WBPro* 53–58.

30. (136) For Pratt, this line "appears to be an interjection by LeFèvre, referring not unsympathetically to the archmisogynist" ("Strains of Defense," 122).

31. (139) See Latin *Lamentations* 4618 and *L* 1.147.

32. (141) As explained by Schmitt, *Matheus von Boulogne*, 16, Mathieu had actually taken part in the Second Council of Lyon at which "bigamous" clerics were condemned to be laicized. Citing Latin *Lamentations* 3917, Schmitt believes that Mathieu was hoping for a dispensation allowing him to keep his benefice after his marriage, a common practice before the crackdown by Pope Gregory X.

33. (142) This term refers to Gratian's *Decretum*, a textbook of canon law divided into "books" and *distinctiones* or chapters.

34. (153) See *L* 1.497–99.

35. (155) See *L* 1.489ff.

36. (161) It's too late to cover your ass when the fart is out] "Tart main a cul, quant pet est hors": See *L* 2.392. Van Hamel notes the same proverb quoted in *Li proverbe au vilain: Die Sprichwörter des gemeinen Mannes*, ed. Adolf Tobler (Leipzig: S. Hirzel, 1890), 90. Le Fèvre introduced this pungent saying into his *L*; it does not appear in the corresponding passage of Mahieu's *Lamentations*.

37. (162) This saying is quite obscene] "Cils proverbes est assés ors": Like Jean de Meun's Lady Reason, Lady Gladness appears to endorse plain speaking. Le Fèvre (and his fictional persona) clearly believed that "parler proprement" on such matters was justified if used with a moral purpose, in this case to discredit the misogyny and misogamy of Mahieu: see the introduction (nn. 76–78) and lines 1023, 2707ff., and 3782, and nn. 144, 332, and 466 below.

38. (167–214) The physical description of Perrenelle follows closely its counterpart in *L* 1.573–622.

39. (219ff.) See *L* 1.655ff. These lines suggest that Mahieu's extreme passion naturally led to his equally extreme disillusionment.

40. (229) they have no bearing on the present case] "ils n'ont point lieu ou cas present": Hasenohr ("La locution," 260) defines this phrase as "s'agissant d'arguments, être pertinents, probants, recevables"; also see line 776 and n. 107 below.

41. (238) Noah, his wife, their three sons, and their wives: Gen. 7:7 and 1 Pet. 3:20.

42. (241) Possibly the Noahide laws of Gen. 9:1–7, which — appropriately for Le Fèvre's purposes — begin and end with the commandment to "be fruitful and multiply." Of course, he may also be referring to the law given to Moses at Mt. Sinai.

43. (243) in reason] "en raison": I have emended the "sans" of Van Hamel's text to the "en" of MS K for better sense.

44. (250) David was bigamous in the modern sense — he was married to more than one woman concurrently (1 Sam. 25:43; 2 Sam. 12:8). However, Le Fèvre focuses exclusively on David's "bigamous" marriage in the patristic/medieval sense, to the widowed Bathsheba, whose husband, Uriah, he had set up to be killed in battle: 2 Sam. 11:2–12:24. The case of David and Bathsheba was a staple of the medieval debate on women: see Blamires, *Woman Defamed*, 8, 15, 32–33, 75, 95–96, 101, 105–6, 116, 267.

45. (264) The prophet Nathan condemned David, not Bathsheba, for adultery and the murder of Uriah: 2 Sam. 12:7. For discussion, see the introduction (nn. 86–89); also see lines 1539ff. and n. 201 below.

46. (267ff.): Le Fèvre's catalog of his "bigamous" contemporaries helps us date the poem. They are identified and discussed in Van Hamel, 2: clxxixff., and by Hasenohr, *Le respit de la mort* (with corrections to Van Hamel's account), xxix–xxx, xl–xliv. Of course, none of these people are "bigamous" in the modern sense — rather, they married widows and/or remarried after the death of a spouse. Le Fèvre's appeal to contemporary real-world experience anticipates Christine's; see the introduction (n. 94). By defending "bigamy," Le Fèvre is also attacking misogyny. These two themes were inseparable in the Middle Ages — see Jerome's *Against Jovinianus*, esp. 1.14 (trans. Fremantle, 358–59), and Chaucer, *WBPro*, esp. 9–94, for examples of misogyny linked with the denigration of widows and propaganda against marriage and especially remarriage.

47. (267) Charles II de Valois, younger brother of Philip VI; he died at Crécy in 1346. He was married for the first time to Jeanne, countess of Joigny. After her death he married a widow, the countess of Estampes (line 269). See *Le respit de la mort*, ed. Hasenohr, xli.

48. (269) Identified by Hasenohr (*Le respit de la mort*, xli) as Marie d'Espagne, daughter of Ferdinand II of Spain and widow of Charles d'Évreux.

49. (269) Counselor at Parliament who married Marote du Bois, daughter of the king's secretary Guillaume du Bois, between 1355 and 1357. He died sometime after 19 March 1379. See *Le respit de la mort*, ed. Hasenohr, xlii.

50. (287) Became fourth president of Parliament on 12 November 1373. He was married for the third time (date unknown) to Marote du Bois, the widow of Anceau Choquart. See *Le respit de la mort*, ed. Hasenohr, xli.

51. (291–97) Lawyer at Parliament and first husband of Jeanne de Dormans, daughter of *chancelier* Guillaume de Dormans. After his death, she became the second wife of Philibert Paillart, who became president of Parliament in 1370. Paillart's first wife was also a widow. See *Le respit de la mort*, ed. Hasenohr, xlii–xliii.

52. (303–8) the [following] two] "ces deux": This description introduces the following lines (on Guillaume de Sens and Pierre de Mainville).

53. (309) Became fifth president of Parliament on 3 February 1380. As explained by Hasenohr (*Le respit de la mort*, liii), the date of *LL* cannot be earlier than this. His first wife, Eude de la Pis d'Oe, must have been a widow when he married her, although the identity of her first husband is unknown. See Hasenohr, xliii–xliv, where she argues that Van Hamel (2: clxxxi) confused Guillaume de Sens with Guillaume de Séris, who became first president in 1371 and died in 1373.

54. (314) Also spelled Pierre de Demeville; became second president of Parliament in 1345 and first president in 1369. He died between 13 July 1370 and 22 March 1371. The identity of his first wife is unknown. He was married for the second time to Idoine de Lisle, who was already three times a widow, her first two husbands

having died at Crécy and Poitiers. His third wife was Perrenelle de Croÿ; see *Le respit de la mort*, ed. Hasenohr, xxix–xxx.

55. (325) Le Fèvre is evidently referring to Mahieu's colleagues who shared his "bigamous" status, the "quam plures" of the Latin *Lamentations* 3920.

56. (345–47) Le Fèvre speaks as a lawyer here. Van Hamel (2: 237) cites the *Digest of Justinian* XXVIII, 1 § 20: "Ne furiosus quidem testis adhiberi potest" (Nor can an angry man be called as a witness).

57. (349) Mahieu defended their case] "Mahieu sustenoit leur partie": Hasenohr ("La locution," 260) explains this expression as "prendre la défense de q[uelqu'u]n, metaphore empruntée de la pratique juridique." Cf. 3654.

58. (351) See *L* 1.647ff.

59. (375–77) Compare *RR* 16592–94. Contra Jean de Meun, Le Fèvre gives credit to wives for providing these amenities (shoes and clothing) to their husbands rather than vice versa. There is an echo of Prov. 31:10–31, a major source for the topos of the wife whose domestic industry brings honor to her husband.

60. (385–89) See *L* 1.659. The famous comparison of woman to a snake in the grass is probably borrowed from *RR* 16502–86. It derives from Virgil, *Bucolics* 3.92–93. Christine would vehemently protest the comparison: "June/July 1401: Christine's Reaction to Jean de Montreuil's Treatise on the *Roman de la Rose*," McWebb, *Debating the* Roman de la Rose, 124, 125.

61. (390ff.) See *L* 1.692ff.

62. (403ff.) See *L* 1.673ff.

63. (419ff.) A digression on the four seasons, the four elements, and the exemplary diligence of the ant. According to Van Hamel (2: cxciv–cxcv), Le Fèvre may be imitating the digressive, encyclopedic style of Jean de Meun's *RR*. He had inserted a longer digression, discussing several of the same subjects, into *Le respit de la mort* 726–2884.

64. (447ff.) The industrious character of the ant was a medieval commonplace. Van Hamel (2: 237) provides a list of analogues in his note on the passage. Le Fèvre had earlier treated this subject as an example that university students should take to heart: *Le respit de la mort* 2563–66.

65. (462) as for me] "pour my": This translation is suggested by Van Hamel (2: 237), who claims that "pour my" means "pour moi." The unusual expression is used for the sake of rhyme. Le Fèvre is probably referring to his poverty, as he did recurrently; see the introduction (n. 31).

66. (487) Le Fèvre returns to his main theme, his response to Mahieu's complaint against Perrenelle.

67. (499–502) See *L* 1.681–84.

68. (517–18) See line 1023 and n. 144 below.

69. (519ff.) See *L* 1.733ff. For the wife as a striking clock, see also line 687 and n. 94 below.

70. (525ff.) See *L* 1.767–68.

71. (531ff.) and truly, so it is] See *L* 1.771ff. Le Fèvre changes the indirect discourse of the source passage in *L* to a statement of fact in order to support his defense of women. According to Pratt, Le Fèvre undercuts the "veracity claim" of this line with "verbs indicating that it is *women's opinion* he is reproducing" ("Strains of Defense," 125). For a contrasting view on Le Fèvre's appeal to "verité," see n. 9 above and Blumenfeld-Kosinski, "Jean le Fèvre's *Livre de Leësce*," 716.

72. (534) Women's affinity for textile production is an ancient topos used both to put them in their place and to praise their intelligence and industry; for examples, see Blamires, *Woman Defamed*, 294 n. 46.

73. (550) but] I have emended the "et" of Van Hamel's edition to the more appropriate "mais" from the corresponding line from *L*, 1.798.

74. (565–68) So it's no great wonder ...] The same line is found at *L* 1.829; Le Fèvre changes his source by describing the wife's anger as justified by the laziness of the husband.

75. (586) See *L* 1.834.

76. (592ff.) See *L* 1.838, 1.843ff.

77. (593–667) And that she misleads the man to five goals] "Et qu'a cinq metes maine l'homme": This passage is awkwardly condensed from *L* 1.843ff., where Le Fèvre awkwardly translates Mahieu's untranslatable wordplay on the locution "ducor ad metam," meaning "I am utterly deceived; I am led to extreme sophistry; I am led to the goal." The first of these meanings is discussed in Hasenohr, "La locution," 265. Following Mahieu's Latin *Lamentations*, Le Fèvre claims that women lead men to their goals (*methes*/Latin *metas*) through five kinds of sophism: of the *la langue* (the tongue), *la veüe* (the sight), *touchier* (touch), *faulx* (falsehood), and *iniquité* (iniquity), also called *cuidier* ([false] belief). Originating in the Latin *Lamentations*, this discussion of Aristotle's five types of sophism and their goals is roughly based on Aristotle's *Elenchi* 1.3, which was known to Mahieu (and thereby Le Fèvre) from Boethius's Latin translation of the work. Boethius uses the term "fines," not "metae": see the passage quoted from *PL* 64, col. 1009, by Alfred Schmitt, *Matheus von Boulogne*, 64 n. 378. The modern edition of Boethius's *Elenchi* is *Sophistical Refutations*, in *Aristoteles Latinus*, ed. L. Minio-Paluello et al. (Bruges: Desclee de Brouwer, later Leiden: Brill, 1961–75), 6: 1–3, 5–60. For more on Boethius's translations of Aristotle, see Stan Ebbesen, "The Aristotelian Commentator," in *The Cambridge Companion to Boethius*, ed. John Marenbon (Cambridge: Cambridge University Press, 2009), 34–36, and John Magee and John Marenbon, "Appendix:

Boethius' Works," in ibid., 304–5. For the reason why Mahieu changed the "fines" of Boethius to the synonym "metae," see n. 90 below. For other examples of word play on "mener a methe," see lines 1137 and 3469.

78. (594) Here is how he names them [the goals] by their fallacies] Somewhat confusingly, the "methe" (goal) *to* which a wicked woman leads a man is also the fallacy or sophism *by* which she leads him. Van Hamel (2: lxxii) explains the five fallacies/goals as "bornes de sophisterie."

79. (598) iniquity] "iniquité": at line 653, Le Fèvre calls this type of sophism by its other name, "cuidier" ([false] belief).

80. (600) See *L* I.850ff., translated by Pratt in Blamires, *Woman Defamed*, 179–80. When Guyon accused his wife of adultery upon catching her in the act, she accused him of merely imagining things in order to have her killed. Using *redargutio*, the sophism of the tongue (see Latin *Lamentations* 378), she convinced him of her innocence against the evidence of his own eyes. A similar tale is found in Marie de France, *Fables*, ed. and trans. Harriet Spiegel (Toronto: University of Toronto Press, 1987), 136–39.

81. (607ff.) See *L* I.903ff. The longer version in *L* explains that Sebille used the sophism of the sight on her husband Werry by persuading him that his eyes had deceived him when he caught her in the act of adultery: for the story, see n. 82 below. Van Hamel (2: 151) cites four sources/analogues, none very similar to Mahieu's version. For other examples of adulterous wives who persuaded their husbands to doubt the evidence of their own eyes, see "The Merchant's Tale and Its Analogues," in *The Literary Context of Chaucer's Fabliaux: Texts and Translations*, ed. Larry D. Benson and Theodore M. Andersson (New York: Bobbs-Merrill, 1971), 203–73.

82. (615ff.) This passage is an abridgement of *L* I.920–66, which tells the ending of the story of Werry and Sebille. After Sebille denied her guilt, the disconsolate Werry went outside to plow a field. There he was met by Baucis, a neighbor woman in alliance with Sebille. As she conversed with him, she spun red wool on her distaff. When Werry turned around to plow a new furrow, she switched the red wool to the white that she had hidden under her girdle. When the wool appeared to change color, he doubted the evidence of his own eyes. Then she told Werry that he had two heads. He touched his head to prove that her statement was untrue, and she replied that people sometimes see things that aren't really there. With the help of Baucis, Sebille persuaded her husband that she was innocent of adultery, even though he had just seen her in the act.

83. (617) In this retelling, Baucis did Werry a favor by relieving his pangs of jealousy even though his wife was actually guilty of adultery.

84. (621ff.) See *L* I.973ff. Framery was deceived through the sophism of the touch when he felt his wife's lover hiding under their bed in the dark of night. Using her quick wits, the wife let her lover escape and substituted the family donkey, which her husband struck and killed. Van Hamel (2: 151) cites two analogues; in currently available editions they are the fabliau of Garin, *Recueil général et complet des fabliaux des XII et XIV siècles*, ed. Anatole de Montaiglon and Gaston Reynaud (1872–90; rpt. Geneva: Slatkine, 1973), 5: 132ff., and chap. 61 in Judith Bruskin Diner, trans., *The One Hundred New Tales (Les cent nouvelles nouvelles)* (New York: Garland, 1990), 230–33.

85. (635ff.) See *L* I.1013ff. The anonymous husband of this example was persuaded through the sophism of falsehood, i.e., his wife's insidious speech, that the moon was a sheet of vellum.

86. (646ff.) See *L* I.1043ff. Solomon was deceived through the sophism of belief. For Solomon's wives and their bad influence on his religious practice, see 1 Kings 1:4–10. Like other medieval misogynists, Mahieu (and his translator Le Fèvre) routinely quote the Bible in their attacks on women and marriage; for an overview of this practice with selected readings, see Blamires, *Woman Defamed*, 31–36. For the example of Solomon in the medieval defense of women, see lines 847ff. and n. 115 below.

87. (648ff.) See *L* I.1043ff.

88. (653) See n. 79 above. "Cuidier" (belief) is another name for the "goal" of "iniquité" (iniquity).

89. (660ff.) See *L* I.1079ff. Pratt identifies the source of this story as Henri d'Andeli's *Le lai d'Aristote*: see Blamires, *Woman Defamed*, 180 n. 102. For more on the topos of "the mounted Aristotle" with sample MS illuminations, see Smith, *Power of Women*, 66–102. For the origin of the story, see ibid., 67–68. She identifies the standard edition of *Le lai* as *Henri d'Andely: Le lai d'Aristote*, ed. Maurice Delbouille (Paris: Les Belles Lettres, 1951).

90. (664) the master of the goals] "des metes le maistre": This untranslatable pun is adopted from the "metarum quinque magistrum" (master of the five goals) as a description of Aristotle at Latin *Lamentations* 463. Now it is clear why Mahieu preferred "meta" to the "finis" of Boethius's Latin; "meta" can mean not only "goal" in a general sense but "goal post in a horse race," just right for the topos of Aristotle mounted like a horse. I am indebted to Lee F. Sherry (personal communication) for explaining the pun.

91. (668) four frivolous stories] "truffes": Apparently a reference to the dubious *fabliau*-like exempla retold in lines 593ff. to explain the five "goals." The same stories are again referred to as "truffes" at 787. Christine scorned the misogyny of *L* as "trufferie" (scurrilous frivolity); see *La città delle dame*, ed. and trans. Richards and Caraffi, 42; and *Book of the City of Ladies*, trans. Richards, rev. ed., 4.

92. (671ff.) See *L* I.1167ff.

93. (681) See *L* I.1197ff.

94. (687) A reference to the woman's relentless vocalizing, like a tolling clock; see also line 519.

95. (689ff.) See *L* 1.1213ff.

96. (697ff.) See *L* 1.1231ff.

97. (711ff.) See *L* 1.1287ff.

98. (720ff.) See *L* 1.1307ff. Pratt ("Strains of Defense," 123) finds the "lascivious description using agricultural and hunting metaphors inappropriate for [Dame] Leesce (ll. 720–32)." It is also possible that Lady Gladness uses ribald language with a serious purpose, to ridicule the misogyny and misogamy of Mahieu.

99. (721–27) dig ... plow ... little garden] Double entendre for sexual activity. Hasenohr ("La locution," 254) notes the occurrence of this expression, "non attesté," at *L* 1.1308. It is included in her catalogue of "locutions" used by Le Fèvre for sexual intercourse when the subject of the locution is a man.

100. (736ff.) See *L* 1.1499, 1505.

101. (742ff.) I have lodged such a case against him] "J'ay contre lui meü tel plait": Van Hamel (2: cxcix) notes that here Le Fèvre uses the pretentious terminology of a lawyer pleading a case before a judge, whom he identifies at line 764 as Lady Reason. According to *LL*, the accusers in the case of "my ladies against the poets" are Le Fèvre, Gladness, and the slandered women, while Mahieu and his "dream team" (Jean de Meun and other great poets, 748–51) are the defendants. Hasenohr ("La locution," 260) notes that the expression is to be taken "au sens juridique."

102. (746) the opposing side is strong] "Et a forte partie a faire": Also a locution borrowed from legal proceedings: Hasenohr, "La locution," 260.

103. (748) See *RR* 10492, where the God of Love endorses the poetry of Gallus, Catullus, and Ovid, among others. (Jean de Meun evidently based this passage on Ovid, *Amores* 3.9, especially 62–64 — see Lecoy's note on the passage in *RR* [2:278–79]). Le Fèvre departed from *RR* by adding Juvenal, who would have been out of place in Jean de Meun's catalog of love poets but fits in well with Le Fèvre's list of misogynistic poets. For an annotated translation of the notorious misogynistic passages from Juvenal's Satire 6, see Blamires, *Woman Defamed*, 25–30. According to Pratt, it "is ironic that in appearing to criticize the great exponents of clerical misogyny Le Fèvre reminds us of a speech that flatters them" ("Analogy or Logic," 65).

104. (749–50) See *RR* 10536.

105. (751) who limped [*clochoit*] just as I do] Le Fèvre alludes to the tradition that Jean de Meun, surnamed "Clopinel" or "the Hobbler," was actually lame. On Le Fèvre's self-described disability and its relation to his authorial self-naming, see the introduction (n. 32).

106. (764) According to the trial metaphor introduced at line 742, Le Fèvre with the help of Lady Gladness has brought a case against Mahieu and his fellow "medsisants" for their slanders against women. Reason is their judge; in accordance with the context, I have capitalized Reason.

107. (776) his statement is irrelevant] "chose qui'il ait dit n'a lieu": See n. 40 above.

108. (801–9) The first of several times in *LL* that Le Fèvre will repeat the argument that it is illogical to blame all women for the sins of one or only a few; see also 1162ff., 1409–20. An important source for the topos, as Le Fèvre surely knew well, is none other than Ovid's *Ars amatoria* 3.9–10. See also notes 459, 469, and 479.

109. (808) it would be a faulty judgment] "la chose seroit mal partie": Hasenohr ("La locution," 272) notes how locutions with "mal parti(e)" refer to the bad outcome of a "lutte ... inégale."

110. (813) his other story] "une autre note": Hasenohr (ibid.,263) glosses "note" as "le mensonge, la tromperie," and the phrase as "raconter une autre histoire, une autre fable."

111. (815) Similar to line 3503 below. Both lines are derived from *L* 2.2632 ff., where Le Fèvre bases his misogynistic argument on the fact that women subdued the two wisest of men, Solomon and Aristotle; for a detailed study of the topos, see Smith, *Power of Woman, passim*.

112. (826ff.) See lines 3004–5 and n. 375 below.

113. (828) See Gen. 2:7.

114. (832–33) See Gen. 1:28. Lady Gladness is appropriately drawn to biblical passages endorsing marriage and procreation.

115. (847ff.) See n. 86 above. Le Fèvre anticipates the daring argument found in the "querelle de la Rose" (1400–1402) that Solomon's involvement with women did nothing to hurt his literary output and may have helped inspire him; see Pierre Col, "Reply to Christine de Pizan's and Jean Gerson's Treatises," McWebb *Debating the* Roman de la Rose, 314, 315, 318, 321, and discussion by Minnis, *Magister Amoris*, 247ff.

116. (850) He didn't want to be a sodomite!] "Si ne voult estre sodomite" : I have translated literally, but the line might also be rendered "he was no sodomite" or "he rejected sodomy." For the construction *vo[u]loir* plus the infinitive in Le Fèvre's Middle French and the problem with literal translation, see my Note on the French Text and Translation, above.

117. (858) The canonical Ecclesiastes and deuterocanonical books of Wisdom, both attributed to Solomon.

118. (859) Both should be capitalized as proper nouns. The "Parables of Solomon" (cf. *WBPro* 679) is Prov. 10:1–22:16 in the Vulgate, while "Proverbs" refers to the book as a whole, especially the portions that precede and follow the Parables.

119. (861) Song of Songs] "Cantiques": Biblical book (on the literal level an erotic poem) attributed to Solomon.

120. (881ff.) See *L* 1.1081ff. These works of Aristotle were known to the Middle Ages through translations by Boethius. On *Elenchi*, see n. 77 above. *Peri hermeneias* was also known as *De interpretatione*; for discussion of Boethius's translation and commentary on this work, see Ebbesen, "Aristotelian Commentator," 36–37. Lady Gladness argues that like Solomon, Aristotle wrote many great books in spite of— or even because of— his subjugation by women.

121. (902) despise] "faire la loupe": Hasenohr ("La locution," 267) notes this as an expression for "mocquerie, mépris, arrogance, domination/admiration." See line 3923 below.

122. (907–8) See *L* 1.1339–40.

123. (9100 purse] "bourse": double entendre for the testicles, especially appropriate given the belief that intercourse was the "debt" owed by spouses to each other; see 1 Cor. 7:3.

124. (910–11) See *L* 1.1350–51. The syntax is unclear owing to awkward condensation of the passage from *L*; the subject of "said" (*disoit*) must be Perrenelle, while the subject of "can't" (*ne puet*) must be Mahieu.

125. (914–15) See *L* 1.1361–62.

126. (918) See *L* 1.1373ff.

127. (921) The subject of the clause is the wet nurse who refused Mahieu's orders to get up and tend to the baby (*L* 1.1436ff.); Perrenelle sided with the wet nurse just to make her husband angry (1.1470ff.) Gladness resorts to sheer bravado in her dubious claim that the negligence of the wet nurse was justified. For more on the wet nurse story, see the introduction (n. 27).

128. (932) On other things than mere trifles] "A autres fais qu'a berbis tondre": literally "other things than sheering sheep." Hasenohr ("La locution," 243–44) identifies the expression as proverbial.

129. (939ff.) See *L* 2.27ff.

130. (946ff.) See *L* 2.67.

131. (948ff.) See *L* 2.68ff. As noted by Hasenohr (*Le respit de la mort*, 192–93, n. 2966–69), Le Fèvre had quoted the same proverb as an autobiographical complaint on his domestic life in that earlier poem; also see her introduction (lix–lx). Hasenohr identifies the immediate source as Innocent III, *De miseria humanae conditione*, ed. M. Maccarone (Lugano, 1955), 23 (17.1.17): "Tria sunt enim quae non sinunt hominem in domo permanere: fumus, stillicidium et mala uxor" (There are three things that make it impossible for a man to stay in his house: smoke, dropping moisture, and an evil wife) (translation mine). The ultimate source is Prov. 27:15–16, quoted (among other misogynistic passages from the books of Solomon) in *Against Jovinianus* 1.28 (trans. Fremantle, 367). The Wife of Bath quotes the same passage in the context of her riposte to a misogynistic husband: (*WBPro* 278–80).

132. (963–68) See *L* 2.98–104.

133. (968) for her nature is deeply ingrained] "Car son viés ploy a pris la heuse": literally "For the boot has taken its old crease." My translation was suggested by Karen Pratt in Blamires, *Woman Defamed*, 183 n. 114. For discussion, see Hasenohr, "La locution," 239.

134. (963–68) See *L* 2.98–104. Neither Van Hamel nor Schmitt (*Matheus von Boulogne*, 82 n. 46) provides a source for the anecdote.

135. (979) For this expression and others like it, see Hasenohr, "La locution," 247.

136. (981ff.) Another instance where Lady Gladness speaks as a lawyer making a case before a judge; cf. line 742 above.

137. (985) the time is suitable and right] "jai assés temps et saison": My translation was suggested by Hasenohr, "La locution," 250.

138. (986) See line 764 and n. 109 above. In both cases, I have capitalized Reason, who acts as judge of the case.

139. (992ff.) Van Hamel (2: 240) identifies the source of this passage as Gratian's *Decretum* pars 2 causa 11 quaestio 3.

140. (1009–11) See 2 Cor. 1:12.

141. (1012–13) See Job 16:19.

142. (1018) so bold with his biting words] "si hardi qu'il donne mors tel": Hasenohr ("La locution," 271) notes that the metaphor for hostile speech is timeless, although this exact expression "n'est pas attestée."

143. (1020) sharpen his lying tongue] "sa faulse langue aguisier": Hasenohr ("La locution," 258) notes "sa langue aguisier" as a common metaphor for speech communication.

144. (1023ff.) Van Hamel identifies this passage as a misinterpretation of Ps. 58:3 (Vulgate 57:4): "Abalienati sunt peccatores a vulva / erraverunt ab utero loquentes mendacium." (Sinners are estranged from the vulva; / they have wandered away from the womb, speaking lies.) (Translation mine.) This is one of four passages in *LL* that argue that every misogynist insults his own mother and thereby himself (517–18, 1017–36, 2775–77, 3013–14). Blamires notes how this is a topos of "the case for women" (*Case*, 38). According to the editor's note on the passage in *The New Oxford Annotated Bible*, 3rd ed., the psalmist is cursing his enemies by deriding them as evil from birth. He is not condemning misogyny, as Le Fèvre apparently believed. Le Fèvre's (mis)use of this explicit passage may anticipate the daring argument found in the "querelle de la Rose" that naming of the private parts, at least with good intentions, is justified by its practice in the Bible: see Pierre Col's "Reply to Christine de Pizan's

and Jean Gerson's Treatises," in McWebb, *Debating the* Roman de la Rose, 314, 315, 316, 319, and Jean Gerson's indignant reply: "Letter" of December 1402, ibid., 354, 355. In Solterer's view (*Master and Minerva*, 143), Le Fèvre's motivation is actually narcissistic: "Slandering women transgresses nature because it vilifies the masculine self generated from women."

145. (1026–27) If a creature forgets] "Ne souvient a la creature": My translation of these lines is based on the note by Van Hamel (2: 240), who explains that their sense is hypothetical.

146. (1032–33) This proverb is also found at *RR* 16502–3, where its import is misogynistic: a wife speaks these words to cajole her husband into the grave mistake of telling her his secret. This is one of many instances in *LL* where Le Fèvre quotes *RR* in a revisionist context sympathetic to women. For Helen Solterer, however, this passage merely proves that "Bad mouthing a woman is a form of self-torture that can be understood only in terms of a masculine self. Blaming *her* damages *him*" (*Master and Minerva*, 143).

147. (1037ff.) See *L* 2.177ff.

148. (1039ff.) Carfania, also known as Calphurnia. In his note to the corresponding passage at *L* 2.183ff., Van Hamel (2: 158) identifies the source of this passage as the *Digest* of Justinian, lex 1, § 5, Dig. de postulando (lib. 2.1). Christine alludes to the story (while softening the scurrilous detail): *Città delle dame*, ed. Caraffi and Richards, 92; *Book of the City of Ladies*, trans. Richards, rev. ed., 31.

149. (1040) Van Hamel (2: 158–59) explains that this racy detail actually originates with Le Fèvre, perhaps as an embellishment of Justinian's "inverecunde postulans" (immodestly pleading). For Le Fèvre's audacious practice of simply fabricating material under the guise of quoting authorities, and the retelling of this story by Martin Le Franc, see the introduction (n. 93). Le Franc's translator Steven Millen Taylor describes a woodcut based on this scene in an early printed text of *Le Champion des Dames*: *The Trial of Womankind*, 129. This is one of the clear cases where Christine treats as historical an incident fabricated by Le Fèvre; the other is Ovid's castration. See introduction (n. 92).

150. (1049ff.) See *L* 2.201ff.

151. (1050ff.) See *L* 2.202ff.; from Num. 12:1–15. Van Hamel proposes the emendation of "qui fu suer" to "la sereur" in his "Corrections et additions," Jehan Le Fèvre de Resson, *Les Lamentations de Matheolus et Le Livre de Leësce* (Paris: Émile Bouillon, 1892–1902), 2: 262.

152. (1053–54) See Ovid, *Met.* 2.531–632.

153. (1059–60) See *L* 2.229–22.

154. (1061ff.) See *L* 2.241ff.

155. (1066) For woman's creation from bone (as opposed to dirt) and this topos as an encomium to women, see line 1205 and n. 171 below.

156. (1069ff.) See *L* 2.241ff.

157. (1070–71) The following lines (both here and in their source at *L* 2.251ff.) don't actually follow the tirade of Le Jaloux in *RR* in any precise detail; but see line 1072 and n. 158 below.

158. (1072) Badel (Le roman de la Rose *au XIV siècle*, 193) notes that this line is a quotation from the tirade of the Jealous Husband, *RR* 8655–56, which Le Fèvre earlier quoted in connection with his own unhappy marriage (real or fictitious) at *L* 1.25.

159. (1073ff.) See *L* 2.314ff. Van Hamel (2: 160) notes exempla similar to the following at Montaiglon and Reynaud, *Recueil général*, 3: 166ff., and Eustache Deschamps, *Le miroir de mariage* 823ff.

160. (1087–90) See *L* 2.347ff.

161. (1093–96) See *L* 2.377–80.

162. (1118–29) Digression on the fall of the angels. The relation to the main theme of *LL* is that the good angels don't share the punishment of those who chose to sin, any more than all women are disgraced by the misbehavior of a few; Christine also uses this argument: *L'epistre au dieu d'amours*, in *Poems of Cupid, God of Love*, ed. and trans. Fenster and Erler, lines 193–96. On digressions in *LL*, see n. 65 above. The story of the angel Lucifer's fall from heaven to become Satan is found in Isa. 14:12 and Luke 10:18.

163. (1134) the law of custom and tradition] "Du droit de coustume et d'usage": In a striking departure from the traditional view of Heloïse as the tragic lover who exercised her vast erudition mostly in disparagement of matrimony (see *RR* 8729ff.), Le Fèvre focuses on Heloïse the accomplished abbess with considerable expertise in the law. This line (1134) has several possible meanings; MS P has "De droit de coustume et d'usage." The latter reading would support Emmanuelle Bonnafoux's suggestion that the line be punctuated "Du droit, de coustume, et d'usage." In this format, it would be translated "in civil law [droit] and customary law." I opted for the most obvious translation, where "coustume" means time-honored local custom, as opposed to "droit," or written law: see *DMF* 2010, s.v. "coustume" B.1. "Usage" means ancient tradition: see *DMF* 2010, s.v. "usage" III. "Coutume et usage" has another possible, quite specialized meaning: usufruct, or more precisely the right to use a forest owned by another party: see *DMF* 2010, s.v. "usage" C.2.a. As abbess, Heloïse concluded a treaty with Norpal, abbot of the neighboring monastery of Vauluisant, regarding "an oak wood ... which Vauluisant ceded to the Paraclete. But the Abbot reserved for his own monastery the acorns, so that the Paraclete could not let its pigs feed there." Enid McLeod, *Héloïse: A Biography* (London: Chatto and Windus, 1971), 215. Usufruct was also important to the economic well-being of Longchamp abbey, so admired by Le Fèvre; Abbess Jehanne de Neuville

in her inventory of assets (1384) noted the abbey's right to use and/or sell the wood cut down from the royal forest at Rouvray; see Jehanne de Neuville, "Inventaire," in Gaston Duchesne, *Histoire de l'abbaye royale de Longchamp (1255–1789)* (Paris: H. Daragon, 1906, 165–66. For more on Jehanne and Longchamp, see *LL* 2853ff. and notes 354–59, below. Whatever the precise meaning intended by this phrase, the author knew from personal experience that an abbess would need intelligence and expertise in the law to fulfill her responsibilities for the financial survival of her abbey as well as the pastoral care of her nuns. See the introduction (n. 29) on the convent adjoining his property in Ressons, and his homage to contemporary Abbess Jehanne de Neuville, lines 2853–88 with nn. 354–57 below.

164. (1135) Jean de Meun acknowledged Heloïse's scholarly attainments at *RR* 8754ff.

165. (1137) They would have led Mahieu to [their] goal] "Car Mahieu a methe menassent": As explained by Hasenohr ("La locution," 265), this expression means that the women's superior arguments would have brought Mathieu to accept defeat. For other examples of Le Fèvre's wordplay on the odd expression "mener a methe," see lines 593–666 and nn. 77 and 90 above. In the earlier passage, Le Fèvre followed Mahieu in treating the women's rhetorical tactics pejoratively; here, he uses the same locution in praise of Heloïse and her learning.

166. (1139) so that they [Mahieu's arguments] would have been useless against them] "Qu'en vers elles n'eüssent lieu": My translation is suggested by Hasenohr, "La locution," 260.

167. (1140–54) The daughter of Jehan Andrieu, professor of canon law at Bologna and Padua, is identified by Van Hamel (2: 241) as Novella (b.1312). According to Hasenohr, *Le Respit* xii, this anecdote is further proof that Le Fèvre "avait frequenté la Faculté de Décret" (attended lectures in canon law.) As noted by Pacchiarotti, *Les Lamentations* 11, the passage accurately describes how such a class was conducted as a debate over *quaestiones*, i.e. a *disputatio*. On the "modern example" as a topos of the "case for women," see Blamires, *Case*, 66–68. Christine deployed the example of this erudite young woman with a similar purpose in *Città delle dame*, ed. Caraffi and Richards, 316; *Book of the City of Ladies*, trans. Richards, rev. ed., 154. She includes details not found in *LL*: the name Novella, the report that her father dedicated his *Novella in Decretales* to her, and the detail that she substituted for her father at lectures, speaking from behind a curtain so that the (male) students wouldn't be distracted by her beauty. It has long been speculated that Christine had independent knowledge of Novella, as her father, Thomas de Pizan, was a professor at Bologna from 1344 to 1356 and could have known Jehan Andrieu. Regarding Christine's report that Novella hid her face behind a curtain, Van Hamel (2: 241) notes that *LL* MS B has "Que l'homme ne la regarda" (such that a man did not look at her) at line 1154, a reading picked up by one of the early printed versions. For more on Novella and the defense of women, see Paul O. Kristeller, who expresses guarded skepticism that such a person actually existed: "Learned Women of Early Modern Italy: Humanists and University Scholars," in *Beyond Their Sex: Learned Women of the European Past*, ed. Patricia H. Labalme (New York: New York University Press, 1984), 102, 114; Curnow, "' Pioche d'Inquisition,'" 169; and Blamires, *Case*, 39–40, 42.

168. (1165) See line 1050 and n. 156 above. In light of Miriam's conduct in Num. 12:1–15, it is hard to understand the claim by Lady Gladness that Miriam wasn't really a scold. Gladness may simply be grasping at straws, or perhaps she means that Miriam told the truth when she accused her brother of marrying a foreign woman, and therefore spoke as a prophetess, not as a harridan.

169. (1198) leave them for a while] "en espace les lairay": Hasenohr ("La locution," 250) notes that this expression, which means to defer or postpone something, is otherwise unattested.

170. (1199) Gladness will keep her promise to treat this subject by enumerating the crimes of men in her closing argument, lines 3496ff.

171. (1205) Woman's superiority because of the material of her creation was a medieval commonplace. See for example Humbert de Romans, "Ad omnes mulieres," in Bede Jarrett, *Social Theories of the Middle Ages, 1200–1500* (1926; rpt. New York: Frederick Ungar, 1966), 71–72; and Christine de Pizan, *L'epistre au dieu d'amour* (trans. Karen Pratt), lines 595ff., in Blamires, *Woman Defamed*, 284 and 284 n. 22.

172. (1221) For the tradition that Adam was created in Hebron, see Brian Murdoch, *The Apocryphal Adam and Eve in Medieval Europe: Vernacular Translations and Adaptations of the* Vita Adae et Evae (Oxford: Oxford University Press, 2009), 126 and 126 n. 75.

173. (1227) Woman's superiority because of the place of her creation was a medieval commonplace; see Humbert de Romans quoted by Jarrett, *Social Theories of the Middle Ages*, 71–72, and Christine de Pizan, *L'epistre au dieu d'amour* (trans. Karen Pratt), line 595ff., in Blamires, *Woman Defamed*, 284 and 284 n. 23. The antifeminist Saint Ambrose disputed this argument in *De paradiso* 1.4 (*PL* 14, col. 284); see the new translation by Alcuin Blamires, "From *Paradise*," in *Woman Defamed*, 61.

174. (1236–40) See *L* 3.2627–30.

175. (1241–43) Le Fèvre plays on the similarity of the Latin word for woman, *mulier*, to Latin *mollire/mollis* (soften/soft). For the defense of woman by etymology, see Blamires, *Case*, 82–83.

176. (1246ff.) This profeminine interpretation of Eve's creation from Adam's side (rather than his head or his feet) was a commonplace; e.g., see Humbert de Romans quoted by Jarrett, *Social Theories of the Middle Ages*, 71–72; Blamires and Pratt, *Woman Defamed*, 261; John Gower, *Mirour de l'omme, Complete Works of John Gower*, ed. Macaulay, vol. 1, lines 17521–32, and Chaucer, *Parson's Tale* 925–29.

177. (1258) I have emended "faire" to "faite"; obvious typographical error.

178. (1267) See lines 2046–48 and n. 260 below.

179. (1287) The subject of the sentence is God.

180. (1288) The subject of the sentence is Adam.

181. (1293–1310) The parallel between Eve's creation from the side of the sleeping Adam and the emergence of the church from the side of the crucified Christ was a commonplace depicted in many pairs of MS illuminations and perhaps most famously in Ghiberti's "Gates of Paradise." Van Hamel (2: 242) cites Augustine, *Ennaratio in Ps.* 56 and *De civ. Dei,* lib. 22 chap. 16.

182. (1321–30) See *L* 2.279–88.

183. (1331ff.) See *L* 2.405–8, 413–16, 435–38, 451–52, 455–56.

184. (1337) ought to get glasses] "devroit prendre yeux de beryl": From *L* 2.415. This detail is original to Le Fèvre and is surely one of the earliest references to eyeglasses in literature. Their earliest known depiction in the visual arts (of a middle-aged scholar at his desk) dates from 1352: see F. Daxecker, "Three Reading Aids Painted by Tomaso da Modena in the Chapter House of San Nicolò Monastery in Treviso, Italy," *Documenta Ophthalmologica* 99, no. 3 (1999): 219–23. The Latin *Lamentations* of 1290–91 has "Qui capit uxorem, cur ergo non speculator, / Heu! Bene primo rem, cum semper decipiatur?" (Whoever takes a wife, why doesn't he look into it — while he still has time? really carefully, because he might be stuck forever!) (808–9, translation mine). By admitting to his familiarity with ocular aids, the author may also be joking about his age.

185. (1339–42) Le Fèvre echoes the blasphemous defense of "trial marriage" at *L* 2.435ff.; see his proof text at 1 Thes. 5:21, which is quoted out of context. In *L* 2.445–50, Le Fèvre notes that postulants to religious orders have a year to change their minds, so why shouldn't the same be true for married men? The *locus classicus* for the complaint that a wife must be taken for life, with no real inspection beforehand, is in "Theophrastus," the misogamous tract quoted in Jerome, *Against Jovinianus* 1.47, trans. Fremantle, 383.

186. (1347–1408) See *L* 2.460ff. The story of "The Widow of Ephesus" derives from Petronius: see *The Satiricon,* ed. Evan T. Sage, rev. ed. Brady B. Gilleland (New York: Meredith, 1969), 95–98, with notes and bibliography on 229–30. It has many imitations, including John of Salisbury, *Polycraticus* 8. There is an annotated English translation of the version in *L* by Karen Pratt in Blamires, *Woman Defamed,* 185–86.

187. (1401) In the longer version in *L* (2.547), Gilbert had told the widow that the stolen corpse had two wounds on its head.

188. (1448) Identified by Van Hamel (2: 243) as Philippe VI (d. 1350.) Although Van Hamel accepts the story as fact, he was not able to find any trace of it in the archives. This "modern example" has a counterpart in *L* 3.1033ff., where Le Fèvre translates Mahieu's eyewitness account of two guilty women burned alive for killing their husbands.

189. (1452) Identified by Van Hamel (2: 243) as Jean le Bon, at that time "lieutenant" to his father the king, which gave him the right to pardon criminals.

190. (1459ff.) Le Fèvre borrowed the story of Lucretia from *RR* 8578ff. Jean de Meun's Friend tells the story as a rare exception to the norm of female disloyalty; Le Fèvre generalizes it as proof by exemplum of women's fidelity.

191. (1474ff.) Penelope is mentioned at *RR* 8622 in a cynical context — even she could be seduced by a skillful suitor. Here she is presented as an example of women's constancy.

192. (1489ff.) See *L* 2.588, 1599–1614; from Ovid, *Met.* 8.1–151.

193. (1495ff.) See *L* 2.618–22.

194. (1501) ff. See *L* 2.643–46.

195. (1505ff.) See *L* 2.667–71.

196. (1506–9) See n. 45 above.

197. (1512–14) See *L* 2.682–86; from Judg. 16:4–21. Le Fèvre has also drawn from the story of Samson at *L* 2.2223–38.

198. (1515ff.) See Ovid, *Met.* 8.1–151. Inspired by her love for Minos, who was besieging her city, Scylla treacherously cut off the purple lock of hair from the head of her father King Nisus; this action caused her father's death and the defeat of her city.

199. (1523) See Ovid, *Met.* 8.151, where she is actually changed into a "ciris" or sea bird. On Le Fèvre's rationalistic dismissal of mere "fable," see introduction (n. 81).

200. (1525) See Ovid, *Met.* 8.146.

201. (1539) On David's fatal order, see 2 Sam. 11:14–17; also see n. 45 above.

202. (1544) The biblical book of 2 Samuel, the source of the story, has the alternate title 2 Kings.

203. (1545ff.) The story of Samson here is partly reminiscent of *L* 2.2223–38. Its biblical source is Judg. 14:20, 15:2, 16:4ff.

204. (1562) His mouth had no restraint at all] "Sa bouche n'ot point de cloison": Hasenohr ("La locution," 274) relates this use of *cloison* to Ecclus. 22:33.

205. (1567) his ordeal] "son orage": For this metaphorical use of "orage" (storm), see Hasenohr, "La locution," 241.

206. (1575–76) Lady Gladness offers no real rebuttal to the charge that women imperil their husbands by

telling their secrets; cf. Chaucer, *WBPro* 434–42, *WBT* 950–80. Christine would repeatedly and fervently dispute this misogynistic canard, using arguments based on both historical examples and current real-life experience: "Christine's Reaction to Jean de Montreuil's Treatise on the *Roman de la Rose*," in McWebb, *Debating the* Roman de la Rose, 126, 127; *Città delle dame*, ed. Caraffi and Richards, 280–86; *Book of the City of Ladies*, trans. Richards, rev. ed., 134–37. Only John Gower appears to have spotted the counterexample of Abigail, who saved her husband's life by learning his secret: *Mirour de l'omme* 13659–68, from 1 Sam. 25:14–38.

207. (1579–80) As noted by Van Hamel (2: clxxxv), this is a quotation of lines 5 and 6 of the opening office of Prime, which Le Fèvre had translated in his *Hymnes de la liturgie*: see *L* 2.2245–49.

208. (1581ff.) See *L* 2.704ff. for the complete version of the story of Solomon and the young man who hid his father. Le Fèvre follows the Latin *Lamentations* except for adding the detail that the young man was ordered to appear "neither dressed nor naked," so he clothed himself in a net (*L* 2.734, 748, *LL* 1596, 1603). Mahieu claims a written source for the Latin version ("prout ipse lego," 924), but Van Hamel (2: 164–65), while providing a list of possibilities, notes the lack of any known source that corresponds with his version in every detail. Schmitt provides a detailed list of analogues (*Matheus von Boulogne*, 92–93, n.243–70), while agreeing that none of these appears to have been used by Mahieu. According to most of the sources/analogues, the king of the story was not Solomon but his son Rehoboam, who scorned the advice of old men: 1 Kings 12:8.

209. (1596–97) On the wise advice of his father, the young man covered his body with a net and rode a donkey to court. A MS illustration of the scene is reproduced on the cover of Pacchiarotti's *Les Lamentations*.

210. (1599) In the longer version found in *L*, the young man identifies his "lord" as his son, his "serf" as his donkey, and his "friend" as his dog. As noted in both *L* and *LL*, his "enemy" is his wife.

211. (1620–21) Does ... defense?] Van Hamel's note (2: 244) describes these lines as "pas très clairs." My translation is in line with his suggestions.

212. (1629–38) See *L* 2.785–94. I have not been able to locate an exact source for this passage in the works of Saint Ambrose.

213. (1635) that state] "tel ordre": Marriage.

214. (1639–46) See *L* 2.847–48, 851–52, 869–70. Cf. Chaucer, *WBPro* 587ff., with the note on the passage in *Riverside Chaucer*, 3rd ed.

215. (1642) and he says she's quick to change her tune] "et assés la fist varier": As noted by Van Hamel (2: 244), the subject of "la fist," meaning "la représente," is "le mesdisant," i.e., Mahieu; see *L* 2.851, 877–80, from Latin *Lamentations* 953, 964–65. According to Mahieu, the widow's tears at her husband's funeral are purely for show; she truly weeps for her first husband only after the second has spent all her money.

216. (1647–72) See *L* 2.884–88, 904–12, 933–44.

217. (1654) Similar to *RR* 7732, where it describes a "damoisele fole" (wanton girl), not a widow.

218. (1663) See Ex. 8:3; Mathieu likens the sexually voracious widows to one of the ten plagues of Egypt.

219. (1668) Patron saint of lunatics. However, as noted by Van Hamel (2: 166), the anecdote is more usually told of the devil and wild horses.

220. (1673–1702) See *L* 2.917–52, 955–66, 998–1004. Male hostility toward women's religious observances, especially the suspicion that they go to worship merely as a way of being seen by and having contact with men, was a staple of antifeminist satire; see Juvenal, *Satires* 6.517–31, and *RR* 13487–98 (based on Ovid, *Ars. am.* 3.387–98, 417–18.) Both Gower and Christine would reverse the topos, claiming that *men* go to church with fake show of piety in order to attract the attention of women: *Confessio amantis* 6.7059–69; *Epistre au dieu d'amours* 48–50.

221. (1702) Along with the corresponding passage in *L*, this is one of the foundational texts for Chaucer's peripatetic Wife of Bath, whose travels on pilgrimage had a decidedly worldly agenda; see the "General Prologue" to the *Canterbury Tales*, lines 463–67, with the note on the passage in *Riverside Chaucer*, 3rd ed.

222. For the notorious misogyny of Saint Ambrose, far more virulent and pervasive than anything in the Bible, see Blamires, *Woman Defamed*, 59–63. Le Fèvre is always careful to prefer the Bible as more authoritative than other sources, including the church fathers.

223. (1712) It is protection from too much heat] "Pour trop grant chaleur fait ombrage": Paraphrase of 1 Cor. 7:9. Hasenohr ("La locution," 258) cites the image as a commonplace.

224. (1713) Le Fèvre/Lady Gladness will keep this promise at 3210.

225. (1721–22) if ... pure luck] "Se mal ... aventure": My translation is based on Van Hamel's note (2: 245). He explains these lines as neighborhood gossip about the widow.

226. (1726–27) Such men ... in arrears] "Et tels leur advantage y quierent ... arrerage": Van Hamel (2: 245) explains that he removed "y" from line 1726 despite its presence in the MSS in order to support his understanding of these lines as a "maxime générale." Contra Van Hamel and with the help of Emmanuelle Bonnafoux, I interpret these lines as applying specifically to the ne'er-do-wells who seek to pay off their debts by marrying a widow for her money; my translation attempts to capture Le Fèvre's wordplay on "advantage ... arrerage."

227. (1728) So it is with [re]marriage] In keeping with my reading of lines 1726–27, I have emended Van Hamel's "aussi" to the "ainsi" of MS B.

228. (1729) it is useless for a woman to be single] "ce n'est rien d'une femme seule": Christine appears to

quote these lines in her warning against remarriage for most widows: "c'est toute folie, quoy que aucunes qui le veulent faire dient ce n'est riens d'une femme seule, et si pou se fient en leur sens que elles se excusent que gouverner ne se sauroient" (remarriage is complete folly. Though some who want to remarry say there is nothing in life for a woman alone, they have so little confidence in their own good sense that they will claim that they don't know how to manage their own lives). *Le livre des trois vertus*, ed. Charity Cannon Willard and Eric Hicks (Paris: Honoré Champion, 1989), 193; *A Medieval Woman's Mirror of Honor: The Treasury of the City of Ladies*, ed. and trans. Charity Cannon Willard and Madeleine Pelner Cosman (New York: Persea Books, 1989), 201.

229. (1761–76) Based on the deuterocanonical OT book of Judith. The citation of Judith as an exemplum of chaste widowhood was commonplace; for examples see Blamires, *Case*, 171 n. 3.

230. (1774–75) Judith used deception to assassinate a sleeping man. This detail is also emphasized, with a possible misogynistic connotation in both works, at Chaucer's *MercT* 1368; for the ambiguity of this passage in *MercT*, but without any reference to *LL*, see the note on the passage in *Riverside Chaucer*, 3rd ed.

231. (1807) women get together and gossip] "Femmes tiennent eschevinage": Hasenohr ("La locution," 260) defines this phrase, "pas autrement attesté," as "se réunir pour parler de q[uelque]ch[ose]," in this case "tous les potins de la ville" (all the gossip of the town).

232. (1813) women hold court] "femmes tiennent senne": Hasenohr ("La locution," 260) explains "senne" as strictly speaking a "synode," but often referring to "toute sorte d'assemblées."

233. (1807–24) See *L* 2.1023–26, 1041–54.

234. (1827–32) See *L* 2.1071–76.

235. (1833–44) See *L* 2.1107–18; the ultimate source is *RR* 16317ff.

236. (1838) make love] "avoir delit": Hasenohr ("La locution," 257) cites this as a phrase meaning sexual intercourse when the locution pertains to both partners.

237. (1839ff.) See *L* 2.1113ff.

238. (1844) we're one flesh] "c'est tout un": Copied from *L* 2.1118. However, in his careless abridgment of the passage, Le Fèvre omitted the following line, *L* 2.1119: "C'est une char; bien est possible" (That is, one flesh — it's very possible). I have translated this line according to the meaning of the original passage in *L*.

239. (1845–56) See *L* 2.1141–54.

240. (1856–60) See *L* 2.1161–64.

241. (1861–68) See *L* 2.1183–84, 1186–92.

242. (1865) she turns her back on him] "le dos luy torne": Hasenohr notes this phrase, but not this particular example, at "La locution," 267.

243. (1869–90) See *L* 2.1195–96, 1213–18, 1221–38.

244. (1878) you turn a deaf ear] "tu fais la sourde oreille": Noted at Hasenohr ("La locution," 267) as an expression for "moquerie, mépris, arrogance, domination/admiration."

245. (1891–92) See n. 206 above.

246. (1905–24) See *L* 2.1251–60, 1267–70, 1273–74, 1276–82.

247. (1905–11) See 1 Cor. 7:32–33, the foundational text for this topos.

248. (1917ff.) See the Parable of the Supper, Luke 14:16–24.

249. (1940) Gladness explains that the passage Mahieu quotes from Luke is a parable, not an exemplum, and thus need not be taken literally as a condemnation of marriage. The interpretation of texts is a constant preoccupation in the medieval debate on women.

250. (1950) See *L* 2.1275. Here in *LL*, Le Fèvre adds "aujourd'hui" to render the married man's case more sympathetic, in contrast to the misogamous rendering of the parable in *L*.

251. (1964–74) See *L* 2.1287ff.

252. (1966ff.) For analogues to the story of the woman who drank poison because she was forbidden to do so, see Van Hamel, 2: cxli. Van Hamel can identify no direct source, and Schmitt (*Matheus von Boulogne*) provides no source note at all. According to Van Hamel (2: 170), the word "recitatur" (Latin *Lamentations* 1071) is a hint that Mahieu drew the story from oral tradition.

253. (1975–89) See *L* 2.1315–36. Mahieu/Le Fèvre changes the source (Ovid *Met.* 10.3ff.) by making Eurydice, not Orpheus, disobey the order, in keeping with his theme of women's disobedience.

254. (1991–2002) See *L* 2.1337–44; from Esther 1:10–19.

255. (2002) made an example] "au doy monstrée," literally, "shown with the finger": See line 2117 and n. 265 below. Hasenohr ("La locution," 268) notes occurrences of this phrase, which she defines as "être en butte à la moquerie publique," in *L*, but not in *LL*.

256. (2003–18) See *L* 2.1381–96.

257. (2007) On Lot's wife, see Gen. 19:15–26.

258. (2028ff.) Van Hamel (2: 246) suggests that Le Fèvre may have been inspired by the digression on free will in *RR* 17029ff. On digressions in *LL*, see n. 65 above. He had earlier produced a digression on free will in *Le respit de la mort* 1174–1276.

259. (2034) put him back on the right path] "remette a voie": My translation follows the suggestion of Hasenohr, "La locution," 240.

260. (2046–48) Woman's subjection to man was said to result from the sin of Eve: Gen. 3:16, 1 Tim. 2:12–14.

261. (2060–62) If Reason ... get in trouble] "Se raison ... trouveroit bataille": This passage is obscure in grammar and meaning. I believe that the "elle" of 2061 refers to the beleaguered individual Reason, while the subject of "s'en aille" is the wayward woman. In *Le respit de la Mort* 1250–61, Le Fèvre expands on the intrapersonal conflict between Will and Reason, with Reason often getting the worst of the contest.

262. (2063–65) A dubious argument echoed by the Wife of Bath: *WBPro* 440–42.

263. (2100) is just giving us a song and dance] "il fait bien entendre la muse": The French literally means "He is just making [us] listen to nonsense," with a pun on *muse* as either nonsense/song or tune/bagpipe. My translation attempts to capture the pun, so appropriate to the exemplum of Orpheus the musician. Hasenohr ("La locution, 261") notes the double meaning of "muse." As noted by Jill Mann, *Feminizing Chaucer*, 30–31, Le Fèvre's objection to Mahieu's exemplum is grounded in the impossibility of return from the dead; he never complains that Mahieu had altered the events of the story as told by Ovid.

264. (2107–12) See *L* 2.1345–67.

265. (2117) Ahasuerus banished Vashti as an example to other wives: see Esther 1:18–22.

266. (2131) Esther's humility (see Esther 8:3 and deuterocanonical Esther 15:5–16) is a topos used to ironic effect in Chaucer's *MercT* 1744–45; see note in *Riverside Chaucer*, 3rd ed. Van Hamel (2: 246) notes another example in Deschamps, *Le miroir de mariage* 9125ff.

267. (2141ff.) Had Eve not sinned, there would have been no need for the Incarnation and redemptive death of Jesus; thus, Eve was our benefactress. For this commonplace defense of Eve as impetus for the *felix culpa* (fortunate fall) and forerunner of Mary, see Blamires, *Case*, 115. Even Christine resorts to it in *Città delle dame*, ed. Richards and Caraffi, 80, 81; *Book of the City of Ladies*, trans. Richards, rev. ed., 24.

268. (2148) Le Fèvre alludes to the tradition (known as "the legend of the true cross") that Jesus' cross was made of wood from a tree originally planted in the Garden of Eden: see Jacobus de Voragine, "De inventione sanctae crucis," *Legenda aurea: Vulgo historia lombardica dicta*, ed. Th. Graesse (1890; rpt. Osnabruck: Otto Zeller, 1969), 303–11, and *The Golden Legend*, trans. William Granger Ryan (Princeton: Princeton University Press, 1993), 1.277–84.

269. (2165) On the cross. Man's sin was crucified with Christ; see Romans 6:6.

270. (2167) Le Fèvre excuses her disobedience on the grounds that she believed that the angel who gave her the command was only a human being; see Heb. 13:2.

271. (2169) stone ... Peter] "pierre ... Pierre": Untranslatable wordplay on pierre (stone) and Pierre/Saint Peter.

272. (2185) On Lot's cohabitation with his daughters, see Gen. 19:30–38.

273. (2194) Lot's grandchildren by his daughters became ancestors of the Ammonites and Moabites, who later fought against the Israelites; see n. 272 above.

274. (2203–46) See *L* 2.1415–24, 1431–36, 1441–46, 1451–58, 1467–68, 1474–82. The locus classicus for the wife's demand for expensive clothing is in "Theophrastus," the misogamous tract quoted in Jerome's *Against Jovinianus* 1.47, trans. Fremantle, 383.

275. (2271) Van Hamel (2: 246) cites "Aristote, éd. Didot II, 314, 9" as the source for the commonplace maxim on order in all things, which could just as easily be derived from 1 Cor. 14:40.

276. (2272–73) A counterargument to lines 2227ff. above; see n. 274 above. Le Fèvre is quite orthodox, not sarcastic, in his defense of a married woman's right to be fashionably dressed by her husband, if we can judge from the views of Christine and Gerson: see *Città delle dame*, ed. Richards and Caraffi, 408–12; *Book of the City of Ladies*, trans. Richards, rev. ed., 204–5; Jean Gerson, "Poenitemini Sermon 3, December 17, 1402," *Oeuvres Complètes*, ed. Mgr. Glorieux (Paris: Desclée, 1960–73), vol. 7* (part 2): 831–32; and Hult, *Debate of the* Romance of the Rose, 205. Gerson considered the wardrobe a compensation for the hazards of childbirth.

277. (2293ff.) See *L* 2.1483ff.

278. (2296) The belief in women's relative coldness is based on Aristotle and Galen; see Blamires, *Woman Defamed*, 39–42.

279. (2304) Le Fèvre/Lady Gladness complains that Mahieu questioned the ancient teaching on women's coldness only to disparage them as hot with avarice.

280. (2306) See *L* 2.1492.

281. (2309) See *L* 2.1495.

282. (2310) See *L* 2.1496.

283. (2313) I.e., the men are robbed by women. Their victimization is described in greater detail at *L* 1.1530–40.

284. (2314–18) Le Fèvre is referring to *L* 2.1541–70, where he interrupted his translation of Matheolus's rant on female avarice to apologize for the scurrilous content of his source.

285. (2327ff.) This expression of sympathy for prostitutes has no analogue in *L*. By contrast, Christine de Pizan rejected poverty as a defense: "que elle [la femme de fole vie] n'aroit de quoy vivre, ne vaut neant: car se elle a corps fort et poissant pour mal faire et pour souffrir males nuis, bateures et assez de mescheances, elle l'aroit bien a gaigner sa vie; mais que ainsi fust disposee comme nous disons. Car chascun la prendroit voulentiers a aidier a faire lessives en ces grans hostelz; si en auroient pitié et voulentiers lui donneroient a gaigner." (That she

[the prostitute] would have no way of earning her living ... is also untrue. If her body is strong enough to perform evil and suffer bad nights, blows, and numerous other misfortunes, she should be strong enough to earn her wages otherwise. If she were willing, people eagerly would take her in to help with the laundry in great houses, pity her, and gladly offer her work.) See *Le livre des trois vertus*, ed. Willard and Hicks, 214; *Medieval Woman's Mirror of Honor*, ed. and trans. Willard and Cosman, 216–17.

286. (2337) when they [the abused prostitutes] can't accomplish] "Quant elles ne peuent acomplir": This is one of two cases where Emil Freymond prefers a reading from Lo., a MS unknown to Van Hamel. He would adopt the eight-syllable "Quant ils [the pimps] ne peuent acomplir" in order to correct the nine-syllable line (as he perceives it) of Van Hamel's edition. However, Freymond's preferred reading seems not to make sense in context. For the other reading from Lo. preferred by Freymond, see line 3981 and n. 492 below.

287. (2339) Van Hamel's note (2: 287) compares these lecherous thugs ("houliers gloutons") to "souteneurs actuels" (modern pimps).

288. (2366) "Envoit" is clearly meant in a subjunctive sense; MSS BPV have "envoie."

289. (2370) I assume that the subject of the sentence is Lady Gladness.

290. (2371ff.) Le Fèvre's version of the Medea story is based on *RR* 13199ff., where the Old Woman tells it as an example of male perfidy. (Both authors may have been influenced by her mostly sympathetic characterization in Benoît de Sainte-Maure, *Le roman de Troie*, ed. Léopold Constans [Paris: Firmin Didot, 1904–12; rpt. New York: Johnson Reprint Co., 1968], 1: 159ff. (lines 715–2078). Jean de Meun's Old Woman tells her stories of deceitful men with a cynical agenda: she is explaining to her young female charge that since men will be unfaithful to you, you don't have to be faithful to them (13235ff.). In *LL*, Le Fèvre recreates several of her stories as straightforward exempla of female virtue. He enhances the profeminist import of Medea's story by making it an example of women's intelligence, generosity, and fidelity. This approach would exert a major influence: Chaucer presents her as a martyr to love (omitting her crimes) in *LGW*; Gower uses her story as an exemplum of Jason's perjury in *Confessio amantis* 5.3147ff.; and Christine de Pizan, in her polemically profeminine works related to the "querelle de la Rose," would repeatedly cite the example of Medea in terms unmistakably reminiscent of the sympathetic portrayal in *LL*: *Epistre au dieu d'amours* 437–44; and *Città delle dame*, ed. Caraffi and Richards, 162, 380–82; *Book of the City of Ladies*, trans. Richards, rev. ed., 69, 189–90).

291. (2390–91) See *RR* 13155–56, which actually refer to Dido. This line also echoes *RR* 4598, where Jean de Meun's Reason warns the Lover that he will risk "sens, tens, chatel, cors, ame, los" (sanity, time, property, body, soul, reputation) if he loves a woman; here, Le Fèvre revises the topos by applying it to Medea's tragic love for a man.

292. (2407ff.) Although Le Fèvre knew the traditional ending of Medea's story (the murder of her children, *L* 2.411–12), he changes it here in order to render her a purely innocent victim. Benoît de Sainte-Maure in his *Roman de Troie* 2028–40 concludes the story of Jason and Medea on a similar note, stressing Medea's kindness and Jason's perfidy while omitting the details of her violent revenge.

293. (2413ff.) For the story of Circe as an exemplum of female generosity and male perfidy, see *RR* 14376–78; Ovid, *Rem. am.* 263ff.: and possibly Benoît de Sainte-Maure's *Roman de Troie* 28479 and 28651. However, none of these passages is very close to Le Fèvre's version. Ovid and Jean de Meun both cite Circe's loss of Ulysses as an exemplum of the futility of witchcraft in retaining a man's affections. Benoît also emphasizes Circe's attempt at controlling Ulysses through her black arts. In keeping with his profeminine agenda in *LL*, Le Fèvre seems to have independently recast the story to make her especially sympathetic.

294. (2423) I have emended "sa mie" to "s'amie," following Van Hamel, 2: 247.

295. (2427) Telegonus, son of Ulysses and Circe, would kill his father; see Benoît de Sainte-Maure, *Roman de Troie* 28701–28825, 29815–30300.

296. (2435ff.) For the story of Dido as an exemplum of female generosity and victimization, see *RR* 13144ff., where the Old Woman tells it as an example of male perfidy. Le Fèvre had told Dido's story in *L* 2.1647–60 as a proof text for women's "fole amour" (sinful passion) (1657); he retells it with an obviously different purpose in *LL*. This later treatment would exert a major influence: Chaucer presents her as a martyr to love in *LGW*, Gower presents her as a victim of Aeneas's negligence in love (*Confessio amantis* 4.87ff.) and as a female martyr to love (8.2552); and Christine, in her profeminine polemics related to the "querelle de la Rose," repeatedly cites the example of Dido in sympathetic terms reminiscent of *LL*: *Epistre au dieu d'amours* 441–60, and *Città delle dame*, ed. Richards and Caraffi, 202–10, 374–78; *Book of the City of Ladies*, trans. Richards, rev. ed., 91–95, 188–89. For the view that Le Fèvre's Dido was influenced by her portrayal in the *Ovide moralisé*, see Eberhard Leube, *Fortuna in Karthago: Die Aeneas-Dido-Mythe Vergils in den romanischen Literaturen vom 14. Bis 16. Jahrhundert* (Heidelberg: Carl Winter, 1969), 51–54. However, Le Fèvre's literalist approach to the myth is very different from the *Ovide Moralisé*, where Dido is glossed as heresy pregnant with error, while Aeneas is the church fleeing from heresy: see C. de Boer, ed., *"Ovide Moralisé," Poème du commencement du quatorzième siècle*, 5 vols. (Amsterdam: Johannes Müller, 1915–38, 14.555ff.; "Dido and Aeneas Moralized," *Medieval English and French Legends: An Anthology of Religious and Secular Narrative*, trans. R. Barton Palmer (Glen Allen, VA: College Publishing, 2006), 294–96. If Le Fèvre consulted this work at all, he consistently ignored the allegorical intercalations.

297. (2447) See lines 2563–76 and n. 311 below.

298. (2466) for my closing argument has yet to be addressed] "Car la queue est a l'escorchier," literally "for the tail has [yet] to be skinned." Giuseppe Di Stefano relates this locution to the proverb "La queue est pire a escorcher, the last is hardest to be done": see *Dictionnaire des locutions en moyen français* (Montréal: CERES, 1993), 741.

299. (2469–73) See *L* 2.1589–97; from Ovid, *Met.* 8.132ff.

300. (2470) laid herself down on her back underneath a bull] "soubz un torel se mist souvine": I have translated literally in keeping with the pornographic context; Hasenohr ("La locution," 257) defines "se mettre souvine" as an expression for sexual intercourse when the subject of the locution is a woman.

301. (2488–90) Le Fèvre/Lady Gladness has already answered Mahieu's allegations on Scylla, Minos, and Nisus (lines 1515–26).

302. (2492ff.) See Judg. 11:30–40. Phillips ("Chaucer and Jehan Le Fèvre," 30) notes that the juxtaposition of Virginia and Jephthah's daughter as exempla of female chastity (also found in Chaucer's *Physician's Tale*) appears to originate with *LL*, important evidence that Chaucer knew this work. Le Franc's account elaborates upon the courage and religious faith of Jephthah's daughter as a credit to women: *Le champion des dames*, ed. Deschaux, 20204 ff.; ed. and trans. Taylor, *The Trial of Womankind*, 171–72 (lines 5377 ff.)

303. (2522ff.) From *RR* 5559ff. Jean de Meun cites the august Roman historian Livy as his source (5564), which doubtless explains why Le Fèvre presents the story as a "chose veritable" (true story) as opposed to the unreliable "fables" (myths) recounted by Mahieu to disparage women. Badel (Le roman de la Rose *au XIV siècle*, 196) notes that Le Fèvre repeats Jean de Meun's mistakes in telling the story; thus, he could not have directly known the version in Livy. Phillips ("Chaucer and Jehan Le Fèvre," 30) notes the echo at Chaucer's *Physician's Tale*, lines 155–56, and its probable indebtedness to Le Fèvre's judgments on the reliability of sources in *LL*.

304. (2537–40) See *L* 2.1615–18.

305. (2539) allowed him to have sex with her] "souffri la couple charnelle": Hasenohr ("La locution," 257) notes this among expressions for sexual intercourse when the subject of the locution is a woman.

306. (2541–44) See *L* 2.1621–26; from Ovid, *Met.* 3.12ff. and *Ars am.* 1.285ff. (Myrrha); *Met.* 4.454ff. and *Ars am.* 1.283ff. (Biblis); *Heroïdes* 11 (Canace and Machaire). The corresponding passage in the Latin *Lamentations* makes no mention of Canace and Machaire. Le Fèvre's allusion to this story is further evidence that he used the *Heroïdes*, a catalogue of wronged heroines that obviously suited the profeminine agenda of *LL*.

307. (2545–52) For Phaedra, see *L* 2.1627–34; from Ovid, *Met.* 15.497–546. The story is mentioned without being retold in the Latin *Lamentations* 1175–76. Le Fèvre changed the usual ending of the story both in *L* and *LL*. In all ancient versions, Hippolytus rejected his stepmother's advances.

308. (2550) After she had drunk that cup to the dregs] "Quant du pot ot les tes eüs": "Tes" is modern French *tesson*, the bottom of the cup or pot. See Hasenohr ("La locution," 257), who notes this expression for sexual intercourse when the subject of the locution is a woman.

309. (2551) she got herself laid] "congnier se fist": A vulgar expression for sexual intercourse; see Hasenohr, "La locution," 256. In his glossary of "locutions" in *Les Lamentations*, 442–43, editor Pacchiarotti defines "congnier" as "foutre": 442–43.

310. (2553–62) See *L* 2.1635–44. Her story is found in Ovid, *Heroïdes* 11 and *Ars. am.* 3.459–60.

311. (2563–76) On Dido, see *L* 2.1647–60 and lines 2435ff. and n. 296 above. The detail that Dido was pregnant at her death is found in Ovid, *Heroïdes* 7.133; Le Fèvre may also have known it from the *Ovide Moralisé* (see n. 296 above), or Machaut, *Judgment of the King of Navarre*, ed. and trans. Palmer, line 2121, unless he simply made it up.

312. (2566) had banged her box] "avoit congnié la coste," literally, "penetrated her basket": Hasenohr ("La locution," 256) notes what she explains as a graphic expression for sexual intercourse when the subject of the locution is a man. Also see n. 309 above.

313. (2577–84) See *L* 2.1695–1702.

314. (2577–78) See Ovid, *Amores* 1.8.43.

315. (2579–84) See *L* 12.1695–1702. According to Van Hamel (2: 172), "the Pope" refers to dispensations by Urban III and Innocent III allowing widows to remarry on account of their weakness; he cites *Decretalium* lib. 4, tit. 21, c. 4 and 5.

316. (2585–94) See *L* 2.1707–14.

317. (2595–2606) See *L* 2.1719–84. For more on hostile criticism of nuns in the Middle Ages, see Jill Mann, *Chaucer and Medieval Estates Satire: The Literature of Social Classes and the General Prologue to* The Canterbury Tales (Cambridge: Cambridge University Press, 1973), esp. 129.

318. (2601) show of piety] "turlupinage": See *L* 2.1765ff. In context, this word appears to have something like its modern French meaning of "a farcical display," in this case the ostentatious piety practiced by the nuns as a ruse to conceal their vices. See *DMF* 2010, s.v. "turlupinage." On the fourteenth-century Turlupin heresy, which allegedly encouraged sexual license and nudism, see Badel, Le roman de la Rose *au XIV siècle*, 458. However, in this passage, Le Fèvre is accusing the nuns of hypocrisy, not heresy.

319. (2605–6) In these two lines, Le Fèvre abridged the attack on the Beguines in the Latin *Lamentations* 1249–62 and *L* 2.1769–84. *LL* contains no other reference to the Beguines, an order of pious laywomen who lived in some respects as nuns and were known for their unorthodox assertiveness (for women) on theological

concerns. Perhaps he believed that the controversy over the Beguines was no longer current, following the severe restrictions placed on the order by early fourteenth-century popes: see Robert E. Lerner, *The Heresy of the Free Spirit in the Later Middle Ages* (Notre Dame: Notre Dame University Press, 1972), 47, 208.

320. (2607–14) See *L* 2.1807–14. The wickedness of old women was a commonplace; for the *loci classici*, see the crafty old bawd Dipsas in Ovid's *Amores* 1.8, the pseudo–Ovidian *De vetula* (which Le Fèvre had translated as *La Vieille*), and the discourse of La Vieille in *RR* 12710–14516.

321. (2615–20) See *L* 2.1831–54.

322. (2621ff.) A variant of the popular "Weeping Bitch" *fabliau*. The full story is told in *L* 2.1855–1950. An old woman agreed to help a young man seduce Galatea, a virgin. Using mustard and onions, she forced her little dog to cry. Then she told Galatea that her own daughter had been changed into that sad little dog as punishment for refusing the love of a young man, who subsequently died of a broken heart. To avoid a similar fate, Galatea met her suitor in a secluded place, and he took her virginity. Schmitt (*Matheus von Boulogne*, 117 n. 729–61) provides a list and discussion of the Latin sources and analogues for the story, the oldest being Petrus Alfonsus, *Die Disciplina clericalis, das älteste Novellenbuch des Mittelalters*, ed. Alfons Hilka und Werner Söderhjelm (Heidelberg: Carl Winter, 1911), 18–19. He omits to mention Jacques de Vitry, *The Exempla, or Illustrative Stories from the Sermones Vulgares*, ed. Thomas Frederick Crane (1890; rpt. New York: Burt Franklin, 1971), 105–6. As usual, Mahieu recasts the story in his own distinctive way; for example, the seduced woman of the possible sources and analogues is a wife, not a virgin. The story found its way into English as "Dame Sirith" and the "Interludium de clerico et puella"; see Eve Salisbury, ed., *The Trials and Joys of Marriage*, TEAMS Middle English Text Series (Kalamazoo, MI: Medieval Institute, 2002), 29–60.

323. (2627) she let him make love to her] "De luy souffri le jeu d'amours": Cited by Hasenohr ("La locution," 257) as an expression for sexual intercourse when the subject of the locution is a woman.

324. (2631–46) See *L* 2.1951–74.

325. (2632) often play at such tricks] "jouent souvent de tels merelles": Literally, *merelles* was a board game with three pieces. Hasenohr ("La locution," 264) explains that the phrase means "user de tels procédés, de tels subterfuges."

326. (2640–46) The story is found in the pseudo–Ovidian *De vetula*, which Le Fèvre had translated as *La vieille*, ed. Cocheris, 2.3151–3296.

327. (2653) Cf. Benoît de Sainte-Maure, *Roman de Troie* 45–46: "Omers, qui fu clers merveillos / E sages e esciëntos ..." For Le Fèvre's knowledge of Homer, which could only have been indirect, see also n. 331 below.

328. (2661ff.) The ultimate source of the [two] kegs is *Iliad* 24.635ff. Le Fèvre's immediate source is *RR* 6783ff. However, as noted by Badel (*Le roman de la Rose au XIV siècle*, 191), Le Fèvre's interpretation of the image is quite original; he transforms the story to mean that a misogynist maligns women only because he has been unlucky in love.

329. (2667) Gladness the loving] "leesce, l'amoureuse": In this passage, "Leesce" obviously connotes erotic satisfaction; however, Le Fèvre's concept of *leesce* or *joye* is far from limited to *jouissance*: see the translation nn.3, 15, and 16, above.

330. (2685–86) Venus's wound is mentioned in Ovid's *Met.* 14.477 and 15.769. Here it seems to be a figure of speech referring to the incurable pangs of love.

331. (2687) Le Fèvre is referring to the fact that Ovid (following Homer) retold many stories of the Trojan War and its aftermath in *Met.*, books 11–14. Although Ovid doesn't mention Homer by name in *Metamorphoses*, Le Fèvre knew from the opening lines of Benoît's *Roman de Troie* (45–46) and Guido delle Colonne's *Historia destructionis Troiae* that Homer was the poet of the Trojan War.

332. (2707ff.) It seems that Le Fèvre simply made up the story that Ovid was castrated. Van Hamel (2: 249) does not know of a source for the claim, although he notes the possible influence of a passage on eunuchs in the pseudo-Ovidian *De vetula* that Le Fèvre had translated. I find no reference to castration in Fausto Ghisalberti's "Medieval Biographies of Ovid," *Journal of the Warburg and Courtauld Institutes* 9 (1946): 10–59. Christine repeated the "fact" of Ovid's mutilation in *Città delle dame*, ed. Caraffi and Richards, 74; *Book of the City of Ladies*, trans. Richards, rev. ed., 21—further evidence that she was influenced by *LL*. Like Le Fèvre, she makes the claim that Ovid became a misogynist because he could no longer enjoy the love of women; cf. *WBPro* 707–10. In an interesting variation on the topos, *Rose* defenders Pierre Col and Jean de Montreuil boldly question the masculinity of *Rose* antagonist Jean Gerson ("Reply to Christine de Pizan's and Jean Gerson's Treatises," McWebb, *Debating the* Roman de la Rose, 310, 311; Jean de Montreuil, Epistle 154, ibid., 346, 347), despite the fact that Gerson *defended* women and marriage in the process of attacking Jean de Meun ("Treatise against the *Roman de la Rose*," ibid., 274, 275; 292, 293). Gerson made an ambiguous response to the slurs on his manhood: Letter (December 1402), ibid., 354, 345. See also n. 149, above, and introduction n. 91.

333. (2723ff.) See Ovid, *Met.* 10.489ff.

334. (2731–36) See n. 306 above.

335. (2737ff.) See Ovid, *Rem. am.* 601ff. However, the passage in Ovid says nothing of a particular tree, only of a wood: 591, 606.

336. (2743–60) See lines 2435ff. and n. 296 above.

337. (2761) See lines 2577–78 and nn. 317ff. above.

338. (2761–64) Cf. *L* 2.1695–1702 and 2.2606–8.

339. (2768–73) See lines 997ff. and 1029ff.

340. (2775–77) He who slanders shames his own mouth; that way ...] See n. 144 above. My translation is based on the emendation suggested by Van Hamel, 2: 250: "putains" to "put ains/i."

341. (2786ff.) Le Fèvre could have known of Abelard and Heloïse from *RR* 8729ff. However, Le Fèvre's purpose here (to praise Abelard for his profeminine views) is very different from the antimatrimonial context of *RR*. Le Fèvre might have considered Abelard as an ally because of Abelard's encomiums to women in Letter 6, "On the Origin of Nuns"; for a translation, see Blamires, *Woman Defamed*, 232–36. For insightful discussion of Abelard's profeminine views, see Mary McLaughlin, "Peter Abelard and the Dignity of Women: Twelfth Century 'Feminism' in Theory and Practice," in *Pierre Abélard, Pierre le Vénérable*, ed. René Louis et al. (Paris: Editions du Centre National de la Recherche Scientifique, 1975), 287–334, and Blamires, *Case*, 199–207.

342. (2792) Where he brought Sister Heloïse] "Ou suer Heloïs voult attraire": An example of Le Fèvre's use of *vouloir* plus the infinitive to denote a completed action, not one merely intended by the subject; see the Note on the Text and Translation in this volume.

343. (2801ff.) Le Fèvre goes on to cite only four "preudes femmes" of the present day, all of them nuns (2852–89) except for the dubious Calabre of Paris (3778–85). Later, he will claim his desire to avoid the sin of flattery as the motive for his relative reticence on contemporary women: see lines 3792ff. and n. 468 below.

344. (2807–8) See line 748 and n. 103 above.

345. (2810–53) Le Fèvre produces a catalog of female saints to support his case for women. As noted by Curnow, "The 'Livre de la Cité des Dames,'" 131, *LL* provided the "hagiographical core for the *Cité des Dames*," although Christine provided more biographical details than Le Fèvre on all the female saints except for Ursula and the eleven thousand virgins. By contrast, Boccaccio explicitly omitted Christian women (with very few exceptions) from *De mulieribus claris*, believing they had been sufficiently discussed elsewhere, and chose to focus on the purely natural achievements of pagan women: see preface, *Famous Women*, trans. Virginia Brown (Cambridge: Harvard University Press, 2003), 6. On Le Fevre's possible use of an expanded *Legenda Aurea* (Golden Legend), see n. 353 below.

346. (2810–24) See Jacobus de Voragine, *Legenda aurea*, ed. Graesse, 701–5; *Golden Legend*, trans. Ryan, 2.256–60. The eleven thousand virgins also appear in *RR* 11081, where False Seeming uses them to support his case that secular women are capable of sainthood. Unlike Le Fèvre (and later Christine, *Città delle dame*, ed. Caraffi and Richards, 460, 462; *Book of the City of Ladies*, trans. Richards, rev. ed., 240), Jean de Meun does not bring up the example of female saints to support a favorable view of women in general.

347. (2819) I have emended Covain to Conain, following Van Hamel, 2: 250.

348. (2825ff.) See Jacobus de Voragine, *Legenda aurea*, ed. Graesse, 789–89; *Golden Legend*, trans. Ryan, 2.334–41. Cf. n. 10 above.

349. (2831ff.) See Jacobus de Voragine, *Legenda Aurea*, ed. Graesse, 400–403; *Golden Legend*, trans. Ryan, 1.368–70.

350. (2835–38) Of the saints mentioned in the following passage, the *Legenda aurea* (claimed by the poet as his source at 2852) names only Agnes, Lucy, Agatha, Geneviève, Christine, Bridget, and Clare (ed. Graesse, 113–17, 29–32, 170–74, 922–26, 419–21, 902–3, 949–50). Le Fèvre's inclusion of saints not cited in the *Legenda* may be due to carelessness, or he may have used an expanded version of that work unknown to us; see n. 353 below.

351. (2837–38) Perpetua (Jacobus de Voragine, *Legenda aurea*, ed. Graesse, 797–99; *Golden Legend*, trans. Ryan, 2.342–43) was married with an infant son at the time of her martyrdom.

352. (2847) Le Fèvre probably means St. Bridget of Ireland; see Jacobus de Voragine, *Legenda Aurea*, ed. Graesse, 902–3. St. Bridget of Sweden would not be canonized until 1391.

353. (2852) The *Legenda aurea* (Golden Legend) of Jacques de Voragine was an extremely popular thirteenth-century collection of saints' lives accepted by Le Fèvre and others as historical. In addition to the 178 biographies found in Jacobus's text, Sherry L. Reames notes the existence of "expanded [versions] containing material on dozens of additional saints ... [with] not just one version per [vernacular] language": The Legenda Aurea: *A reexamination of its paradoxical history* (Madison: University of Wisconsin Press, 1985), 4. Pierce Butler describes some of the expanded Latin and French versions in his Legenda Aurea-Légende Dorée-Golden Legend: *A study of Caxton's* Golden Legend *with special reference to its relations to the earlier English prose translation* ((Baltimore: John Murphy, 1899), 1–49. I have cited Graesse's edition of the Latin *Legenda* because it includes saints' lives added later to the collection, including Geneviève, Bridget, and Clare (see n. 350 above); thus, it most likely approximates the expanded version evidently used by Le Fèvre. The recent critical edition of the Latin *Legenda* includes only the original legends: Iacopo da Varazze, *Legenda Aurea*, ed. Giovanni Paolo Maggioni, 2 vols. (Florence: SISMEL, 1998). For more studies of additions to the *Legend*, see the bibliography.

354. (2853–88) Jehanne de Neuville was a contemporary of Le Fèvre who was born near his hometown. According to archival research (see *Le respit de la mort*, ed. Hasenohr, xlv–xlvi), she became Abbess Johanna VII at the Minorite (that is Franciscan) convent of Longchamp (near Paris) on 16 October 1375, resigned as abbess

on 22 April 1387 (*terminus ante quem* for the composition of *LL*— see ibid., liii), and died in 1400. During her sixty-one years at Longchamp, she supervised the repairs of war damage to the bell tower and cloister, arranged for the construction of "nouvelles chambres," and reorganized the kitchen and infirmary. To accomplish all this, she managed to borrow 2,200 *livres*. On her death, she willed to the abbey a seven-*livre* annuity and two books, "un bon collectaire et unes bonnes heures de Nostre-Dame." On Jehanne's abbacy, see also n. 163 above. For the "modern example" in the medieval defense of women and Jehanne de Neuville as a case in point, see Blamires, *Case*, 66–68. For Christine's transcendent recreation of the topos in the *Ditié de Jehanne d'Arc*, see Alan P. Barr, "Christine de Pisan's *Ditié de Jehanne d'Arc*: A feminist exemplum for the *querelle des femmes*," *Fifteenth Century Studies* 14 (1988): 1–12, which doesn't mention Le Fèvre. Christine's life story would be retold as a "modern example" and inserted into a MS of *L*; see the appendix to this volume.

355. (2856) escoliere] "student": Le Fèvre's honorific use of this word in the feminine gender is quite original. According to *DMF* 2010, "écolier" (m.) means student or disciple, while "écolière" (f.) means a younger woman who takes a dubious lesson from an older woman. This description of Jehanne may allude to the excellent library and program of education at Longchamp: see Gertrud Młynarczyk, *Ein Franziskanerinnenkloster im 15. Jahrhundert: Edition und Analyse von Besitzinventaren aus der Abtei Longchamp* (Bonn: Ludwig Röhrscheid Verlag, 1987), esp. 139, 144, 235–38. Le Fèvre refers to male escolliers/students in a respectful context at *L* 4.70.

356. (2877) pastourelle] "shepherdess": Le Fèvre's honorific use of this word in the feminine gender is quite original. According to *DMF* 2010, "pasteur" (m.) can refer to a pastor of souls, while "pastourelle" (f.) means young female shepherd or a lyric poem about such a person. I submitted this example with an appropriate new definition to the editors of *DMF*; it appears in the *DMF* 2012.

357. (2884) Inspired by her mentor, Saint Francis of Assisi, Saint Clare was the first to expand the Franciscan or Minorite life to women.. Her story appears in expanded versions of the *Legenda aurea* (Golden Legend): ed. Graesse, 700–702, and *The Golden Legend (Aurea Legenda), Compiled by Jacobus de Voragine, 1275, Englished by William Caxton, 1483, www.fordham.edu/halsall/basis/goldenlegend/index.asp*, vol. 6. I have emended the punctuation of this line (replacing a comma with a period) in accordance with Van Hamel's note on the passage, 2: 251, explaining how he discovered, after already editing the text, that "Celle de Gueux et la Moisie" were two individuals (nuns in Jehanne's convent.)

358. (2885) The lady of Gueux and the one called Moisie] "Celle de Gueux et la Moisie": Hasenohr (*Le respit de la mort*, xlvi–xlvii) identifies the first of these two women as Jeanne des Gueux, whose grandmother, great-aunt, and aunt were nuns at the same convent. At her death in 1389, she willed to the convent library "un livre en françois que en apelle *gracia dei*." "La Moisie," as also explained by Hasenohr, was Margarete la Musie, who also made bequests to the abbey at her death in 1396. Hasenohr speculates that Le Fèvre had met these women in the course of his work as *procureur en Parlement*. For recent scholarship on these two nuns, see Gertrud Młynarczyk, *Ein Franziskanerinnenkloster*, 90, 92, 202, 197, 212, 230, 291, 294.

359. (2887) are following closely in her footsteps] "Ensuivent de bien près la trace": I have emended "En suivant" to "Ensuivent," following Van Hamel, 2: 251–52. See n. 357 above. Hasenohr ("La locution," 269) notes how this ancient expression means "to follow someone's example."

360. (2889ff.) worthies] "preuses" Van Hamel (2: 252) cites a similar catalog of "neuf preuses" (nine female worthies) in Eustache Deschamps: *Oeuvres complètes*, ed. Gaston Reynaud, SATF (Paris: Firmin Didot, 1994), 11: 225–27. (These were counterparts to the better-known Neuf Preux or Nine [Male] Worthies, a roster of military heroes from the Bible, pagan history, and medieval times.) However, Van Hamel discounts the possibility of direct borrowing between the two poets on the grounds that the "neuf preuses " were well known to popular culture. Le Fèvre never actually uses the word "neuf" (nine), although nine women are cited in lines 2992–99 below.

361. (2892–93) Hippolyta and Menalippe were Amazons noted for their courage; see Boccaccio, *Famous Women*, trans. Brown, 42. Sinope is missing from Boccaccio but included in Christine's *Book of the City of Ladies* among the Amazons along with Hippolyta and Menalippe: *Città delle dame*, ed. Richards and Caraffi, 110 (Sinope); 116–22 (Hippolyta and Menalippe); *Book of the City of Ladies*, trans. Richards, rev. ed., 42 (Sinope); 43–47 (Hippolyta and Menalippe).

362. (2894) to make fun of the evil-speakers] "Pour mesdisans faire la lippe": Hasenohr ("La locution," 267) defines this locution as "se moquer de lui."

363. (2896ff.) In *L* 2.1578–88, Le Fèvre vilified Semiramis as guilty of incest with her son. Here she is rehabilitated as a "preuse" (female worthy); her sexual transgression goes unmentioned. For the full story on her half-disheveled hair, see lines 3534–57 below. The source appears to be Boccaccio's *De mulieribus claris (Famous Women*, trans. Brown, 8–12). Like Le Fèvre, Christine picks and chooses material from *De claris* in order to recreate Semiramis as a fully admirable character (*Città delle dame*, ed. Richards and Caraffi, 106–110; *Book of the City of Ladies*, trans. Richards, rev. ed., 38–40). Although Christine admired Dante's *Divine Comedy* as far superior to *RR* ("Response to Pierre Col" in McWebb, *Debating the* Roman de la Rose, 1/6, 1/9), she follows *LL* and not *Inferno* 5.52–60 in her portrayal of Semiramis, whose incestuous union she excuses as acceptable under pre–Christian law. For other ancient and medieval treatments of the Semiramis story, as well as an independent edition of the relevant passages in Boccaccio and Christine, see Liliane Dulac, "Un mythe didactique." Dulac

refers to *LL* only in passing: 320 and 330 n. 27. In fact, Le Fèvre's completely sympathetic revision of the story of Semiramis was clearly a prototype for Christine's.

364. (2898) See lines 3558ff., 3580ff., and n. 437 below.

365. (2899) I am unable to identify Teuca and Deïphile except that Van Hamel (2: 252) denotes them as "preuses" (female worthies). For Lampito, see line 3592 and n. 441 below.

366. (2913) 1 Sam. 1–3:21. Hannah fits Le Fèvre's polemical purpose because she was falsely accused by a male, the high priest Eli.

367. (2914–22) See the deuterocanonical OT book of Susannah.

368. (2923ff.) See John 8:3–11.

369. (2941) Le Fèvre draws his own unconventional moral from a story that would seem to be a warning against the hypocrisy of the religious elders.

370. (2966) follow the right path] "aler bonne voye": On this expression, see Hasenohr, "La locution," 241.

371. (2993) See *L* 2.1968ff. For the deception of Ovid by an old woman, see the introduction (n. 37) and n. 326 above.

372. (3004–5) Badel (*Le roman de la Rose au XIV siècle*, 199) notes the connection of this passage and lines 826ff. above with the endorsement of procreation in *RR* 16527–28. Badel notes at 115 and 115 n. 3 that the same topos (pleasure as a "ruse de la nature" to ensure the propagation of species) appears in the pseudo-Ovidian *De vetula*, which Le Fèvre had translated: *La vieille*, ed. Cocheris, 1.542–54. Unlike Jean de Meun, as noted by Badel (198), Le Fèvre would align his argument with Christian orthodoxy by explicitly linking the good of procreation with marriage; see lines 3011–12 below.

373. (3013–14) See n. 144 above.

374. (3017ff.) Adaptation from *L* is especially careless here; see *L* 2.1993ff., especially 2005–9, 2011–18.

375. (3035ff.) See *L* 2.2033–36, 2027–29, 2039–42, 2047–56.

376. (3041) Elsewhere in *LL*, Le Fèvre mentions Medea only as a faithful helper to Jason and a wronged heroine; here she is praised for her intelligence and skill. Both in Benoît de Sainte-Maure's *Roman de Troie* (1216–28) and *RR* (13207, 13217–19), Medea is described as highly learned, especially in magic. Christine also celebrates Medea's skills: *L'epistre au dieu d'amours* 437–44; *Città delle dame*, ed. Caraffi and Richards, 162; *Book of the City of Ladies*, trans. Richards, rev. ed., 69.

377. (3043) Elsewhere in *LL*, Le Fèvre mentions Circe only as a faithful helper to Ulysses and a wronged heroine. Christine discusses Circe's magical skills in a respectful way: *Città delle dame*, ed. Richards and Caraffi, 164, *Book of the City of Ladies*, trans. Richards, 69–70.

378. (3045) See Lucan, *Pharsalia* 507–830.

379. (3051ff.) See *L* 2.2073–76.

380. (3054) This supernatural figure appears in *RR* 18397, albeit in a different context (as the figment of a disordered dream state.)

381. (3055ff.) Fearing the loss of his kingdom, Saul had the prophet Samuel called up from the dead by the witch of Endor; Samuel gave a hostile answer to his former protégé because God had withdrawn his support as punishment for Saul's disobedience. 1 Sam. 28:6–20. See *L* 2.2115–20.

382. (3061) frown] "a mate chiere," literally "with a sad expression." According to the Bible, it was Samuel, not the witch, who channeled the judgment of God.

383. (3063) See *L* 2.2121.

384. (3065–67) Le Fèvre returns to the claim that women have loose tongues, a recurring theme of *L*; see 2.2215ff. For other examples and commentary, see n. 206 above.

385. (3067–78) See *L* 2.2249–72 and Van Hamel, 2: 179–80. Le Fèvre may have called this story "tout neuf" for the sake of rhyme, or he may have considered it "new" because it was unknown to him outside of the Latin *Lamentations*. Van Hamel cites several possible sources and analogues. The story is well-known as a result of its inclusion in La Fontaine's *Fables*, 8.6. Alfred Schmitt (*Matheus von Boulogne*, 125 n. 909 ff.) believes that Mahieu's version most closely resembles *Gesta Romanorum*, ed. Hermann Oesterley (1872; rpt. Hildesheim: Georg Olms, 1963), 475–76 (chap. 125).

386. (3079–94) See *L* 2.2273–2308. Van Hamel (2: 180) provides a list of possible sources and analogues, most of them with significant differences from Mahieu's version.

387. (3095–3102) See *L* 2.2309–22.

388. (3102) I have emended "mentir" (lying) to the "jangler" (reckless talking) of the corresponding passage at *L* 2.2322. Le Fèvre's mistake may be due to his haste in copying the source — two lines later, the word "mentir" appears in *L*. Christine resented this misogynistic understanding of why the risen Christ appeared first to women: see *Città delle dame*, ed. Caraffi and Richards, 88; *Book of the City of Ladies*, trans. Richards, rev. ed., 28–29. As noted in Blamires (*Case*, 108–12), both the appearance of the risen Jesus first to Mary Magdalene, and his commandment that she inform his male disciples, were generally perceived as an honor to women.

389. (3103–52) See *L* 2.2325–89. Van Hamel (2: 180–81) provides several possible sources and analogues for the *fabliau* known as "Puteus," beginning with *Disciplina clericalis*, ed. Hilka and Söderhjelm, 20–21 (chap. 14).

390. (3153–76) See *L* 2.2395–2432. Van Hamel (2: 182) notes two possible sources or analogues for this story: August Preime, *Die Frau in den altfranzösischen* Fabliaux (Cassel: L. Döll, 1901), 133f., and Montaiglon and Reynaud, *Recueil général*, 1: 173ff.

391. (3177) This line and the entire passage that follows (through 3209) depend grammatically on the main clause at line 3210.

392. (3179–95) that they go out on pilgrimage] This whole passage constitutes a capsule summary of Mathieu's complaints against women; see the parallel summary at *L* 2.2121ff., especially 2.2145–46, 2149–53.

393. (3199–3208) except for anything against religion] This entire passage is a lawyerly condition placed by Le Fèvre on his defense of women: i.e., he will defend women against Mahieu's charges, those he has just summarized in lines 3179–95, with the proviso that no one should think he makes excuses for bad behavior or discourages good.

394. (3210) I strongly answer thus] Main clause to the sentence beginning at line 3177.

395. (3214) As proof, I will tell you a true story] "Si en diray vray exemplaire": In a digression lasting through line 3418, Le Fèvre will firmly situate his defense of women within the mainstream of Christian theology, especially its prohibition on slander; see line 3411 and n. 417 below.

396. (3215–3418) A digression on theology parallel in some respects to book 3 of *L*. Its theme is human sin, free will, and God's judgment. For its relevance to the work as a whole, see nn. 395 above and 417 below. For digressions in *LL*, see n. 63 to the translation.

397. (3236ff.) The story of Lucifer's fall is from Isaiah 14:12 and Luke 10:18.

398. (3241) See *L* 3.1508.

399. (3243–44) See *L* 3.1511–12.

400. (3247–48) See lines 3386–87 for a resumption of this theme. Le Fèvre alludes to the devil in his role as accuser or prosecutor of humanity; for the *loci classici*, see Job 1:6–11 and Zech. 3:1.

401. (3256) See lines 1250 and 1264 above.

402. (3258) As noted by Van Hamel (2: 254), Le Fèvre apparently believes the rational and understanding ("raisonnable et intellective") souls to be one and the same thing, the *anima intellectiva*.

403. (3267ff.) The conundrum is explained at line 3670: "absent" and "future things" may be learned about and remembered with the help of books.

404. (3278) See lines 2027ff. above.

405. (3303–10) The theory of macrocosm (the physical universe) and microcosm (the individual human being) and their common composition from the four elements was a medieval commonplace. Le Fèvre also recycled it in *Respit de la mort* 967–80. As noted by Hasenohr (*Le respit de la mort* 163 n. 970–80), Le Fèvre could have found the same information in the pseudo–Ovidian *Vetula* 3.262–64, which he had translated as *La vieille* 3.4403ff.

406. (3315–18) Le Fèvre goes on to explain that on Judgment Day, God will be the judge, man the defendant, and the devil the accuser: see lines 3247–48, 3382–87, and n. 400 above.

407. (3317–18) then the accuser or plaintiff] "Et accuseur ou demandeur": Van Hamel (2: 254) notes the lawyerly distinction between criminal and civil trials. In either case, there will be a defendant.

408. (3319–20) See *L* 2.1511–12. For more on the "fortunate fall," a staple in the medieval defense of Eve and all her female descendants, see n. 267 above.

409. (3342–43) A combined reference to Gen. 3:22–24 and Gen. 2:17.

410. (3352ff.) See *L* 3.1550ff.

411. (3368) See *L* 3.1600.

412. (3376) At Pentecost; see Acts 2:1–4.

413. (3337–39) See John 14:16–17, 26. In Catholic theology, the Paraclete or Comforter of John's Gospel is synonymous with the Holy Spirit, which descended on the disciples at Pentecost: see n. 414 below.

414. (3378) encourage them in joy] "en joye ennorter": See nn. 15 above and 428 below. In orthodox theology, *joye* (Latin *gaudium/gaudia*), also called *leesce* (Latin *laetitia*), is the reward of a faithful Christian life and even a mandate for the Christian: for example, see 1 Thess. 5:16, "semper gaudete." In *LL*, Le Fèvre is always careful to stress the Christian legitimacy of "joy" and "gladness" and not merely their erotic connotation.

415. (3381) Literally "a language suitable for him"; see Acts 2:4.

416. (3386–87) See lines 3247–48 and n. 400 above.

417. (3411) evil speakers] "mesdisans," literally "slanderers": Through this warning that God will judge the sin of slander, Le Fèvre brings his digression back to the main theme: his rebuttal of Mahieu the *mesdisant* and, embedded in that subject, his defense of women.

418. (3426) Van Hamel (2: 254) cites Cato's *Distichs* 1.3: "Virtutem primam esse puta compescere linguam" (Believe that the essential virtue is controlling your tongue). Le Fèvre had translated the *Distichs* of Cato; see the introduction (n. 36).

419. (3429) The quotation from Ptolemy is from *RR* 7007ff.

420. (3433) There is no exact source in the Pauline epistles. Van Hamel (2: 254) cites Titus 1:10. Le Fèvre is probably thinking of Mat. 12:34 or James 3:2; the closest parallel in Paul's writings is Rom. 3:13–14 (where

the Apostle quotes Ps. 5:9, 140:3, and 10:7). I am indebted to Virginia Barney (personal communication) for the latter reference.

421. (3447) I will hammer all my life] "Je forgeray toute ma vie": A hitherto unnoticed pun on the author's name. "Forgeray" may have a sexual connotation; see *RR* 21335ff. Elsewhere in his works, however, Le Fèvre used it to denote the professional activity of a smith, as in "Je, Jehan Le Fevre qui ne sçay forgier ..." in the prologue to *La vieille*, ed. Cocheris, 3, and metaphorically to describe his craft as a poet: see La vieille, 3.5985–86, "J'ay tant forgié que j'ay parfait / Ceste oeuvre par dit et par fait," and his "Cato" lines 25–29. For further discussion, see line 3974 and n. 490. This line may contain a promise to write more on the subject of *Gladness* (a pledge repeated at 3990), a promise he was unable or unwilling to fulfill.

422. (3464ff.) See lines 338ff. In both cases, the metaphor is the same — evil speaking is a wind that blows trouble right back at the speaker.

423. (3468) Here Lady Gladness begins her closing argument.

424. (3469) bring my treatise to the goal] "mon propos mener a methe": Another example of Le Fèvre's wordplay on the locution "mener a methe"; for other examples of this locution with discussion, see lines 593–666 and 1137 and nn. 77, 90, and 165 above. Followed by Le Fèvre as translator, Mahieu had used "ducor ad metam" to disparage women; at line 1137 above and here, Le Fèvre places it in the context of an encomium to women.

425. (3479ff.) See lines 43ff. above; Gladness echoes her opening statement.

426. (3481) Truth is personified here as another name for the judge to whom Le Fèvre and Lady Gladness make their appeal. I have capitalized her name in keeping with the context.

427. (3482) Le Fèvre appealed to Reason as his judge at line 764. Now she will hear his closing argument. I have capitalized Reason in keeping with the context.

428. (3487) encourage them in joy] "a joye ennorter": See n. 15 above. Linking the defense of women with Christian theology, Le Fèvre and Lady Gladness channel the Holy Spirit, also known as the Paraclete or Comforter; see n. 414 above. In this context, "joye" (and by extension, its synonym "leesce") appears in one of its possible meanings, i.e., earthly happiness in accordance with a virtuous Christian life.

429. (3488) a merry jest] "une bonne gogue": According to Karen Pratt ("Strains of Defense," 124), the closing argument by Lady Gladness "may be being presented tongue-in-cheek, for 'bonne gogue.' . . can mean 'a joke' as well as 'a source of pleasure.'"

430. (3489) no dialogue] Le Fèvre promises that Lady Gladness will speak her closing argument *sola*, with no interpolated misogynistic arguments. He (mostly) adheres to this promise, but see lines 3713–17 and 3794–3800, where Le Fèvre interrupts her monologue with "the competing voice of a devil's advocate" (Pratt, "Strains of Defense," 124–25).

431. (3501ff.) See lines 816ff. above; also *L* 2.2643, 2631–32.

432. (3506) The subject of "dit" (says) is Lady Gladness; what Mahieu has alleged against women — that they overpowered the best of men — really proves her case for the superiority of women.

433. (3514) See *L* 2.2633ff.

434. (3517) He has to sing a different tune] "Chanter luy convient aultre note": Hasenohr ("La locution," 259) notes this early occurrence of a phrase meaning "tenir un discours tout différent."

435. (3522) his libelous little book] "libelle diffamatoire": the Latin *Lamentations*, which Le Fèvre extolled as "l'euvre du sage" (the wise man's work) at *L* 1.5.

436. (3534ff.) See lines 2896ff. and n. 363 above.

437. (3558ff.) See line 2598 above and Benoît de Sainte-Maure's *Roman de Troie* 24047ff. Penthesilea praised in Boccaccio *De mulieribus claris* (*Famous Women*, trans. Brown, 64–65), and Christine's *Città delle dame*, ed. Caraffi and Richards, 122–30; *Book of the City of Ladies*, trans. Richards, rev. ed., 47–51.

438. (3580) See line 3586 and n. 440 below.

439. (3583) made such trouble for him] luy fist tel essoine: For the possible meanings of this phrase, see Hasenohr, "La locution," 270.

440. (3586) Van Hamel (2: 256) cites "Justin I c. 8" as the source of Le Fèvre's story of Thamiris. This work is now available online: M. Iunianus Iustinus, *Historiarum Phillippicarum T. Pompeii Trogi Libri XLIV in epitomen redacti*, http://www.thelatinlibrary.com/justin.html. Also see Boccaccio, *De mulieribus claris* (*Famous Women*, trans. Brown, 98–100), and Christine, *Città delle dame*, ed. Caraffi and Richards, 112–14; *Book of the City of Ladies*, trans. Richards, 42–43.

441. (3592) Queen of the Amazons; see *De mulieribus claris* (*Famous Women*, trans. Brown, 25–27), and Christine, *Città delle dame*, ed. Richards and Caraffi, 110–12; *Book of the City of Ladies*, trans. Richards, 40–42. I am unable to identify Arsionne; perhaps Le Fèvre meant Alcyone.

442. (3594) See lines 2893, 2899 above with nn. 361 and 365.

443. (3595) The Italian maiden who bravely fought against Aeneas; see Virgil's *Aeneid* 11.532ff., Boccaccio, *De mulieribus claris* (*Famous Women*, trans. Brown, 76–78), and Christine's *Città delle dame*, ed. Caraffi and Richards, 146–48; *Book of the City of Ladies*, trans. Richards, 60–61.

444. (3598ff.) For the battle between Hercules and Cacus, see *RR* 15543ff. and 21592ff.

445. (3606ff.) Probably an allusion to Hercules' subservience to Omphale; Ovid, *Fasti* 2.305. A similar story is told of Hercules and Iole in *De mulieribus claris* (*Famous Women*, trans. Brown, 45–48), but not in Christine's *Book of the City of Ladies*.

446. (3623ff.) See Boccaccio, *De mulieribus claris* (*Famous Women*, trans. Brown, 52–56); also see Christine's *Città delle dame*, ed. Caraffi and Richards, 164–68; *Book of the City of Ladies*, trans. Richards, 71–73. In his profeminine polemic of 1440–42, Martin Le Franc would include with Carmentis and other learned women the example of Christine de Pizan: see *Le champion des dames*, ed. Deschaux, 18942ff.; ed. and trans. Taylor, *The Trial of Womankind*, 135–36 (lines 4118ff.).

447. (3629) found the way] "trouva le chemin": See Hasenohr, "La locution," 241.

448. (3632) Le Fèvre uses characters from ancient mythology, i.e. "fable," to support his case, a tactic he deplored when used by the opposing side; see the introduction (n. 81).

449. (3637) Medea was described in all the sources used by Le Fèvre as highly skilled in the "arts" or branches of knowledge; see n. 376 above.

450. (3642–43) Probably the Sybil of *Aeneid* 6.99ff., also known in the Middle Ages as Almathea the prophet. She is the subject of Boccaccio, *De mulieribus claris* (*Famous Women*, trans. Brown, 50–52), and Christine's *Città delle dame*, ed. Richards and Caraffi, 224–28; *Book of the City of Ladies*, trans. Richards, 102–4.

451. (3645) Here Le Fèvre seems to have confused the Cumaean Sibyl Almathea (the Sybil of Virgil's *Aeneid*) with the Sybil Erithrea, who was said to have foretold the birth of Christ; on Erithrea, see Boccaccio, *De mulieribus claris* (*Famous Women*, trans. Brown, 42–43), and Christine's *Città delle dame*, ed. Caraffi and Richards, 222–24; *Book of the City of Ladies*, trans. Richards, 101–2. Another possibility is that Le Fèvre credits the Cumaean Sibyl Almathea, the Sybil most associated with Virgil, with his supposed prediction of the birth of Jesus in the Fourth Eclogue. Curnow believes that these lines refer to Proba, who rearranged the works of Virgil to tell the story of the Old and New Testaments; see Christine's *Livre de la cité des dames*, ed. Curnow, 725–28, 1068 nn. 84–84a.

452. (3646) *De mulieribus claris* (*Famous Women*, trans. Brown, 95–96) is a possible source, although Boccaccio makes no claim that Sappho was more truthful than her male counterparts. Perhaps this claim originates with Le Fèvre. Christine also tells the story of Sappho: *Città delle dame*, ed. Caraffi and Richards, 294–96; *Book of the City of Ladies*, trans. Richards, 67–68.

453. (3650–52) To bolster his case for women, Le Fèvre may be euhemerizing the example of Pallas (also known as Athena or Minerva) as a historical woman so brilliant that she was later believed to be the goddess of wisdom. Boccaccio, *De mulieribus claris* (*Famous Women*, trans. Brown, 17–19), is a possible source for this approach. If Le Fèvre/Lady Gladness is referring to the pagan goddess rather than a historical human being, she is using a mythical figure to support her case, after repeatedly condemning this tactic when used by misogynistic authors; see introduction n. 81 and n. 479 below. Christine unequivocally euhemerizes Pallas as a historical person later believed to be a goddess: *Città delle dame*, ed. Caraffi and Richards, 170–74; *Book of the City of Ladies*, trans. Richards, 73–75.

454. (3654) and defends the case for women] "Et des femmes tient la partie": see 349 and n. 57 above.

455. (3655–61) Lady Gladness bases her case for women's intelligence on the feminine grammatical gender of names for the branches of learning, a frivolous argument she would have decried if used by the opposing side: see n. 479 below.

456. (3662) Here Le Fèvre unambiguously refers to the Sibyl Erithrea; see n. 451 above.

457. (3666ff.) Mentioned in Guido's *Historia destructionis Troiae* 1.7; Le Fèvre might have also used Boccaccio, *De mulieribus claris* (*Famous Women*, trans. Brown, 67–68). Christine cites her as a truthful prophet in *Città delle dame*, ed. Caraffi and Richards, 232–34; *Book of the City of Ladies*, trans. Richards, 106–7.

458. (3675) The story is from *RR* 6459ff. In *RR*, the fall of Croesus is an example of Fortune's fickle wheel. Le Fèvre makes it an encomium to women's gift of prophecy.

459. (3688–91) Christine uses the same topos (a catalog showing men's near-monopoly on violent crimes): *L'epistre au dieu d'amours* 641–49, 659–61. However, she never generalizes that all men are violent.

460. (3692–3707) A series of positive generalizations about women as the gentle sex. Christine would use this topos repeatedly: *L'epistre au dieu d'amours* 168–78; also see the introduction (n. 97).

461. (3731–33) See lines 1222–27 and n. 173 above.

462. (3750) See line 534 and n. 72 above.

463. (3762) Men love the pleasures of life] "Les hommes aiment miel et cire": My free translation is based on *RR* 17019, where a similar phrase (miel et çucre) refers to the pleasures of life, and the definition provided by Di Stefano for "le miel et le cire": "l'un et l'autre, tout": *Dictionnaire des Locutions*, 545.

464. (3764) See line 534 and n. 72 above.

465. (3763–75) Mann (*Feminizing Chaucer*, 28) cites Le Fèvre's "appeals to daily experience" as evidence for the originality and "sincerity" of the work: "His picture of women slaving away at their weaving and cheese-pressing while their husbands drink in the tavern or waste their time in blood-sports (3763–75) would fit comfortably into the pages of today's *Guardian*." For more on Le Fèvre's "empiricism," see introduction, especially n. 94.

466. (3782–83) has made many a vagina small again and perked up the breasts] "A fait maint con rapeticier

/ Et les mamelles estrecier." "Calabre of Paris" is otherwise unidentified; not surprisingly, Christine makes no mention of her. Like both *RR* authors, Le Fèvre articulates a fetish for a pubescent body type, a rosebud rather than a rose in bloom (e.g. *RR* 1644–45, 21638–39). See lines 193–96 above, where the youthful Perrenelle is praised for her girlish figure; compare the "tetinettes rondettes" of Ovid's youthful love object at *La vieille*, trans. Jehan Le Fèvre, ed. Cocheris, 2.2755–56. Generally no prude, Van Hamel (2: 257) seems taken aback by the details of Calabre's "louche art." Blamires (*Case*, 6) insightfully suggests of this passage on Calabre: "perhaps Le Fèvre does not have tongue in cheek here: he is deliberately shocking the reader with an extraordinary example of altruistic female behaviour in a context where the entire point has been to contrast that altruism (fulfilling the received function as 'helper' [*LL* 3735]) with egotistical male indolence and destructive male *fureur* [*LL* 3736]." In line with this respectful reading, I have translated "con," usually an obscenity often punned with "conil" (rabbit), as a medical term. Such a nonscurrilous meaning is possible in Middle French: see *DMF* 2010, s.v. "con." In keeping with her view that the closing argument of Lady Gladness is generally ironic, Karen Pratt ("Strains of Defense," 124) complains that "her language is no less bawdy than Matthew's or LeFèvre's as she describes the gynaecological skills of Calabria de Paris." As noted elsewhere, however, Le Fèvre clearly subscribed to the view of some late medieval exegetes that such plain speaking could be acceptable if used for a good purpose; see the introduction (n. 76) and n. 144 above.

467. (3785) to appease the jealous husbands] "pour les jalous faire taisans": Here and elsewhere, "jalous" seems to connote "cruel" or "abusive" as much as "jealous." The *locus classicus* for this male archetype is the rant of Le Jaloux in *RR* 8437ff. The male partners of Calabre's patients are labeled as "débauchés raffinés" in Van Hamel's note (2: 257).

468. (3792) Lady Gladness says she will avoid the sin of flattery by praising virtuous women of the distant past while omitting to mention the many now living in France. This passage opens Le Fèvre to the charge that he joined with misogynistic authors by insinuating that such exemplary women are no longer to be found. However, Le Fèvre's assertion here is not quite true; Lady Gladness has cited the examples of honorable contemporary Frenchwomen at 267ff., 1427ff., 2853ff., 2885, and (more questionably) at 3778ff., not to mention the daughter of the fourteenth-century Italian Jehan Andrieu (1140ff.). Christine would run the risk of flattering her contemporaries by listing many names of then-living women as proof of women's capacity for virtue: *Città delle dame*, ed. Caraffi and Richards, 222–26; *Book of the City of Ladies*, trans. Richards, 212–14.

469. (3796–97) Gladness ... names only the good women] Mann (*Geoffrey Chaucer*, 38) notes that "this is only fair, since men are equally silent about such male villains as Nero or Herod (3794–819)." She argues that this "one-sidedness" is "necessary," here as in Chaucer's *LGW*, to "redress the balance of male-oriented literature," a strategy used by both Le Fèvre and Chaucer "without any hint of incongruity or irony."

470. (3804–10) are they worthy of belief] I have cleaned up Le Fèvre's grammar here by turning "Desquelles il ne font a croire" into a main clause. Though mostly skeptical of Le Fèvre's sincerity as a champion of women, Helen Solterer (*Master and Minerva*, 149) finds this passage "points to a nascent understanding of the symbolic damage inflicted textually on women... . it even goes so far as to suggest that [the crime of] defamation may apply to an entire literary tradition."

471. (3812) The ancient Roman accused of treason by Cicero.

472. (3815) The villain of 1 Mac. 3:13–24.

473. (3818) Probably Flavius Rufinus (d. 395), who allowed Alaric to sack the Roman Empire.

474. (3812–19) With the same purpose, Christine provides a similar catalog of wicked and violent men in *Città delle dame*, ed. Caraffi and Richards, 338–46; *Book of the City of Ladies*, trans. Richards, 164–70.

475. (3821) Cleopatra, who was good] "Cleopatra, qui fu bonne": The queen of Egypt was also included in Chaucer's *LGW*; see *De mulieribus claris* (*Famous Women*, trans. Brown, 178–84). Mann (*Feminzing Chaucer*, 31) notes that "Cleopatra is the only one to be dignified with this epithet ["bonne"]." Mann's assertion is true of the immediate context, but elsewhere in LL, other heroines are called "bonne(s)": Medea (2385), Jephthah's daughter (2506), and women religious (2841). The epithet "good" is clearly foundational to the defense of women as a genre.

476. (3822–26) A catalog of unimpeachably historical women from the Old Testament and ancient Rome; Christine likewise includes both biblical and Greco-Roman heroines in her *Book of the City of Ladies*.

477. (3846–51) As Le Fèvre was surely well aware, this truthful commonplace is found in Ovid, *Ars am.* 3.29–30. Christine would use it at *Epistre au dieu d'amours* 348–54.

478. (3849) men catch in their traps] "Les males prennent en leurs naces": According to Hasenohr ("La locution," 264), this is an inversion of the topos that women ensnare men with their wiles; she notes that the latter is especially frequent in *The Fifteen Joys of Marriage*, trans. B. A. Pitts (New York: Peter Lang, 1985). See n. 483 below.

479. (3863) See also nn. 459 and 469 above. Speaking as an attorney defending women, Lady Gladness makes a statement indicting all men equally for the sins of a few — the same fallacy she repeatedly decried when applied to women by the opposing side (lines 800–809, 1115ff., 1409ff.). Le Fèvre is apparently making a lawyer joke when he has Lady Gladness resort to the same fallacious type of argument she has previously condemned. At *L* 2.2684ff., however, Le Fèvre produced an original defense of argument by generalization from a single case.

By contrast, Christine always acknowledges the existence of good men in her works defending women. Karen Pratt remarks, "While it is possible that Le Fèvre has here slipped unconsciously into the type of masculine analogical thought usually associated with misogynistic discourse, he may well have deliberately placed untenable generalizations in Leësce's mouth in order to ridicule her" ("Analogy or Logic," 64).

480. (3868) Le Fèvre resorts to hyperbole, even heterodoxy, in his defense of chaste widowhood. In Catholic theology, chaste widowhood (the sixtyfold fruit) occupies the middle rung of a hierarchy, superior to faithful marriage (the thirtyfold fruit) but inferior to virginity (the hundredfold fruit): see for example Jerome, *Against Jovinianus* 1.3, trans. Fremantle, 347. Jean Gerson, among many other medieval theologians, reaffirms this inequality of merit, while advising his parishioners of all three categories "loer et honnorer l'autre sans orguel" (to praise and respect the others without pride): see "Poenitemini V," in McWebb, *Debating the* Roman de la Rose, 370, 371. A cruel double standard applied to widowhood; at *L* 2.579ff., Lefèvre translates Mahieu's argument that a man is not obligated to mourn for his wife.

481. (3870) A general aspersion on men for the crimes of a few: see nn. 459 and 479 above.

482. (3880–81) as long as he can get his John Thomas up] "Tant que maistre jobart puist tendre": For Karen Pratt, Lady Gladness's use of "bawdy" language "as she describes … the root cause of misogyny" is evidence for a lack of seriousness in her defense of women ("Strains of Defense," 124). It is equally possible that Le Fèvre/Gladness is joking at the expense of male "mesdisants," not women.

483. (3910) fall into the traps of women] "es las des femmes ne cheïst": Hasenohr ("La locution, " 267) traces this expression to Ecclus. 9:3. See 3849 and n. 478 above.

484. (3912) Allusion to the legend of Virgil in the chest or basket. For the late medieval tradition of Virgil's humiliation by a woman, and its frequent association in literature and visual arts with the topos of the mounted Aristotle, see Domenico Comparetti, *Virgil in the Middle Ages*, trans. E. F. M. Benecke (London: Swan Sonnenschein, 1908), 325–39, and Smith, *Power of Women*, 156–59.

485. (3923) See 902 and n. 121 above.

486. (3927–28) Mann (*Feminizing Chaucer*, 36) notes how Le Fèvre "makes nothing more of this point," while Chaucer will repeatedly focus on rape as the "constant touchstone for determining justice between the sexes."

487. (3929–32) I believe that the subject of "tendent" (set out) is understood to be "femmes" (women), while the subject of "ne s'en peuent deffendre / Ne doivent" (can't defend their case against them, nor should they try) is understood to be "hommes" (men).

488. (3949–54) Le Fèvre invites some future author, perhaps a woman, to complete and correct his work. Christine de Pizan would take up this challenge, most explicitly in her *Book of the City of Ladies*. Karen Pratt finds the "humility" topos excessive and intended to cast doubt on the veracity of his profeminine argument ("Strains of Defense," 126).

489. (3973) if I have to pay the expenses] "S'il m'estuet payer la lamproie": This strange locution (literally "to pay the lamprey") is discussed, with many examples including this one, in *DMF* 2010, s.v. "lamproie." According to this source, it means "Payer une gratification, d'où en être pour ses frais" (to pay a tip, on receiving nothing for one's money). A *lamproie* can also be a gold chain; see *DMF* 2010 B. Exactly how *lamproie* in either sense relates to the meaning of this expression is discussed in detail, but scarcely elucidated, at Hasenohr, "La locution," 253. She glosses the expression as "être a l'amende, payer une amende" (owe a fine, pay a fine). The context would support the translation "pay court costs." Karen Pratt ("Strains of Defense," 127) notes that Le Fèvre may be referring to "Machaut's *Jugement dou Roy de Navarre*, in which Largesse tells Guillaume that because he has slandered women: 'Vous n'estes pas avouez; / Si devez paier la lamproie.' [You are not endorsed; thus you must pay the piper; ll. 3088–89 (Palmer translation.)]" In her view, this passage "underlines the mercenary nature of the defender of women he [Le Fèvre] has created." The accusation runs both ways; Le Fèvre attacks the "mesdisants" for their "avarice" at 3989.

490. (3974) Mercy, mercy on poor Smith] "Merci, merci au povre fevre": Le Fèvre is punning on his name. For other examples, see the introduction (n. 32).

491. (3975) See Luke 16:24. Here and at 3972, Le Fèvre may be complaining of illness, or he may be "thirsty" for patronage.

492. (3978) parchment] "peaulx," literally "skins." Citing this and other examples, Cerquiglini-Toulet notes that "The materiality of the manuscript — the skin of the animal that was used to make it — plays a large role in the imagination": *A New History*, 19.

493. (3981) who carry both purses and sacks] "Qui portent et bourses et males": Standard slang for the male genitalia, also used in *RR*. Emil Freymond prefers the reading from Lo., a MS unknown to Van Hamel: "Soient blesmes sanguins ou pasles" (Be they white, ruddy, or pale). I find Van Hamel's choice of readings (from MS V) more in keeping with Le Fèvre's generally racy style. For the other reading from Lo. preferred by Freymond, see 2337 and n. 286 above.

494. (3984) someone wiser] "plus sage": Helen Phillips ("Chaucer and Jean Le Fèvre," 35) comments on this line: "Would it be ridiculous to suggest that there might be a precedent here for the advent of that 'man of gret auctorite' at the end of Chaucer's *House of Fame*?" In the same passage, she notes that Chaucer may have

found a model in this passage for his own "inability to finish works, or bring them to satisfactory 'closure.'" I suggest that both Le Fèvre and Chaucer may be quite purposeful and protomodern in their avoidance of finality and their closing appeals for an active reader-response to their works.

495. (3987) resolved] "determinée": Swift (*Gender, Writing, and Performance*, 150) notes how this word refers to a *determinatio*, the scholastic term for the final judgment at a disputation.

496. (3989) Le Fèvre accuses other writers (and by implication himself, the translator of *Lamentations*) of writing attacks on women in order to make money. Unfortunately nothing is known of Le Fèvre's literary patrons or customers with the exception of "Aubery Bernay, dit l'enfant de Tonnerre," otherwise unknown, who requested his *Hymnes de la Liturgie*: see Hasenohr, *Respit de la mort*, liii.

497. (3991) take my leave] "j m'en vois": Swift prefers to translate this phrase with the more informal "now I'm off," a "playfully bathetic conclusion ... [that] highlights how the debate's verdict will never be fixed one way or the other" (*Gender, Writing, and Performance*, 150); however, see the alternate understanding of Le Fèvre's open-ended conclusion at n. 494 above.

Appendix

A Unique Interpolation on Christine de Pizan in a Manuscript of Jehan Le Fèvre's *Lamentations* and *Livre de Leesce* (Prague, National Library of the Czech Republic, XXIII D 74)

In the opening chapter of her *Livre de la cité des dames* (Book of the City of Ladies), author Christine de Pizan describes how she took a rest from her more arduous studies by leafing through a volume of lighter material identified only as "Matheolus," which had been recommended to her as some kind of encomium to women.[1] To her horror and dismay, she discovered it to be just another male-authored work among many that recycled a series of "diableries et de vituperes de femmes et de leurs condicions" (devilish and wicked thoughts about women and their behavior).[2] Christine explains how she was inspired by "Matheolus" and other misogynistic authors to create her literary "City of Ladies," a thoroughgoing text- and experience-based rebuttal to the entire antifeminine tradition.

To understand the intertextuality of *The Book of the City of Ladies*, it is important first to identify the work she repeatedly cites as "Matheolus." (It was an act of scholarly integrity that she did so, even if she failed to acknowledge the full extent of her borrowing[3]; by contrast, her close contemporary Chaucer, while also substantially indebted to Le Fèvre, not once admits to knowing his works under any name.) Is she alluding to the original Latin *Lamentations* by Mahieu of Boulogne, known derisively (for his wretched life circumstances) as "Matheolus"? This is unlikely. All evidence indicates that the Latin work was not nearly as widely copied or read as its fourteenth century French translation, the *Lamentations* of Jehan Le Fèvre.[4] Much more probably, Christine perused a volume that included both Le Fèvre's French *Lamentations* and his original sequel or palinode, *Le livre de Leesce*, a point-by-point profeminine rebuttal to the virulently misogynistic *Lamentations*. As we know from surviving MSS of the companion poems, they were frequently bound as a unit.[5] Christine's description of "Matheolus," as well as the content of her *Book of the City of Ladies*, supports the assumption that she had access to both the *Lamentations* and its sequel; by "Matheolus," she almost certainly referred to both poems in a single-volume format. As copiously documented in this book, there can be no doubt that she borrowed extensively from *Le livre de Leesce* as a paradigm for her masterpiece of profeminine argument, while correcting what she perceived (not without some justice) as its errors and deficiencies. She even repeated as fact two fictitious stories that Le Fèvre had slipped into his poem and claimed as historical truth.[6] Furthermore, she tells us that "Matheolus" had been recommended to her as a work in praise of women[7]; of the companion poems, only *Le livre de Leesce* could possibly be described in such a way. The evidence also supports her knowledge of the *Lamentations*, if only through the hasty perusal she describes in her *Book*.[8] In the person of Lady Reason, Christine excoriates "Matheolus" as heretical in its attack against "l'ordre de mariage, qui est saint estat digne et de Dieu ordené" (the estate of marriage — which is a holy estate, worthy and ordained by God).[9] Of the companion poems, only the *Lamentations* gives free rein to un–Christian views on marriage; in *Leesce*, Le Fèvre is staunchly orthodox in his accolades to wedlock, referring to Mahieu's misogamous opinions only to shoot them down.[10]

In her *Book of the City of Ladies*, Christine's citations of "Matheolus" are relentlessly scornful and dismissive. She calls it a "little book ... of no authority ... of a bad name," full of "lies," "of no use in developing virtue or manners," "lack[ing] integrity in diction and theme," and in short, a mere "trufferie."[11] Like a number of modern critics, she speculates on whether the misogynistic rants of "Matheolus" should be taken to heart as serious invective against women, or treated with detachment as some kind of literary game.[12] However, for Christine, the real-world consequences of antifeminine discourse — rejection of marriage, promiscuity, even wife-beating — were too serious to be neutralized with a hermeneutics of evasion.[13] Her polemics on women are passionately designed to refute the topoi of the misogynistic tradition in their most obvious literal meaning.

But what did the scholarly "Matheolus" think of Christine? Taken literally, of course, the question is absurd. Neither Mahieu de Boulogne (fl. 1290) nor Jehan Le Fèvre (b. ca. 1326) could have lived long enough to comment on her life as an author. Still, the relationship between Le Fèvre and Christine was reciprocal and intertextual in the most literal sense of the term. I am referring to a unique twenty-six-line scribal interpolation on Christine in a MS of the *Lamentations* and *Livre de Leesce*, discovered by Emil Freymond in 1908,[14] three years after an edition of the companion poems had been completed and published by A.-G. Van Hamel as the two-volume work we still use today. Freymond describes how the MS turned up quite unexpectedly in the Bibliothek des Fürsten [Prince] Georg Lobkowitz of Prague, in the course of a scholarly search through the private and monastic libraries of that city for medieval MSS in German. Noted in the library catalogue only under the cryptic phrase "enthaltend Werk in provinzialischer Sprache" (containing a work in the provincial language), the MS had gone unnoticed up to then.[15] As described by Freymond, the paper MS is composed of 260 folios copied by two scribes, "S¹" for folios 1–87v, and "S²" ("der nachlässige Kopist" [the careless copyist])[16] for the remainder. Around one thousand lines of *Leesce* were copied from pages evidently assembled out of order.[17] Freymond dates the MS to 1430 at the earliest, as the interpolation refers to Christine as already deceased[18]; he named it "MS Lo." after the library where he discovered it. Today, the MS is housed in the National Library of the Czech Republic.

Channeling "Matheolus" as translated by Le Fèvre, the anonymous scribe inserted a twenty-six-line encomium to Christine amid a passage from the *Lamentations* that she would have rightly perceived as slanderous, heretical, and obscene. Appearing at folio 110v, the interpolation must be the work of S², who in Freymond's conjecture "wohl aus dem Osten stammte" (may well have come from the East).[19] Of course, it is also possible that the lines were not composed by the Careless Scribe, but copied by him (or her) from an exemplar lost or yet to be discovered. The passage immediately preceding the interpolation (2.4035ff.) can be paraphrased as follows: once you marry, your wife will want to dominate you in all things; keeping tabs on your wife is like plowing sand; if you absolutely must get married, take a hundred wives, not just one; if you have a thousand wives, it's as good as having none at all. Solomon and Ovid agree on this advice. All of this leads up to *Lamentations* 2.4098: "N espouses pas aiez amies" (Don't get married — have girlfriends!).

Following this line, without a hint of conscious irony, the penman (or her) has placed his interpolation in praise of Christine de Pizan, evidently unnoticed since its publication in 1908. Here is Freymond's transcription, followed by my translation:

> A ce propos je te diray
> un exemple qui est tout vray
> Que je vy en mon temps durant
> Et dune femme proprement
> (5) Nommee fu dame cristine
> En nom et en science digne
> Et bien lettree et bien saichant
> Et bien amee et bien amant
> Elle fist de moult beaulx volumes
> (10) Bien auctorises que nous leumes
> Son pere sembla de prudence
> Maistre Thomas qui tant science
> En france apporte de boulongne
> Qui fu retenu sans eslongne
> (15) Astronomien du bon roy
> Charles le quint et sans desroy
> Bien le servi toute sa vie
> Mais bien te dy quonques envie
> Neust cristine de marier
> (20) Franchement voult studier
> Elle voult fuir bigamie
> Tant que vesqui et fu en vie
> Elle complia plusieurs liures
> Moult gracieux se tu as vivres[20]
> (25) Bien aise je lo que ty tiengnes
> Et que cest exemple retiengnes

Here the MS resumes with *Lamentations* 2.4099: "Se tu es de fraile nature."[21] These lines may be translated as follows:

> In this connection I will give you an example that is completely true, that I saw in my lifetime, of a woman whose right name was Lady Christine, of good repute and profound knowledge, both loving and well loved. She wrote many beautiful and most author-itative books that we read. By her prudence she resembled her father, Master Thomas, who brought much learning to France from Bologna. He was employed without interruption as astronomer by the good King Charles the Fifth, whom he served all his life without misdeed. I tell you in no uncertain terms that Christine never had any desire to [re]marry. She strongly preferred to study in freedom and to reject bigamy for as long as she lived and was in life. She finished many wonderful books. If you have the means to live on, I recommend you heed and remember this example.

The discussion that follows will focus on two questions: how fairly did the interpolator impersonate the translator-author of the *Lamentations* and *Le livre de Leesce*? And how accu-rately did he or she understand and represent the life choices of Christine de Pizan?

Despite the incongruity of a tribute to Christine in such a context, the themes of the interpolation fit in most likely quite seamlessly with both the French translation and its sequel. (Of course, the Scribe had yet to copy *Le livre de Leesce* as he worked on the *Lamentations*—*Leesce* did not necessarily serve as a direct influence on the interpolation.) As noted elsewhere in this volume, Le Fèvre was intensely concerned with the factual truth of his sources. To support his profeminine argument, he even recounted the examples of several real-life contemporary women.[22] By citing Christine's well-known story as an "exemple ... tout vray," the Scribe (not so "Careless" here) displays a similar preoccupation. In historical fact, Christine avoided "bigamy" in the patristic sense of the term; on the death of her husband, she chose to live the rest of her life as a single woman, as she writes in her autobiographical *L'advision de Christine*: "N'oubliant ma foy et bonne amour promise a lui deliberay en sain propos de jamaiz autre n'avoir" (Mindful of my vow and the good love I promised him, I decided in a sound determination never to take another [husband]).[23] The moral of the exemplum as told by the Scribe—it is best to avoid marriage, especially "bigamous" unions—also fully conforms with the professed agenda of the *Lamentations*. Christine's reported motive for eschewing "bigamy"—"franchement voult estudier"—is deeply rooted in the topos established by Paul, Jerome, and Mahieu de Boulogne (among many others), on the distracting and mentally corrosive ordeal of a life with spouse and children, for the scholar above all.[24]

The Scribe's fidelity to Christine's life history and self-understanding is much more questionable. On the one hand, the passage is composed of nothing but accurate information. It may even be a summary-paraphrase of several chapters in Christine's own *L'advision*. In those chapters, Christine praised her accomplished father,[25] affirmed her promise never to remarry,[26] and described her prolific authorship (fifteen books and counting) as compensation for her lonely existence as a single woman. Through the persona of Lady Philosophy, Christine consoles herself on the untimely death of her husband:

> ... il n'est mie doubte que, se ton mary t'eust duré jusques a ore, l'estude tant comme tu as n'eusses frequenté, car occupacion de mainage ne le t'eust souffert, auquel bien d'estude tu te mis comme a la chose plus eslevé selon ton jugement aprés la vie qui est de tous poins pour les pafaiz, c'est la contemplative, laquelle est vraie sapience.

> ... if your husband had survived until the present, you would undoubtedly have spent less time on your studies; for the household chores would not have allowed you this benefit of scholarship, to which you set yourself as to the thing you judged the noblest after the life that is in all respects for the perfect, or the contemplative life.[27]

In other respects, of course, the judgment of the Careless Scribe would have deeply offended the author of *The Book of the City of Ladies*. Christine did not subscribe to Jerome's hateful ideology on "bigamy"; as far as I know, she never used the word at all. In her *Livre des Trois Vertus*, a work of advice for women of all stations, her statement on remarriage is cautionary, not judgmental: it may be necessary or suitable for the youngest widows to remarry, while the others are generally better off as they are.[28] No doubt her relatively tolerant position was influenced by the ubiquity of serial matrimony among the noble class where she found her patrons.[29] On the subject of widows, Christine departed from her usual rhetorical practice, seen especially in *The Book of the City of Ladies*. This was to repeat the most outrageous allegations of the misogynistic authors as rhetorical straw men in order to demolish them with an impassioned argument of her own.[30] However, at no point in the *City of Ladies* (or anywhere else to my knowledge) did she quote or otherwise engage with the topos of widows as inconstant in love and sexually voracious, not even as a pretext for counterargument. There is no reference to the subject at all. For example, the much-maligned Bathsheba is conspicuous by her absence from Christine's profeminine polemics, despite her prominent role in their sources, although she does appear (along with Esther) as a model intercessor and peacemaker in a letter of advice by Christine to Queen Isabeau.[31] Through her strategic silence, Christine most likely expressed her personal discomfort with this material as well as her utter contempt for it. It is safe to say that she would have indignantly rejected the use of her life story as a case in point for the misogamous theme of Mahieu/Le Fèvre's *Lamentations*. She would have been even more disgusted by the possible innuendo at line 8, "Bien amee et bien amant," that she followed the practice of "free love" recommended as a healthy alternative to marriage in the lines immediately preceding the interpolation. We can be sure she would have been much better pleased with her capsule biography in Martin Le Franc's *Le champion des dames* (1440–42), where she is praised along with Carmentis and others as exemplary proof of women's capacity for excellence in learning.[32] Quite suitably, Christine herself has become a "modern example" to support a profeminine polemic, after using the device so prolifically and skillfully in her *Book of the City of Ladies*.

On one theme, however, Christine and the Careless Scribe were in perfect accord: her choice of the single life was not only well founded in biblical and patristic tradition but a good career move. It led to her "finish[ing] books" (line 23), no easy task for anyone. Although the topos of marriage as a hindrance to study is just that, a commonplace, its employment by Christine and later by the Scribe is, if not unique, at least uncommon and ahead of its time.[33] Other writers, including Heloïse, had quoted authoritative sources to discourage a gifted *man* from disrupting his pursuit of philosophy by taking on the burdens of a spouse and children.[34] Informed by the "true example" of Christine, the Scribe has produced a rare affirmation of the scholarly life as a legitimate choice for a *woman*, and not only a woman but an author whose works were produced in and for the secular world.

In the tradition of my author, I plan to work with a colleague "plus sage" in examining MS Lo., along with all the fascinating issues in social and literary history involved with the manuscript.

NOTES

1. An earlier draft of this appendix was presented to a session of the Christine de Pizan Society chaired by Benjamin F. Semple at the 46th International Congress of Medieval Studies, Kalamazoo, MI, 15 May 2011, under the title "An Intertextual Affair: Christine de Pizan Reads 'Matheolus,' 'Matheolus' Reads Christine." Attendees at the session contributed their helpful insights, acknowledged below. I also wish to thank codicologist Tina-Marie Ranalli for her help with the appendix, along with Petr Slouka and Jindřich Marek for tracing the present location of MS Lo.

2. *Città delle dame*, ed. Caraffi and Richards, 42; *Book of the City of Ladies*, trans. Richards, rev. ed., 4.

3. See the introduction (n. 9).

4. The Latin *Lamentations* survives in five MSS: see *Matheus von Boulogne*, ed. Schmitt, 22–27.

5. For a list of surviving MSS of *Lamentations* and *Le Livre de Leesce* bound together, see the bibliography in this volume.

6. See the introduction (nn.91–93); also see notes to the translation 149 and 332.

7. *Città delle dame*, ed. Caraffi and Richards, 40; *Book of the City of Ladies*, trans. Richards, rev. ed., 3.

8. *Città delle dame*, ed. Caraffi and Richards, 40; *Book of the City of Ladies*, trans. Richards, rev. ed., 3.

9. *Città delle dame*, ed. Caraffi and Richards, 48; *Book of the City of Ladies*, trans. Richards, rev. ed., 7.

10. See *LL* 221–26, 244–47, 374–82, 1241–70, 1423–26, 1706–12, 1905–62; introduction (nn. 65, 67).

11. *Città delle dame*, ed. Caraffi and Richards, 40, 42; *Book of the City of Ladies*, trans. Richards, rev. ed., 3–4.

12. In the voice of Lady Reason, Christine speculated that "Matheolus" might have used the figure of "antiphrasis" to express one thing by saying the opposite: *Città delle dame*, ed. Caraffi and Richards, 48; *Book of the City of Ladies*, trans. Richards, rev. ed., 7. For modern critics who question whether the misogyny of Mahieu or Le Fèvre should be taken literally as a statement of the author's views, see the introduction (nn. 28 and 45).

13. On the destructive real-life consequences of misogynistic discourse as perceived by Christine and her

ally Gerson, see the introduction (nn. 67 and 68). On husbands spurred by misogynistic reading to beat their wives, see Christine de Pizan, "October 2, 1402: Christine's Reponse to Pierre Col," in Christine McWebb, "*Debating the* Roman de la Rose," 174, 177.

14. See Emil Freymond,"Eine Prager Handschrift der Lamentations de Matheolus und des Livre de Leësce," *Prager Deutsche Studien* 8 (1908): 565–83. The interpolation is transcribed at 581–82.

15. Ibid., 568.

16. Ibid., 573.

17. Ibid., 572.

18. Ibid., 571.

19. Ibid., 572. He considers "S¹" to be "ein Pikarde."

20. In our discussion of my paper at Kalamazoo 2011 (see n. 1 above), we found lines 23 and 24 rather puzzling. The Middle French word *vivres* (the plural of *vivre*) usually means "food," although it sometimes rather connotes "means to live on." I initially translated the lines as "She finished many wonderful books if you can afford them." Bernard Ribémont suggested the full stop after "liures," which I have adopted here.

21. The following lines advise the male reader who is weak in nature to have many mistresses; if he is strong, he should just avoid women.

22. See *LL* 2873–88 and notes. For Le Fèvre's concern for the veracity of his examples, see also the introduction (000). For the "real-life example" in *LL* and related works, see *LL* 1140–54 and n. 167 to the translation; also *LL* 2853–88 and n. 354 to the translation.

23. For the French text, see Christine de Pizan, *Le livre de l'advision de Christine*, ed. Christine Reno and Liliane Dulac (Paris: Honoré Champion, 2001), 100; for the English version quoted here, see *Christine's Vision*, trans. Glenda McLeod, Garland Library of Medieval Literature 68B (New York: Garland, 1993), 11. This comparison with *L'advision* was suggested in the discussion of my paper at Kalamazoo (see n. 1 above) by Julia Nephew.

24. 1 Cor. 7:32–33; Jerome, *Against Jovinianus* 1.47, trans. Fremantle, 383–84; and Mahieu's Latin *Lamentations* 42–66, 1057ff.

25. The Scribe's capsule biography of Christine more closely resembles *L'advision*, book 3, chaps. 6–18 than it does her autobiographical passage in *Le livre de la mutacion de fortune*, ed. Suzanne Solente, Société des Anciens Textes Français (Paris: A. J. Picard, 1959), lines 51–1460, although of course it has much in common with both. Christine tells us of her father at *L'advision*, book 3, chap. 17; ed. Reno and Dulac, 121; *Christine's Vision*, trans. McLeod, 127; also in *Mutacion de fortune* 157–210.

26. In *Mutacion de fortune* 1395–99, Christine sounds a little more open to the possibility of returning to the life of a married woman.

27. *L'advision*, book 3, chaps. 8, 10, and 18; ed. Reno and Dulac, 123; *Christine's Vision*, trans. McLeod, 129. Elsewhere in *L'advision*, she writes of her prolific authorship as the result of her painful bereavement: *L'advision*, ed. Reno and Dulac, 108, 111; *Christine's Vision*, trans. McLeod, 117, 119–20. Christine's view of widowhood as potentially liberating is explored in Liliane Dulac, "Les ouvertures closes dans le *Livre de la cité des dames* de Christine de Pizan: Le *topos* du 'veuvage qualifiant,'" *Vers un thesaurus informatisé: Topique des ouvertures narratives avant 1800*, Actes quatrième colloque international SATOR, 25–27 October 1990, ed. Pierre Rodriguez and Michele Weil (Montpellier: Université Paul-Valéry, 1990), 35–45; and Kevin Brownlee, "Widowhood, Sexuality and Gender in Christine de Pizan," *Romanic Review* 86 (1995): 339–53.

28. *Le livre des trois vertus*, ed. Willard and Hicks, 193 (book 3, chap. 4); *A Medieval Woman's Mirror of Honor: The Treasury of the City of Ladies*, ed. and trans. Willard and Cosman, 201. She reserves her scorn for the widow who marries a younger man. On Christine's view of widowhood as a direct response to a passage in *LL*, see 1729ff. and translation n. 228.

29. For example, the dedicatee of her *L'épistre de la prison de la vie humaine*, Mary of Berry, was married three times; see Christine de Pizan, The Epistle of the Prison of Human Life *with* An Epistle to the Queen of France *and* Lament on the Evils of the Civil War, trans. Josette A. Wisman (New York: Garland, 1984), 3 n. 1. At no point does Christine disparage her as a trigamist.

30. For an example of how Christine repeatedly quoted misogynistic topoi to introduce her counterarguments, see the introduction (n. 100). Many of her chapter titles in *The Book of the City of Ladies* consist of misogynistic arguments, to be refuted in the chapter that follows.

31. See "An Epistle to the Queen of France," ed. and trans. Wisman, 76, 77. There is but dubious biblical evidence for Bathsheba in this innocent role: see 1 Kings 1:15–17 and 1 Kings 2: 13, 22.

32. *Le champion des dames*, ed. Deschaux, 18942ff.; ed. and trans. Taylor, 135–36 (lines 4118ff.).

33. Christine's opinion, echoed by the Careless Scribe, that the single state was best for a woman scholar as well as a man, is early but not unheard of in Western literary history; see for example Anne R. Larsen, "With Camille Morel (1547–after 1611) and later Marie de Gournay (1565–1645), Catherine des Roches is the first major woman writer in France to refuse marriage": *From Mother to Daughter*, ed. and trans. Larsen (Chicago: University of Chicago Press, 2006), 81. I am indebted to Susan Tarcov (personal communication) for the reference.

34. Abelard quotes Heloïse's antimatrimonial arguments in his *Historia calamitatum*, in *Letters of Abelard and Heloise*, trans. Radice, 70–74.

Annotated Bibliography

Manuscripts of the French *Lamentations* and *Livre de Leesce* Discovered to Date

[These designations only take into account LL and L. In some cases, there other texts present in the codex.]

LL only

P   Paris, Bibliothèque nationale de France (BnF), Français 2243

V   Rome, Biblioteca Apostolica Vaticana, Reginensi 1519

L only

A   Paris, BnF, Français 12479

C   BnF, Français 1657

D   BnF, Français 12480

G   Geneva, Bibliothèque de Genève, Comites Latentes 169

L   London, British Library, Add MS 30985 [formerly British Museum 30985]

M   Montpellier, Bibliothèque universitaire de médecine, H254

T   Tours, Bibliothèque municipale, 897

[new]   Cambridge, Harvard University, Houghton Library, French 169

[new]   London, British Library, Harley 6298

L and LL

B   Paris, BnF, Français 24312

F   Florence, Biblioteca Medicea Laurenziana, Ashburnham 119

N   London, British Library, Royal MS 20 B XXI

Lo   Prague, National Library of the Czech Republic, XXIII D 74 [formerly Prague Lobkowicz Library 448]

K   Carpentras, Bibliothèque municipale inguimbertine, Duhamel 376 [Lambert 372]

Aug.   Wolfenbüttel, Herzog August Bibliothek, Codex Guelferbytanus 5. Augusteus 4to. [Heinemann 2948]

The Works of Jehan Le Fèvre

Le Fèvre, Jehan, trans. "Der Cato Jean Lefèvre's nach der Turiner Handschrift I. III. 14. zum erstenmal herausgegeben." Ed. J. Ulrich. *Romanische Forschungen* 15 (1904): 70–106. [Edition of Le Fèvre's French translation of "Cato." Same issue of journal includes Ulrich's editions of three other medieval French "Catos."]

[_____?]. "Chants royaux, ballades et rondeaux prononcés en l'honneur de la sainte Vierge au Puy de Rouen." MS Bibliothèque impériale 6989. [Hippolyte Cocheris (*La vieille*, xxxvi) claims without explanation that two unsigned ballades in this MS were Le Fèvre's work. Van Hamel, *Les Lamentations* 2.clxxxvi, argues that these are not the work of our Le Fèvre.]

[_____?]. *La danse macabré*. [Not extant. Critics have inferred that Le Fèvre wrote a work of this title from *Respit de la mort* 3078, "Je fis de Macabré la dance." For the debate on whether this work ever actually existed, see Paris, "La *dance macabré*," and Batany, "Les danses macabres."]

_____, trans. *Ecloga Theoduli*. Bibliothèque Nationale fr. MSS 572, 19123, 24864 and nouv. Acq. Lat. 1107. [Described in Hasenohr, xlviii–xlix.]

[_____, trans.?] *L'epistre sur les miseres de la vie*. Bibliothèque Nationale MS fr. 19137.] [Gröber ("Französische Literatur," 1067) mysteriously cites this work as "vielleicht nur ein Abschnitt" (possibly only a section) of the *Lamentations*. Aside from this remark and the inclusion of this title on the Arlima website (http://www.arlima.net/il/jean_le_fevre_de_ressons.html), there is no other critical reference to this work, and no explanation of its attribution to Le Fèvre.]

_____, trans. *Hymnes de la liturgie*. Bibliothèque Nationale MS fr. 964.

_____, trans. "From the *Lamentations of Matheolus*." [Excerpts.] Trans. Karen Pratt. In *Woman Defamed and Woman Defended: An Anthology of Medieval Texts*, ed. Alcuin Blamires with Karen Pratt and C. W. Marx, 177–97. [Includes 1.732–64, 824–902, 1079–1166, 2.1–114, 177–250, 451–

578, 847–946, 1107–1242, 1315–36, 1671–1702, 2589–2648, 2759–90, 4095–4142, and 3.1399–1459. This is the only English translation of *L* outside of short quotations embedded in critical works.]

_____, trans. *Les Lamentations de Matheolus*. Studi e Ricerche 86. Ed. Tiziano Pacchiarotti. 2nd ed. Alessandria: Edizioni dell'Orso, 2010. [With introduction and glossary but without textual notes. Includes the Latin *Lamentations*. Lineation identical to that of Van Hamel. Does not acknowledge MSS discovered post–Van Hamel.]

_____, trans. *Les lamentations de Mathéolus*. Ed. A.-G. Van Hamel. *Les lamentations de Matheolus et Le livre de Leësce, par Jehan Le Fevre, de Resson*. Vol. 1. Paris: Émile Bouillon, 1892. [Republished electronically, http://www.archive.org/details/leslamentations00hamegoog. Includes an edition of the Latin *Lamentations* based on the single MS known to Van Hamel.]

_____. *Le Livre de Leesce*. [Excerpt.] *Romvart. Beiträge zur kunde mittelalterlicher Dichtung aus italienischen Bibliotheken*. Ed. Adalbert Keller. Paris: Jules Renouard & Cie, 1844. 368–79. [Included in an anthology of medieval poems found in MSS from Italian libraries.]

_____. *Le livre de Mathéolus, poème français de xive siècle par Jean Lefevre, nouvelle édition, revue sur les manuscrits et les éditions gothiques*. 2 vols. Ed. Ed. [*sic*] Tricotel. Brussels: Imprimerie de A. Mertens et Fils, 1846, 1864. [Edition of *Lamentations* superseded by Van Hamel's edition.]

_____. *Le livre de Leësce*. Ed. A.-G. Van Hamel. *Les lamentations de Matheolus et Le livre de Leésce, par Jehan Le Fevre, de Resson*. Vol. 2. Paris: Émile Bouillon, 1905. Republished electronically, http://www.archive.org/details.leslamentations00hamegoog. [To date, the only complete edition of *Le Livre de Leesce*.]

_____. *Le respit de la mort. Poèmes de la mort de Turold à Villon*. Ed. and trans. Jean-Marcel Paquette. Bibliothèque Médiévale. Paris: Union Générale d'Éditions, 1979. 160–63. [Lines 3071–94, in Middle French with glossary.]

_____. *Le respit de la mort de Jehan LeFèvre*. Ed. Geneviève Hasenohr. Paris: A. & J. Picard, 1969. [Introduction is a work of scholarship with information on Le Fèvre biography and MSS.]

_____, trans. *La vieille, ou Les dernières amours d'Ovide: Poeme français du XIVe siècle traduit du latin de Richard de Fournival par Jehan LeFèvre*. Ed. Hippolyte Cocheris. Paris: Auguste Aubry, 1861. [Edition of Le Fèvre's French translation of the Pseudo-Ovidian *De vetula*.]

_____, trans. "*La Vieille* de Jean Le Fèvre, édition et étude de la traduction versifiée de *De Vetula*, poème attribué a Richard de Fournival." Ed. Marie-Madeleine Huchet. Diss. Paris, École Pra-

tique des Hautes Études, 2009. [Thesis directed by Geneviève Hasenohr, cited in Pacchiarotti, ed., *Les Lamentations* 123.]

Other Primary Sources

Abelard. "Abelard's Letter of Consolation to a Friend." Ed. J. T. Muckle. *Mediaeval Studies* 12 (1950): 175–211. [Latin text of the *Historia calamitatum*.]

_____. From Letter 6, "On the Origin of Nuns." Trans. Alcuin Blamires. In Alcuin Blamires et al., *Woman Defamed and Woman Defended*, 232–36. [Abelard's encomium to women; probably the source for Le Fèvre's view of Abelard as sympathetic to women, *LL* 2786ff.]

_____. "The Letter of Heloise on Religious Life and Abelard's First Reply." Ed. J. T. Muckle. *Mediaeval Studies* 17 (1955): 240–81. [Has Latin text of Abelard's encomium to women.]

_____. "The Personal Letters of Abelard and Heloise." Ed. J. T. Muckle. *Mediaeval Studies* 15 (1953): 47–94. [The Latin text.]

Abelard and Heloise. *The Letters of Abelard and Heloise*. Trans. Betty Radice. Harmondsworth: Penguin, 1974. [Probably the source for Le Fèvre's view of Heloïse as a "philosopher," *LL* 1135.]

Aristoteles Latinus. Ed. L. Minio-Paluello et al. Bruges: Desclee de Brouwer, later Leiden: Brill, 1961–75. [Includes the works of Aristotle in the form known to Le Fèvre and his Western European contemporaries.]

Baird, Joseph L., and John R. Kane, eds. and trans. *La querelle de la Rose: Letters and Documents*. University of North Carolina Studies in the Romance Languages and Literatures 199. Chapel Hill: University of North Carolina, 1978. [English translation of *querelle* documents.]

Benoît de Sainte-Maure. *Le roman de Troie, pub. d'après tous les manuscrits connus*. Ed. Léopold Constans. Société des Anciens Textes Français 52, 55, 57, 62, 67. Paris: Firmin Didot, 1904–12. [Possible source for some details on Medea and Circe in *LL*.]

Benson, Larry D., and Theodore M. Andersson, eds. *The Literary Context of Chaucer's Fabliaux: Texts and Translations*. New York: Bobbs-Merrill, 1971. [Does not mention Le Fèvre; provides a literary context and some analogues for his *fabliaux*.]

Bersuire, Pierre. "The *Ovidius Moralizatus* of Petrus Berchorius: An Introduction and Translation." Trans. William Donald Reynolds. Diss., University of Illinois, 1971. [Fourteenth century mythographer uses an allegorical approach quite different from Le Fèvre's literalism.]

Biblia sacra iuxta vulgatam versionem. Stuttgart: Deutsche Bibelgesellschaft, 1994.

Blamires, Alcuin, ed., with Karen Pratt and C. W. Marx. *Woman Defamed and Woman Defended: An Anthology of Medieval Texts.* Oxford: Clarendon, 1992. [Well-annotated anthology of primary sources for and against women.]

Boccaccio, Giovanni. *Concerning Famous Women.* Trans. Guido A. Guarino. New Brunswick, NJ: Rutgers University Press, 1963.

_____. *The Corbaccio, or the labyrinth of love.* Rev. ed. Trans. Anthony K. Cassell. Binghamton, NY: Medieval and Renaissance Texts & Studies, 1993. [Misogynistic screed having many commonalities with *L*.]

_____. *De mulieribus claris.* Ed. Vittorio Zaccaria. 2nd ed. *Tutte le opere di Giovanni Boccaccio*, vol. 10. Verona: Mondadori, 1970.

_____. *Famous Women.* Ed. and trans. Virginia Brown. I Tatti Renaissance Library I. Cambridge: Harvard University Press, 2001. [Dual language edition.]

_____. *Famous Women.* Trans. Virginia Brown. I Tatti Renaissance Library. Cambridge: Harvard University Press, 2003. [English translation only.]

Chaucer, Geoffrey. *The Canterbury Tales. The Riverside Chaucer.* 3rd ed. Ed. Larry D. Benson. Boston: Houghton Mifflin, 1987.

_____. *The Legend of Good Women. The Riverside Chaucer.* 3rd ed. Ed. Larry D. Benson. Boston: Houghton Mifflin, 1987: 587–630.

_____. *The Romaunt of the Rose. The Riverside Chaucer.* 3rd ed. Ed. Larry D. Benson. Boston: Houghton Mifflin, 1987: 685–767. [Translates *leesce* as "gladness," the reading I have chosen for my book.]

Christine de Pizan. *The Book of the City of Ladies.* Trans. Rosalind Brown-Grant. Harmondsworth: Penguin, 1999.

_____. *The Book of the City of Ladies.* Trans. Earl Jeffrey Richards. Rev. ed. New York: Persea Books, 1998. [Christine's profeminine masterpiece; has many borrowings from *LL*.]

_____. *Christine's Vision.* Trans. Glenda K. McLeod. Garland Library of Medieval Literature, Series B 68. New York: Garland, 1993. [Translation of *L'advision Christine*. Describes how Christine was freed by her widowhood to study and write books.]

_____. *La città delle dame.* Ed. Earl Jeffrey Richards. Trans. Patrizia Caraffi. 2nd ed. Trento: Luni, 1998. [First published edition of the original French text, in a dual-language format with Italian translation.]

_____. *The Epistle of the Prison of Human Life with An Epistle to the Queen of France and Lament on the Evils of the Civil War.* Ed. and trans. Josette A. Wisman. Garland Library of Medieval Literature 21A. New York: Garland, 1984. [Dual language edition.]

_____. *Epistre au dieu d'amours* and *Dit de la Rose.* In *Poems of Cupid, God of Love*, ed. and trans. Thelma S. Fenster and Mary Carpenter Erler.

New York: E. J. Brill, 1990. [Polemical responses to *RR*, with many parallels to *LL*.]

_____. *Epistre Othea.* Ed. Gabriella Parussa. Geneva: Librairie Droz, 1999. [Provides an allegorical interpretation of pagan mythology quite distinct from the literalist readings in *LL* and Christine's own polemics on women.]

_____. *"Le livre de la cité des dames:* A Critical Edition." Ed. Maureen Curnow. Ph.D. diss., Vanderbilt University, 1975. [Indispensable edition of the original French text; to date the only fully annotated edition, with documentation of Christine's debt to *LL*.]

_____. *Le livre de l'advision de Christine.* Ed. Christine Reno and Liliane Dulac. Études Christiniennes 4. Paris: Honoré Champion, 2001. [Annotated edition of the French text.]

_____. *Le livre de la mutacion de fortune.* Ed. Suzanne Solente. 4 vols. Société des Anciens Textes Français. Paris: A. J. Picard, 1959. [Christine describes (lines 1313ff.) how the trials of widowhood transformed her into a man.]

_____. *Le livre des trois vertus: Édition Critique.* Ed. Charity Cannon Willard and Eric Hicks. Paris: Honoré Champion, 1989. [Sequel to *Le livre de la cité des dames.* Christine's views on widows and prostitutes contrast with those of Mahieu and Le Fèvre.]

_____. *A Medieval Woman's Mirror of Honor: The Treasury of the City of Ladies.* Trans. Charity Cannon Willard. Ed. and intro. Madeleine Pelner Cosman. New York: Persea Books, 1989. [Translation of *Le livre des trois vertus*, the sequel to Christine's *Livre de la cité des dames.*]

_____. *The Selected Writings of Christine de Pizan.* Ed. and trans. Renate Blumenfeld-Kosinski. New York: Norton, 1997.

_____. *The Writings of Christine de Pizan.* Ed. Charity Cannon Willard. New York: Persea Books, 1994. [English only. Includes Christine's account in *Le livre de la mutacion de fortune* of how the trials of widowhood transformed her into a man.]

Deschamps, Eustache. *Le miroir de mariage. Oeuvres complètes*, vol. 9, ed. Gaston Raynaud. SATF. Paris: Firmin Didot, 1894. [A work contemporary with and having many parallels to *L* and *LL*.]

"Dido and Aeneas Moralized." *Medieval English and French Legends: An Anthology of Religious and Secular Narrative.* Trans. R. Barton Palmer. Glen Allen, VA: College Publishing, 2006. 283–96. [Translation of the *Ovide Moralisé* 1.1–57 and 14.302–601.]

Diner, Judith Bruskin, trans. *The One Hundred New Tales (Les cent nouvelles nouvelles).* Garland Library of Medieval Literature 30B. New York: Garland, 1990. [Fifteenth-century collection of stories; chap. 61 is an analogue to *LL* 621ff.]

Fiero, Gloria K., Wendy Pfeffer, and Mathé Allain,

ed. and trans. *Three Medieval Views of Women: La contenance des fames, Le bien des fames, Le blasme des fames.* New Haven: Yale University Press, 1989. [Dual language edition of two antifeminist *dits* and one defense, *Le bien des femmes*, a 96-line poem of the early fourteenth century with parallels to *LL*.]

The Fifteen Joys of Marriage. Trans. B. A. Pitts. New York: Peter Lang, 1985. [A fifteenth-century antimatrimonial satire.]

Geoffroy de la Tour Landry. *The Book of the Knight of the Tower.* Trans. William Caxton. Ed. M. Y. Offord. EETS supplementary series 2. New York: Oxford, 1971.

_____. *Le livre du Chevalier de La Tour Landry, pour enseignement de ses filles.* Ed. M. Anatole de Montaiglon. Paris: Guiraudet et Jouaust, Librairie Jannet, 1854; rpt. Charleston, SC: Nebo Press, 2010. Also published electronically, http://www.kobobooks.com. [A book of advice for young women with parallels to *L* and *LL*.]

Gerson, Jean. *Oeuvres complètes.* Ed. Mgr. Glorieux. 10 vols. in 11. Paris: Desclée, 1960–73.

Gesta Romanorum. Ed. Hermann Oesterley. 1872; rpt. Hildesheim: Georg Olms, 1963. [Has sources and/or analogues to Mahieu/Le Fèvre exempla.]

Gower, John. *The Complete Works of John Gower.* Ed. G. C. Macaulay. 4 vols. Oxford: Clarendon, 1899–1902.

_____. *Confessio amantis.* Ed. Russell A. Peck. TEAMS Middle English Text Series. 3 vols. Kalamazoo, MI: Medieval Institute Publications, 2000–2004.

Guido delle Colonne. *Historia destructionis Troiae.* Ed. Nathaniel Griffin. Cambridge: Harvard University Press, 1936.

_____. *Historia destructionis Troiae.* Trans. Mary Elizabeth Meek. Bloomington: University of Indiana, 1974.

Guillaume de Lorris and Jean de Meun. *Le roman de la Rose.* Ed. Félix Lecoy. 3 vols. Classiques Français du Moyen Age 92, 95, 98. Paris: Champion, 1976–82.

_____. *Le Roman de la Rose: Édition d'après les manuscrits BN 12786 et BN 378.* Ed. Armand Strubel. Lettres gothiques. Paris: Le Livre de Poche, 1992. [Dual language text with modern French.]

_____. *The Romance of the Rose.* Trans. Charles Dahlberg. Princeton: Princeton University Press, 1971.

Henri d'Andely. *Le lai d'Aristote.* Ed. Maurice Delbouille. Paris: Les Belles Lettres, 1951. [Source of "mounted Aristotle" topos.]

Hicks, Eric, ed. *Le debat sur le "Roman de la Rose."* Paris: Honoré Champion, 1977. [Edition of the *querelle* documents in the original French.]

Iacopo da Varazze [Jacobus de Voragine.] *Legenda Aurea.* Ed. Giovanni Paolo Maggioni. 2 vols.

Tavarnuzze: SISMEL, 1998. [Critical edition of the Latin text; includes only the chapters (mostly biographies) accepted as authored by Jacobus.]

Jacobus de Voragine. *The Golden Legend (Legenda Aurea) Compiled by Jacobus de Voragine, 1275, Englished by William Caxton, 1483.* www.fordham.edu/halsall/basis/goldenlegend/index.asp [Online edition of Caxton's *Golden Legend*, an expanded version probably similar to the one used by Le Fevre.]

_____. *The Golden Legend: Readings on the Saints.* Trans. William Granger Ryan. 2 vols. Princeton: Princeton University Press, 1993. [Includes only the chapters (mostly biographies) accepted as authored by Jacobus.]

_____. *Legenda aurea.* Ed. Theodor Graesse. 3rd ed. 1890. Rpt. Osnabrück: Zeller, 1969. [Edition in Latin of the collection of saints' lives cited by Le Fèvre in his defense of women; includes chapters authored by Jacobus, plus chapters added later to the book and evidently known to Le Fèvre.]

Jacques de Vitry. *The Exempla, or Illustrative Stories from the Sermones Vulgares of Jacques de Vitry.* Ed. Thomas Frederick Crane. 1890; rpt. New York: Burt Franklin, 1971. [In Latin. Has possible sources or distant analogues for several of Le Fèvre's *fabliaux*.]

Jehanne de Neuville. "Inventaire dressé par Jeanne de la Neuville (22 avril 1384)." In Gaston Duchesne, *Histoire de l'abbaye royale de Longchamp (1255–1789).* Paris: H. Daragon, 1906. 165–69. [Inventory of convent properties drawn up by the abbess.]

Jerome. *Against Jovinianus. The Principal Works of St. Jerome.* Trans. W. H. Fremantle. New York: Christian Literature Company, 1893. 346–416.

_____. *Epistola adversus Jovinianum.* Ed. J. P. Migne. *Patrologia Latina,* cols. 211–337. [Important source for the medieval palinode. This work includes the antifeminist tract *Liber aureolus de nuptiis*, attributed to Theophrastus, an influential attack on remarriage, and influential examples of historical women both good and bad.]

Juvenal. Excerpts from the Satires. Trans. Rolfe Humphries. In Blamires et al., *Woman Defamed and Woman Defended,* 25–30.

Klopsch, Paul, ed. *Pseudo-Ovidius 'De Vetula': Untersuchungen und Text.* Leiden: E. J. Brill, 1967. [Edition of the Latin text translated by Le Fèvre.]

Le Franc, Martin. *Le champion des dames.* Ed. Robert Deschaux. 5 vols. Paris: Honoré Champion, 1999. [Profeminine polemic of 1440–42 with borrowings from Le Fèvre and a homage to Christine.]

_____. *The Trial of Womankind: A Rhyming Translation of Book IV of the Fifteenth-Century* Le Champion des Dames. Ed. and trans. Steven Millen Taylor. Jefferson, NC: McFarland, 2005.

Machaut, Guillaume de. *The Judgment of the King of Bohemia.* Ed. and trans. R. Barton Palmer. New

York: Garland, 1984. [Retracted for its alleged misogyny by Machaut in his palinode, *The Judgment of the King of Navarre*. Dual language edition.]

———. *The Judgment of the King of Bohemia. An Anthology of Medieval Love Debate Poetry*. Trans. and ed. Barbara K. Altmann and R. Barton Palmer. Gainesville: University Press of Florida, 2006. 11–68.

———. *The Judgment of the King of Navarre*. Ed. and trans. R. Barton Palmer. New York: Garland, 1988. [Dual language edition of Machaut's palinode, where he retracts the claim from his *Jugement du roy de Behaigne* (Judgment of the King of Bohemia), supposedly derogatory to women, that a man whose sweetheart has left him suffers more than a woman whose beloved has died. Probably one of the models for *LL* and Chaucer's *LGW*.]

———. *The Judgment of the King of Navarre. An Anthology of Medieval Love Debate Poetry*. Trans. and ed. Barbara K. Altmann and R. Barton Palmer. Gainesville: University Press of Florida, 2006. 69–176.

———. *Le jugement du roy de Behaigne and Remede de fortune*. Ed. and trans. James I. Wimsatt and William W. Kibler. Music edited by Rebecca A. Baltzer. Chaucer Library. Athens: University of Georgia Press, 1988. [Dual language edition.]

———. *Le livre dou voir dit (The Book of the True Poem)*. Ed. Daniel Leech Wilkinson. Trans. R. Barton Palmer. New York: Garland, 1998. [Dual language edition.]

Mahieu de Boulogne [Matheolus]. *Les lamentations de Matheolus*. [Latin text.] In *Les lamentations de Matheolus et le Livre de Leësce de Jehan Le Fèvre, de Resson*. Ed. A.-G. Van Hamel. Vol. 1. Paris: Émile Bouillon, 1892. [Republished electronically at www.archive.org/details/leslamentations00 hamegoog. The Latin text appears on the corresponding pages of Le Fèvre's French translation.]

———. *Lamenta. Les Lamentations de Matheolus*. Ed. Tiziano Pacchiarotti. Alessandria: Edizioni dell'Orso, 2010. [The Latin *Lamentations*, which the editor calls the *Lamenta*, in dual language format with Le Fevre's French. Based on the sole MS known to Van Hamel.]

———. *Matheus von Boulogne: 'Lamentationes Matheoluli' (kommentierte und kritische Edition der beiden ersten Bücher)*. Ed. Alfred Schmitt. Bonn: Druck Rheinischen Friedrich-Wilhelms-Universität, 1974. [Edition of the Latin *Lamentations*, first two (out of four) books only, with helpful introduction and annotations; based on five MSS, four discovered post–Van Hamel.]

Marie de France. *Fabeln*. Ed. Karl Warnke with Eduard Mall. Halle: Niemeyer, 1898; rpt. Slatkine, 1974. [Also published electronically.]

———. *Fables*. Trans. Mary Lou Martin. Birmingham, AL: Summa, 1984. [Dual language text based on the Warnke edition cited by Van Hamel.]

———. *Fables*. Trans. Harriet Spiegel. Toronto: University of Toronto Press, 1987. [Dual language edition.]

McWebb, Christine, ed. *Debating the* Roman de la Rose: *A Critical Anthology*. New York: Routledge, 2007. [Dual language edition of documents from the "querelle de la Rose," which is broadly interpreted to include many works discussing that text. Includes text and translation of Le Fèvre's *Lamentations* 2.1765–1801, an attack on the Beguines.]

Miller, Robert P., ed. *Chaucer: Sources and Backgrounds*. New York: Oxford, 1977. [Still-useful anthology containing pro- and antifeminist primary sources — biblical, patristic, and medieval.]

Montaiglon, Anatole de, and Gaston Reynaud, eds. *Recueil général et complet des fabliaux des XIIIe et XIVe siècles*. 6 vols. 1872–90; rpt. Geneva: Slatkine, 1973. [Has several analogues to *fabliaux* of Mahieu/Le Fèvre.]

Ovid. *Amores*. In *Heroides and Amores*, trans. Grant Showerman. 2nd ed. revised by G. P. Goold. Cambridge: Harvard University Press, 1977. [Contains the influential monologue by Dipsas, the *vetula* or old female bawd.]

———. *Ars amatoria and Remedia amoris. The Art of Love and Other Poems*. Trans. J. H. Mozley. 2nd ed. revised by G. P. Goold. Cambridge: Harvard University Press, 1979.

———. *Fasti*. Trans. James G. Frazer. Rev. G. P. Goold. Cambridge: Harvard University Press, 1989.

———. *Heroides. Heroides and Amores*. Trans. Grant Showerman. 2nd ed. revised by G. P. Goold. Cambridge: Harvard University Press, 1977. [Important influence on the palinode. A collection of letters by abandoned heroines; a hostile revisionist treatment of "heroes" such as Aeneas.]

———. *Metamorphoses*. Trans. Frank Justus Miller. 3rd ed. revised by G. P. Goold. Cambridge: Harvard University Press, 1984.

"Ovide Moralisé": *Poème du commencement du quatorzième siècle*. Ed. C. de Boer. 5 vols. Verhandelingen der Koninklijke Akademie van Wetenschappen te Amsterdam, Afdeeling Letterkunde, Nicuwe Reeks, Deel XV. Amsterdam: Johannes Müller, 1915–38. [French translation of Ovid's *Metamorphoses* with additional material including allegories quite different from Le Fèvre's literalist approach. Also see R. Barton Palmer, trans., "Dido and Aeneas Moralized."]

Petrus Alfonsus. *Die Disciplina clericalis des Petrus Alfonsi, das älteste Novellenbuch des Mittelalters*. Ed. Alfons Hilka and Werner Söderhjelm. Heidelberg: Carl Winter, 1911. [Exempla collection with several distant analogues in *L* and *LL*.]

"Le rebours de Matheolus." Van Hamel, 2: 136–37.

[Anonymous lyric included in an early printed version of *LL*, B.N. Inv. Réserve Yᵉ 257 (anc. 4421).]

"Le resolu en mariage." In Van Hamel, 2: 129–36. [Anonymous lyric included in an early printed version of *LL*, B.N. Inv. Réserve Yᵉ 257 (anc. 4421).]

Robathan, Dorothy M., ed. *The Pseudo-Ovidian 'De vetula': Text, Introduction, and Notes*. Amsterdam: A. M. Hakkert, 1968. [Edition of the Latin text translated by Le Fèvre.]

Salisbury, Eve, ed. *The Trials and Joys of Marriage*. TEAMS Middle English Text Series. Kalamazoo, MI: Medieval Institute, 2001. [Has analogues of "Weeping Bitch" *fabliau* and other satires on women and marriage.]

Theoduli Eclogum. Ed. Joannes Osternacher. Urfahr: Verlag des bischöflichen, 1902. [Edition of the Latin text or a schoolbook translated by Le Fèvre.]

Tobler, Adolf, ed. *Li proverbe au villain: Die Sprichwörter des gemeinen Mannes; altfranzösische Dichtung nach den bischer bekannten Handschriften*. Leipzig: S. Hirzel, 1895.

Vincent of Beauvais. *Speculum Historiale. Speculum Quadruplex sive Speculum Maius*. 1624; rpt. Graz: Akademische Druck, 1964–65. [The *Speculum Historiale* is a possible source for biographies of famous women in *LL*.]

Secondary Sources

Allen, Prudence. *The Concept of Woman*, vol. 2: *The Early Humanist Reformation, 1250–1500*. Grand Rapids: Eerdmans, 2002. [Brief chapter on the denigration of woman in Le Fèvre's *L*.]

Badel, Pierre-Yves. *Le roman de la Rose au XIVe siècle: Étude de la réception de l'oeuvre*. Geneva: Droz, 1980. [Documents in detail, showing parallel passages, Le Fèvre's debt to *RR*; claims that Le Fèvre's *L* was largely responsible for misogynist reputation of *RR* in later Middle Ages.]

Barr, Alan P. "Christine de Pisan's *Ditié de Jehanne d'Arc*: A Feminist Exemplum for the *querelle des femmes*." *Fifteenth Century Studies* 14 (1988): 1–12.

Batany, Jean. "Bonheur et malheur dans les 'estats' sociaux: Le gauchissement hédoniste d'une problematique morale." In *L'idée de bonheur au moyen âge: Actes du Colloque d'Amiens de mars 1984*, ed. Danielle Buschinger. Göppingen: Kummerle, 1990. [Relates *Le respit de la mort* among many other works to the presence or absence of happiness in different estates of society.]

_____. "'Les danses macabres': Une image en negatif du fonctionnalisme social." In *Dies Illa: Death in the Middle Ages*, ed. Jane H. M. Taylor, 15–27. Liverpool: Francis Cairns, 1984. [Argues that *Le respit de la mort* 3078 should be understood as a metaphor for the human condition; Le Fèvre did not write a now-lost *Dance macabré*.]

Blamires, Alcuin. *The Case for Women in Medieval Culture*. Oxford: Clarendon, 1997. [Excellent study on the medieval defense of women. Has the most complete analysis to date of Le Fèvre's influence on Christine. Finds Lady Gladness a weak character and her author's sincerity questionable.]

_____. Introduction. *Woman Defamed and Woman Defended: An Anthology of Medieval Texts*, ed. Blamires, with Karen Pratt and C. W. Marx, 1–15. Oxford: Clarendon, 1992.

Blumenfeld-Kosinski, Renate. "Jean le Fèvre's *Livre de Leësce*: Praise or Blame of Women?" *Speculum* 69 (1994): 705–25. [Argues that *Gladness* is a serious and mostly successful defense of women.]

Brown-Grant, Rosalind. "Christine de Pizan as Defender of Women." In *Christine de Pizan: A Casebook*, ed. Barbara K. Altman and Deborah L. McGrady, 81–100. New York: Routledge, 2003.

Brownlee, Kevin. "Discourses of the Self: Christine de Pizan and the *Rose*." *Romanic Review* 79 (1988): 199–221. [Describes how Christine coopted characters and themes from Jean de Meun to serve her own purposes.]

Bruni, Francesco. "Dal 'De vetula' al 'Corbaccio': L'idea d'amore e i due tempi dell'intellettuale." *Medioevo Romanzo* 1 (1974): 161–216. [Discusses the Latin *De vetula* as an influence on Boccaccio's *Corbaccio*.]

Burke, Linda Barney. "Bohemian Gower: The *Confessio Amantis*, Queen Anne, and Machaut's Judgment Poems." *Machaut's Legacy: The Judgment Poetry Tradition in Late Medieval Literature*. Eds. R. Barton Palmer and Burt Kimmelman. University Press of Florida. Forthcoming.

_____. "Counter-Defamation: Women and Truth in Gower's *Confessio amantis* and Jehan Le Fèvre's *Le livre de Leësce*. [Abstract.] *John Gower Newsletter* 20, no. 2 (2001): 20–21.

_____. "An Intertextual Affair: Christine de Pizan Reads 'Matheolus,' 'Matheolus' Reads Christine." Presented at the 46th International Congress on Medieval Studies, Kalamazoo, MI, 15 May 2011. [Compares Christine's disparagement of "Matheolus" in her *Book of the City of Ladies* with a unique interpolated encomium to Christine in a late MS of Le Fèvre's *L*.]

_____. "'She is the second St. Clare': The Exemplum of Jehanne de Neuville, Abbess of Longchamp, in a Fourteenth-Century Defense of Women by Jehan Le Fèvre." *Franciscan Studies* 2013. Forthcoming.

_____. "The Sources and Significance of 'The Tale of King, Wine, Woman, and Truth' in John Gower's *Confessio amantis*." *Greyfriar: Siena Studies in Literature* 21 (1980): 3–15.

_____. "Women in John Gower's *Confessio amantis*." *Mediaevalia* 3 (1977): 239–60.

Butler, Pierce. Legenda Aurea-Légende Dorée-Golden Legend: *A Study of Caxton's Golden Legend* with *Special Reference to its Relations to the Earlier English Prose Translation*. Baltimore: John Murphy, 1899. [Describes the expanded versions of the Latin *Legend* and its French translations. Le Fèvre likely used one of these.]

Cerquiglini-Toulet, Jacqueline. *A New History of Medieval French Literature*. Trans. Sara Preisig. Baltimore: Johns Hopkins University Press, 2011. [Integrates brief examples from Le Fèvre's works into a wide-ranging history of medieval French literature.]

Comparetti, D. *Vergil in the Middle Ages*. Trans. E. F. M. Benecke. With an Introduction by Robinson Ellis. London: Swan Sonnenschein, 1908. [Has a chapter on Virgil's humiliation by a woman and its relation to similar stories of Aristotle *et al.*]

Curnow, Maureen Cheney. Introduction. In "The *Livre de la Cité des Dames*: A Critical Edition." Ph.D. diss., Vanderbilt University, 1975. [Only complete introduction to *The Book of the City of Ladies* and only one to elucidate Christine's debt to *LL*.]

Daxecker, F. "Three Reading Aids Painted by Tomaso da Modena in the Chapter House of San Nicolò Monastery in Treviso, Italy." *Documenta Ophthalmologica* 99, no. 3 (1999): 219–23. [Provides context on fourteenth-century eyeglasses.]

Delany, Sheila. *The Naked Text: Chaucer's* Legend of Good Women. Berkeley: University of California Press, 1999. [The subject of women is the subject of literature, especially understood as patriarchal authority; does not mention Le Fèvre.]

Dictionnaire du Moyen Français, version 2010. ATILF CNRS — Nancy Université. http://www.atilf.fr/dmf. [Online interactive Middle French dictionary with many citations to literature of the period, including Le Fèvre.]

Dictionnaire du Moyen Français, version 2012 (DMF 2012). ATILF-CNRS & Université de Lorraine. http://www.atilf.fr/dmf. [Online interactive Middle French dictionary with many citations to literature of the period; includes my submission for entry for "pastourelle."]

Di Stefano, Giuseppe. "À propos de: Jean Le Fèvre de Resson, *Les Lamentations de Matheolus*, édition critique par T. Pacchiarotti, Alessandria, Edizioni dell'Orso, 2010, 470 pp." *Le Moyen Français* 70 (2012): 156–58. [Unfavorable review of Pacchiarotti's edition of *L*.]

———. *Dictionnaire des Locutions en Moyen Français*. Bibliothèque du Moyen Français 1. Montréal: Éditions CERES, 1991. [Includes many examples from the *L* and *LL*.]

Donovan, Michelle. "Rewriting Hagiography: The *Livre de la cité des dames*." *Women in French Studies* 4 (Fall 1996): 14–26.

Duchesne, Gaston. *Histoire de l'Abbaye Royale de Longchamp (1255–1789)*. Paris: H. Daragon, 1906. [Includes information on Jehanne de Neuville.]

Dulac, Liliane. "Un mythe didactique chez Christine de Pizan: Semiramis ou La veuve heroïque (du *De mulieribus claris* à *La cité des dames*)." In *Mélanges de Philologie Romane offerts à Charles Camproux*, ed. Robert Lafont et al., 1: 315–43. Montpelier: Université Paul-Valery, 1978. [Otherwise exhaustive study completely overlooks the revisionist and sympathetic treatment of Semiramis in Le Fèvre's *LL* and its obvious role as the prototype for Christine's.]

Ebbesen, Stan. "The Aristotelian Commentator." In *The Cambridge Companion to Boethius*, ed. John Marenbon, 34–36. Cambridge: Cambridge University Press, 2009. [Explains the transmission of Aristotle's works, including those cited by Le Fèvre, to the Western European Middle Ages.]

Economou, George D. "The Character Genius in Alan of Lille, Jean de Meun, and John Gower." *Chaucer Review* 4 (1970): 203–10.

Fehse, Erich. "Sprichwort und Sentenz bei Eustache Deschamps und Dichtern seiner Zeit." *Romanische Forschungen* 19, no. 2 (1906): 5435–94. [A collection that includes the works of Le Fèvre and is thus a valuable complement to Hassell's *Middle French Sentences*.]

Field, Sean L. *Isabelle of France: Capetian Sanctity and Franciscan Identity in the Thirteenth Century*. Notre Dame, IN: University of Notre Dame Press, 2006. [Background information on Longchamp abbey.]

Fleith, Barbara. *Studien zur Überlieferungsgeschichte der lateinischen* Legenda Aurea. Brussels: Société des Bollandistes, 1991. [Explains how many MSS of the Latin *Legenda* include additional saints' lives.]

Freymond, Emil. "Eine Prager Handschrift der Lamentations de Matheolus und des Livre de Leësce." *Prager Deutsche Studien* 8 (1908): 565–83. [Describes a newly discovered MS, christened "Lo.," unknown to Van Hamel because it was tucked away and miscataloged in a small private library in Prague.]

Ghisalberti, Fausto. "Mediaeval Biographies of Ovid." *Journal of the Warburg and Courtauld Institutes* 9 (1946): 10–59.

Green, R. P. H. "The Genesis of a Medieval Textbook: The Models and Sources of the *Ecloga Theoduli*." *Viator* 13 (1982): 49–106. [Detailed documentation of the sources of the Latin *Ecloga*.]

Gröber, Gustav. "Französische Literatur." In *Grundriss der romanischen Philologie*, ed. Gustav Gröber, 2.1: 433–1247. Strassburg: K. J. Trübner, 1897. [Discussion of Le Fèvre, 1066–67, claims without explanation that Le Fèvre wrote an *Epistre sur les miseres de la vie humaine*.]

Guglielminetti, Marziano. "Jean le Fèvre et Machiavel: Matheolus et Belphégor." In *L'aube de la*

Renaissance, ed. Dario Cecchetti et al., 225–32. Bibliothèque Franco-Simone. Geneva: Slatkine, 1991. [Compares Machiavelli's tale of Belphégor with a possible source, Le Fèvre's exemplum of a devil who went back to hell rather than stay with his wife, *L* 2.3853ff. Elucidates how Le Fèvre et al. understood the genres of *fable* and *exemple*.]

Hamilton, George L. "Les sources du *Tiaudelet*." *Romania* 48 (1922): 124–27. [Argues that Le Fèvre's French *Ecloga Theoduli* must have been translated from a Latin MS containing introduction and commentary.]

———. "Theodulus: A Medieval Textbook." *Modern Philology* 7 (1909–10): 169–85. [Discusses the Latin *Ecloga Theoduli*, which Le Fèvre translated into French.]

———. "*Theodulus* in France." *Modern Philology* 8 (1911): 611–12. [Provides hitherto unnoted examples of allusions to the Latin *Ecloga Theoduli* in medieval French literature.]

Hanning, Robert W. "The Question of Women in the *Decameron*: A Boccaccian *Disputatio ad utramque partem*." Presented at the 46th International Congress on Medieval Studies, Kalamazoo, MI, 14 May 2011.

———. *Serious Play: Desire and Authority in the Poetry of Ovid, Chaucer, and Ariosto.* New York: Columbia University Press, 2010. [Discusses the palinodes of Ovid and Chaucer as playful yet profound in their comic challenge to literary authority.]

Hasenohr, Geneviève. Introduction. In Jean Le Fèvre, *Le respit de la mort*, ed. Hasenohr, ix–clii. Paris: A. & J. Picard, 1969. [Indispensable biography of Le Fèvre and chronology of his works.]

———. "Jean Le Fèvre." In *Dictionnaire des lettres françaises: Le moyen âge*, ed. Hasenohr and Michel Zink, 802–4. Paris: Fayard, 1994. [Summary of Le Fèvre's life and works, with updated bibliography on all topics.]

———. "La locution verbale figurée dans l'oeuvre de Jean Le Fèvre." In *La locution: Actes du Colloque International Université McGill, Montréal. Le Moyen Français 14/15*, ed. Giuseppe Di Stefano and Russell G. McGillivray, 229–81. Montréal: Ceres, 1984. [A glossary and helpful discussion of "locutions" or stock phrases in the works of Le Fèvre, including *LL*.]

———. "Tradition du texte et tradition de l'image: À propos d'un programme d'illustration du *Theodolet*." In *Miscellanea codicologica F. Masai dicata MCMLXIX*, ed. Pierre Cockshaw, Monique-Cécile Garand, and Pierre Jodogne, 2: 451–67. Ghent: E. Story-Scientia, 1979. [Although mainly concerned with the unique MS of a translation by an unknown author, this article also summarizes the scholarship on Le Fèvre's *Theodolet*.]

Hassell, James Woodrow, Jr. *Middle French Sentences, Proverbs, and Proverbial Phrases.* Toronto: Pontifical Institute of Medieval Studies, 1982.

Hazelton, Richard. "The Christianization of 'Cato': The *Disticha Catonis* in the Light of Late Medieval Commentaries." *Mediaeval Studies* 19 (1957): 157–73. [Discusses the Latin *Cato* and its medieval Latin commentaries.]

Hill, Jillian M. L. *The Medieval Debate on Jean de Meung's* Roman de la Rose: *Morality versus Art.* Studies in Mediaeval Literature 4. Lewiston, ME: Edwin Mellen Press, 1991. [Documents how *RR* was mostly known for its moral teachings before Le Fèvre's *L* established its reputation for scurrility, misogamy, and misogyny.]

Huot, Sylvia. *The* Romance of the Rose *and Its Medieval Readers.* Cambridge Studies in Medieval Literature 16. Cambridge: Cambridge University Press, 1993. [Essential for its discussion of revisionist responses to *RR*, including outright reworkings of the text itself.]

———. "Seduction and Sublimation: Christine de Pizan, Jean de Meun, and Dante." *Romance Notes* 25 (1985): 361–73. [Explains that for Christine, the value of a literary work is in its effect, not the intention of its author.]

Jarrett, Bede, O.P. *Social Theories of the Middle Ages, 1200–1500.* 1926; rpt. New York: Frederick Ungar, 1966. [Has still-useful chapter on conflicting medieval attitudes toward women.]

Kelly, Joan. "Early Feminist Theory and the *Querelle des Femmes*, 1400–1789." *Signs: Journal of Women in Culture and Society* 8 (1982): 4–28.

Kiser, Lisa J. *Telling Classical Tales: Chaucer and* The Legend of Good Women. Ithaca: Cornell University Press, 1983. [The subject of women is the subject of literature.]

Kristeller, Paul. "Learned Women of Early Modern Italy: Humanists and University Scholars." In *Beyond Their Sex: Learned Women of the European Past*, ed. Patricia H. Labalme, 102–14. New York: New York University Press, 1984. [Discusses the daughter of Jehan Andrieu, a figure treated as historical by Le Fèvre and Christine.]

Langlois, Ch.-V. *La vie en France au moyen âge: De la fin du XII siècle au milieu du XIV siècle d'après des moralistes du temps.* 4 vols. 1926–28; Geneva: Slatkine Reprints, 1970. [Vol. 2 contains an annotated summary and discussion of the *Lamentations* in Latin and French.]

Lehmann, Paul. "Zur Überlieferung der Lamentationes Matheoli." *Zeitschrift für romanische Philologie* 46 (1926): 696–99. [Reports discovery of four MSS of the Latin *Lamentations* and one MS of Le Fèvre's *L* and *LL*.]

Lerner, Robert E. *The Heresy of the Free Spirit in the Later Middle Ages.* Notre Dame: Notre Dame University Press, 1972. [Historical context on the Beguines.]

Leube, Eberhard. *Fortuna in Karthago: Die Aeneas-Dido-Mythe Vergils in den romanischen Literaturen vom 14. bis zum 16. Jahrhundert*. Studien zum Fortwirken der Antiken, vol. 1. Heidelberg: Carl Winter, 1969. [Argues that *L* and *LL* were influenced by the *Ovide Moralisé*.]

Lynn, Beth. "Clare of Assisi and Isabelle of Longchamp: Further Light on the Early Development of the Franciscan Charism." *Magistra* 3 (1997): 71–98.

Maddocks, Hilary. "Pictures for Aristocrats: The Manuscripts of the *Légende Dorée*." *Medieval Texts and Images: Studies of Manuscripts from the Middle Ages*. Eds. Margaret A. Manion and Bernard J. Muir. Chur, Switzerland, and Sydney, Australia: Academic Publishing and Craftsman House, 1991. 1–23. [Describes MSS of the French *Golden legend* such as Le Fèvre might have consulted.]

Magee, John, and John Marenbon. "Appendix: Boethius' Works." In *The Cambridge Companion to Boethius*, ed. John Marenbon, 304–5. Cambridge: Cambridge University Press, 2009. [Explains how the works of Aristotle were transmitted in Latin to the Western European Middle Ages.]

Mann, Jill. *Apologies to Women*. Cambridge: Cambridge University Press, 1990. [Places *LL* within the tradition of the medieval palinode, which she argues to be less than serious.]

_____. *Chaucer and Medieval Estates Satire: The Literature of Social Classes and the General Prologue to the* Canterbury Tales. Cambridge: Cambridge University Press, 1973. [Provides context on estates satire against women, with passing reference to Le Fèvre.]

_____. *Feminizing Chaucer*. Chaucer Studies XXX. Cambridge: D. S. Brewer, 2002.[Updated version of 1991 edition. Discusses *LL* as an original and serious defense of women, and thus a prototype for Chaucer, especially his *LGW*; she questions actual influence.]

McLaughlin, Mary M. "Peter Abelard and the Dignity of Women: Twelfth-Century 'Feminism' in Theory and Practice." *Pierre Abélard Pierre le Vénérable: Les courants philosophiques, littéraires et artistiques en occident au milieu du xii siècle*, ed. René Louis and Jean Jolivet, 287–334. Colloques Internationaux du Centre National de la Recherche Scientifique, 546. Paris: Éditions du Centre National de la Recherche Scientifique, 1975.

McLeod, Enid. *Heloïse: A Biography*. London: Chatto and Windus, 1971. [Has good information on Heloïse's career as an abbess.]

McLeod, Glenda. *Virtue and Venom: Catalogs of Women from Antiquity to the Renaissance*. Ann Arbor: University of Michigan Press, 1991.

McRae, Laura Kathryn. "Interpretation and the Acts of Reading and Writing in Christine de Pisan's *Livre de la cité des dames*." *Romanic Review* 82 (1991): 412–33.

Meyer, P. "Notice du Manuscrit Canonici Miscell. 278 de la Bibliothèque Bodleienne, à Oxford." *Bulletin de la Société des Anciens Textes Français* 3 (1877): 38–40. [Describes a newly discovered dual language French-Flemish MS of Le Fèvre's *Cato*.]

Minnis, Alastair. *Fallible Authors: Chaucer's Pardoner and Wife of Bath*. Middle Ages Series. Philadelphia: University Pennsylvania Press, 2008. [Argues that for Chaucer, the value of a literary work resides in its wisdom, not in the gender or other personal qualities of its author.]

_____. *Magister amoris: The* Roman de la Rose *and Vernacular Hermeneutics*. New York: Oxford, 2001. [Has a chapter on the *querelle de la Rose* with brief discussion of Le Fèvre's role.]

_____. *Medieval Theory of Authorship*. 2nd ed. Philadelphia: University of Pennsylvania Press, 1988. [Useful material on exegesis of biblical stories, including David and Bathsheba.]

_____, with V. J. Scattergood and J. J. Smith. *Oxford Guides to Chaucer: The Shorter Poems*. Oxford: Clarendon, 1995. [Chapter on *LGW* has helpful material on the medieval palinode.]

Młynarczyk, Gertrud. *Ein Franziskanerinnenkloster im 15. Jahrhundert: Edition und Analyse von Besitzinventaren aus der Abtei Longchamp*. Pariser Historischer Studien 23. Bonn: Ludwig Röhrscheid Verlag, 1987. [Includes a history of the convent library from the foundation of the abbey and information on the fourteenth-century sisters mentioned by Le Fèvre.]

Moore, Arthur K. "Chaucer and Matheolus." *Notes and Queries* 190 (1946): 245–48. [Discussion limited to *L*.]

Morse, Ruth. *The Medieval Medea*. Woodbridge, Suffolk: D. S. Brewer, 1996. [Valuable overview with brief mention of *LL*.]

Murdoch, Brian. *The Apocryphal Adam and Eve in Medieval Europe: Vernacular Translations and Adaptations of the* Vita Adae et Evae. Oxford: Oxford University Press, 2009.

Neff, Theodore Lee. *La satire des femmes dans la poésie lyrique française du moyen âge*. Paris: Giard et Brière, 1900.

Pacchiarotti, Tiziano. Introduction. *Jean Le Fèvre de Ressons: Les Lamentations de Matheolus*. Ed. Tiziano Pacchiarotti. Alessandria: Edizioni dell'Orso, 2010: 1–127. [Argues that *L* is no mere antifeminist satire; rather, criticism of women is integrated into a complex work of general estates satire and reaction to new developments in law and theology.]

_____. "Les Manuscrits du Matheolus et leur réception." In *Le Recueil au Moyen Âge: La fin du Moyen Âge*. Texte, Codex & Contexte 9, eds. Tania Van Hemelryck and Stefania Marzano, 253–61. Turnhout, Belgium: Brepols, 2010. [Describes the rediscovery of the Geneva MS of *L*.]

_____. "Traduction et écriture personelle dans les *Lamentations de Matheolus.*" In *La traduction vers le moyen français: Actes du Colloque de l'AIEMF, Poitiers, 27–29 avril 2006.* ed. Claudio Galderisi and Cinzia Pignatelli, 411–19. The Medieval Translator/Traduire au Moyen Age 2. Turnhout, Belgium: Brepols, 2007. [Le Fèvre's *L* is so much embellished from its Latin source as to constitute a "reécriture"; through his ubiquitous first-person translator-persona, Le Fèvre actually distances himself from the misogyny of Mahieu and *RR.*]

Palmer, R. Barton. Introduction. In Guillaume de Machaut, *The Judgment of the King of Navarre*, ed. and trans. Palmer, xi–l. New York: Garland, 1988. [Much helpful information on the medieval palinode.]

Paris, Gaston. "La *Dance macabré* de Jean Le Fevre." *Romania* 24 (1895): 129–32. [Argues that Le Fèvre's *Le respit de la mort* 3078 refers to his now-lost poem, *Dance macabré.*]

Payen, Jean-Charles. "La crise du mariage à la fin du XIII siècle d'après la littérature française du temps." In *Famille et parenté dans l'Occident médiéval: Actes du Colloque de Paris (6–8 juin 1974)*, ed. Georges Duby and Jacques Le Goff, 413–30. Collection de l'École Française de Rome, 1977, Vol. 30. Rome: École Française de Rome, 1977.

Percival, Florence. *Chaucer's Legendary Good Women.* Cambridge Studies in Medieval Literature 38. Cambridge: Cambridge University Press, 1998. [Places *LL* in the context of the ancient and medieval palinode.]

Phillips, Helen. "Chaucer and Jean le Fèvre." *Archiv für das Studium der neueren Sprachen und Literaturen* 232 (1995): 23–36. [Includes brief comparison of *LL* to *WBPro* and *WBT.*]

Phillipy, Patricia A. "Establishing Authority: Boccaccio's *De claris mulieribus* and Christine de Pizan's *Le livre de la cité des dames.*" *Romanic Review* 77 (1986): 167–93.

Pratt, Karen. "Analogy or Logic; Authority or Experience? Rhetorical Strategies for and against Women." In *Literary Aspects of Court Culture: Selected Papers from the Seventh Triennial Congress of the International Courtly Literature Society*, ed. Donald Maddox and Sara Sturm-Maddox, 57–66. Cambridge, Eng.: D. S. Brewer, 1994. [Explicates the ambiguity and dubious sincerity of *LL*. Insightful and indispensable.]

_____. "The Strains of Defense: The Many Voices of Jean LeFèvre's *Livre de Leësce.*" In *Gender in Debate from the Early Middle Ages to the Renaissance*, ed. Thelma S. Fenster and Clare A. Lees, 113–33. New York: Palgrave, 2002. [Powerful argument that Lady Gladness presents a weak and questionable defense of women.]

_____. "Translating Misogamy: The Authority of the Intertext in the *Lamentationes Matheoluli* and Its Middle French Translation by Jean LeFevre." *Forum for Modern Language Studies* 35, no. 4 (Oct 1999): 421–35. [Argues that Le Fèvre's *L* intensified the merely theoretical misogyny of Mathieu's *Lamentations* with its strategic additions of material from *RR.*]

Quilligan, Maureen. "The Name of the Author: Self-Representation in Christine de Pizan's *Livre de la cité des dames.*" *Exemplaria* 4, no. 1 (Spring 1992): 201–28.

Quinn, Betty Nye. "Ps. Theodulus." In *Catalogus translationum et commentariorum*, ed. Paul O. Kristeller et al., 2: 383–408. Washington, DC: Catholic University of America Press, 1971. [A list of medieval and early modern translations and commentaries on the *Ecloga Theoduli.*]

Reames, Sherry L. *The* Legenda Aurea: *A Reexamination of its Paradoxical History.* Madison: University of Wisconsin, 1985. [Notes the existence of expanded versions like the one evidently used by Le Fèvre in his catalog of female saints.]

Richards, Earl Jeffrey. "Introduction: Returning to a 'Gracious Debate': The Intellectual Context of the Epistolary Exchange of the Debate about the *Roman de la Rose.*" In *Debating the Roman de la Rose: A Critical Anthology*, ed. Christine McWebb, xxi–xxxvi. New York: Routledge, 2007.

Robathan, Dorothy M. "Introduction to the Pseudo-Ovidian *De vetula.*" *Transactions and Proceedings of the American Philological Association* 88 (1957): 197–207.

Ruhe, Ernstpeter. *Untersuchungen zu den altfranzösischen Übersetzungen der Disticha Catonis.* Beiträge zur Romanischen Philologie des Mittelalters 2. Munich: Max Huber, 1968. [Discusses seven medieval French translations of *Cato* including Le Fèvre's, the most popular with over thirty MSS.]

Schmitt, Alfred. Introduction. In *Matheus von Boulogne: "Lamentationes Matheoluli" (Kommentierte und kritische Edition der beiden ersten Bücher)*, 1–36. Bonn: Druck Rheinischen Friedrich-Wilhelms-Universität, 1974. [Helpful summary of scholarship to date on the Latin *Lamentations.*]

Schmitz, Götz. *The Fall of Women in Early English Narrative Verse.* Cambridge: Cambridge University Press, 1990.

Smith, Susan L. *The Power of Women: A* Topos *in Medieval Art and Literature.* Philadelphia: University of Pennsylvania Press, 1995. [Discusses the legends of Solomon, David, Aristotle, Virgil, et al. as helpless against the power of women. Brief discussion of *LL.*]

Solterer, Helen. *The Master and Minerva: Disputing Women in French Medieval Culture.* Berkeley: University of California Press, 1995. [Discusses *LL* as questionable in intention and heavily contaminated with misogyny.]

Swift, Helen J. *Gender, Writing, and Performance: Men Defending Women in Late Medieval France, 1440–1538.* Oxford: Clarendon, 2008. [Although focused on a later period, this book is relevant for its discussion of revisionist approaches to *RR* and their connection to *LL*.]

Thundy, Zacharias P. "Chaucer's *Corones Tweyne* and Matheolus." *Neuphilologische Mitteilungen* 86, no. 3 (1985): 343–47. [Discussion limited to *L* and *Troilus and Criseyde*.]

_____. "Matheolus, Chaucer, and the Wife of Bath." In *Chaucerian Problems and Perspectives: Essays Presented to Paul E. Beichner C.S.C.*, ed. E. Vasta and Z. P. Thundy, 24–58. Notre Dame: University of Notre Dame Press, 1979. [Detailed comparative charts, almost entirely limited to *L*.]

Vaillant, V.-J. *Maistre Mahieu (Matheolus), satirique boulonnais du XIII siècle: Essai de biographie.* Boulogne-sur-mer: Simonnaire, 1894.

Van Hamel, A.-G. Introduction, in *Les Lamentations de Matheolus et Le Livre de Leësce*, by Jehan Le Fèvre, de Resson, ed. A.-G. Van Hamel, vol. 1, i–xxv, vol. 2, xxvii–ccxxv. Paris: Émile Bouillon, 1892. [Includes the only general introduction to *LL* outside the present volume.]

_____. "Le poème latin de Matheolus." *Romania* 17 (1888): 284–85. [Describes how Van Hamel discovered the Utrecht MS of the Latin *Lamentations*, a work hitherto believed lost.]

Yeager, Robert F. *John Gower's Poetic: The Search for a New Arion.* Woodbridge, Suffolk: D. S. Brewer, 1990.

Young, M. Joy. "Portraits of Woman: Virtue, Vice, and Marriage in Christine de Pizan's *Cité des dames*, Matheolus' *Lamentations* and Lefèvre's *Livre de leësce*." Ph.D. diss., Catholic University of America, 1992. [Argues that Christine knew "Matheolus" only through *LL*.]

Index of People, Places and Writings

Numbers refer to lines of the poem *Le Livre de Leesce* (French text) located on pages 35–73.

A

Abelard, Peter 2786
Abraham 2183
Acarius, St. 1668, 1756
Achilles 3569, 3572, 3914
Adah 119
Adam 1219, 1249, 1274, 1281, 1286, 1299, 2153, 3344, 3495
Aeneas 2435, 2446, 2459, 2565, 2568, 2575, 2744, 2747, 2752
Agatha, St. 2835
Agnes (girl about town) 1814
Agnes, St. 2835
Ahasuerus 1991, 2106
Alexander 877
Alithia 45, 51
Almageste 3429
Amazonia 3562
Ambrose, St. 1630, 1707
Ammon 2190, 2192
Ammonites 2192
Anceau Choquart 276, 283
Antigone 3820
Aristotle 69, 660, 814, 819, 867, 2271, 3516, 3908
Arsionne (?) 3592
Assyrians 1766
Athens 47

B

Babylonia 3582
Bathsheba 252, 1541
Beatrice (girl about town) 1814
Beelzebub 3032
Bertha (*fabliau* character) 3153, 3158, 3161, 3175
Bertha (girl about town) 1814
Bible 1544
Biblis 2542, 2731
Bridget, St. 2847
Britain 2813

C

Cacus 3598
Camilla 3595
Cain 121, 228
Calabre 3778
Canacee 2543, 2731
Carfania (Calphurnia) 1039, 1106, 1113, 1162
Carmentis 3623, 3629
Carthage 2441
Cassandra 3666
Catiline 3812
Cato 3825
Cerberus 3600
Christine, St. 2836
Circe 2415, 2416, 2421, 2432, 3043
Claire, St. 2884
Clement (*fabliau* character) 3154, 3162, 3169
Cleopatra 3821
Colchos 2377
Conain 2819
Count of Alençon 267
Countess of Estampes 269
Crete 18343, 2545
Croesus, daughter of 3675
Cyrus 3581, 3582, 3585

D

Darius 59
David 250, 264, 1022, 1508, 1539, 3515
de Bailleul, chevalier de 1432
Decretum 992
de Dormans, Jeanne 293
Deïphile 2899, 3594
Delilah 1513, 1546, 1550, 1554
Demophon 2558, 2736
Dido 2442, 2454, 2563, 2743
Dionysius (the tyrant) 3814
Dulichium 2413

151